Practical OCaml

Joshua B. Smith

Apress®

Practical OCaml

Copyright © 2006 by Joshua B. Smith

ISBN-13: 978-1-4302-1194-5

ISBN-10: 1-4302-1194-6

Lead Editor: Matt Wade

Technical Reviewer: Richard Jones

Editorial Board: Steve Anglin, Ewan Buckingham, Gary Cornell, Jason Gilmore, Jonathan Gennick, Jonathan Hassell, James Huddleston, Chris Mills, Matthew Moodie, Dominic Shakeshaft, Jim Sumser, Keir Thomas, Matt Wade

Project Manager: Sofia Marchant

Copy Edit Manager: Nicole Flores

Copy Editor: Nancy Sixsmith

Assistant Production Director: Kari Brooks-Copony

Production Editor: Katie Stence

Compositor: Linda Weidemann, Wolf Creek Press

Proofreader: April Eddy

Indexer: Brenda Miller

Artist: April Milne

Cover Designer: Kurt Krames

Manufacturing Director: Tom Debolski

Distributed to the book trade worldwide by Springer-Verlag New York, Inc., 233 Spring Street, 6th Floor, New York, NY 10013. Phone 1-800-SPRINGER, fax 201-348-4505, e-mail orders-ny@springer-sbm.com, or visit http://www.springeronline.com.

For information on translations, please contact Apress directly at 2560 Ninth Street, Suite 219, Berkeley, CA 94710. Phone 510-549-5930, fax 510-549-5939, e-mail info@apress.com, or visit http://www.apress.com.

The source code for this book is available to readers at http://www.apress.com in the Source Code/ Download section.

For Carol and Aaron

Contents at a Glance

Contents

▊CHAPTER 20 Digression: Functional Programming 261

▊CHAPTER 21 Practical: Web Programming 273

About the Author

JOSHUA B. SMITH is a writer and consultant. He completed an undergraduate degree in English and proceeded to use those skills in tech support. Joshua became a Unix administrator and programmer in the financial industry. After completing his MBA, he moved to the suburbs of Washington DC, where he now works and lives with his wife and son.

About the Technical Reviewer

RICHARD JONES studied mathematics and computer science at Imperial College, London, before working at a number of companies involved in everything from crystallography to high-speed networks to online communities. He is currently employed by Merjis, studying web site usability and search engine advertising, and training developers in the finer points of the Google AdWords API.

Richard's significant contributions to OCaml include mod_caml (bindings for Apache), perl4caml (using Perl code within OCaml), PG'OCaml (typesafe bindings for PostgreSQL), and the Merjis AdWords Toolkit.

Acknowledgments

Without the resources created and provided by the OCaml team and the larger OCaml community, this book would not have been possible. My thanks also go to INRIA for providing so much to the OCaml community. I would like to thank everyone who helped answer my questions and correct my misunderstandings.

My technical reviewer, Richard Jones, deserves many thanks for all his hard work. Sofia Marchant, Nancy Sixsmith, Matt Wade, and Katie Stence all improved this book in innumerable ways. I also thank everyone at Apress for all you have done. Any errors that remain in this book are all mine.

Finally, I would like to thank my family for being so understanding and supportive during this project.

## CHAPTER 1

Why Objective Caml (OCaml)?

It's a fair question. You have picked up this book, so I assume that you are (at a minimum) interested in Objective Caml (OCaml). That interest is enough for some to cover the "why" question. If you write programs to make a living, perhaps the glib, navel-gazing answer is not what you were looking for.

"Why not OCaml?" will probably not cover it, either. OCaml is not a popular language in the way that Java is a popular language. Flame wars rarely break out over non-Lisp languages that are not in the mainstream. Artificial languages do not become popular because of their technical merits—probably because defining the "technical merits" of a language can be very difficult to do and is often more opinion than fact. Artificial languages, much like human languages, become popular in ways that leave us to figure out why they became popular only after the fact.

For example, nobody designed Italian to be the language of the opera; it was the language of the opera because people decided it was so. The justification was constructed later. Lucky for us, artificial languages are not quite as capricious as other human languages.

Returning to the title question, if I were to answer the question in more mundane terms, I would say that OCaml helps the programmer to easily express normal concepts and actually express difficult concepts. This expressiveness enables a program to do what programs are supposed to do, which is to solve problems with software. Another part of the answer is that in OCaml, safety and correctness are not sacrificed on the altar of expressiveness.

To answer in not-so-mundane terms, we can compare what an architect might want in building materials versus what a carpenter might want in building materials. An architect wants the best materials to *build* with, but a carpenter wants the best materials to *work* with. This is as it should be—the carpenter values the work and wants to do it well. The architect, however, might not have the specific concerns the carpenter does. This is as true in software as it is in wood.

As a programmer, I want good materials. OCaml is one of the best materials I can think of. If this book is your first real exposure to OCaml, you might have to take my word for it—at least in the beginning.

Who Benefits from Learning OCaml?

OCaml is a functional programming language. It is garbage collected and statically typed, although the type information is inferred at compile time. This inference means you don't have to specify the types and you can't create functions that take the wrong types. The compiler will catch a lot of errors for you and make you create your functions correctly.

Programming in OCaml will also make you much more aware of types in your code, even if the other languages you program in are not statically typed. A solid understanding of types and their meanings can help nearly all programmers.

OCaml will not—at least yet—provide you with shiny resume bullet points. But it will enable you to solve problems faster, with less code and fewer bugs.

What Is OCaml Good For?

OCaml is a general-purpose programming language, which means that you can program anything in it. However, programming languages are often designed with certain problem domains in mind, and OCaml has areas in which it excels more than others.

One of these is in the area of "safe" applications (used here to indicate more than security-related safety). Not only is OCaml garbage collected, but most types are boxed. This means that buffer overruns and similar runtime failures cannot happen in OCaml programs. Safety in OCaml extends beyond this, though. The static typing and compile-time checks by the OCaml compiler make certain classes of errors impossible. Type conversion or mismatch errors cannot happen in OCaml because automatic type coercions cannot happen.

OCaml code is also verifiable. There are automated proof utilities that can test your code and verify that it is type correct. This testing goes beyond syntax checkers such as Lint; it delves into static analyses of programs on a level that other languages (except maybe Ada) can only hope to accomplish some day.

All this safety also comes with speed. The optimizing compiler generates very fast code. OCaml entries in the International Conference on Functional Programming (ICFP) programming contest have taken many prizes over the years.

With speed and safety also comes a highly developed module system and standard library. The module system provides incremental compilation and type signatures. The type signatures go well beyond what can be accomplished with header files and promote data privacy by enforcing function visibility at compile time. This means that private functions stay private—the compiler makes it so. Without unsafe pointers (which do not exist in OCaml), this security is strong.

The module system also enables you to write large applications using multiple developers and teams. This large-scale programming support is essential for developing any application of real complexity.

OCaml has a very advanced Foreign Function Interface (FFI) and an Interface Definition Language (IDL) compiler, which enable you to write application logic in OCaml and interface with legacy or vendor code safely and cleanly. It also means you don't have to rewrite existing applications to start benefiting from OCaml.

Data-driven applications are easily expressed in a functional style. Add in the FFI and you can access your data from your custom database or use Open Database Connectivity (ODBC) to access it in a standard way. There are also drivers for many popular database management systems (DBMSs) for OCaml.

Using OCaml will also make you a better programmer. This may sound like a snake-oil sales pitch, but remember that programming is about algorithms and data structures. Learning a new programming language expands your understanding of these concepts, resulting in a better programming you.

This abstract benefit aside, OCaml programs are often smaller than their counterparts. If the number of bugs in any code base is a function of its length, fewer lines of code mean fewer bugs. OCaml is a terse language, and with exception handling and pattern matching you often don't need to write as much code as you do in other languages. This shortening of the code base means you can get more done faster—and with fewer bugs.

Another of the problem domains OCaml excels at handling is text processing. Not just text processing such as Perl or AWK, but also projects such as writing compilers. With ocamllex and ocamlyacc as part of the standard distribution, the OCaml system is a compiler construction kit in a box. It also has tools for dealing with very complicated and difficult semantic processing tasks and text manipulation. These tools can be very helpful for data mining applications and "messy" data problems that are more and more frequent. OCaml supports regular expressions, and strings are a native type.

Let's not forget research and analysis applications. Many companies write their applications in another language and then write verification and analysis code in OCaml (or another meta-language [ML] dialect).

Functional programming in general is designed to make computer programs more like mathematical processes (for example, complex numbers and arbitrary precision-number modules are in the standard library). The precedence features mimic normal mathematical precedence. Also, real numbers and floats are treated differently.

Who Uses OCaml?

This is often the second question people ask about OCaml. The answer is this: a lot of people. From hedge fund users to graduate students, the list of people using OCaml to solve problems grows every day.

Airbus and Microsoft are two of the many companies that use OCaml to help avoid problems in programs written in languages other than OCaml. The shopping engine for NBCi is written in OCaml. The Coq proof assistant is, too. The OCaml community maintains a web site devoted to showcasing these success stories at http://caml.inria.fr/about/successes.en.html.

Most of the people using OCaml do not show up on that page. Companies often do not care how the solutions to their problems arrive, as long as they do arrive.

Where Did OCaml Come From?

The OCaml language is a descendent of ML. ML, originally designed by Robin Milner, was implemented in a Lisp dialect in the late 1970s when Milner and his team were working on the LCF proof assistant. It was later that ML was written to run on standard Lisp compilers and when Guy Cousineau first got involved.

Guy Cousineau added algebraic data types and pattern matching. He also later defined an ML based on the Categorical Abstract Machine (CAM). This CAM-ML could be described, proven to be correct, and then optimized—all of which represented a major improvement to the ML.

Now, fast forward to the 1990s; Xavier Leroy designed a new implementation of the Caml (a pun on CAM-ML). This new implementation was built around a C-based, byte code interpreter. With the addition of memory management, this new language was dubbed Caml Light. The *Light* part of the name came from the new, highly portable, efficient interpreter that could run on desktop PCs.

Caml Light was used in education and research for many years. Caml Special Light was then released to address some of the shortcomings of the original Caml Light system. *Special* meant that the language now had an optimizing native-code compiler and an ML-inspired high-level module system.

In 1996, objects were added to Caml Special Light, which added the *O* in OCaml. This object system added the power of object-oriented programming (OOP) to the existing static typing and inference system. In 2000, more features were added (polymorphic variants and methods, optional arguments, and more).

These features are all now part of the current OCaml system, which is actively maintained by the Institut National de Recherche en Informatique et en Automatique (INRIA).

What Is the Current State of the Art?

OCaml is not a dead language; it is constantly updated and worked on by a small group of full-time researchers and the community at large. The small but active community develops the language and the standard library.

INRIA is the core of OCaml development, but OCaml is used inside academic projects the world over. The language is also being improved, with a lot of work going into the type inference engine and tools such as Camlp4.

Why This Book?

Apress is committed to publishing the books that programmers need, and this book is one of the few English language books available on OCaml. Now is a good time for OCaml because the focus on security and correctness of programs will only become greater. As more and more of our world runs on software, the need for safe and verifiable programming and languages will increase. Luckily, OCaml is already there.

This book also fills a gap in the type of books available. Most of the available books are highly academic. This book is, as the title suggests, a practical book. We will not be discussing computer science; we will be talking about code and programming.

To go back to the carpenter analogy, we are talking about wood. We might mention metallurgy and physics, but that is not what we are focused on.

What Is Covered?

Now, let's take a look at the upcoming chapters and what will be covered in each one. This will give you a good idea of what to expect and what you will be learning in this book.

Interacting with OCaml: The Toplevel (Chapter 2)

This chapter introduces the various interfaces to OCaml and the different distributions (and where to get them). We focus on the command line (with Ledit) and the Microsoft Windows toplevel. We also cover creating a custom toplevel and create the first "Hello World" program in OCaml. We also discuss the basic files, focusing on the code files instead of the interface files for now.

Syntax and Semantics (Chapter 3)

This chapter covers types, records, and control flow. We also introduce let bindings, variables, and comparison operators. We cover them with an eye to the fact that OCaml is a constant language. We spend some time talking about the math problem in OCaml, which is one of the more commonly complained-about aspects of OCaml: namely that the operators for float and int are different. This problem often causes grief for students of the language.

Understanding Functions (Chapter 4)

This chapter covers both let and let rec function definitions. We also cover curried functions: what they are and why the programmer should care. Given that OCaml is a constant language, we demonstrate accumulators and other recursive methods that do not require mutability.

Practical: Creating a Simple Database (Chapter 5)

This chapter creates a simple database by using functions, records, and the toplevel. This database includes functions for interacting with the data and saving it to a file via the OCaml serialization library.

Primitive and Composite Types (Chapter 6)

This chapter covers the primitive types found in OCaml, including int, float, bool, string, and so on. It is more detailed than Chapter 3 and covers actually doing stuff with these types. We also cover composite types in a more detailed fashion and include some discussion of why types matter and how they help the programmer.

Practical: Simple Database Reports, Exports, and Imports (Chapter 7)

Using the simple database from the earlier example, we create reports and imports from strings using printf and scanf, as well as the things we have learned about primitive types. Using examples from the previous chapters, we refactor the database records to better reflect the problem.

Collections (Chapter 8)

OCaml has a rich set of collections and functions for operating on them. We cover iteration, folding, sequences, and implications of the collection's features (when to use what and why).

Files and File I/O (Chapter 9)

This chapter is an introduction to channels and their properties, including sockets. We look at interacting with the file system and pathnames. We also include discussions about the problems file input/output (I/O) presents to functional programming languages.

Exception Handling (Chapter 10)

This chapter discusses stack unwinding, exceptions, and all the scary stuff that isn't so scary because OCaml is a constant language. We also cover exception handling in classes.

Practical: A URI Library (Chapter 11)

In this chapter, we implement a URI parsing library that handles file:// URIs (using the OCaml Filename module) and has stubs for handling other URI types as well.

Using OCamldoc (Chapter 12)

Ocaml includes literate programming features with its documentation-generation tool, Ocamldoc. This is a short chapter that discusses the OCamldoc tool. We give examples in Chapter 11, but here we discuss the specifics of OCamldoc and how to make the documentation better.

Modules and Functors (Chapter 13)

This chapter covers modules and interfaces. We use the example code in Chapter 10 to create a documented module with an interface. We also introduce functors. We cover how to distribute and install modules, as well as findlib basics and creating a findlib META file.

Practical: A Spam Filter (Chapter 14)

This is the obligatory naive Bayesian spam filter, with a small twist: the module is a functor that takes the scoring function as an argument.

Practical: A Network-Aware Scoring Function (Chapter 15)

Using the client socket support in OCaml, we create a network-based scoring function that allows for querying and updating token scores. This chapter also provides a basic server to complete the application.

Ocamllex and Ocamlyacc (Chapter 16)

This is a basic introduction that covers the differences between Lex and Yacc. It features an example, but *not* a four-function calculator. This chapter does not cover Abstract Syntax Trees (ASTs).

Practical: Complex Log File Parsing (Chapter 17)

Using ocamllex and ocamlyacc, we create a fast and flexible log file scanner. The log files are spread across multiple lines, with other log entries interleaved. We also use a contrived log file that is appropriately complex.

The Objective Part of Caml (Chapter 18)

As you might expect, Objective Caml includes a robust and complete object system that is integrated with the Ocaml type system. This chapter discusses the use and limitations of objects (and OOP) in Ocaml.

Digression: OCaml Is Not Pure (Chapter 19)

OCaml is not a pure functional programming language. We cover mutability, references, and using classes to hide this impurity.

Digression: Functional Programming (Chapter 20)

This chapter discusses functional programming (FP) and what its ramifications are to the world of programming. There are many people who say wild and breathless things about FP, yet there are many who say nasty things, too. What is a programmer to do? And how can a programmer get a chance to use these less-popular languages? This digression is somewhat evangelical.

Practical: Web Programming (Chapter 21)

Now we're back in the saddle. Just because Ocaml is a functional language doesn't mean you can do web programming with it. In this chapter, we discuss Common Gateway Interface (CGI) programming in Ocaml. We also talk about Apache modules and basic web programming.

Practical: A Shoutcast Server (Chapter 22)

In this chapter, we write a Shoutcast server, which also creates a generic server framework from which users can implement their own arbitrary servers. We also talk about the high-level socket functions.

Using Threads (Chapter 23)

OCaml supports threads natively, but they are not "real" threads. This chapter tries to help the reader understand what this means. We also discuss multiprocess concurrency, mutexes, and the Event module, which provides for synchronous communication.

Practical: A Concurrent Web Crawler (Chapter 24)

We implement a concurrent web crawler that uses threads to crawl many sites simultaneously. Our web crawler doesn't give Google a run for the money, but it does provide an excellent way to understand threads and Ocaml programming.

Interfacing with OCaml (Chapter 25)

This chapter is a brief tutorial on CamlIDL and wrapper writing in C for OCaml directly. We also talk about why FFI matters in a language such as OCaml.

Practical: Time and Logging Libraries (Chapter 26)

Now that there is an understanding of how to interface Ocaml and C code, we present several more-complicated examples, including a time library that provides formatting time strings, parsing strings into time values, and other functions. A logging library loosely modeled after the Log4j library for Java is also presented.

Practical: Processing Binary Files (Chapter 27)

We've done a lot of complex text parsing, but what about binary data? We search for strings and present a library that finds the longest identical sections of two binary files.

OCaml Development Tools (Chapter 28)

We talk about OCaml Makefile, findlib, and other tools (including integrated development environments [IDEs]). Here we talk about profiling and debugging, too. This chapter also shows you how to set up your own Ocaml development environment.

Camlp4 (Chapter 29)

Camlp4, the Ocaml preprocessor and pretty printer, is one of the most powerful and difficult-to-understand parts of the Ocaml system. This application and library set enables you to create domain-specific languages (DSLs) on-the-fly and actually rewrite the Ocaml language. This chapter provides a basic understanding of the functionality that Camlp4 provides.

Conclusion (Chapter 30)

A wrap up of all things OCaml.

What Isn't Covered?

This book is more than just a tutorial. I have tried to cover all of the areas of normal OCaml programming. We will not be covering extending the OCaml language in languages other than Ocaml and C. If that sounds confusing, don't worry about it, it is. Much of the OCaml distribution is written in OCaml, but there are ways of writing your own functions in languages other than Ocaml (Perl, for instance).

Other than this chapter, this book does not cover OOP design and patterns in depth. OCaml has support for objects, and we cover that. However, patterns and OOP design are both subjects that have many books written about them. Unfortunately, this is not one of them. This book is also not a general computer science textbook.

What Are My Expectations for You?

I expect that OCaml is not the first programming language you have learned. Although sections of this book can and do function as a tutorial, this book is more directed at experienced programmers who want to understand more about OCaml.

That being said, I don't expect you to have a formal background in computer science. The FP community has more than its fair share of computer scientists, but this book is targeted at programmers. There are many resources for computer scientists who want to know more of the theoretical underpinnings of OCaml (not the least of these is the core group). These folks are quite approachable and good to work with.

Conclusion

Now that you know what to expect and what is expected of you, the next step is installing and running OCaml. Then we move on to a series of chapters that cover most of the OCaml programming language and give complete working examples to demonstrate it. Although this sounds simple enough, some parts of it will be easier than others. Would you have it any other way?

■ ■ ■

## CHAPTER 2

Interacting with OCaml: The Toplevel

The OCaml toplevel, the interactive OCaml interpreter, is one of the many powerful features of OCaml that can help you be more productive. This interactive interpreter enables you to enter OCaml code and have it evaluated immediately. You can then prototype code on-the-fly (much like Python, which has a similar system) instead of relying on the compile-run-debug cycle found in languages such as Java or C. The toplevel provides an interactive read/eval/print loop and gives you access to all features of the language.

OCaml has two compilers: a byte-code compiler and a native-code compiler. In most circumstances, native code cannot be debugged under the OCaml debugger, but it runs faster and does not rely on the OCaml interpreter. Thus, native code can be installed on a computer that does not have OCaml installed. All the examples in this book work the same way under byte code or native code, so you do not need to worry about this. In fact, most of the examples provided can be examined in the toplevel interpreter while you read the text. Before that, however, you'll need to get the OCaml compilers and development utilities.

OCaml is freely available, although it is not released under the General Public License (GPL) or a Berkeley Software Distribution (BSD)–style license; it is distributed under a set of Open Source Initiative (OSI)–certified free licenses. The compiler is distributed under the Q Public License (QPL) 1.0 (with a change to the Choice of Law provision, choose France instead of Norway), and the library is distributed under a slightly modified Lesser General Public License (LGPL).

OCAML LICENSING

Calling it a "slightly modified" LGPL is somewhat misleading. It is actually the LGPL with the "linking exception." This "exception" is a clause in the LGPL that requires you to provide object files for linking. The OCaml maintainers have simplified the license to not require this exception.

Much more information about the LGPL and its ramifications can be found at the Free Software Foundation web site at http://www.fsf.org/licensing/licenses/lgpl.html.

Distributions of OCaml

The only official distribution of OCaml comes from the Institut National de Recherche en Informatique et en Automatique (INRIA). All the source code and documentation contained within the official release can be found at `http://caml.inria.fr` (this source should be considered authoritative).

Official Distribution

Official binaries exist for Microsoft Windows (for both the MinGW and Microsoft compiler tool chains), Linux, and Mac OS X. The full source code is also available and should build on any Portable Operating System Interface (POSIX)–compliant operating system.

Many Linux distributions have up-to-date packages for OCaml, and there are ports in the BSDs for OCaml and many associated libraries.

Note The native-code compiler, `ocamlopt`, is not available on as many platforms as the interpreter.

Unofficial Releases

There is one popular unofficial release, Great Outdoors Digital Indoors (GODI), which can be found at `http://godi.ocaml-programming.de`. GODI is a source-only distribution that provides automated package install and simplifies the process of getting many of the libraries that you want when developing applications.

We will be using the official distribution of OCaml throughout this book. This is not a critique of GODI; it is an acknowledgment that the INRIA team's work has created the fastest way for new users to get started with OCaml.

Installing OCaml

The Windows distribution comes in two flavors: one that is compiled with the free MinGW tools and one that works with Microsoft Visual Studio. The difference between the two rests in the way native code is generated. If that sounds confusing, don't worry about it right now— you can choose either one.

Windows

The Windows distribution of OCaml comes with a graphical shell for the toplevel called OCamlWinPlus. The OCamlWinPlus environment enables easy transfer of interactive sessions to source files. It handles this transfer either through simple cut and paste or by two save options. The first option is to save the transcript, which saves the entire session to a text file—including error messages, warnings, and output. You can also choose to save just the meta-language (ML) code, which enables you to save your files as loadable files (it preserves non-ML code in the comments in the file). The OCamlWinPlus environment is also a

Windows native application, which means it looks and feels more like a Windows application than the command-line version.

After installing the OCaml Windows package (assuming that you've installed the package on a Windows 9x or higher system), you can start the OCamlWinPlus environment by choosing Start➤Programs➤Objective Caml➤Objective Caml in the Windows Start menu. You then see a window that looks the one shown in Figure 2-1.

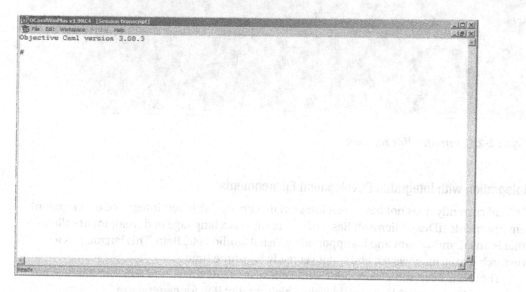

Figure 2-1. *OCamlWinPlus environment*

■**Tip**   Although it is not required, installing a supported version of Tk enables you to run the OCamlbrowser, which lets you browse through the functions in the OCaml library. At the time of this writing, the current version of OCaml is 3.09 and uses Tk version 8.4. The Tk runtime libraries are available from ActiveState or directly from Scriptics (the company in charge of Tcl and Tk commercialization). Even if you don't have Tk installed, however, you can still use the OCamlWinPlus toplevel.

Command-line Toplevel

Figure 2-2 shows the command-line toplevel executed and running.

You can run the command-line toplevel from a command prompt on Windows. You should use the OCamlWinPlus toplevel if you are running OCaml on Windows.

You can find the command-line version of the OCaml toplevel in the default installed location of `c:\program files\objective caml\bin\ocaml.exe`. This application can be run by all users after installation and should be in the default path, so running it from its installation directory is not necessary.

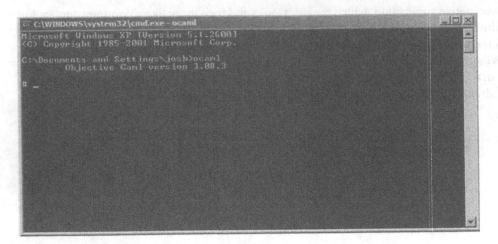

Figure 2-2. *Command-line toplevel*

Integration with Integrated Development Environments

OCaml currently does not have great integration with any Windows integrated development environments (IDEs). Microsoft Research currently has a language in development called F# that is an OCaml variant and is supported by Visual Studio 2005 Beta. This language is a research platform, however, and is not yet ready for prime time.

There has been some work done with Eclipse to create an OCaml IDE, but it is also not yet ready. When available, it should yield a high-quality IDE for general use.

There is an available IDE written in OCaml called Cameleon, which can be downloaded from http://pauillac.inria.fr/~guesdon/tools/cameleon/cameleon.html. Cameleon comes with several useful libraries, although the IDE itself has not caught on widely within the OCaml community. Many people use XEmacs instead of IDEs.

One problem is that the most-requested environment features, Intellisense and code completion, are not readily available in any of these IDEs. The documentation is very good, however, and you should keep it handy.

Emacs and XEmacs Interfaces

There are a couple of XEmacs interfaces to OCaml. There is an OCaml mode that comes in the OCaml source distribution, as well as one that comes with XEmacs. However, the most widely used is Tuareg mode, which can be used on any platform that supports XEmacs and OCaml.

Tuareg mode, which can be downloaded from http://www-rocq.inria.fr/~acohen/tuareg, is maintained by Albert Cohen, a research scientist at INRIA.

You can download GNU Emacs from http://www.gnu.org and XEmacs from http://www.xemacs.org.

Linux

Installation of OCaml on Linux is often done via the packaging system for the distribution you are using. You can also install GODI on any almost any POSIX-compliant operating system (OS) and architecture. The source code for the official distribution is available as well, and it too can be compiled and run on nearly any POSIX-compliant OS and architecture. Because OCaml is itself written in C and OCaml, it is highly portable.

Note I have even installed OCaml on a Sharp Zaurus running Linux.

Getting It

You can download the binary packages and the OCaml source from the INRIA site. You can also download the source packages, which at the time of this writing can be found at `http://caml.inria.fr/download.en.html` (this link is for the English language pages).

If you download the source, you can build it via the standard `./configure;make;make install` sequence that many autotools-built applications use.

On many Linux distributions, there are OCaml binary packages available. For Debian (and Debian-derived) users, you can get the compilers via Advanced Package Tool (APT) like so:

```
# apt-get install ocaml
# apt-get install ledit
# apt-get install tuareg-mode
```

These three packages contain the OCaml compliers and interpreters, the Ledit program, and an improved XEmacs editing environment.

For users of RPM-based distributions, you can download RPMs of the OCaml distribution from `http://caml.inria.fr/download.en.html`. Contributed RPMs exist for most RPM-based distributions.

Running It

After you install the application and include the binaries in your PATH, you can start the toplevel by calling the `ocaml` command.

Ledit

Ledit is not part of the official OCaml distribution. It is, however, an invaluable tool for using the OCaml toplevel interactively. Ledit is an application that gives you command-line editing that is similar to the library readline. Readline support is not available in the OCaml toplevel because of GPL restrictions.

Ledit is written in OCaml, so it can be compiled and used anywhere OCaml exists. However, it is most often seen used in Unix and Unix-like operating systems. Ledit can be downloaded from the INRIA web site and is freely available. You start OCaml using Ledit by calling `ledit` with `ocaml` as an argument: `ledit ocaml`.

Ledit can be downloaded from `ftp://ftp.inria.fr/INRIA/Projects/cristal/Daniel.de_Rauglaudre/Tools/`.

Interacting with the Toplevel

The toplevel is designed to be an interactive interpreter and can process any code that will compile.

What the Screen Shows

When you start the toplevel, you see a message about the version of OCaml you are using and the prompt. The toplevel waits for input. The toplevel also displays type information in the output. The following is a typical prompt (you can enter code at the # and it will be evaluated after you type ;; and return):

```
        Objective Caml version 3.09.0
#
```

Using the Toplevel As a Calculator

The toplevel is a full OCaml environment that is also fully interactive. You can enter code into the toplevel just as you would enter it into a source file. The code is then interpreted, and the result is displayed to the screen.

Note OCaml makes distinctions between integers and floating-point numbers. The immediate side effect is that commands relating to math are different for floating-point numbers and integers.

```
# 1 + 1;;
- ; int = 2
```

In the previous code, I typed in 1 + 1, and the toplevel gave me the answer (2) and told me that it has type int (for integer). Some more examples follow:

```
# 2 + 1;;
- ; int = 3
# 3 / 4;;
- ; int = 0
```

+, -, *, and / work only on integers. To do floating-point arithmetic, you have to use the floating-point operators: +. (a plus sign followed by a period); -. (a minus sign followed by a period); *. (an asterisk followed by a period); and /. (a slash followed by a period). Numbers are also followed by a decimal point (period). The minimum representation of a float is a number followed by a period, but trailing zeros are allowed.

```
# 1. +. 1.;;
- ; float = 2.
```

As you can see, the floating-point operators result in a very similar output.

Hello World

The canonical first program is the "Hello World" program. Really, just typing **"Hello World"** into the interpreter creates this program because the string "Hello World" is evaluated and returned by the toplevel. With that in mind, the previous examples have actually been your first program. However, you probably want to interact with more than the OCaml type inference engine.

WHAT IS TYPE INFERENCE?

Type inference is the process by which the OCaml compiler figures out type information from your code. The compiler does this for two reasons: so that the programmer does not have to specify type information, and so that the types are used correctly. These compile-time type checks are what prevent you from using a function with the wrong type. In a language such as Python, these errors would show up only during runtime.

Type inference is part of the polymorphic type checker found in ML dialects. The consequence and benefits of type are discussed in more detail in Chapter 6.

OCaml uses a `printf` style of command to output information to `stdout`. OCaml `printf` is similar in style to that of C, but OCaml's `printf` is typesafe (as all OCaml functions are). `printf` is also a library, or module, in OCaml and has many other features that will be covered later. For now, you will be using only the `Printf.printf` function.

This example also introduces you to OCaml's dot notation for modules and functions. The `printf` library is compiled into the toplevel, so it is always available for your use.

From Toplevel

The three `printf` format strings you should know right off the bat are for strings, integers, and floats (see Table 2-1). There is a return type of unit, which is a similar concept to void in C, except that unit is a type instead of an absence of type.

Table 2-1. *printf Type Specifiers*

Type Specifier	Description
%s	String
%i	Integer
%f	Floating-point number

The `printf` command takes a format string followed by arguments. So "Hello World" can be run like so:

```
# Printf.printf "%s" "Hello, World";;
Hello, World- : unit = ()
```

If you have more format characters than arguments, OCaml will return a function object. This is a higher-order function (or *curried* function), which is discussed later.

```
# Printf.printf "%s %s" "hello";;
hello - : string -> unit = <fun>
```

You should always look at the return types from input. You often know you have made a semantic error if the return types are not what you expect them to be.

Final Notes

The OCaml toplevel does not have overly verbose error messages about what is wrong with your code. This lack of information can be frustrating for new users, but it is important to remember that the OCaml compiler is usually correct.

The toplevel will give you all the information it has about the problem with your code. In the following example, it even points to the exact point at which the problem appears:

```
# let func x = match x with
  Foot y -> Meter x;;
Characters 44-45:
    Foot y -> Meter x;;
                    ^
```

This expression has type distance but is here used with type int

The error message only tells you in which character position the error appears (this character position is between the start of the definition and the ;;, which signals the end of the let binding):

```
# let convert x = match x with
  Foot y -> Meter (int_of_float ((float_of_int y) *. 0.3048))
  | Meter y -> Foot (int_of_float ((float_of_int y) /. 0.3048))
  _ -> x;;
Characters 157-158:
    _ -> x;;
    ^
```

Syntax error

Code Files

Similar to most programming languages, OCaml can use source files stored in plain text, and they are no different from any other programming language source files. They often have the extension .ml for source files and .mli for interface files. Interface files are discussed in later chapters.

■**Note** All ML dialects, not just OCaml, use the .ml convention for the file extension. There are other file extensions that OCaml uses that other ML dialects do not use (these other files are covered in depth in upcoming chapters).

Basic Code Files

In this code segment, you'll notice a couple of extra keywords. We will cover these later, but for now you should focus on the similarities with the previous interactive examples.

You can cut and paste the following lines into a text file by using your favorite editor and then save it. Under either Linux or Windows, compile the file into a byte-code executable using the OCaml byte-code compiler ocamlc.

```
let _ = Printf.printf "Hello World\n";;
```

Let's say you saved this file as firstprog.ml in your user directory on Windows. You would then compile the file into a byte-code executable and run it. The command is ocamlc -o firstprog.exe firstprog.ml. This code uses the byte-code compiler (ocamlc) and outputs the executable file into firstprog.exe (the .exe extension does not need to be present on Linux).

This code would create an output file called firstprog.exe (or ./firstprog if you are on Linux), which can be executed on the same command line, as shown in Figure 2-3.

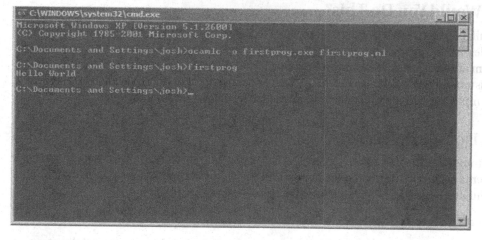

Figure 2-3. *Compiling your first OCaml program*

Congratulations—you have created your first OCaml program!

OCaml File Extensions

OCaml commonly uses other file extensions, too. The most common extensions are listed in Table 2-2 (they will be covered in more depth later in the book).

Table 2-2. *Common File Extensions*

Extension	Description
.ml	Source code
.mli	Interface code
.cmo	Byte-compiled library or file
.cmi	Compiled interface code
.cma	Native code–compiled library or file

Custom Toplevel

The toplevel that we have been interacting with is not a special toplevel. You can create your own toplevel files by using ocamlmktop. This is really a more advanced topic and we mention it here mostly for completeness.

Why Would You Do This?

The main reason to create a custom toplevel is to have easy access to various modules and code files. Although you can manually load libraries in the toplevel, some people prefer loading them automatically. There are also platforms that do not support dynamic loading.

Custom toplevels can also link in libraries and modules that are not loaded by default. For example, the code you just wrote is not loaded by default into the toplevel.

How Do You Do This?

The command to create custom toplevels is called ocamlmktop, which takes the same set of arguments as the OCamlc compiler. For example, if you have two libraries you want to bundle into your custom toplevel—foo.cmo and bar.cmo—execute the following:

```
ocamlmktop -o custom_toplevel foo.cmo bar.cmo
```

This command creates an executable named custom_toplevel in the current directory. You can then use your custom toplevel in place of running the ocaml command.

Conclusion

The OCaml toplevel provides an interactive system that is well suited for prototyping and learning. Although it presents some usability issues, utilities to make using the toplevel easy are available for all platforms.

Now that you can install and run the OCaml system, you're ready to move on to actually writing OCaml code and using the toplevel to prototype applications and functions.

Chapter 3 looks at creating a small database system and delves into the built-in types and functions of the OCaml language.

CHAPTER 3

■ ■ ■

Syntax and Semantics

So, now that you know how to install and start the OCaml toplevel, you will learn how to actually do things in the language.

This chapter covers types—the concept of types is one of the most important in OCaml. It also covers variables and discusses the ramifications of the fact that OCaml is a constant language (meaning that data values are not really variable).

Types in OCaml are important because they are the foundation upon which many of the compile-time checks are built. The type inference engine makes sure that the function return and input types are correct, eliminating a certain class of error. The OCaml type system is very flexible and enables the programmer to define types easily.

An example of a class of error that can be eliminated by using types occurs in distance calculation. Let's say you have an application that calculates distances, and you can input these distances in metric or imperial units. To prevent problems, you can define a distance type that does not allow these units to be confused.

Variables in a Constant Language

OCaml is a constant language, which means that variables are really just named values that cannot change within a scope during runtime. Although it might sound like hedging, it means that you do not have to worry about a value getting stepped on in OCaml. You know that after a value is set, it cannot change in the scope you are in—so you do not have to check it.

When combined with automatic garbage collection, this constancy protects you from a raft of problems that can occur in other programming languages. For example, in many languages, a function might modify data when you call it, resulting in side effects. In OCaml, a function is prevented from modifying those data structures by the language itself.

OCaml does have mutable references, which are more like very safe pointers than variables. They do not have the same problems that pointers in other languages have, however. You cannot, for example, perform operations on the pointer other than setting and retrieving data.

What Variables Are Not

There are some variables that are mutable, which are called references or mutable values. They are not considered a pure functional construct; they exist because OCaml is a practical language, and there are times when having mutability (with a buffer, for example) can be very handy.

Note OCaml is not a purely functional language; it is a practical language. So if you are set on being pure, you should not use mutable references.

Let Bindings

If you have ever used a functional programming (FP) language, you know about the let binding. It means in OCaml what it means in English: *let* (*allow*) this name to be associated with this value. The simplest let binding binds a basic type to a name:

```
# let a = 1;;
val a : int = 1
```

Note the new kind of return message: val. This is a message from the OCaml compiler that a is now bound to something. Binding a name to something makes that name a value and then the type information of the binding is displayed.

All values are constant within their scope. References are also constant, although the value they refer to can be mutable. References are displayed as a special record type:

```
# let b = ref 1;;
val b : int ref = {contents = 1}
```

References always point to another type and they are modifiable. You can assign a new number to this example by using the assignment operator:

```
# b := 20;;
-- : unit = ()
# b;;
-- : int ref = { contents = 20 }
#
```

References can also be modified via their contents attribute. A more idiomatic method of assigning to a reference is by using the assignment operator shown previously.

```
# b := 10;;
-- : unit = ()
# b;;
-- : int ref = {contents = 10}
# b.contents <- 20;;
-- : unit = ()
# b;;
-- : int ref = {contents = 20}
```

The special := operator is used to assign references. You also can use the <- operator to assign a value to the contents of a given reference. However, for clarity, the := operator is preferred. For now, we will not discuss the difference between the = operator and the other assignment operators (but it is discussed in later chapters). The let bindings are all pretty simple here; you will see more complicated examples as we move forward.

Mutable References Should Be Used Sparingly

It can be tempting to use mutable references, but I suggest that you resist that temptation. I have generally found that, except in a few cases, the use of a mutable reference could be removed by fixing my designs.

This is not a rule in any sense of the term because sometimes a mutable reference is really the best choice. File input/output (I/O) is a good example because file I/O is often a nonfunctional chore. Some other functional languages deal with these nonfunctional chores by using monadic computation, but that might not always be necessary.

You can hide mutable references in OCaml classes to make their use less problematic (this is discussed in more detail in Chapter 19).

Understanding Scope

It can sometimes be difficult to think about scope in OCaml because there are comparatively few syntactic notations to help indicate scope. However, when you understand that only a new let or a function call can be the demarcation of scope, the elegance begins to appear.

The following example shows how a new scope is introduced:

```
Objective Caml version 3.09.0

# let someval = "hello";;
val someval: string = "hello"
# let otherval = "world" in let someval = "Bummer, " in
  Printf.printf "%s %s\n" someval otherval;;
  Bummer, world
- : unit = ()
#
```

The binding of the same name (in this case, someval) inside the new scope overrides the one outside. In practice, this situation doesn't happen very often in real programs. However, in OCaml (as in almost all programs) it is important to keep variable names unique and clear. The compiler will not generate a warning or an error if you occlude a variable using scoping.

Records and Types

Let's start by creating a basic record type called first_example:

```
# type first_example = { foo: string; bar: int};;
type first_example = { foo : string; bar : int; }
# {foo = "hello";bar = 10};;
- : first_example = {foo = "hello"; bar = 10}
# {foo = 10; bar = 10 };;
This expression has type int but is here used with type string
```

Types are intrinsic attributes in OCaml—everything has a type. Records are special collections of types. Types can be user-defined and can be arbitrarily complicated. Enumerated values (enums) can be represented easily in the OCaml type system. In the preceding example, you see the creation of a record type called first_example that has two elements: a string and an integer. After you define the type, the interpreter shows the signature of the type, which lets you know that it is available and okay to use.

When you enter data that conforms to the type specification (or signature), the interpreter recognizes it as the type defined. If you try to enter the wrong type for the elements, the interpreter gives an error because you tried to use the wrong type for that element.

You also can define types that are very similar to enums in other languages, which enables you to create types for symbolic processing or enumerating.

```
# type second_example = Jack | Queen | King | Ace;;
type second_example = Jack | Queen | King | Ace
# Jack;;
- : second_example = Jack
# Ten;;
Unbound constructor Ten
#
```

The preceding example creates an enumerated type describing four different playing card values. The type name must be lowercase, but the types must be uppercase. Not every uppercase word will work, however, as demonstrated by the error using the Ten type (this happens because you haven't defined it yet).

Accidentally redefining types is something to watch out for. There will be no warnings if you have redefined a type, although you might get compiler errors that make little sense. If you find that you are getting errors compiling a bit of code, and the compiler tells you that it got a type but was expecting the same type, you should look closely at your type definitions.

Now that you have seen types in action, they can be discussed in greater detail. A *type* is a thing (or a collection of things) or value. In OCaml, every entity has a specific type, and that type is known at compile time. In many languages, the type of each entity must be specified in the code (Java and C are examples). This situation can lead to the programmer doing work that the compiler will later check (at least in languages such as Java), and a mistake in the type specification can lead to errors when the program is run.

Other languages (Python, for example) do not require this specification. They do, however, figure out the type of a given element at runtime. These languages usually do not have to know all the type information at compile time, which can also lead to errors at runtime.

OCaml avoids these kinds of runtime errors by ensuring that the type of each entity is known at compile time. It does this by inferring type information at compile time, which is also the reason why you do not have to specify type information in the code. The compiler also enforces these types, requiring all types to be correct and known. This part of the compiler is referred to as the *type inference engine* (discussed later in this chapter and in other chapters).

Basic Types

Basic (or built-in) types in OCaml are identifiers such as integers, floats, and strings (see Table 3-1). These are the types that OCaml knows about already (and it has functions to handle them).

Table 3-1. *OCaml Basic Types*

Type	Description
int	31-bit signed integer
float	Floating-point number, equivalent to the C language double
bool	True (true) or false (false)
char	8-bit unsigned integer, character
string	Character strings
unit	Special type (typesafe type)

OCaml integers are 31 bits because OCaml uses 1 bit to distinguish between integers and pointers. However, if you need 32-bit integers, there is a 32-bit integer library called Int32 (and a 64-bit integer library called Int64).

Aggregate Types

Aggregate types, which are composed of basic types, are most often types that you have defined. OCaml enables you to define types in a couple of ways.

```
# type aggregate = Rock of (int * string);;
type aggregate = Rock of (int * string)
```

The preceding type is made up of integer and string types. Classes are also types. (The OCaml object system is covered in later chapters.) Aggregate types can even be recursive, which is very handy when you want to use a type to represent data structures such as trees. The following is a recursive type:

```
# type tree = Leaf of tree | Node of string;;
type tree = Leaf of tree | Node of string
# Leaf (Leaf (Node "terminal"));;
- : tree = Leaf (Leaf (Node "terminal"))
#
```

Polymorphic Types

Data types in OCaml can also be *polymorphic*, which allow for aggregate types to contain different types without having to specify every possible combination. This kind of polymorphism is similar to (but not the same as) templates in C++ and Java.

The important thing about polymorphic types is that you do not have to define a unique type for each combination if your type will be really polymorphic. The type inference engine within OCaml will enforce this for you, as with all types.

```
# type fish = Fish of int;;
type 'a polyfish = Polyfish of 'a;;
type fish = Fish of int
```

```
# type 'a polyfish = Polyfish of 'a
# Fish 10;;
- : fish = Fish 10
# Polyfish "hello";;
- : string polyfish = Polyfish "hello"
# let printpolyfish x = match x with
    Polyfish n -> Printf.printf "%s\n" n;;
  val printpolyfish : string polyfish -> unit = <fun>
# printpolyfish (Polyfish 10);;
Characters 24-26:
  printpolyfish (Polyfish 10);;
                         ^^
This expression has type int but is here used with type string
#
```

OCaml has polymorphic classes similar to C++ and Java, but the polymorphism at the type level in OCaml is *parametric polymorphism* instead of *object polymorphism*. The subtleties of the differences are well beyond the scope of this book, but if you want to know more, the Usenet newsgroup comp.lang.ml is a good starting place for discussions about the complex issues of parametric polymorphism.

For now, it is enough to understand that OCaml has the capability to use polymorphism so that the programmer does not have to enumerate every possible type that a structure or function can deal with. You should also be aware that polymorphism in OCaml is not the same as what other languages call polymorphism.

Creating Enums and Simple User-Defined Types

In C (and many C-like languages) you have the option of defining *enumerated values* (*enums*), which are often groupings of values such as RED, BLUE, and GREEN that you would otherwise have to assign another value to.

Using the example from the chapter introduction, you might do the following to create a distance type:

```
# type distance = Meter of int | Foot of int | Mile of int;;
type distance = Meter of int | Foot of int | Mile of int
# Foot 10;;
-- : distance = Foot 10
# Meter 20;;
-- : distance = Meter 20
# (Meter 20) + (Foot 10);;
Characters 0-10:
  (Meter 20) + (Foot 10);;
  ^^^^^^^^^^
This expression has type distance but is here used with type int
#
```

Although the type can be used after it is defined, you cannot simply add two values together and get any result.

This type definition is also called a *variant* in some OCaml documentation. Variants can also be used to describe recursive data types. For example, you could add a polymorphic distance variant to the distance data type by creating the definition like so:

```
# type 'a distance = Meter of int | Foot of int | Mile of int | ➥
Distance of 'a distance;;
type 'a distance =
    Meter of int
  | Foot of int
  | Mile of int
  | Distance of 'a distance
# Distance (Foot 10);;
- : 'a distance = Distance (Foot 10)
# Distance 10;;
Characters 9-11:
  Distance 10;;
          ^^
This expression has type int but is here used with type 'a distance
#
```

Adding this definition to the type doesn't provide much, but it demonstrates the function of recursive types. In real life, you will often see recursive data structures used to describe trees and similar structures.

If you want to encode a type to describe a tree-like structure similar to the one shown in Figure 3-1, you can use the following type definition (and associated code) to do it:

```
# type tree = Node of tree * tree | Terminal of int;;
type tree = Node of tree * tree | Terminal of int
# Node ((Terminal 10),(Node ((Node ((Terminal 11),(Terminal 7))),Terminal 5)));;
- : tree =
Node (Terminal 10, Node (Node (Terminal 11, Terminal 7), Terminal 5))
```

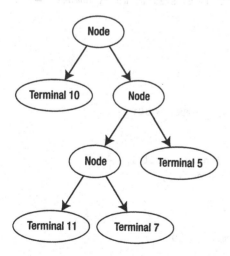

Figure 3-1. *Representation of a tree structure*

Defining Records

A record is much like a C-style struct. As an aggregate type, you can make records starting with any other types (including other records). A record is a collection of labels and types. These labels must be unique within the current module so the type inference engine can infer types correctly. You will create an example record that uses the 'a distance type from the last example to demonstrate this:

```
# type 'a part_with_length = {part_name: string; part_number: int; ➡
part_length: 'a distance };;
type 'a part_with_length = {
  part_name : string;
  part_number : int;
  part_length : 'a distance;
}
```

This example uses two basic types, strings and ints, as well as the aggregate type distance. Now that you have the part_with_length type, you can begin to define parts. Notice that you do not have to specify that you are creating this type because the type inference engine will do it for you:

```
# let crescent_wrench = {part_name="Left Handed Crescent Wrench";part_number=1; ➡
part_length=(Foot 1)};;
val crescent_wrench : 'a part_with_length =
  {part_name = "Left Handed Crescent Wrench"; part_number = 1;
   length = Foot 1}
#
```

Mutability and Records

Records can have mutable elements, which are defined with the mutable keyword. To use the earlier example, to have a mutable part record type, you could define it like this:

```
# type 'a mutable_part_with_length = {mutable mpart_name: string; mpart_number: ➡
int; mpart_length: 'a distance };;
type 'a mutable_part_with_length = {
  mutable mpart_name : string;
  mpart_number : int;
  mpart_length : 'a distance;
}
# let mcrescent_wrench = {mpart_name = "hello";mpart_number = 10; ➡
mpart_length = (Foot 1)};;
val mcrescent_wrench : 'a mutable_part_with_length =
  {mpart_name = "hello"; mpart_number = 10; mpart_length = Foot 1}
# mcrescent_wrench.mpart_name <- "Mutable Crescent Wrench";;
- : unit = ()
# mcrescent_wrench;;
- : 'a mutable_part_with_length =
{mpart_name = "Mutable Crescent Wrench"; mpart_number = 10;
 mpart_length = Foot 1}
#
```

The new part now has a name that can be changed. Although purists might stay away from mutability, it is important to know that the feature exists in the language.

Name Clashes

One of the side effects of the type inference engine is that you cannot create a record definition with fields that are the same name as another. For this reason, you should not define two records that contain a field called id in the same module. The compiler will not complain if you do this, however.

More About Math

OCaml is designed to be provable, and there is at least one publicly available automated theorem solver in OCaml for OCaml programs.

■**Note** OCaml is designed to be provably correct. The Coq proof assistant, which is available from http://coq.inria.fr/, is a formal proof management system. Among other things, it includes the capability to automatically generate certified programs from proofs of their specifications.

Operator overloading is not possible in OCaml, and the concept is not considered a "Good Thing" by the OCaml community. This is one notable break from other meta-languages (MLs), many of which treat all numbers the same.

Integers and Floats

Integers have certain semantics. One of the most important is that they do not have fractional parts. Integer operators are the familiar math operators such as +, /, and >.

Floating-point numbers (floats) in OCaml have the same resolution as a double in the operating sysem (OS) you are using. Floats should not be used when high precision is required, however, even though they have high resolution. The main problem with floats is that they have rounding issues common to such numbers.

All standard mathematical operators working on floats have a . suffix. For example, adding floats is done through the +. operator to prevent type confusion.

Others

OCaml handles complex numbers via a standard library appropriately named Complex. This library includes types and routines for dealing with complex numbers. You also can use the type system to create numerical types.

For example, suppose you want to create a fractional type. You could use a record type for this:

```
# type fraction = { numerator: int; denominator: int };;
```

However, there are libraries with OCaml (called Ratio libraries) that handle fractions and arbitrary precision numbers. This record type using fractions is just an example of record types instead of mathematical capabilities.

Defining Functions

Functions are defined by using let the same way other values are defined. Functions have to take at least one argument. Simple functions are covered here; the next chapter gets into more detail. A very simple function just adds 1 to any integer passed to it:

```
# let add x = x + 1;;
val add : int -> int = <fun>
# add 5;;
- : int = 6
#
```

Flow control in FP can be a strange thing if you are used to imperative styles. FP often makes heavy use of recursion instead of iteration (although sometimes this is "six of one and half dozen of the other").

Imperative Programming

OCaml has all the normal flow control statements. For example, you can rewrite the simple addition function to add a given number if the passed parameter is greater than a given value:

```
# let add_plus x = if (x > 10) then
  x + x
  else
  x + 1;;
val add_plus : int -> int = <fun>
# add_plus 15;;
- : int = 30
# add_plus 10;;
- : int = 11
#
```

Other flow control operators are discussed in Chapter 4, which focuses on functions.

Recursion

Recursion, which is a key concept in OCaml, involves calling a function from within itself. One of the best-known recursive algorithms (in certain circles, at least) is Euclid's algorithm for finding the greatest common divisor of two integers:

```
# greatest_c_div 7 21;;
- : int = 7
# greatest_c_div 200 324;;
- : int = 4
```

```
# greatest_c_div 200 323;;
- : int = 1
# greatest_c_div 200 321;;
- : int = 1
# greatest_c_div 200 320;;
- : int = 40
# let rec greatest_c_div x y = match x with
  0 -> y
| _ -> greatest_c_div (y mod x) x;;
    val greatest_c_div : int -> int -> int = <fun>
#
```

The difference between defining a function as recursive or not recursive is the addition of the rec keyword.

Why Use Recursion?

Some algorithms are best expressed recursively. Although all recursive algorithms can be solved by using imperative programming, it is not always the best way to express these algorithms. For example, the greatest common divisor function shown previously is three lines when expressed recursively. If you expressed it imperatively, it would take eight lines and would not be nearly as clear:

```
let imperative_gcd x y = let a = ref x in let b = ref y in
  while (a.contents > 0) do
    let m = a.contents in
      (
                a := b.contents mod a.contents;
                b := m
      )
  done;b.contents;;
```

They both yield the same answers, though, and both perform the same task:

```
# greatest_c_div 5436 7212;;
- : int = 12
# imperative_gcd 5436 7212;;
- : int = 12
```

Chapter 4 covers recursion extensively in the function discussion. If you are having some trouble with recursion, don't be discouraged; almost everyone has some difficulty with the concept.

Pattern Matching

Pattern matching is a very powerful tool. Using a distance type similar to the one you defined earlier, you can write a function to convert between feet and meters:

```
# type distance = Meter of float | Foot of float
type distance = Meter of float | Foot of float
```

```
# let convert x = match x with
  | Foot y -> Meter (y *. 0.3048)
  | Meter y -> Foot (y /. 0.3048) ;;
val convert : distance -> distance = <fun>
# let result = convert (Meter (float_of_int 3));;
val result : distance = Foot 9.84251968503937
# convert result;;
- : distance = Meter 3.00000000000000044
```

This example also demonstrates the float_of_int function, which is used to convert integers to floating-point numbers. There is also an int_of_float function that does the reverse.

Signatures

Signatures are descriptions of a function, value, module, or class that use type information only. They are used in a variety of ways in OCaml programming, not the least of which is as a pseudocode when talking about OCaml code.

Signatures are generated automatically by the toplevel interpreter when you enter code. They are then displayed and show the inferred type information. The following example shows a value one being set to an integer:

```
# let one = 1;;
val one : int = 1
```

The second line shows that one is a value (rather than an object or something else), that its type is int, and that its value is 1. If you were to define a function, it might look like this:

```
# let one x = x + 10;;
val one : int -> int = <fun>
```

This example shows that one is a function that takes an integer argument and returns an integer value (the last type in the sequence is the return type). The type of this expression is also indicated as a function type (or fun). This book often refers to code using signatures, which are used to show type information and are almost always easier to understand than implementation code. Much of the OCaml documentation uses signatures in a similar fashion, as do many programmers. It is important that you become familiar with reading and signatures.

Conclusion

Now you have the tools to do actual computation in OCaml. You have begun to learn about type and what the type system in OCaml can do for you, as well as defining your own types and functions to operate on them.

The next chapter is where you will dive into functions and learn how to actually create programs in OCaml.

CHAPTER 4

■■■

Understanding Functions

Functions are the main part of OCaml, which is not surprising because OCaml is a functional programming (FP) language. Functions in OCaml have signatures that are displayed in the OCaml toplevel and are used extensively in the module language.

For now, you'll focus on function signatures displayed in the toplevel. These function signatures enable you to know what parameters a function will accept and the return type of the function. They do not indicate whether a given function is recursive, however.

Creating Values and Functions

Functions are data items that take arguments and return a data item of a given type. A function can take and return any valid OCaml type, including other functions. (This capability to take and return functions will be discussed in more detail later in this chapter.) A *value* is a data item of a given type that contains some data. Values can be thought of as variables, although they are not really "variable" in the sense of being able to be changed.

Values are a label for a given collection of data. They are *immutable*—they cannot be changed once assigned. They can, however, be overridden. Values are created by using the let function and can be defined statically (for example, assigning a value to a string or number) or from the result of computation (for example, the result of a function).

If you go to the OCaml toplevel, you can assign some values by using the let keyword:

```
# let a = 5;;
val a : int = 5
# let b = 10;;
val b : int = 10
#
```

■**Note** Keywords such as let are not really functions. Although they take arguments and return items, they do not perform computations. You can think of them as prepositions (where values are nouns and functions are verbs).

The preceding code assigned the value a to be 5 and the value b to be 10. You can now use a and b in other functions.

```
# a + b;;
- : int = 15
#
```

You can define functions in the same way as values by using the `let` keyword. In the following code, the function `myfunc` is defined with `()` as the first argument. This is shorthand for a unit argument, which is very similar in concept to `void` (found in languages such as Java). This function performs some simple math and returns an integer:

```
# let myfunc () = 1 + 1;;
val myfunc : unit -> int = <fun>
```

Pay careful attention to the line after the definition. This line, which is called the *signature*, shows what type of arguments a given function takes (and how many) and the return type. It also shows that `myfunc` is a special value of the `fun` type, which indicates that `myfunc` is a function instead of a simple value.

If you call this function with the `unit` argument, you get the expected result, which is a value. The signature of the return tells you the value of the return and its type:

```
# myfunc ();;
- : int = 2
```

You can explicitly define a function by using the `fun` keyword:

```
# let myfunc = (fun () -> 1 + 1);;
val myfunc : unit -> int = <fun>
# myfunc ();;
- : int = 2
```

No matter how you define functions, their properties are the same.

Most functions are like these—prefix functions—because the default is to define functions as prefix functions. However, infix functions are easy to define. This chapter will cover both prefix and infix functions.

The previous example shows the difference between functions and values: functions must take parameters. The function signature of both definitions is the same. The function signature says that the function `myfunc` takes one parameter of type `unit` and returns an `int`. The special `()` is the `unit` type, which can serve as a placeholder for a value you have no intention of passing. This is a way to make functions that don't actually take any real parameters.

You can also have `let` bindings inside of your functions, which can be any allowed value. A common use for the bindings is to have values defined within your functions, which is done like so:

```
# let myfunc x y =
    let someval = x + y in
    Printf.printf "Hello internal value: %i\n" someval;;
val myfunc : int -> int -> unit = <fun>
# myfunc 10 20;;
Hello internal value: 30
- : unit = ()
#
```

This code creates the equivalent of temporary variables in a function. The garbage collection will handle their destruction, so you need only to define them. These definitions can be arbitrarily deep, although you might want to create new functions if your definitions get too complicated.

Functions Must Have One Return Type

A nonpolymorphic function can have only one return type in OCaml. Even polymorphic functions have only one return type, although this return type can be a polymorphic type. Polymorphism is enforced by the type inference engine, and it is very easy for a novice to try to create functions that do not return the type you think they do. Fortunately, the compiler will give you an error message if you attempt to do this (this is shown in the next example).

Function return types will be automatically figured out by the compiler. The compiler will find the most generic type a function can return and then use it. If your function is polymorphic, it will automatically be designated as such, and you cannot force a function to be polymorphic simply by defining it.

This automatic determination of return type can lead to some frustrating situations in which you and the compiler disagree with what a given function returns. As shown in the following example, if you try to create a function that does not have one return type, the compiler gives you an error. The error message the compiler gives can sometimes appear unhelpful (in this example, the error is that a string is returned if an exception is encountered).

```
# let errorprone x = try
    while !x < 10 do
      incr x
    done
    with _ -> "Failed";;
Characters 100-108:
      with _ -> "Failed";;
             ^^^^^^^^
This expression has type string but is here used with type unit
# let errorprone x = try
    while !x < 10 do
      incr x
    done
    with _ -> ();;
val errorprone : int ref -> unit = <fun>
#
```

Constraining Types in Function Calls

You can specify a function's parameter types for a couple of reasons (the most important reason is that you might have to). Although the compiler attempts to infer the types used in your functions, it does not always succeed, especially when mutable values are used and in certain other cases (this topic is discussed in more detail in Chapter 5).

Another reason to specify the type is to make the type clear. If you know that a given parameter will be a given type, you can define it and know that the compiler will give an error if it is used incorrectly.

In most cases, however, the explicit definition of a parameter type is not required. Although there are some cases in which constraining the type will yield performance benefits, it is not often done because the development benefit of having the compiler do the work is frequently greater. The compiler will still infer the type information and verify that it is correct, even if you have specified it. The compiler will give you errors if the inferred type is incompatible with the specified type:

```
# let mismatching (x:int) (y: float) = x + (int_of_string y);;
Characters 56-57:
  let mismatching (x:int) (y: float) = x + (int_of_string y);;
                                                        ^
This expression has type float but is here used with type string
#
```

Using Higher-Order Functions

OCaml has support for *higher-order functions (HOFs)*, which take other functions as arguments. OCaml can do this because functions are first-class types. For example, the following (somewhat contrived) example is a function that takes three arguments. The first argument is a function that takes two arguments; the other two arguments are then passed as arguments to the first argument. In this case, the example just uses the numeric comparison arguments to demonstrate. Because the > and < operators are infix operators, they must be enclosed in parentheses (if you don't do this, you get the shown error):

```
# let bigger f x y = f x y;;
val bigger : ('a -> 'b -> 'c) -> 'a -> 'b -> 'c = <fun>
# bigger (>) 10 20;;
- : bool = false
# bigger (<) 10 20;;
- : bool = true
# bigger < 10 20;;
Characters 9-11:
  bigger < 10 20;;
         ^^
This expression is not a function, it cannot be applied
#
```

Another example of a HOF is when some (but not all) of the arguments that a function needs are passed to it. This function is called a *curried function*.

```
# let add_one = (+) 1;;
val add_one : int -> int = <fun>
# add_one 10;;
- : int = 11
# (fun x y -> x * y);;
- : int -> int -> int = <fun>
```

You can define anonymous functions and use them in much the same way. An anonymous function that is assigned to a name is indistinguishable from a function defined any other way. The preceding code shows both a curried function and an anonymous function. Read on for more on their creation and use.

Using Lists

Lists are used to create some of the examples in this chapter. However, the syntax for dealing with lists will not be covered for a few chapters yet. To make the examples more understandable, here is a quick introduction to OCaml lists:

- List elements must be of the same type.

- Lists are defined by using square brackets, with elements separated by semicolons.

- Lists are indexed starting at 0 (not 1).

- Lists are a basic type and a very important data structure.

- List elements cannot be modified.

- Lists are of fixed length and cannot be resized.

```
# [1;2;3;4;5];;
- : int list = [1; 2; 3; 4; 5]
# List.sort compare [4;5;6;2;4;2;0];;
- : int list = [0; 2; 2; 4; 4; 5; 6]
# List.nth [0;1;2;3;4] 3;;
- : int = 3
# List.nth [0;1;2;3;4] 0;;
- : int = 0
```

Lists also have comparing/sorting functions. The compare function shown in the preceding code is a built-in function that can be used for sorting any valid OCaml type. Lists are covered in much greater depth later in the book, but this introduction should give you enough information to understand the examples in this chapter.

Anonymous Functions

Anonymous functions are very useful in OCaml. Sometimes referred to as *generic* functions, anonymous functions are functions that do not have a name so they are not assigned to any value. There are many reasons to use and create anonymous functions.

Many functions take functions as arguments, and anonymous functions are an easy way to pass those functions.

The compare function for sorting lists is a good example—it takes two arguments and returns an integer of 1 if the second value is less than the first. It returns 0 if the values are equal and -1 if the second value is greater than the first.

You can pass your own compare function to other functions, such as the List.sort function, and have them sort based on your compare function. This example sorts a list by a reversing anonymous function and by the default compare function.

```
# List.sort (fun x y -> if x = y then
  -1
  else if x < y then
  1
  else
  0) [1;4;9;3;2;1];;
- : int list = [9; 4; 3; 2; 1; 1]
# List.sort compare [1;4;9;3;2;1];;
- : int list = [1;1;2;3;4;9]
```

Although anonymous functions are used a great deal in OCaml, they can sometimes hurt code readability. Functions are basic types in OCaml and (like other values in OCaml) also do not have to be assigned to a name. Unlike other values, unnamed or anonymous functions have many uses.

This property of functions is one of the differences between OCaml (and FP languages in general) and other kinds of programming languages. Functions can be passed to other functions and returned from functions. These passed and returned functions can also be anonymous functions. In this book, you will see anonymous functions used with the scanf commands in many chapters.

```
# Scanf.sscanf "hello world" "%s %s" (fun x y -> Printf.printf "%s %s\n" y x);;
world hello
- : unit = ()
```

The anonymous function used here reversed the strings. This function was created on-the-fly by using the fun keyword. The only difference between anonymous functions and named functions is that one has a name and the other does not. Because the naming of functions is a help to the programmer more than it is a technical requirement, you could write all your programs using only anonymous functions. Doing that is not recommended—for obvious reasons.

Putting the *Fun* in Functions

The fun keyword can be used to define functions that are assigned to a name and it can create them without assigning them to a name. Functions in OCaml must take an argument. This property is one of the attributes that separate functions from plain values. You do not have to use the fun keyword when defining anonymous functions if you are currying functions (which is discussed later in this chapter).

In an interactive session, you can see the results:

```
# (fun x -> 10);;
- : int -> int = <fun>
# (fun x -> 10 + x) 30;;
- : int = 40
# Printf.printf "%s\n";;
- : string -> unit = <fun>
# let funclist = [Printf.printf "%s\n"];;
val funclist : (string -> unit) list = [<fun>]
```

```
# (List.nth funclist 0) "hello world";;
hello world
- : unit = ()
#
```

Why Use Anonymous Functions?

You can use anonymous functions when you are creating functions that operate on functions. HOFs can be very useful for solving problems, especially when you want to build up a group of operations and results. They can also be used for complicated operations and lists of functions and/or callbacks.

List folding is an example of when using an anonymous function is very handy. (*Folding* is referred to as *reducing* in some languages.) Although the map function applies a given function to each element in a collection, the fold function takes two arguments—the first is the list element and the second is the result of the previous function call (and so on). The initial value is specified as an argument to the fold function. This value is also the return value if you have an empty list. In the following example, the + function is used (indicate to the compiler that it is a function by enclosing it in parentheses).

```
# List.fold_left (+) 0 [1;2;3;4;5];;
- : int = 15
```

This is equivalent to doing 0 + 1 + 2 + 3 + 4 + 5. You can curry this function and create a new function, sum, that does it all in a simple-to-call manner.

```
# let sum = List.fold_left (+) 0;;
val sum : int list -> int = <fun>
# sum [1;2;3;4;5;6];;
- : int = 21
#
```

Understanding Consequences of Functions As Data

As shown in the callback example, when the functions are registered, they are anonymized. Although they lose their name, you can find the name of a function that has been stored in a data structure or passed as an argument to another function using physical equality (the = operator). This doesn't change anything about the function. For example, the following example creates a simple function and stores it into a list. Once stored in the list, the function is not accessible from that list by its name. Physical equality also distinguishes the function from another function, even if that function is otherwise the same.

```
# let f x y = x + y;;
val f : int -> int -> int = <fun>
# let m = [f];;
val m : (int -> int -> int) list = [<fun>]
# (List.hd m) == f;;
- : bool = true
# let b = f;;
val b : int -> int -> int = <fun>
```

```
# b == f;;
- : bool = true
# let c x y = x + y;;
val c : int -> int -> int = <fun>
# c == f;;
- : bool = false
#
```

Although functions cannot be decomposed, you can compose functions however you like. Take care when you do this—function composition can yield results that are difficult to figure out. The compiler can do the composition if the code is syntactically valid and can sometimes present error messages that are equally difficult to understand. This is a situation in which the syntax (the structure) of the code might be mostly correct, but the semantics (the meaning) is almost certainly incorrect.

To illustrate, here is a simple test case. This case really doesn't do anything except highlight the ease in which you can get yourself in trouble with composition. You start with a simple function: compose:

```
# let compose m y = y m;;
val compose : 'a -> ('a -> 'b) -> 'b = <fun>
```

This function reorders a pair of functions that are passed to it and returns a third, newly composed function:

```
# compose (fun x -> x 3.14159) (fun m n o -> (m n) o);;
- : (float -> '_a -> '_b) -> '_a -> '_b = <fun>
# let b = compose (fun x -> x 3.14159) (fun m n o -> (m n) o);;
val b : (float -> '_a -> '_b) -> '_a -> '_b = <fun>
# b 3.123;;
Characters 2-7:
  b 3.123;;
  ^^^^^
This expression has type float but is here used with type float -> 'a -> 'b
# b (fun n m o -> o);;
- : '_a -> '_b -> '_b = <fun>
# (b (fun n m o -> o)) "hi" "there";;
- : string = "there"
#
```

The only way you know that a given value is actually a function is by paying careful attention to the signatures. You can also pay attention to the compiler errors, although doing so makes the process take much longer.

Caution If you find yourself often composing functions, you might want to review your functions and break them down. They might be too complicated.

Functions cannot be serialized via the Marshal module. This is a limitation of the Marshal module that is difficult to overcome because functions require abstract values (which also cannot be serialized). If you need to have anonymous functions serialized, you have to do it manually or convert the functions into a data structure (which is often much easier said than done).

Curried Functions

Currying is when you take a function that takes multiple arguments and turn it into a function that takes only one argument. The term *curried function* is often used to describe any situation in which you transform a function into a function that takes different arguments. You can do more than simply pass functions as parameters to other functions—you can assign a value from a function with some of its parameters passed to it and then use it as if it were a function with different arguments.

Looking back at the example given earlier in the chapter, here is a new function that takes only one argument from a function that originally took two arguments:

```
# let add_one = (+) 1;;
val add_one : int -> int = <fun
# add_one 10;;
- : int = 11
#
```

In this case, you fixed one of the two arguments (by setting it to 1) in the function. The function is not evaluated until all its arguments are complete.

Why Curried Functions Are Important

By using curried functions, you can build up the arguments to your functions at runtime, so you do not have to resort to list processing to build a runtime-defined list of arguments.

Curried functions also enable you to refactor your code more effectively. Because you can easily redefine how function arguments appear to any given function, you can restructure your code accordingly.

Working with the Distance Type

You will be working with the nonpolymorphic version of the distance type created in the last chapter. You will start with conversions between the different variants and then go on to create a four-function distance calculator.

```
# type distance = Meter of int | Foot of int | Mile of int;;
type distance = Meter of int | Foot of int | Mile of int
```

Converting Between Kinds of Distances

Simple conversion functions enable you to convert to meters, feet, and miles (for clarity, this example uses the naming convention _* instead of the more standard distance_of_* convention):

```
# let to_meter x = match x with
  Foot n -> Meter ( n / 3)
  | Mile n -> Meter (n * 1600)
  | Meter n -> Meter n;;
val to_meter : distance -> distance = <fun>
# let to_foot x = match x with
  Mile n -> Foot (n * 5000)
  | Meter n -> Foot (n * 3)
  | Foot n -> Foot n;;

val to_foot : distance -> distance = <fun>
# let to_mile x = match x with
  Meter n -> Mile (n / 1600)
  | Foot n -> Mile (n / 5000)
  | Mile n -> Mile n;;
val to_mile : distance -> distance = <fun>
#
let meter_of_int x = Meter x;;
val meter_of_int : int -> distance = <fun>
# meter_of_int 10;;
- : distance = Meter 10
```

You might wonder whether you can just define an int_of_distance function, pull out the number, and be done with it. The reason for not doing this is type preservation. The distance example was created to show how type can prevent certain types of programming errors from occurring. By erasing the type of the distance (Foot or Meter), you can have a situation in your code in which distances get added that shouldn't be, which might cause a very subtle error in your output (or worse). If you were really working with these kinds of measurements, you might not even want a distance type; you might want a Meter type and a Foot type, and so on.

Because it is a safe language, OCaml gives you tools to avoid these kinds of errors right out of the gate. You should always think very hard before reverting to type erasure to solve a problem. You might be opening yourself up to future problems.

Creating a Four-Function Distance Calculator

You will define a default match for most of these functions, which will prevent a warning being generated by the compiler. The warning that would be generated from these definitions if you did not include a default match is the following: Warning: this pattern-matching is not exhaustive. Here is an example of a value that is not matched: (Mile _|Foot _).

Although there is no operator overloading in OCaml, it is easy to define your own infix functions. There are no restrictions on defining infix functions, although you should not use (* or *) because they can cause confusion with the comment character in OCaml. In fact, you should always put spaces around any use of * to avoid confusion. Take care to not redefine any built-in functions. Although redefining is not prohibited, it is a bad practice and will confound anyone after you who must maintain the code.

The first function you will define is addition. You will use the infix syntax for all of these functions. These are examples of how HOFs can simplify code. The function names imply that they are strictly mathematical functions, but you can pass arbitrary functions as long as they take two arguments and return the correct type.

```
# let math_on_meter x y z = match x,y with
  Meter n, Meter m -> Meter (z n m)
  | _ -> raise Not_found ;;
val math_on_meter : distance -> distance -> (int -> int -> int) -> distance =
  <fun>
# let math_on_foot x y z = match x,y with
  Foot n,Foot m -> Foot (z n m)
  | _ -> raise Not_found;;
val math_on_foot : distance -> distance -> (int -> int -> int) -> distance =
  <fun>
# let math_on_mile x y z = match x,y with
  Mile n,Mile m -> Mile (z n m)
  | _ -> raise Not_found;;
val math_on_mile : distance -> distance -> (int -> int -> int) -> distance =  <fun>
#
```

Having defined infix functions, you can now clearly implement the math functions:

```
# let ( %+ ) x y = match x with
  Meter n -> math_on_meter x (to_meter y) ( + )
  | Foot n -> math_on_foot x (to_foot y) ( + )
  | Mile n -> math_on_mile x (to_mile y) ( + );;
val ( %+ ) : distance -> distance -> distance = <fun>
# let ( %- ) x y = match x with
  Meter n -> math_on_meter x (to_meter y) ( - )
  | Foot n -> math_on_foot x (to_foot y) ( - )
  | Mile n -> math_on_mile x (to_mile y) ( - );;
val ( %- ) : distance -> distance -> distance = <fun>
# let ( %* ) x y = match x with
  Meter n -> math_on_meter x (to_meter y) ( * )
  | Foot n -> math_on_foot x (to_foot y) ( * )
  | Mile n -> math_on_mile x (to_mile y) ( * );;
val ( %* ) : distance -> distance -> distance = <fun>
# let ( %/ ) x y = match x with
  Meter n -> math_on_meter x (to_meter y) ( / )
  | Foot n -> math_on_foot x (to_foot y) ( / )
  | Mile n -> math_on_mile x (to_mile y) ( / );;
val ( %/ ) : distance -> distance -> distance = <fun>
#
```

You see an example of these functions together here:

```
# (Meter 3) %* (Mile 1);;
- : distance = Meter 4800
# (Foot 12) %- (Foot 3);;
- : distance = Foot 9
#
```

Creating Recursive Functions

Recursion is very important in OCaml. In particular, *tail recursion* is significant because it can create enormous performance improvements in your code.

Anonymous functions cannot be recursive because you cannot call what has no name. We will talk about how you can do many other equally interesting things with anonymous functions in this chapter.

Recursion is used extensively in functions, data structures, and types. Also, because of performance gains that can be realized via tail recursion, recursive solutions are often chosen over iterative solutions. However, recursion does not automatically make programs perform better. In fact, recursive solutions that are not tail-recursive often perform poorly compared with other solutions.

The Fibonacci sequence is often solved via recursion:

```
# let rec fib n = if (n < 2) then
  1
  else
  (fib (n - 1)) + (fib (n - 2));;
val fib : int -> int = <fun>
# fib 6;;
- : int = 13
#
```

But when was the last time you needed to use the Fibonacci sequence? Recursion is used very often in OCaml code to solve a variety of problems and is often used to replace iterative loops. The following example presents two functions that explode strings into lists of chars and collapse lists of chars to strings:

```
let explode_string x =
  let strlen = String.length x in
  let rec es i acc =
    if (i < strlen) then
      es (i+1) (x.[i] :: acc)
    else
      List.rev acc
  in
  es 0 [];;
```

```
let collapse_string x =
  let buf = Buffer.create (List.length x) in
  let rec cs i = match i with
    [] -> Buffer.contents buf
  | h :: t -> Buffer.add_char buf h;cs t
  in
  cs x;;
```

These two functions also show the common practice of wrapping a recursive function in a nonrecursive one to keep the accumulator variable out of the function called by the programmer.

Why Do Recursive Functions Need a Special Designation?

Recursive functions are special in the OCaml world. You must tell the compiler that the function is recursive so the name of the function is available to itself (otherwise, you get an error). The following example shows that without defining the function as recursive, the compiler does not know the function exists when the function is called recursively:

```
# let wrong_recursive lst acc = match lst with
    [] -> acc
  | h :: t -> wrong_recursive t ((String.length h) :: acc);;
  Characters 75-90:
    | h :: t -> wrong_recursive t ((String.length h) :: acc);;
                ^^^^^^^^^^^^^^^
Unbound value wrong_recursive
# let rec wrong_recursive lst acc = match lst with
    [] -> acc
  | h :: t -> wrong_recursive t ((String.length h) :: acc);;
    val wrong_recursive : string list -> int list -> int list = <fun>
#
```

There are also optimizations that the compiler can make on recursive functions. The best-known of these are tail-recursion optimizations, which allow for very fast constant stack operations.

Tail Recursion and Efficient Programming

When a function is called, the arguments it was called with remain on the execution stack until the function returns; then they are popped off. Because the memory available to any given machine is finite, there is a real limit to how many times a function might recur until the machine runs out of memory and OCaml throws a Stack_overflow exception.

Tail recursion is a type of recursive call in which there is no further computation required on the result of the call, so the values of the function arguments are no longer required and can be popped. The OCaml compiler can detect tail-recursive calls and optimize for them, making recursive calls run in a constant stack.

A function is tail-recursive if it meets two criteria. The first criterion is the easiest: the recursive call cannot be within a try/with block. The following example, therefore, cannot be tail-recursive:

```
# let rec scan_input scan_buf acc_buf = try
                Scanf.bscanf scan_buf "%c" (fun x -> Buffer.add_char acc_buf x);
                scan_input scan_buf acc_buf
                with End_of_file -> Buffer.contents acc_buf;;
val scan_input : Scanf.Scanning.scanbuf -> Buffer.t -> string = <fun>
#
```

The second criterion for tail recursion is that the returned value is the unmodified return value. The Fibonacci function defined previously is not tail-recursive because the return value requires recursive calculations. However, the explode and collapse functions are tail-recursive.

Doing More Pattern Matching

Although your functions do not have to do pattern matching, it is a powerful tool and is used widely within the world of OCaml code. So far, you have done pattern matching only on types, but you can pattern match on values as well.

Pattern matches must be static; that is, they must be known at compile time. You can, however, use guarded matches to provide for extended matching.

Pattern matching must be used to access data structures other than pairs, for example. You can define triplets and quadruplets on-the-fly and then access them by using pattern matching. These sequence types are enforced by the compiler, although they do not have a name. You can name these types if you want, although these kinds of structures are often anonymous. You can also use them as components in any aggregate type.

```
let myfunc x = match x with
  n,m,z -> (n+m,z+. 4.);;
val myfunc : int * int * float -> int * float = <fun>
# myfunc (1,2,3.);;
- : int * float = (3, 7.)
# myfunc 1;;
Characters 7-8:
  myfunc 1;;
       ^
This expression has type int but is here used with type int * int * float
#
```

The preceding function can also be written (and is more commonly written) this way:

```
# let myfunc (n,m,z) = (n+m,z+. 0.4);;
val myfunc : int * int * float -> int * float = <fun>
```

You can have a default match, which matches anything. The previous examples used the default match to throw an exception when a parameter is not the right kind of variant of a given type. That is not all you can do, however.

If you have a match that is not used, the compiler will tell you about it, too. For example, if you want to define a polymorphic function that is similar to the previous one but takes three integers, you could write this:

```
# let myfunc x = match x with
  n,m,z -> n+m+z
  | n,m,_ -> n+m;;
Characters 49-54:
Warning: this match case is unused.
    | n,m,_ -> n+m;;
      ^^^^^
val myfunc : int * int * int -> int = <fun>
```

This code does not work, however. If you want the third argument to be polymorphic, you have to use type constraints or not operate on that argument with type-specific operations. Polymorphism is denoted by 'a in the function signature.

```
let myfunc x = match x with
  n,m,_ -> n+m;;
val myfunc : int * int * 'a -> int = <fun>
# let myfunc (n,m,z) = n+m;;
val myfunc : int * int * 'a -> int = <fun>
```

Lists can also be used in pattern matching. A very LISP-ish kind of function definition can be created by using recursion and pattern matching. For example, the following introduces the :: operator, which splits a list into its head and tail. This function is like the LISP car and cdr folded into one operation:

```
# let rec lispy x acc = match x with
  [] -> acc
  | head :: tail -> lispy tail (acc + head);;
val lispy : int list -> int -> int = <fun>
# lispy [1;2;3;4;5] 0;;
- : int = 15
#
```

Understanding the Default Match

The *default match* is present if there are no matches defined. The compiler also gives a warning if your pattern matches are not exhaustive and if you have matches that will never hit.

Having a default match does not make your functions polymorphic. The compiler infers the most generic type the arguments can be and assigns them accordingly. Having a default match doesn't change the fact that a function can have only one return type.

Bindings Within Pattern Matches

You can pretty much do anything you would normally do in OCaml inside an inner let binding, but you need to always be aware of scoping issues. Like most languages, you should use parentheses to clearly show scope:

```
# let b x y = match x with
  0 -> (let q = x in match y with
               0 -> 1
             | _ -> q)
  | 1 -> y
  | _ -> x * y;;
val b : int -> int -> int = <fun>
# b 0 3;;
- : int = 0
# b 0 0;;
- : int = 1
#
```

Guarded Matches: A Return to the Distance Calculator

So, let's say you want a special addition function that adds only distances that are positive. You could rewrite the math functions or you could add another set of functions with guards.

Guards are ways to limit the allowed values in pattern matches. Guards are Boolean functions that create a match if and only if the function is true. Guards do have a performance penalty, and it is considered bad form to have a function with all pattern matches guarded.

Those items aside, guards are an excellent way to communicate allowed ranges in your functions. The following example shows that an exception is raised if the first parameter is less than or equal to 0:

```
# let ( %%+ ) x y = match x with
  Foot n when n > 0 -> math_on_foot x (to_foot y) ( + )
  | Meter n when n > 0 -> math_on_meter x (to_meter y) ( + )
  | Mile n when n > 0  -> math_on_mile x (to_mile y) ( + )
  | _ -> raise (Invalid_argument "Not a distance type I have defined");;
val ( %%+ ) : distance -> distance -> distance = <fun>
# (Foot 0) %%+ (Mile 3);;
Exception: Invalid_argument "Not a distance type I have defined".
# (Foot 3) %%+(Mile 3);;
- : distance = Foot 15003
#
```

Writing code for both sides is left as an exercise for the reader.

Understanding Built-in Functions

We have not formally introduced many of the built-in functions in OCaml. Some are included where needed, but this book is not intended to be a full language primer.

You should consult the OCaml reference manual for documentation about the myriad built-in functions that exist. The OCaml standard library is quite large and contains many convenience functions you might be tempted to write.

Using Labels and Optional Arguments

In OCaml, most function parameters are *sequential*, which means they are used in the order in which they are supplied. However, you can change this order and provide optional arguments and default values by using *labels*.

Functions with labels have a slightly different syntax, as can be seen in the following examples. To designate code with labels, add the ~ flag to the parameters.

```
# let add_some_labeled ~x ~y = x + y;;
val add_some_labeled : x:int -> y:int -> int = <fun>
# add_some_labeled 10 20;;
- : int = 30
# add_some_labeled ~x:10 30;;
Characters 10-12:
  add_some_labeled ~x:10 30;;
            ^^
Expecting function has type y:int -> int
This argument cannot be applied without label
# add_some_labeled ~x:10 ~y:10;;
- : int = 20
#
```

You can call the function with or without labels, but you cannot mix them because the labels are not commutated. However, you can define one as an optional argument and the other as unlabeled, like so:

```
# let increment ?(by = 1) v = v + by;;
val increment : ?by:int -> int -> int = <fun>
# increment 10;;
- : int = 11
# increment ~by:30 10;;
- : int = 40
```

One of the problems with labels is that you cannot call those parameters without labels after they are labeled. There is also a performance penalty for optional arguments, but it is small. If the labels provide greatly improved readability, I recommend their use.

```
# increment 30 10;;
Characters 13-15:
  increment 30 10;;
              ^^
Expecting function has type ?by:int -> int
This argument cannot be applied without label
#
```

After the function has a labeled argument, it must be called using the label. This is one of the reasons why libraries that provide labeled variants often provide them in a separate version of the library.

Conclusion

You can now define a variety of functions and work with them. You also should have a basic understanding of the semantics of values and functions in OCaml. So armed, you can go on to the next chapter, in which you will build a simple database of parts using some of the types covered in the past few chapters.

Functional programming depends on functions. In other languages, developers sometimes feel it is important to limit the number of functions they create. Remember that functions are the building blocks of complex systems in FP. They should be like bricks: small and simple. It is the assembly of those bricks that is important; if you try to limit your bricks, you might not be able to create programs that are as flexible as you want.

## CHAPTER 5

Practical: Creating a Simple Database

Now that you have a basic overview of the OCaml language under your belt, it's time to actually write code that does something. In this chapter, you will write a small database of securities trades and accounts. You will be able to add and remove (buy and sell) quantities of a given stock. There is also a simple network-based client to retrieve current price information from the web.

Keep in mind that this chapter does not represent the most sophisticated OCaml code. The examples are designed to provide a clear understanding of how to actually accomplish the tasks you have. Although you might get lucky and you have a burning need to build a simple database this example is applicable to a wide range of real-world tasks.

Two Modules You Need

You will be using two modules from the OCaml standard library. The first is the Hashtbl module, which provides hash tables (no surprise there). Hash tables in OCaml can have a key of any hashable type. Most types are hashable, and you can define your own hash function if you are so inclined. Why and how you would do that are beyond the scope of this book, but you should know that it can be done.

The other module is the Marshal module, which enables the storage of arbitrary data structures directly onto disk. OCaml encodes the structure with a special encoding that can be stored in a string, transmitted over a network, saved to disk—whatever you want to do. The encoding is also portable across different OCaml platforms, but changes between OCaml versions sometimes make the data incompatible. Also, serialization of some data structures requires that the same binary be used to store and recover the data. For these reasons, it is often inappropriate to use the Marshal module as your only persistent storage method.

Using the Hashtbl Module in OCaml

Hash tables are not used in OCaml as often as they are in other languages. They are not strictly functional (which means that some of the functions that operate on hash tables have side effects), so some people avoid them for that reason. They are, however, fully supported by OCaml and are a valid idiom.

Hash tables in OCaml are much like hash tables in other programming languages—they are a store of key/value pairs. The key for a hash table and the value can be any valid type in OCaml, and you can nest them, too. Hash table keys can have more than one value. Hash tables are unordered, so you cannot rely on them if you need an ordered collection.

Using the Marshal Module

OCaml provides a standard library for the serialization of data structures. This library is the Marshal module, and it provides the capability to serialize data structures into files or strings. The Marshal functions are not totally typesafe, however. This lack of type safety comes when you read or write a marshaled data stream. You must give the type information to the OCaml system when reading this stream, which means that you can be wrong and cause a problem in your code. The Marshal module is one of the few places where this is possible.

The benefits of using marshaling are great enough to offset this danger, especially in less complex code. In more complex code and in places where safety is more important, using marshaling might not be advisable. This is a decision you must make when you are writing your application.

Marshaling is very fast, both in the sense of development speed and in performance. Marshaling is also very easy to use and understand. It is this module that enables you to add persistence to the database in four lines of code.

How to Use These Modules

Both of these modules are usable immediately from the toplevel environment. You can call the functions from these modules by using their full names, which is what was done in this chapter. You can also open the module as follows:

```
#open Marshal;;
#
```

After you open a module, you can access the functions and types within that module without specifying the module name (this can be especially helpful when using the toplevel because it reduces the amount of typing you have to do). Other complicated effects and issues with opening are addressed in Chapter 13.

Working with Files

OCaml uses buffered input/output (I/O) channels to access items such as files and sockets. Buffered I/O is the default for performance and garbage collection reasons. You can access unbuffered I/O, although it is available only in the Unix module and might not be totally cross-platform (because not all platforms have complete functionality in the Unix module). Unbuffered I/O, especially for file system access, is not generally recommended. The buffering provided by OCaml is highly optimized for performance.

One important thing to know about OCaml channels: they do not get closed automatically; you must close them explicitly if you want to free up the resources they consume. If you do not close the file, your program will "leak" file descriptors. Resource leaks should always be avoided.

Opening and Closing Channels

There are two types of channels: input channels and output channels. Not surprisingly, input channels are channels from which data is read, and output channels are channels to which data is written.

One problem with functional programming is that processes such as file access (an inherently imperative action) can sometimes be problematic in purely functional languages. OCaml is not purely functional, so it does not have this problem.

Another note is that some operating systems (OSs) prefer to have files opened in binary or text mode, depending on the type of I/O. The examples provided use the binary opening method because Marshal requires it under Windows. However, the binary opening flag does nothing on an OS that doesn't require the binary opening method.

Accounts Database

The database is an OCaml hash table that is serialized to disk via the Marshal library with two record types for organizing our data. The first is the `position` type:

```
# type position = { symbol:string;holding:int;pprice:float};;
type position = { symbol : string; holding : int; pprice : float; }
```

The `position` type holds a stock symbol, the quantity the `position` is holding (an integer), and the purchase price (a floating integer). The holding quantity is an integer because you cannot have a fractional share in U.S. markets (you can have the value of a fractional share in certain cases, but not when you are buying or selling a security directly).

The next type is the `account` type, which has a name for the account, a maximum individual holding amount, and a list of positions in given stocks. The maximum individual holding is a way to say that you do not want any position to be more than that percentage of the total value of the account. For example, if you own $10,000 worth of stocks, you might not want any one stock to make up more than 25 percent of the total value. This is a risk strategy designed to keep you from having all your eggs in one basket. It is not a sophisticated strategy, however.

```
# type account = {name:string;max_ind_holding:float;pos:position list};;
type account = {
  name : string;
  max_ind_holding : float;
  pos : position list;
}
#
```

Some Sample Data

You need some sample data. The following is a list of stock symbols and closing price data. Most of these are symbols in the Russell 1000 Index, and you can find a dizzying array of stock price data on the Internet for free. These prices and symbols are what you will use in the examples in this chapter:

```
let cur_prices = [("IBM", 82.48); ("GOOG", 406.16); ("AMAT", 18.04);
                                ("INTC", 19.24);("MMM", 81.03); ("AMD", 33.69);
                                ("AAPL", 69.79); ("GS", 161.02);("AMZN", 37.09);
                                ("ALD", 30.75); ("Y", 278.9); ("AFC", 0.);
                                ("BCO", 51.05); ("BSX", 21.57); ("CC", 24.65);
                                ("CSCO", 20.81);
                                ("C", 47.66); ("CZN", 13.22); ("DO", 91.22);
("DELL", 29.76);
                                ("COO", 53.18); ("CA", 26.8); ("DYN", 4.83);
("FAST", 46.64);
                                ("FDX", 117.1)];;
```

Important Functions for Handling Data

First, you need to be able to create new accounts easily.

```
# let gen_account acdb accname max_holding init_pos =
    if (Hashtbl.mem acdb accname) then
      raise (Invalid_argument "Account Name Already In Use")
    else
      Hashtbl.add acdb accname
        {name=accname;
         max_ind_holding=max_holding;
         pos=init_pos};;
val gen_account :
  (string, account) Hashtbl.t -> string -> float -> position list -> unit =
  <fun>
#
# let db = Hashtbl.create 10;;
val db : ('_a, '_b) Hashtbl.t = <abstr>
# gen_account db "first" 0.40 [];;
- : unit = ()
# gen_account db "first" 0.40 [];;
Exception: Invalid_argument "Account Name Already In Use".
#
```

Now that you have created an account, you have to add and remove positions from it, which you can do by buying or selling the security. Note that accounts must have unique names. Although an OCaml hash table can have multiple values for a given key, you should make sure that accounts are unique in this system. If you try to create a nonunique account, an exception is thrown.

Manipulating the Database Contents

The following defines buy and sell functions that add or remove positions from a given account. The sell function also returns additional information about the quantity sold and the profit (which might be negative, meaning a loss). The buy function also calculates the simple average price of a security. This method is fine for this kind of project, but if you were making your livelihood from this, you would probably want a more robust accounting system.

```
# let account_buy (symb,price) quant acc =
    {acc with pos =
        ({symbol=symb;holding=quant;pprice=price} :: acc.pos)};;
  val account_buy : string * float -> int -> account -> account = <fun>
# let account_sell (symb,price) acc =
  let rec seller sym prc pos_list soldq soldv newposlst =
    match pos_list with
                [] -> ((soldq,soldv),{acc with pos = newposlst})
    | h :: t -> if (h.symbol = sym) then
        seller sym prc t (soldq + h.holding) (
                ((float_of_int h.holding) *.
                 (prc -. h.pprice)) +. soldv) newposlst
      else
                seller sym prc t soldq soldv (h :: newposlst)
  in
    seller symb price acc.pos 0 0. [];;
# let buy db account_name (symbol_name,price) quantity =
    let acc = Hashtbl.find db account_name in
    Hashtbl.replace db account_name (account_buy (symbol_name,price)
        quantity acc);;
val buy : ('a, account) Hashtbl.t -> 'a -> string * float -> int -> unit =
  <fun>
# let sell db account_name (symbol_name,price)  =
    let acc = Hashtbl.find db account_name in
    let ((quant,profit),newacc) =
     account_sell (symbol_name,price) acc in
    Hashtbl.replace db account_name newacc;(quant,profit);;
    val sell : ('a, account) Hashtbl.t -> 'a -> string * float -> int * float =
  <fun>
#
```

Now that you have a way to add and remove items, you can add some items and then present functions for finding information out about your accounts.

```
# buy db "first" ("CSCO",16.30) 100;;
- : unit = ()
# buy db "first" ("IBM",92.0) 100;;
- : unit = ()
# buy db "first" ("MMM",75.30) 200;;
- : unit = ()
# buy db "first" ("GOOG",386.50) 100;;
- : unit = ()
# buy db "first" ("GS",160.2) 100;;
- : unit = ()
#
```

Saving and Loading the Database

You now need to define the store and load functions that will provide the database with persistence. These two functions are very simple, mostly because the Marshal module takes care of most of the complexity for you.

```
# let store_db accounts_db filename =
    let f = open_out_bin filename in
    Marshal.to_channel f accounts_db [];
    close_out f;;
val store_db : 'a -> string -> unit = <fun>
# let load_db filename =
    let f = open_in_bin filename in
    let v = ((Marshal.from_channel f): (string, account) Hashtbl.t) in
    close_in f;
    v;;
val load_db : string -> (string, account) Hashtbl.t = <fun>
#
```

Note the type definition in the load function. It is there because the Marshal module does not store type information. To make sure that the type is converted correctly from the marshaled output, indicate the type. If the file you specify cannot be converted into that type, an exception is raised. In some cases, the program can even crash (segfault). The kind of bad outcome is determined by the file; if it looks like valid Marshal data with the wrong type, a crash is more likely.

```
# load_db "map_reduce.ml";;
Exception: Failure "input_value: bad object".
#
# store_db db "example.db";;
- : unit = ()
#
```

When loading a file that is not a stored database, an exception is raised. Storing the database, however, simply returns unit and does not modify the database in any way.

Interacting with the Database

The defined function tells you what symbols are in a given account.

```
# let symbols_in_account acc =
    List.map (fun x -> x.symbol) acc.pos;;
val symbols_in_account : account -> string list = <fun>
# symbols_in_account (Hashtbl.find db "first");;
- : string list = ["GS"; "GOOG"; "MMM"; "IBM"; "CSCO"]
```

It returns a list, and uses the fold function.

```
# let value_at_purchase acc =
  List.fold_left (fun y x -> ((float_of_int x.holding) *. x.pprice) +. y)
    0. acc.pos;;
val value_at_purchase : account -> float = <fun>
# value_at_purchase (Hashtbl.find db "first");;
- : float = 80560.
```

Let's face it; you're more interested in the value of the account. The first value function tells you the value of the account at the purchase price. This function basically just sums up the values in the positions and returns that float. The next function tells you the value of the account at any given price. One of the arguments is a data structure (specifically an association list) that maps a stock symbol name to a price. Every symbol in the account must also be in that list; otherwise, an exception will be thrown.

```
# let current_value acc cur_prices =
  List.fold_left (
    fun y x ->
    ((float_of_int x.holding) *. (List.assoc x.symbol cur_prices)) +. y
  ) 0. acc.pos;;
val current_value : account -> (string * float) list -> float = <fun>
# current_value (Hashtbl.find db "first") cur_prices;;
- : float = 83253.
# current_value (Hashtbl.find db "first") (List.remove_assoc "GS" cur_prices);;
Exception: Not_found.
#
```

The next two functions enable you to calculate a profit and loss (P&L) for a given account or for the whole database of accounts. The first function shows the P&L for a given account; the second shows all accounts in a given database (this example has only one account, so the two are the same):

```
# let profit_and_loss acc cur_prices =
    (current_value acc cur_prices) -. (value_at_purchase acc);;
val profit_and_loss : account -> (string * float) list -> float = <fun>
# let total_pandl accdb cur_prices =
  List.fold_left (+.) 0. (Hashtbl.fold (fun x y z -> ➥
        (profit_and_loss y cur_prices) :: z) accdb .[]);;
  val total_pandl : ('a, account) Hashtbl.t -> (string * float) list -> float =
  <fun>
# profit_and_loss (Hashtbl.find db "first") cur_prices;;
- : float = 2693.
# total_pandl db cur_prices;;
- : float = 2693.
```

```
# let percent_holding acc cur_prices =
    let curval = current_value acc cur_prices in
    List.map (fun x ->
        (x.symbol,(((float_of_int x.holding) *. ➥
(List.assoc x.symbol cur_prices)) /. ➥
            curval))) acc.pos;;
    val percent_holding :
  account -> (string * float) list -> (string * float) list = <fun>
# percent_holding (Hashtbl.find db "first") cur_prices;;
- : (string * float) list =
[("GS", 0.19341044767155541); ("GOOG", 0.48786229925648322);
 ("MMM", 0.19465965190443588); ("IBM", 0.099071504930753243);
 ("CSCO", 0.02499609623677225)]
```

The preceding function returns a list of each symbol and the fraction of the total account value that it represents. This function is important because you indicated in your account data type that there is a maximum percentage holding that you want enforced. The data structure cannot enforce that, so you want to have another function that tells you which symbols exceed your limits.

```
# let needs_rebal acc cur_prices =
    let percnt_hold =
      percent_holding acc cur_prices in
    List.filter (fun x -> (snd x) > acc.max_ind_holding) percnt_hold;;
val needs_rebal : account -> (string * float) list -> (string * float) list =
  <fun>
# needs_rebal (Hashtbl.find db "first") cur_prices;;
- : (string * float) list = [("GOOG", 0.48786229925648322)]
```

Here is where the information in the account about the maximum individual holding comes in. If a given position is more than the maximum, it needs to be rebalanced. This function returns a list of symbols in a given account that need to be rebalanced:

```
# let contains_symbol symb acc =
    List.fold_left
      (fun x y -> if (x) then x else y) false
                  (List.map (fun x -> x.symbol = symb) acc);;
  val contains_symbol : string -> position list -> bool = <fun>
# let accounts_holding symb accdb =
  Hashtbl.fold (fun x y z ->
                  if (contains_symbol symb y.pos) then
                      (x :: z)
                  else
                      z) accdb [];;
  val accounts_holding : string -> ('a, account) Hashtbl.t -> 'a list = <fun>
# accounts_holding "CSCO" db;;
- : string list = ["first"]
#
```

You can use these last two functions to find out which account is holding a given symbol. You can also get a list of all the accounts that hold a position in a given symbol. These two functions are important for finding where a given position might be.

Quick Note About Code Length

In many ways, OCaml is a very terse language. At this point, you've seen slightly fewer than 100 lines of OCaml. In that amount of code, you have defined a set of types and a simple database, complete with on-disk persistence.

This terseness is one of the major aspects of OCaml that makes it such a practical and productive language. OCaml enables you to do more with less, yet the code is still typesafe and easy to inspect.

Getting Price Information

Although the methods needed to write network clients will not be introduced for several chapters, the following code is still useful. This code implements a very, very simple HTTP client for downloading stock price data from Yahoo Finance. It relies on the Unix module, which you can load from the toplevel using the following syntax:

```
#load "unix.cma";;
#
```

You can now access these functions. If you are using a platform that does not allow dynamic linking, such as Windows, it will not work. Instead, you have to make a custom toplevel that includes the Unix module.

```
C:\Documents and Settings\josh>ocamlmktop -o mytop.exe unix.cma
C:\Documents and Settings\josh>mytop
        Objective Caml version 3.09.0
# Unix.open_connection;;
- : Unix.sockaddr -> in_channel * out_channel = <fun>
#
```

You can now use the following code to download price information from Yahoo. If you enter a symbol that does not exist, you might get a bogus price or an exception.

```
let rec split_content str lastpoint totalsize = let nxt =
  String.index_from str (lastpoint + 1) '\013' in
  if (nxt = (lastpoint + 2)) then
    (* remember, the +4 is because I don't care about the last parts *)
    String.sub str (nxt+2) (totalsize - (nxt+4))
  else
    split_content str nxt totalsize;;
let get_price symb =
  let buf = Buffer.create 20 in
    Buffer.add_string buf "GET /d/quotes.csv?s=";
    Buffer.add_string buf symb;
    Buffer.add_string buf "&f=sl1d1t1c1ohgv&e=.csv HTTP/1.0\n";
```

```
      Buffer.add_string buf "HOST: finance.yahoo.com\n\n";
      let hostname = Unix.gethostbyname "finance.yahoo.com" in
      let address = Unix.ADDR_INET (hostname.Unix.h_addr_list.(0),80) in
      let (i_conn,o_conn) =
        Unix.open_connection address in
        output_string o_conn (Buffer.contents buf);flush o_conn;
        let nstr = String.create 1024 in
        let leng = input i_conn nstr 0 1024
        in Scanf.sscanf (split_content nstr 0 leng) "\"%s@\",%f"
                    (fun x y -> x,y);;
# get_price "BADSYM";;
- : string * float = ("BADSYM", 0.)
# get_price "CSCO";;
- : string * float = ("CSCO", 20.81)
#
```

Conclusion

This chapter demonstrated how functions can be used to build up systems. You also learned about two powerful modules included in the OCaml standard library.

This is far from being a complete database. In later chapters, you will build a complex query mechanism and import/export facility for this database. You can probably think of many features it is missing as well.

The point of this chapter was to give you an introduction to some of the OCaml features in the form of working code. This is more interesting than that exhaustive description and more fun than "hello world". The next chapter goes into the language in more depth to provide building blocks for more complicated examples to come.

CHAPTER 6

███

Primitive and Composite Types

Chapter 3 introduced you to the OCaml concept of type; here you will learn more about types—their importance and things you can do with and about them. This chapter discusses the *primitive* types in OCaml (they are sometimes referred to as *basic* types; both terms are used interchangeably here).

OCaml is strongly and statically typed, which means that all type information in a given program must be known at compile time. Further, the type information cannot change within the program while it is running. The compiler enforces this type information, and there are restrictions on which operations can operate on a given type.

The benefit of this feature is that certain types of errors are not possible in a strongly typed language. For example, the following code in C compiles and runs, but outputs the wrong answer:

```
#include <stdio.h>

int main() {
        int b = 0;
        float c = 10.;

        printf("%i\n",b+c);
        return 0;
}
```

This program prints 0 (on some systems, it might print a random number or other garbage) to the screen and returns normally. This kind of error is pretty easy to make and can be very difficult to find unless you are specifically looking for it. C++ handles the situation and prints out the correct answer, but it does so because of implicit conversion. Dynamically typed languages such as Perl and Python handle the situation and print out a correct answer—again due to implicit conversion.

"Wait a minute," you might say. "This example is faulty because it has numbers, and OCaml is one of the few languages that make a real distinction between ints and floats." Although it is true that OCaml differentiates, this program is still fundamentally wrong. You can make a more detailed case by looking at strings.

If you switch variable b to be a string, the C and C++ code no longer compile. The C++ code could be made to compile, though, via operator overloading. In the case of operator overloading, the programmer might never even know it happened.

These languages take a different view of type safety than OCaml does. No language can be ignorant of types because types are a very important part of computation and computer science. (Even machine language deals with types, although a given machine language might have only one type.) However, no single rule covers the way any given language deals with types.

In fact, there is no "One True Way" when talking about types. In the computer language world, there is often disagreement about what the term *strongly typed* even means. After you come to terms with the definition of the strength of the typing, you come to the difference between latently typed and dynamically typed behavior.

OCaml takes a particular stance about the importance of knowing type information: type information should be constant. The compiler should enforce the rules, and the runtime environment should, too. This is part of the OCaml design goal of safety.

Constant Type, Dynamic Data

The OCaml compiler knows all the type information in a program at the time it is compiled. This static typing does not mean that the data your program operates on must be static as well.

Much of the type checking and verification is done in the name of safety. Being safe means you can do away with a lot of the code that you would have to write to verify without these checks. Compile-time checks are more rigorous and much faster than runtime checks, (which is why OCaml code is so fast).

Integers (Ints)

In OCaml, *integers (ints)* are 31 bits because OCaml uses the 32nd bit for its own purposes.

Ints in OCaml are very fast; they just aren't as big as they are in some other languages. Precision is used to describe numeric types, but precision has nothing to do with accuracy when calculations are concerned.

The OCaml normal int might not be enough for your task, so OCaml supports three other integer types in the core library. The first is int32, which is a 32-bit signed integer. There are utilities to operate on int32 values in the Int32 module. You can define an int32 by simply adding an l (lowercase L) to the end of your number.

The int64 integer type is much like int32, except that it supports 64-bit ints (if your platform does). You append an L to the end of your int to create one. The last type of integers OCaml supports are nativeints, which are the native integers on the platform you are using. They are very similar to int32 and int64 types and can be defined by adding an n to your integers.

```
# 10l
;;
- : int32 = 10l
# 10L;;
- : int64 = 10L
# 10n;;
- : nativeint = 10n
# 10;;
- : int = 10
# let (+) x y = Int32.add x y;;
val ( + ) : int32 -> int32 -> int32 = <fun>
# 10l + 10l;;
- : int32 = 20l
# 10 + 10;;
Characters 0-2:
  10 + 10;;
  ^^
```

This expression has type int but is here used with type int32
```
#
```

Defining high-precision ints is very easy. You can also convert freely to and from the different ints using the specific module, though some information may be lost.

Operator overloading is not possible (if you have code that uses these other integers, you cannot use the + operator and have it work automatically), but operator overriding works very well. You can override the + operator to work on Int32 or Int64 by just redefining it in your code.

Caution You cannot mix code modules with this kind of redefinition in place.

Floating-Point Numbers (Floats)

The mathematical operators for *floating-point numbers (floats)* are different from the ones for ints, which can sometimes be frustrating for both new and seasoned programmers (especially when you are prototyping and are not yet sure what type you want to use for a given number).

I strongly caution against joining ints and floats in real code. You can easily define your own numeric type and make it behave however you want; the problem is that ints and floats really are different.

People who are used to coding in languages that unify ints and floats might disagree with this recommendation. This separation is also a source of flame warfare on Usenet (and will probably continue for many years).

Think of this: you do not have to round ints. The rounding problem present in floats has been a situation for a long time. It is such a big problem that languages such as Java have a standard library for handling arbitrary precision math and numbers. Equality is also an issue:

when is a float really equal to a float? When you add rounding into the mix, you can easily get a situation in which things are close to equal—but not quite. An example can be found in modf, which in OCaml is the same as in C (basically). This function takes a float (a double in C) and returns the integer part and the fractional part.

A good example of the rounding and equality problems inherent in floats is with modf, as follows:

```
# Printf.printf "%.16f\n" (fst (modf 1.2));;
0.2000000000000000
- : unit = ()
# fst (modf 1.2);;
- : float = 0.19999999999999996
# 0.2 = fst (modf 1.2);;
- : bool = false
# 1 = 1;;
- : bool = true
#
```

This example shows one of the other insidious issues with floating-point math: it might display correctly. If you debug by printf, you might never even see the subtle rounding problems that are causing trouble. Although rounding might never cause problems, this attitude is pretty far from the OCaml philosophy. This code is correct and valid code, showing once again that "correct" and "doing what I want" are not always the same thing.

Strings and Chars

Chars and strings are supported natively by OCaml. *Chars* are ASCII chars and can be defined using '\<NUMBER>'. The number can be any number from 000 to 255 and it must always have three digits. To display ASCII char 1, you use '\001', and so on. Pattern matching has full support for chars and even supports a range operator (which enables inclusive matching of a given character range). Although strings are supported natively, there is a string-manipulation module (called String) in the standard library. The String module has many of the string operations you would expect, except for regular expressions.

```
# char_of_int 1;;
- : char = '\001'
# '\001';;
- : char = '\001'
# int_of_char '\001';;
- : int = 1
#
```

You can use chars in pattern matching. The following example also demonstrates the range operator (..). The range operator, which is used instead of enumerating each value in the range, works on chars and ints. In this example, the first pattern match is true on 'a', 'b', and 'c', but nothing else:

```
# let charfunc x = match x with
  'a' .. 'c' -> Printf.printf "You got a passing grade\n"
  | 'd' -> Printf.printf "You've got some academic trouble\n"
  | 'f' -> Printf.printf "Would you like fries with that?\n"
  | _ -> Printf.printf "Better a quitter than a failure, eh?.\n";;
val charfunc : char -> unit = <fun>
# charfunc 'a';;
You got a passing grade
- : unit = ()
# charfunc 'b';;
You got a passing grade
- : unit = ()
#
```

Regular expression support does not exist in the String module. In fact, many string operations that users of languages such as Python would expect are entirely absent from this module. However, these functions exist in the Str module. There is also a module that provides Perl-compatible regular expressions, although it is not part of the standard distribution.

Strings can be concatenated, searched, and otherwise manipulated. Strings also can be indexed like arrays via the normal OCaml indexing syntax:

```
# let b = "aalflfld";;
val b : string = "aalflfld"
# b.[1];;
- : char = 'a'
# b.[1]<-'d';;
- : unit = ()
# b;;
- : string = "adlflfld"
#
```

Strings are mutable, which is very important because many OCaml programmers use strings as buffers to pass mutable data. This practice can be very useful when working with data that might need to be mutable, but you don't want to use input/output (I/O) to handle.

String elements are modified via the OCaml assignment operator <-, which enables you to modify one element of a string. There is no built-in way to get a char list from a string (or vice versa).

OCaml does not know anything about Unicode; it uses ISO-8859-X to encode characters and strings. There are several third-party libraries that provide support for Unicode. You will need to use these (or implement your own) if you want to work with anything but ISO-8859-X.

Using the Pervasives Module

The *Pervasives module* is the module that is open by default in the OCaml toplevel. The Pervasives module includes functions that are, well, pervasive. For example, the open_in function is actually a function in the Pervasives module. You do not have to prefix it with the module name because the Pervasives module is open by default.

This section did not cover modules in depth, but don't worry. There is more coverage later on, and right now this information isn't critical to your use of OCaml.

Lists and Arrays

Lists are very powerful tools in OCaml. Lists can contain elements of only a single type (for example, a list of all integers or a list of all strings). However, you can make a type that suits your needs and then make a list of it. Most of the operations on lists are found in the List module instead of in the Pervasives module.

Lists in OCaml are implemented underneath by using a singly linked list, making the traversal of OCaml lists very efficient.

Arrays are much like mutable lists. Unlike lists, arrays allow for efficient random access. Arrays should be used when you want random access to elements in the container. Lists provide the capability to access random elements, but that access is not efficient.

Both arrays and lists are *polymorphic*, which means that they can be used with any OCaml type (even other polymorphic types).

Which tool should you use? This subject is not something I can easily give advice about. I usually use lists until I find the need to do a lot of random access. In my work, this does not happen often, so I normally just use lists. However, I always use arrays in the area of matrix manipulation because the Array module has matrix support.

Exceptions

Exceptions are their own type. This type, exn, is the type of all exception values.

The fact that exceptions are their own type has several ramifications for the OCaml programmer. You can, for example, write a function that takes an exception as an argument:

```
# let raise_if_unequal x y e =
    if not (x = y) then raise e;;
  val raise_if_unequal : 'a -> 'a -> exn -> unit = <fun>
# raise_if_unequal 10 30 Not_found;;
Exception: Not_found.
# raise_if_unequal 10 30 (Invalid_argument "hello?");;
Exception: Invalid_argument "hello?".
# raise_if_unequal 30 30 (Invalid_argument "hello?");;
- : unit = ()
#
```

This somewhat contrived example shows that exceptions are just like any other OCaml type. (Exceptions are covered in depth later in this book.) Just remember that the OCaml exception type is just like any other type in OCaml and is subject to the same limitations.

Other Types

OCaml has other types—some simple and some more specialized. For example, OCaml has a Boolean type called `bool` that can have only two possible values: `true` and `false`. You can convert a string to a `bool` using the function `bool_of_string`. If you are familiar with `bool` types in other languages, the `bool` types in OCaml will not be strangers to you.

The lazy type is another type. Although OCaml normally uses eager evaluation to evaluate all function arguments, there are times when it is easier to use `lazy` evaluation (especially in situations in which you want to defer computation until later). A simplistic example that highlights the difference between eager and `lazy` evaluation follows:

```
# let somef x = 100;;
val somef : 'a -> int = <fun>
# somef (lazy (1 / 0));;
- : int = 100
# somef (1 / 0);;
Exception: Division_by_zero.
#
```

When the function is called by using `lazy` evaluation, it yields to the correct answer. However, when eager evaluation is used, an exception is raised because the argument is evaluated first. Evaluation of the `lazy` value is performed by the `Lazy.force` function. After a `lazy` expression is evaluated, it does not get evaluated again, even if you force it. This is convenient because multiple forces do not result in multiple calculations. Also, after a `lazy` value is forced, it evaluates to that value from then on.

```
# let b = lazy (10 + 30);;
val b : int lazy_t = <lazy>
# Lazy.force b;;
- : int = 40
# b;;
- : int lazy_t = lazy 40
# Lazy.force b;;
- : int = 40
```

Polymorphic Types

OCaml supports polymorphic types natively. You can define your own polymorphic types as you define other types. For example, if you want to define a polymorphic type, you create the following:

```
# type 'a polytype = Dataitem of 'a;;
type 'a polytype = Dataitem of 'a
# Dataitem 10;;
- : int polytype = Dataitem 10
# Dataitem "hello";;
- : string polytype = Dataitem "hello"
```

These types are polymorphic until they are used with a concrete type (such as an int). The type is then concrete, so it can no longer operate on more than one type. However, you can use a polymorphic type, too. OCaml provides the option type, which is a polymorphic type, to handle many of the more common situations programmers face:

```
# Some 10;;
- : int option = Some 10
# None;;
- : 'a option = None
#
```

You can define a polymorphic type with more than one polymorphic element. You do this by adding more polymorphic notes:

```
# type ('a,'b) morestuff = MNone | MSome of 'a | MSomeMore of 'b;;
type ('a, 'b) morestuff = MNone | MSome of 'a | MSomeMore of 'b
# MSomeMore 1;;
- : ('a, int) morestuff = MSomeMore 1
#
```

Polymorphic functions can operate on polymorphic types. They are more difficult to define in practice, however, because so many of the OCaml operators are bound to a specific type that it can be difficult to write a function that does something valuable and have it be polymorphic. (You will learn more in later chapters.)

Composite Types

Previous chapters discussed records and variants. *Composite types* can be polymorphic and are defined in the same way as other polymorphic types.

You can define a type that is just a grouping of other primitive types. These kinds of types are represented much like tuples.

The elements of these types are inaccessible except via pattern matching, which has an important impact on how you write your code. This access is also one of the reasons why pattern matching is so important in OCaml.

Unlike other types you might define, naming composite doesn't bind them to this name. Although you can assign a name to a given composite type, the compiler doesn't report everything that matches that pattern as that type. However, you can use the named type to provide restrictions on function parameters, which can be very helpful to prevent confusion in polymorphic types.

```
# type 'a polytype = int * float * 'a;;
type 'a polytype = int * float * 'a
# let b x = match x with
  m,n,o -> m+n+o;;
val b : int * int * int -> int = <fun>
#
```

```
# let b (x:'a polytype) = match x with
  m,n,o -> (m,o);;
val b : 'a polytype -> int * 'a = <fun>
# b (10,10.,"hello");;
- : int * string = (10, "hello")
# b (10,10,"hello");;
Characters 2-17:
  b (10,10,"hello");;
  ^^^^^^^^^^^^^^^
This expression has type int * int * string but is here used with type
  'a polytype = int * float * 'a
#
```

This is an error that would have been caught at compile time instead of runtime. In this case, the error is not particularly important because the function drops that element. This restriction could have been done without using a named type and by substituting the type information directly into the function definition. However, named types can be helpful for documentation purposes.

The function is defined using pattern matching explicitly in the previous example. You also can define the function a different way and get the same signature (and thus the same functionality):

```
# let b (m,n,o) = m + n + o;;
val b : int * int * int -> int = <fun>
```

How you do this is up to you, although it is more convenient for many functions (especially functions using pattern matching for data structures) to do the latter (it is also more idiomatic for OCaml).

Polymorphic Variant Types

Some polymorphic types, referred to as *variant* types, can be created without using the type keyword. These types do not belong to a specific type the way that named types do. Instead, they are tagged with a value, and the compiler will ensure that the tag is valid and correct.

```
# [`Heart;`Club;`Diamond;`Spade];;
- : [> `Club | `Diamond | `Heart | `Spade ] list =
[`Heart; `Club; `Diamond; `Spade]
```

These types also can be named by using the type keyword; this type name can then be used for pattern matching:

```
# type suit = [`Heart | `Club | `Diamond | `Spade];;
type suit = [ `Club | `Diamond | `Heart | `Spade ]
# let winner m = match m with
    `Heart -> true
  | #suit -> false;;
    val winner : [< suit ] -> bool = <fun>
```

The variant tag does not belong to a particular type, although the type system ensures that the tag used is valid and correct. A variant type is inferred for every use of the type.

Why not use these types? Although they are somewhat efficient, it is harder to make optimizations without static typing information. Another problem with polymorphic variants is that they weaken the type discipline in your code. They are still typesafe, but they do more than simply ensure type safety. These other operations make them more heavyweight, so some kinds of errors are more difficult to detect. This is especially true because standard type definitions require more explicit type definitions that cannot be modified. For example, the following function definition is probably not correct:

```
# let winner m = match m with
    `Unknown -> true
  | `Heart -> true
  | #suit -> false;;
      val winner : [< `Club | `Diamond | `Heart | `Spade | `Unknown ] -> bool =
  <fun>
# winner `Unknown;;
- : bool = true
```

It does compile and it even works. You can make the compiler generate a warning if you specify the type (but it is probably not what you want):

```
# winner `Unknown;;
- : bool = true
# let winner (m:suit) = match m with
    `Unknown -> true
  | `Heart -> true
  | #suit -> false;;
    Characters 39-46:
Warning U: this match case is unused.
      `Unknown -> true
      ^^^^^^^
val winner : suit -> bool = <fun>
# winner `Unknown;;
Characters 7-14:
  winner `Unknown;;
        ^^^^^^^
This expression has type [> `Unknown ] but is here used with type suit
#
```

It compiles, but then fails when it is used. This is one of the biggest reasons to use polymorphic variants with care.

Conclusion

Take a look at a short example that displays an actual program and uses some of the concepts discussed in this chapter (some random number generation was added). Note that self_init is very important. Without this initialization, the OCaml pseudo-random-number generator is more pseudo than random.

```
open Random;;
Random.self_init ();;


let situations = [| "Ship about to explode";
                               "Ship Hailing Us";
                               "Klingons off the Starboard bow"|];;
let responses = [| "Hail Ship";
                               "Send Friendship Message";
                               "Shoot To Kill";
                               "Abandon Ship"|];;

let display_current_situation () =
  Printf.printf "Captain! %s\nWhat do we Do?\n"
    (Array.get situations (Random.int (Array.length situations)));;

let show_menu lst =
  Array.iteri (fun x y -> Printf.printf "%i     %s\n" x y) lst;
  Printf.printf "\nResponse? ";;

let respond x = match x with
  "Hail Ship" -> "Hailing, Sir."
  | "Send Friendship Message" -> "They like me,  they really like me!"
  | "Shoot To Kill" -> "But, we come in Peace!?!"
  | "Abandon Ship" -> "Iceberg, right ahead!"
  | _ -> "Captain, I just don't understand you!";;

let _ =
  display_current_situation ();
  show_menu responses;
  Printf.printf "%s\n"
    (respond (Array.get responses (int_of_string (read_line ()))));;
```

As you move forward, you'll see that many of the techniques used in this light-hearted example are useful in many areas. This is especially true now that you have a good grounding in the OCaml built-in types and how to create your own. A good understanding of the OCaml type system takes you a long way toward fully understanding OCaml.

■ ■ ■

## CHAPTER 7

Practical: Simple Database Reports, Exports, and Imports

Now that you have a solid grounding in the OCaml types and functions, you will revisit the simple database from Chapter 3 and Chapter 5. One of the major things missing from that database was any way to import or export data. Sure, you can add and remove items, but if you really want to use this database, you will want more functionality.

You will implement your reporting and importing via the Printf and Scanf functions, which bear a strong functional resemblance to their C counterparts (although they do not share their counterparts' weaknesses).

Neither Printf nor Scanf can be a source of buffer overruns or other security faults that are present in other languages. Printf and Scanf are very fast, which make them well-suited for a variety of speed-sensitive applications. They are also part of the standard library, which means they are portable across all OCaml platforms.

Function signatures will be used in this chapter to discuss functions. Function signatures have been shown in past examples, and they are given as output from the OCaml toplevel. When you discuss functions and algorithms with people who know OCaml, they will often use function signatures to illustrate ideas and information. Function signatures are also very useful when you are trying to understand documentation, especially if it is ocamldoc-generated documentation.

Format Codes

Both Printf and Scanf use % prefixed conversion characters as formatting codes. They can be intermixed with regular text, and there is support for range operators and other operations specific to each one.

Table 7-1 contains the codes that are common to both functions (specific codes are shown later). The formatting is also very similar to the Portable Operating System Interface (POSIX) Scanf codes.

Table 7-1. *Scanf/Printf Formatting Codes*

Formatting Code	Description
d, i, n, or N	Converts integer (int) to signed decimal
u	Converts int to unsigned decimal
x	Converts int to unsigned hexadecimal (lowercase letters)
X	Same as x with uppercase letters
o	Converts int to unsigned octal
s	String
S	String (OCaml-style escaped syntax)
c	Char
C	Char (OCaml-style escaped syntax)
f	Floating-point number (float) with decimal notation
F	Float with decimal notation and mandatory decimal point
e or E	Float in scientific notation
g or G	Float in the most compact representation (either f, F, e, or E)
%	Matches or outputs a percent symbol
B	Boolean, converts to string true or false

The integer-conversion codes can also be prefixed with an l, L, or n for int32, int64, and nativeint, respectively.

Printf

Table 7-2 gives a list of formatting codes specific to Printf.

Table 7-2. *Printf-Specific Codes*

Printf-specific Code	Description
-	Left-justifies output
0	Pads numerical conversion with zeros
+	Prefix + sign to positive numbers
a	Calls a type-specific pretty printer (covered in later chapters)
[space]	Prefix numbers with a space if they are positive (basically a one-space padding)
.[number]	Width/precision of a numeric field; for example, %.2f prints 0.00 for a zero, and %.3i prints 000 for zero

The Printf module contains functions for creating formatted output, which supports most of the basic types in OCaml and is syntactically similar to the C language Printf functions.

Printf is typesafe and does not implicitly convert arguments to the types represented in the format string. This can be painful for some; however this is much like other OCaml functions and is focused on safety rather than magic.

Both Printf and Scanf use formats that are basic types and they look like strings to the programmer. Formats are not strings, even though they look like strings, which can lead to some confusion. There are three functions that can be important if you want to manipulate format strings:

```
string_of_format
format_of_string
^^
```

The last one is the concatenation operator, which is very useful because it enables you to build up a format programmatically.

You probably do not need to manipulate format strings programmatically. A later chapter will discuss pretty printers, which take much of the burden of representing custom types away from the programmer.

fprintf

```
val fprintf: Pervasives.out_channel -> ('a, Pervasives.out_channel, unit) ➥
    Pervasives.format -> 'a
```

Printf.fprintf stdout "%i %s" 10 "hello world\n";; would display "10 hello world" on stdout. This function is used to write formatted output to any out_channel such as a file or a socket.

eprintf

```
val eprintf: ('a, Pervasives.out_channel, unit) Pervasives.format -> 'a
```

This function is the same as fprintf, except it writes its output to stderr. This function does not take an out_channel as an argument.

printf

```
val printf: ('a, Pervasives.out_channel, unit) Pervasives.format -> 'a
```

This function is the stdout version of eprintf; it does not take an out_channel as an argument. This is the function used for most of the examples.

sprintf

```
val sprintf: ('a, unit, string) Pervasives.format -> 'a
```

This function writes its output to a string instead of an out_channel. It enables you to build up formatted strings programmatically. This function also features prominently in the examples.

bprintf

```
val bprintf: Buffer.t -> ('a, Buffer.t, unit) Pervasives.format -> 'a
```

Instead of a string, this function writes its output to a buffer, which is much faster than a string for this kind of input/output (I/O). If you have large amounts of formatted output, you should use a buffer instead of a string. Strings are quite convenient, however.

kprintf

```
val kfprintf : (out_channel -> 'a) ->
      out_channel ->
      ('b, out_channel, unit, 'a) format4 -> 'b
```

This function enables you to specify a function that takes a string. The return type of this function is the return type of kprintf.

Why would you want to do this? For one thing, this function provides a mechanism to write filters using a convenient syntax.

Scanf

Scanf is (unsurprisingly) the opposite of Printf. Scanf reads from a buffer, string, or channel; converts the input according to the format string; and passes the converted input to a function.

Table 7-3. *Scanf-Specific Codes*

Scanf-specific Codes	Description
[range]	Indicates a range; for example [0-9] is the range from 0 to 9; the dash is not matched. The ^ is used to negate the range ([^0-9] matches anything *not* 0 to 9).
L	Passes the number of lines processed so far to a function.
n	Passes the number of characters processed so far to a function.
N	Passes the number of tokens (or codes) processed so far to a function.
!	Matches the end of the input.
%	Matches a percent symbol (%) in the input.

Scanning Module

The Scanning module has various functions for dealing with different types of input and buffering. The functions to create buffers from strings, functions, and channels are found in this module.

fscanf

```
val fscanf: Pervasives.in_channel ->  ('a, Scanning.scanbuf, 'b) ->
                                           Pervasives.format -> 'a -> 'b
```

This function is the analog of fprintf. Any in_channel works with it, including sockets and files.

scanf

```
val scanf: ('a, Scanning.scanbuf, 'b) Pervasives.format -> 'a -> 'b
```

This function is the equivalent of using `fscanf` with `stdin`.

sscanf

```
val sscanf: string -> ('a, Scanning.scanbuf, 'b) Pervasives.format -> 'a -> 'b
```

This function uses a string to scan from. It is used a lot in the examples.

bscanf

```
val bscanf: Scanning.scanbuf -> ('a, Scanning.scanbuf, 'b) Pervasives.format -> 'b
```

Using a buffer instead of a string, this function is faster for many applications. It is also more efficient because the OCaml buffers are highly optimized.

kscanf

```
val kscanf: Scanning.scanbuf -> (Scanning.scanbuf, exn, 'a) ->
('b, Scanning.scanbuf, 'a) -> Pervasives.format -> 'b -> 'a
```

This is a very interesting function. Because you pass a second function to `kscanf` that is called on error, this function enables you to do error recovery or further processing.

Why Use These Functions?

After seeing these functions, you might think, "Gee, that's nice, but I would have used regular expressions." Regular expressions provide a pattern-matching facility for strings that is very powerful. With the popularity of Perl, regular expressions have become quite popular in their own right.

Why Not Regular Expressions?

Regular expressions are great tools, although they are not the best tools for every job. Pattern matching is different from the `Scanf` type of input handling. For one thing, patterns can match incorrectly while returning a result. This might not matter so much when you are dealing only with string data. However, because OCaml is typesafe, it can lead to problems. `Scanf` does not even scan the data if it does not match, leaving you to handle the data in a different way. With regular expressions, the failure can occur much later in your function.

None of this should be considered an implication about anything. The best reason why regular expressions are not used here is because these examples are designed to teach you about OCaml. Regular expressions are just that: regular. They are a standard; if you understand them, all that's left is the idiosyncratic implementation of regular expressions in the language you are using (discussed later in this book). However, this chapter is about the specifics of OCaml and how to apply the tools in the language to actually do something.

What About Line-Oriented I/O?

Okay, but what about line-oriented I/O? Surely everything doesn't have to be scanned? The read_line function does just that. This function works only on stdin, though; for other channels, you can use input_line or Scanf.

The following is a short example of using the input_line function. The signature for input_line is simply: input_line : in_channel -> string, and it will raise an End_of_file exception when it encounters the end of the given channel. This function can be used on any OCaml in_channel. After you input the line, you can perform further processing if you need to.

```
# let load_file filename =
  let ic = open_in filename in
  let rec lf ichan acc =
    try
      lf ic ((input_line ic) :: acc)
    with End_of_file -> acc
  in
  let res = lf ic [] in
    close_in ic;res;;
            val load_file : string -> string list = <fun>
# load_file "testfile";;
- : string list = ["world"; "hello"]
```

The preceding example loads a file that has hello and world on two separate lines. Because of the way the function accumulates lines, it displays the file backward. One nice thing about input_line is that it automatically handles Unix- or DOS-style newlines in files for you.

The Right Tool for the Right Job

The Scanf and Printf functions are very useful when you want formatted I/O. Regular expressions and ad hoc methods work for some things. You also do not need to use these functions if you want to code in OCaml. A good place to use formatted output is when processing files with fixed length fields. You can do this with substrings in OCaml, too, but using Printf and Scanf can be much easier.

Here is a quick example. The following is a (very small) subset from an archive of data from the Storm Prediction Center (http://www.spc.noaa.gov/archive/tornadoes/), which is a National Oceanic and Atmospheric Administration (NOAA) program. This data segment represents a set of fixed-length fields that are the two-digit year (two chars), the sequence number of the storm (three chars), the state code (two chars), the two-digit month (two chars), the two-digit day (two chars), the time (four chars), the time zone (one char), a time plus/minus factor (one char), and a storm type (one char).

```
# let example_fixed_len = "500013901031600311";;
val example_fixed_len : string = "500013901031600311"
# let parse ex = Scanf.sscanf ex "%2s%3s%2s%2s%2s%4s%1s%1s%1s"  ➥
        (fun a b c d e f g h i -> (a,b,c,d,e,f,g,h,i));;
```

```
val parse :
  string ->
  string * string * string * string * string * string * string * string *
  string = <fun>
# parse example_fixed_len;;
- : string * string * string * string * string * string * string * string *
    string
= ("50", "001", "39", "01", "03", "1600", "3", "1", "1")
# let hard_parse ex = (
  (String.sub ex 0 2),
  (String.sub ex 2 3),
  (String.sub ex 5 2),
  (String.sub ex 7 2),
  (String.sub ex 9 2),
  (String.sub ex 11 4),
  (String.sub ex 15 1),
  (String.sub ex 16 1),
  (String.sub ex 17 1) );;
                    val hard_parse :
  string ->
  string * string * string * string * string * string * string * string *
  string = <fun>
# hard_parse example_fixed_len;;
- : string * string * string * string * string * string * string * string *
    string
= ("50", "001", "39", "01", "03", "1600", "3", "1", "1")
#
```

Although both functions yield the same result, the Scanf version is much easier to understand (and much easier to maintain). The OCaml community and the language itself are quite pragmatic. You should also use the right tool for the right job—which is where these functions come in. Ad hoc methods are often easy to write but difficult to debug. Typesafe-formatted I/O provides a way for you to write code with the confidence that you are getting what you think you are getting. Although it is not a substitute for validation at a later step, it does take some of the burden away from the scanning and output stages.

For these examples, you are basically defining a protocol. It is not a rigid protocol and it might change in the future, which makes using formatted output both appropriate and desirable.

Third-party libraries that enable typesafe regular expressions are also available. The most notable one is the Micmatch library written by Martin Jambon. This library can be found at http://martin.jambon.free.fr/micmatch.html and is distributed under a Berkeley Software Distribution (BSD) type of license. You'll find a lot of documentation and examples on the site if you want to learn more.

More About Buffers

The buffers used by both `Printf` and `Scanf` are not the same kind of buffers used in buffered I/O. There is also no reason not to use these buffers for your own purposes.

These buffers exist because using strings is often slow for concatenation. When you have a buffer that you want to shove data into, it is tempting to use a string. Buffers are much faster than strings and are linear (most of the time) for appending. Strings are quadratic when appending, which is fine for few or small appends, but not for real buffering. Chapter 8 discusses buffers in more detail.

Writing a Report

Just to refresh your memory, here are the two types you will be working with and the data structure that stores all the items that you will use (the type constraint on the hash table is there for clarity).

```
type position = { symbol : string; holding : int; pprice : float; };;
type account = {name:string;max_ind_holding:float;pos:position list};;
# let (db: (string,account) Hashtbl.t) = Hashtbl.create 100;;
val db : (string, account) Hashtbl.t = <abstr>
```

You should write a pretty printer for the two main types. A pretty printer is used at the toplevel so that the information is nicely formatted by default. Printers for any given type can be added and removed using the #install printer and #remove_printer directives. Notice that these commands are prefixed with #, which means they are special commands used in the toplevel. You shouldn't use these directives in code that is not intended to be run via the toplevel.

Note You should have the code from Chapter 5 loaded for the following examples.

```
# let print_position pos = print_string "Holding: ";print_int ➥
      pos.holding;print_string (" " ^ pos.symbol ^ "@");
      print_float pos.pprice;print_newline ();;
val print_position : position -> unit = <fun>
# let example = {symbol="IBM";holding=100;pprice=85.5};;
val example : position = {symbol = "IBM"; holding = 100; pprice = 85.5}
# example;;
- : position = {symbol = "IBM"; holding = 100; pprice = 85.5}
# #install_printer print_position;;
# example;;
Holding: 100 IBM@85.5
val example : position =
# #remove_printer print_position;;
# example;;
val example : position = {symbol = "IBM"; holding = 100; pprice = 85.5}
#
```

Notice that the pretty printer changes the display of type but nothing else. You can add a pretty printer for accounts, too.

```
# let print_account acct = print_string ("Account_ID: " ^ acct.name); ➥
        print_newline ();List.iter print_position acct.pos;;
val print_account : account -> unit = <fun>
# let acc_example = {
      name="example";
      max_ind_holding=0.40;
      pos = [example;
                      {symbol="GOOG";holding=100;pprice=406.10};
                      {symbol="AMAT";holding=1000;pprice=18.00}]
};;
val acc_example : account =
  {name = "example"; max_ind_holding = 0.4;
   pos =
    [{symbol = "IBM"; holding = 100; pprice = 85.5};
     {symbol = "GOOG"; holding = 100; pprice = 406.1};
     {symbol = "AMAT"; holding = 1000; pprice = 18.}]]}
# #install_printer print_account;;
# acc_example;;
Account_ID: example
Holding: 100 IBM@85.5
Holding: 100 GOOG@406.1
Holding: 1000 AMAT@18.
val acc_example : account =
#
```

Your pretty printers can use other pretty printers in their definitions. In fact, your pretty printers can be almost anything you want them to be. They are still not really reports, nor do they use any formatted output. You can't expect all your users to use the OCaml toplevel, so you'll need more.

For starters, you define a small function that will give you some descriptive statistics from a list of information. In this case, the list of information is a list of floats.

```
let summary_stats items =
  let total = List.fold_left (+.) 0. items in
  let mean = (total /. (float_of_int (List.length items))) in
  let median = List.nth items ((List.length items) / 2) in
  let std_dev =
    sqrt (
      (
        List.fold_left (
          fun y n -> ((n -. mean) *. (n -. mean)) +. y
        ) 0. items)
      /. (float_of_int (List.length items))
    ) in
  total,mean,median,std_dev;;
```

```
let rec top_n source acc counter =
  match source with
    h :: t when (counter = 0) -> List.rev acc
  | h :: t when (counter > 0) -> top_n t (h :: acc) (counter - 1)
  | _ -> assert(false);;
```

Next, you write a function that finds the top 10 earning accounts from the database. The best way to do this is to write a function that can find the top or the bottom set of values. You can then write functions to return the top or bottom 10 quite easily. These examples use functions (such as the profit_and_loss function) that were defined in Chapter 5 when these types were initially defined.

```
# let rec top_n source acc counter =
  match source with
    h :: t when (counter = 0) -> List.rev acc
  | h :: t when (counter > 0) -> top_n t (h :: acc) (counter - 1)
  | _ -> assert(false);;
      val top_n : 'a list -> 'a list -> int -> 'a list = <fun>
# let top_10 db new_prices =
  let lst = List.sort (fun (m,n) (x,y) -> compare y n)
    (Hashtbl.fold (fun x y z -> ((x,profit_and_loss y new_prices) :: z)) db []) in
  top_n lst [] 10;;
val top_10: ('a, account) Hashtbl.t ->
                        (string * float) list ->
                        ('a * float) list = <fun>
# let bottom_10 db new_prices = let lst = List.sort (fun (m,n) (x,y) -> compare n y)
    (Hashtbl.fold (fun x y z -> ((x,profit_and_loss y new_prices) :: z)) db []) in
  top_n lst [] 10;;
val bottom_10 : ('a, account) Hashtbl.t ->
                        (string * float) list ->
                        ('a * float) list = <fun>
```

By using these functions, you can now write a reporting function. The first one is pretty simple: it creates a report of the top or bottom items and displays it, formatted, along with the descriptive statistics. You have to either import the database you used in Chapter 5 or enter some new data. At the end of the chapter, there are routines for generating data programmatically.

```
# let print_top_report title lst = let rec toprep buf items =
  match items with
    [] -> let (sum,mn,med,stdev) = summary_stats (List.map
                                            (fun (x,y) -> y) lst)
      in
                Buffer.add_string buf "------------------\n";
                Buffer.add_string buf (Printf.sprintf "Sum:\t%-0.2f\n" sum);
                    Buffer.add_string buf (Printf.sprintf "Mean:\t%-0.2f\n" mn);
                        Buffer.add_string buf (Printf.sprintf "Median:\t%-0.2f\n"
med);
```

```
                  Buffer.add_string buf (Printf.sprintf "Stdev:\t%-0.2f\n\n"
                                                              stdev);
                      print_string (Buffer.contents buf)
    | (sy,pr) :: t ->
              Buffer.add_string buf (Printf.sprintf "%s\t%-0.2f\n" sy pr);
              toprep buf t
in
let newbuf = Buffer.create 100 in
  Buffer.add_string newbuf title;
  Buffer.add_string newbuf "\n------------------\n";
  Buffer.add_char newbuf '\n';
  toprep newbuf lst;;
 val print_top_report : string -> (string * float) list -> unit = <fun>
# print_top_report  "Top 10 Accounts" (top_10 db current_prices);;
Top 10 Accounts
------------------

w3045      5278.88
2t7v0      2997.70
0816r      2732.56
w5vl4      2158.85
o6q47      1672.16
2a3ka      1632.47
q6rrg      1614.69
8mf4k      1390.25
452y6      1378.56
770e0      1275.63
------------------
Sum:       22131.75
Mean:      2213.18
Median:    1632.47
Stdev:     1163.08

- : unit = ()
#
```

Writing Export Functions

Although you already have persistence in your database, you don't have the ability to export it in a platform-neutral way. You can take some of the formatting strings from the report to use for the exports:

```
# let price_to_string (m,n) = Printf.sprintf "%s %0.4f" m n;;
val price_to_string : string * float -> string = <fun>
# let string_of_position pos = Printf.sprintf "%s %i %0.4f" pos.symbol ➥
        pos.holding pos.pprice;;
val string_of_position : position -> string = <fun>
```

```
# let price_from_string s = Scanf.sscanf s "%s %f" (fun x y -> x,y);;
val price_from_string : string -> string * float = <fun>
# let position_of_string s = Scanf.sscanf s "%s %i %0.4f" (fun x y z -> ➡
    {symbol=x;holding=y;pprice=z});;
val position_of_string : string -> position = <fun>
# let string_of_account acct =
  let rec build_pos poslist accum =
    match poslist with
        [] -> Buffer.contents accum
      | h :: t ->
            Buffer.add_char accum '|';
                Buffer.add_string accum (string_of_position h);
                build_pos t accum
  in
  let temp_buf = Buffer.create 100 in
  Buffer.add_string temp_buf acct.name;
  Buffer.add_char temp_buf '|';
  Buffer.add_string temp_buf (string_of_float acct.max_ind_holding);
  build_pos acct.pos temp_buf;;
                        val string_of_account : account -> string = <fun>
# let export_accounts db filename =
    let oc = open_out filename in
    Hashtbl.iter (fun key data ->
                    Printf.fprintf oc "%s\n" (string_of_account data)) db;
    close_out oc;;
val export_accounts : ('a, account) Hashtbl.t -> string -> unit = <fun>
# export_accounts db "testfile";;
- : unit = ()
#
```

The export that this code creates is easy to import. This function can be modified to output XML or any other output type you want to use. It also can be processed by other text-processing tools or even imported into Excel as a delimited file.

Writing Import Functions

Now that you can export these items, you need a way to bring them back in and also import items from other systems. You can take most of the format strings used in the export example and plug them into the import code, which is one of the reasons why using Printf and Scanf is so appealing.

Import functions are a little harder to write and they tend to need more code. This is partly because you have to validate the input data in some way and also because you need to re-create some of the data structures.

```
# let account_of_string str =
  let rec build_pos sb accum =
    let getnextch = try
      Scanf.bscanf sb "%c" (fun issep -> match issep with
                                        '|' -> Scanf.bscanf sb "%s %i %f"
                                                   (fun x y z -> Some
                                                      {symbol=x;holding=y;pprice=z})
                                      | _ -> raise (Invalid_argument "Malformed position"))
      with End_of_file -> None
    in
    match getnextch with
            None -> accum
      | Some p -> build_pos sb (p :: accum)
  in
  let scan_buffer = Scanf.Scanning.from_string str in
  let acc_name,mih = Scanf.bscanf scan_buffer "%s@|%f" (fun x y -> x,y) in
  let pslist = build_pos scan_buffer [] in
  {name=acc_name;max_ind_holding=mih;pos=pslist};;
val account_of_string : string -> account = <fun>
# let import_accounts dstore filename =
  let ic = open_in filename in
  let rec iaccts chan store =
    let newacc = try
      Some (account_of_string (input_line ic))
    with End_of_file -> None
    in
    match newacc with
      None -> ()
    | Some p -> Hashtbl.add store p.name p;
                    iaccts ic store
  in
  let res = iaccts ic dstore in close_in ic;res;;
val import_accounts : (string, account) Hashtbl.t -> string -> unit = <fun>
# let newdb = Hashtbl.create 100;;
val newdb : ('_a, '_b) Hashtbl.t = <abstr>
```

After you create the database, you can either import the data from Chapter 5 or you can generate data. The routines for generating data are covered later in the chapter. For now, you will call the function to generate the data.

```
# populate_db 10 newdb cur_prices;;
- : unit = ()
# Hashtbl.fold (fun x y z -> y :: z) newdb [];;
- : account list =
```

```
[{name = "okkx0"; max_ind_holding = 0.884100708693;
  pos = [{symbol = "AMAT"; holding = 140; pprice = 18.04}]};
 {name = "770e0"; max_ind_holding = 0.311912812725;
  pos =
   [{symbol = "CC"; holding = 652; pprice = 24.65};
    {symbol = "BCO"; holding = 28; pprice = 51.05};
    {symbol = "GS"; holding = 426; pprice = 161.02};
    {symbol = "GS"; holding = 0; pprice = 161.02};
    {symbol = "CSCO"; holding = 445; pprice = 20.81}]};
 {name = "zb650"; max_ind_holding = 0.472736468921;
  pos ....
```

This is another advantage of the bottom-up programming that functional programming encourages. When you create a component, it can be useful in many places. Code reuse at the functional level can be very useful, especially when refactoring code.

The code here could probably be rewritten in a number of ways. This is by design because this short example provides an actual working application upon which you can experiment and build.

Generating Data

When testing applications such as the one presented in this chapter, you often want to use data that is realistic, but perhaps not production data. An easy way to get this kind of data is to generate it (you can even generate pathologic data, too).

```
# let rand_char () =
    let flip = Random.bool () in
             match flip with
                  true -> Char.chr ((Random.int 9) + 48)
                  | false -> Char.chr ((Random.int 26) + 97);;
      val rand_char : unit -> char = <fun>
# let random_acct_name len =
    let rec ran indx str =
             match indx with
          0 -> str.[0] <- rand_char ();str
             | _ -> str.[indx] <- rand_char ();ran (indx - 1) str
     in
            ran (len - 1) (String.create len);;
            val random_acct_name : int -> string = <fun>
# let rec gen_random_pos_list len accu price_list =
    match len with
                0 -> accu
            | _ ->
               let (sym,price) = List.nth price_list
```

```
                    (Random.int (List.length price_list)) in
                        gen_random_pos_list (len - 1)
                                    ({symbol=sym;
                    holding=(Random.int 1000);
                    pprice = price} :: accu) price_list;;
                    val gen_random_pos_list :
  int -> position list -> (string * float) list -> position list = <fun>
# let gen_random_account current_prices =
      {name=(random_acct_name 5);
       max_ind_holding=((Random.float 0.8)+.0.2);
       pos = gen_random_pos_list ((Random.int 9) + 1) [] current_prices};;
      val gen_random_account : (string * float) list -> account = <fun>
# let rec populate_db rand_cands store current_prices=
      match rand_cands with
                    0 -> ()
                | _ -> let newacc = gen_random_account current_prices in
                    Hashtbl.add store newacc.name newacc;
                    populate_db (rand_cands - 1) store current_prices;;
          val populate_db :
  int -> (string, account) Hashtbl.t -> (string * float) list -> unit = <fun>
#
```

You would have to modify this code to make it generate pathologic data. However, as it stands, it enables you (along with the functions in the previous chapter) to generate a great deal of data and manipulate it to your heart's content.

Conclusion

Now you have created a database with input, output, and reporting. You also should have a solid foundation in the display and import of data in OCaml. The functions discussed in this chapter provide many of the building blocks for a wide variety of applications.

■**Note** Because you used OCaml I/O channels, this application is implicitly networkable.

Chapter 8 talks about OCaml collections and about the design of your database. It points out the things that you could have done and why you didn't. The OCaml collections are not as vast as those of Java, but they provide many of the items you would expect from a high-level programming language.

■■■

Collections

OCaml has a standard library that provides for several collections to handle everything from lists to sets. Although not all these collections are purely functional, the purity of a given container isn't all that important to many programmers.

These collections are all part of the OCaml standard library that is distributed with OCaml. They are not the only collection types availed in OCaml, nor are they the only collections that can be created. There are many implementations available on the Internet, such as Event queues and Priority queues. Many of these implementations are based on the standard library containers discussed here.

Note If you don't have a background in functional programming, the periodic mention of what is (or is not) "pure" can be confusing. Although purity has wide implications when writing code, the implications of purity while learning a language are relatively unimportant.

You will continue to expand your use of signatures as a mechanism to show what code does. Each collection gives a (mostly) complete signature for the functions available for that kind of collection.

Note Function signatures basically consist of a display of type information. They tell you (and the compiler) the type of arguments, values, and return of a given function or value. They can be particularly useful in the toplevel, which displays them after each closure.

Although all programs do not need all collections, it is a good idea to understand the basic attributes of the collections. Not only does a basic understanding save you from implementing your solutions but often these standard collections also give you ideas on how to solve problems later.

What Are Collections?

A collection is used to group multiple data items so that you can operate on them as a single unit. Collections are useful when you want to store, retrieve, and manipulate data in the aggregate instead of individually. They are used to represent data that can be considered a natural group, such as a hand of cards, a gaggle of geese, or a bag of chips.

There are many reasons to use the standard collections when writing programs—one of the most important is that they are standard. They enable programmers to write code that will work with other code people have written. If you write your own list implementation, and I write my own, there is no guarantee that our code will work together. Using the standard collections also reduces the learning curve (for the same reasons). If I understand how standard OCaml arrays work, I don't have to learn new array-handling semantics if your library uses arrays. This standardization translates directly into reduced time and effort when writing your own code. You don't have to reinvent the wheel every time you want to use a hashtable.

This reduced effort extends into a general reduction in effort when designing and using new APIs. You also can avoid bugs because you can be pretty sure that the standard collections are well-tested and used. Using standard collections also encourages code reuse because your code already works with the standard collections and can be used by others. You also can use other code that uses the standard collections.

Comparison Functions

OCaml uses the idea of comparison functions in many of the container modules. A comparison function is one that when given two arguments, it returns an integer indicating the relative value. There is a generic comparison function in the Pervasives module that works on most OCaml data types (even types you create). You can, however, write your own comparison function and use it in the modules described in this chapter. The returned integer is -1 if the second value is greater than the first, 0 if they are equal, and 1 if the second value is less than the first.

```
# compare 3 1;;
-: int = 1
# compare 3 6;;
-: int = -1
# compare 3 3;;
-: int = 0
```

For a more illustrative example, suppose that you have a type that represents people at a university. They are orderable based on the priority you assign to them. If you use the built-in compare function, they are compared based on the order they are given in their enumerated type. However, you can write your own function and order them in any way you like.

```
# type university = Grad_Student | Undergrad_Student |AtLarge_Student ➡
| Adjunct_Professor | Professor | Staff;;
type university =
    Grad_Student
  | Undergrad_Student
  | AtLarge_Student
  | Adjunct_Professor
```

```
  | Professor
  | Staff
# let assortment = [Grad_Student;Staff;Adjunct_Professor;Undergrad_Student];;
val assortment : university list =
  [Grad_Student; Staff; Adjunct_Professor; Undergrad_Student]
# List.sort compare assortment;;
- : university list =
[Grad_Student; Undergrad_Student; Adjunct_Professor; Staff]
# let rank uni = match uni with
      Grad_Student -> 0
  | Undergrad_Student -> 1
  | AtLarge_Student -> 2
  | Adjunct_Professor -> 4
  | Professor -> 5
  | Staff -> 3;;
              val rank : university -> int = <fun>
# let compare_students s s' = compare (rank s) (rank s');;
val compare_students : university -> university -> int = <fun>
# List.sort compare_students assortment;;
- : university list =
[Grad_Student; Undergrad_Student; Staff; Adjunct_Professor]
#
```

Lists

Although lists were used in previous examples, they were not discussed in much depth. Lists are implemented as single-linked lists in OCaml. They are quite fast for sequential access, but are not suited for random access.

Lists are a purely functional data structure. There are some functions in the List module that are sometimes surprising for new OCaml programmers. Before getting into those functions, this section covers some of the more basic list actions.

Caution Lines of code that can be entered into the OCaml toplevel have a pound sign (#) prompt at the beginning of the line and continue until two semicolons (; ;) mark the closure. Otherwise, the information shown are responses from the toplevel or signature information describing functions and values.

Lists are defined using square brackets, with each element separated by semicolons. The length function returns the index of the last element. (Remember that OCaml lists are indexed starting from 0, not 1.) In this example, the list is 9 elements long, so the length function returns 9.

```
# let example_list = [10;20;30;40;50;60;70;80;90];;
val example_list : int list = [10; 20; 30; 40; 50; 60; 70; 80; 90]
```

```
    val length : 'a list -> int
```

```
# List.length example_list;;
- : int = 9
```

The signature shows that the value example_list is a list of integers containing the displayed values. Two important list operations are the functions that return the head and the tail of a list. The head is the first value, the tail is all values after the first value, and the tail can be an empty list [] (although in this case, it is not). You can see that lists are polymorphic because of the 'a instead of a specific type in the following signature:

```
  val hd : 'a list -> 'a
  val tl : 'a list -> 'a list
# List.hd example_list;;
- : int = 10
# List.tl example_list;;
- : int list = [20; 30; 40; 50; 60; 70; 80; 90]
```

You can access the head and tail of a given list explicitly by using the List.hd and List.tl functions. Because the head of a list must be an element, calling List.hd on an empty list raises an exception.

```
# List.hd (List.tl example_list);;
- : int = 20
# List.hd [];;
Exception: Failure "hd".
```

Lists also can be reversed—the reversed list is returned from the List.rev function. Although lists cannot be modified, the :: command also can be used to add an element to a list, returning a new list and leaving the old list unchanged. This command is also used in pattern matches to give the head and tail of a list, and this behavior is available only in pattern matches.

```
# 100 :: example_list;;
- : int list = [100; 10; 20; 30; 40; 50; 60; 70; 80; 90 ]
# List.rev example_list;;
- : int list = [90; 80; 70; 60; 50; 40; 30; 20; 10]
```

Although you can access specific elements of a list, you should not do it very often. If you need random access to the data in a list, you should probably use an array instead. If you try to access an element that is outside of the list bounds, a Failure exception is raised.

```
  val nth : 'a list -> int -> 'a
# List.nth example_list 10;;
Exception: Failure "nth".
# List.nth example_list 5;;
- : int = 60
```

Although lists cannot be modified in place, there are functions that will return a new list with added, concatenated, and flattened operations performed. The append function appends one list to the end of the other. The rev_append function appends the list to the reversed list and enjoys a performance advantage over the normal append function. The concat and flatten functions are essentially the same—given a list of lists, they return one list with all the elements from the interior lists. Like all lists, all the elements in the lists must be the same type.

```
val append : 'a list -> 'a list -> 'a list
val rev_append : 'a list -> 'a list -> 'a list
val concat : 'a list list -> 'a list
val flatten : 'a list list -> 'a list
```

```
# List.append example_list [0;0;0];;
- : int list = [10; 20; 30; 40; 50; 60; 70; 80; 90; 0; 0; 0]
# List.rev_append example_list [0;0;0];;
- : int list = [90; 80; 70; 60; 50; 40; 30; 20; 10; 0; 0; 0]
# let nlist = List.rev_append example_list [0;0;0] in
List.rev_append nlist [0;0;0];;
- : int list = [0; 0; 0; 10; 20; 30; 40; 50; 60; 70; 80; 90; 0; 0; 0]
# List.concat [example_list;example_list];;
- : int list =
[10; 20; 30; 40; 50; 60; 70; 80; 90; 10; 20; 30; 40; 50; 60; 70; 80; 90]
# List.flatten [example_list;example_list];;
- : int list =
[10; 20; 30; 40; 50; 60; 70; 80; 90; 10; 20; 30; 40; 50; 60; 70; 80; 90]
```

Lists can be iterated over, map'd, and fold'd. The iter function calls a function on each element of a given list. The result of that function must be the unit type, which means that you cannot get information returned to you via iteration. If you want information returned, you must use the map function, which maps a function onto each element in the list and returns a list of the results of each function call. Almost all the OCaml collections have iter and map functions. iter and map are also common expressions in functional programming languages.

The same is true of the fold functions, which for lists come in right-handed and left-handed versions. If this is the first time you've seen fold operations, ensure that you understand them because they can be very powerful and confusing. The fold_left function applies the given function to each element of the given list and to an initial argument. The result and the initial argument must be the same type. Consider the following code:

```
# let add x y = x + y;;
val add : int -> int -> int = <fun>
# let a = [10;20;30];;
val a : int list = [10; 20; 30]
# add 10 (add 20 (add 30 0));;
- : int = 60
#
```

In the example, the zero added to 30 is the "first" argument. Each add call takes two arguments: one is a number, and the other is the result of another call to the add function.

The left-handed version of the fold command processes the list elements from left to right, whereas the right-handed version does the opposite. These two functions are very powerful. The folding examples provided use the addition function to create a sum of the elements in the list.

```
val iter : ('a -> unit) -> 'a list -> unit
val map : ('a -> 'b) -> 'a list -> 'b list
val rev_map : ('a -> 'b) -> 'a list -> 'b list
val fold_left : ('a -> 'b -> 'a) -> 'a -> 'b list -> 'a
val fold_right : ('a -> 'b -> 'b) -> 'a list -> 'b -> 'b
```

```
# List.iter print_int example_list;;
102030405060708090- : unit = ()
# List.map string_of_int example_list;;
- : string list = ["10"; "20"; "30"; "40"; "50"; "60"; "70"; "80"; "90"]
# List.rev_map string_of_int example_list;;
- : string list = ["90"; "80"; "70"; "60"; "50"; "40"; "30"; "20"; "10"]
# List.fold_left (+) 0 example_list;;
- : int = 450
# List.fold_right (+) example_list 0;;
- : int = 450
```

The next two functions are interesting. The for_all function returns true if the given function evaluates as true for every element in the given list; otherwise, it is false. The exists function evaluates as true if one of the elements results in true in the given list.

```
val for_all : ('a -> bool) -> 'a list -> bool
val exists : ('a -> bool) -> 'a list -> bool
```

```
# List.for_all (fun x -> x > 0) example_list;;
- : bool = true
# List.exists (fun x -> x < 0) example_list;;
- : bool = false
```

You can test for membership (that is, whether this list contains a given value) and get the element in the list by using the mem and find functions. The find function raises a Not_found exception if the element is not found.

```
val mem : 'a -> 'a list -> bool
val find : ('a -> bool) -> 'a list -> 'a
```

```
# List.mem 50 example_list;;
- : bool = true
# List.mem 100 example_list;;
- : bool = false
```

```
# List.find (fun x -> x = 50) example_list;;
- : int = 50
# List.find (fun x -> x > 50) example_list;;
- : int = 60
```

The filter function returns all elements of a given list that evaluate to true given a function. The find_all function is equivalent to the filter function. The partition function is like the filter function, with the addition of returning all the elements that don't match the function. Imagine that you have one bucket filled with black and white marbles. The filter function would give you a new bucket filled with only black or white marbles. The partition function would give you two buckets, each filled with only black or white marbles.

```
val filter : ('a -> bool) -> 'a list -> 'a list
val find_all : ('a -> bool) -> 'a list -> 'a list
val partition : ('a -> bool) -> 'a list -> 'a list * 'a list
```

```
# List.filter (fun x -> x > 40) example_list;;
- : int list = [50; 60; 70; 80; 90]
# List.find_all (fun x -> x > 40) example_list;;
- : int list = [50; 60; 70; 80; 90]
# List.partition (fun x -> x > 40) example_list;;
- : int list * int list = ([50; 60; 70; 80; 90], [10; 20; 30; 40])
```

Association (or assoc) lists, which are important data structures in OCaml, are key/value pairs and are often used instead of hashtables. Assoc lists are faster than hashtables when there are only a few keys to search. Assoc lists can be treaded like any other list, too.

The associated value of a key can be returned by using the assoc function (or Not_found if there is no key). You also can check for membership using the mem_assoc function. The remove function does not remove the item from the list, but it does return a list with that association removed. Only the first key/value pair is accessible using these functions, so multiple key/value pairs with the same key just waste memory.

```
val assoc : 'a -> ('a * 'b) list -> 'b
 val mem_assoc : 'a -> ('a * 'b) list -> bool
val remove_assoc : 'a -> ('a * 'b) list -> ('a * 'b) list
```

```
# let pair_examples = [[(20, "20"); (30, "30"); (40, "40"); (50, "50"); ➥
 (60, "60"); (70, "70");
 (80, "80"); (90, "90")]];;
- : (int * string) list =
[(20, "20"); (30, "30"); (40, "40"); (50, "50"); (60, "60"); (70, "70");
 (80, "80"); (90, "90")]
```

```
# List.assoc 10 pair_examples;;
- : string = "10"
# List.mem_assoc 10 pair_examples;;
- : bool = true
# List.remove_assoc 10 pair_examples;;
- : (int * string) list =
[(20, "20"); (30, "30"); (40, "40"); (50, "50"); (60, "60"); (70, "70");
 (80, "80"); (90, "90")]
```

These lists can be created from and returned to lists using the split and combine functions (example_list is used from the earlier example).

```
val split : ('a * 'b) list -> 'a list * 'b list
 val combine : 'a list -> 'b list -> ('a * 'b) list
```

```
# List.combine example_list (List.map (fun x -> string_of_int x) example_list);;
- : (int * string) list =
[(10, "10"); (20, "20"); (30, "30"); (40, "40"); (50, "50"); (60, "60");
 (70, "70"); (80, "80"); (90, "90")]
# let pair_examples = List.combine example_list (List.map (fun x -> ➥
string_of_int x) example_list);;
val pair_examples : (int * string) list =
  [(10, "10"); (20, "20"); (30, "30"); (40, "40"); (50, "50"); (60, "60");
   (70, "70"); (80, "80"); (90, "90")]
# List.split pair_examples;;
- : int list * string list =
([10; 20; 30; 40; 50; 60; 70; 80; 90],
 ["10"; "20"; "30"; "40"; "50"; "60"; "70"; "80"; "90"])
```

Lists can be sorted and merged. The sort function takes a comparator function (as discussed earlier) and returns a sorted list. The merge function takes a comparator function, too. It returns a sorted list with the values from both lists sorted together (merged).

```
val sort : ('a -> 'a -> int) -> 'a list -> 'a list
val merge : ('a -> 'a -> int) -> 'a list -> 'a list -> 'a list
```

```
# List.sort compare example_list;;
- : int list = [10; 20; 30; 40; 50; 60; 70; 80; 90]
# List.merge compare example_list [ 33;44;55;66];;
- : int list = [10; 20; 30; 33; 40; 44; 50; 55; 60; 66; 70; 80; 90]
```

Although lists must contain elements of a single type, you can create union types if you really need a list that contains more complex information.

■Caution Don't abuse union types. Type safety is important in OCaml code; circumventing it does not do you any favors.

Arrays and Matrices

Although OCaml lists are not good for random access, OCaml arrays are. Arrays can be indexed and modified in place, but they share the same restriction that elements must be of the same type. Because arrays can be modified in place, you can write functions that have side effects with arrays.

You can create arrays directly (using the [| and |] notation) with semicolons separating the elements, or they can be created by Array module functions. The make and create functions are equivalent. The init function enables you to generate values via a function that takes the current array index as an argument.

```
external make : int -> 'a -> 'a array = "caml_make_vect"
external create : int -> 'a -> 'a array = "caml_make_vect"
val init : int -> (int -> 'a) -> 'a array
```

```
# let my_array = Array.make 10 0;;
val my_array : int array = [|0; 0; 0; 0; 0; 0; 0; 0; 0; 0|]
# let my_array = Array.init 10 (fun x -> x);;
val my_array : int array = [|0; 1; 2; 3; 4; 5; 6; 7; 8; 9|]
# let my_array = Array.init 10 (fun x -> Random.int 100);;
val my_array : int array = [|34; 47; 14; 28; 48; 25; 0; 17; 65; 57|]
```

The length function returns the number of elements in a given array. Like lists, it returns the true number of elements. You can use the GET and SET methods to get a specific element in an array. You also can use the subscript syntax, which enables you to get the value of the element in a cleaner style—by using .(N) where N is the index.

```
external length : 'a array -> int = "%array_length"
external get : 'a array -> int -> 'a = "%array_safe_get"
external set : 'a array -> int -> 'a -> unit = "%array_safe_set"
```

```
# Array.length my_array;;
- : int = 10
# Array.get my_array 50;;
Exception: Invalid_argument "index out of bounds".
# Array.set my_array 5 0;;
- : unit = ()
# my_array;;
- : int array = [|34; 47; 14; 28; 48; 0; 0; 17; 65; 57|]
# my_array.(4);;
- : int = 48
```

Arrays cannot be appended to, even though they can be modified in place. The append and concat functions return new arrays.

```
val append : 'a array -> 'a array -> 'a array
val concat : 'a array list -> 'a array
# Array.append [|1;2;3;4;5|] my_array;;
- : int array = [|1; 2; 3; 4; 5; 34; 47; 14; 28; 48; 0; 0; 17; 65; 57|]
# Array.concat [[|1;2;3;4;5|];my_array];;
- : int array = [|1; 2; 3; 4; 5; 34; 47; 14; 28; 48; 0; 0; 17; 65; 57|]
```

A subarray can be taken from an array using the sub function. This function returns a new array with the number of elements specified. If you provide bad indexes for the function, it raises the somewhat vague Invalid_argument exception.

```
val sub : 'a array -> int -> int -> 'a array
```

```
# Array.sub my_array 3 3;;
- : int array = [|28; 48; 0|]
# Array.sub my_array 3 10;;
Exception: Invalid_argument "Array.sub".
```

Arrays can be filled with a given value or blitted from another array. In both cases, the target array is modified in place.

```
val fill : 'a array -> int -> int -> 'a -> unit
val blit : 'a array -> int -> 'a array -> int -> int -> unit
```

```
# Array.fill my_array 0 10 9;;
- : unit = ()
# my_array;;
- : int array = [|9; 9; 9; 9; 9; 9; 9; 9; 9; 9|]
# let my_array = Array.init 10 (fun x -> Random.int 100);;
val my_array : int array = [|76; 60; 32; 74; 92; 20; 75; 83; 12; 88|]
# let other_array = Array.init 10 (fun x -> Random.int 100);;
val other_array : int array = [|14; 22; 24; 78; 16; 62; 0; 90; 4; 21|]
# Array.blit other_array 3 my_array 3 6;;
- : unit = ()
# other_array;;
- : int array = [|14; 22; 24; 78; 16; 62; 0; 90; 4; 21|]
# my_array;;
- : int array = [|76; 60; 32; 78; 16; 62; 0; 90; 4; 88|]
```

Like lists, arrays can be iterated and mapped. Unlike lists, functions that also provide the index of the given value are available. The folding functions do not have the capability to tell what index they are at, however.

```
val iter : ('a -> unit) -> 'a array -> unit
val map : ('a -> 'b) -> 'a array -> 'b array
val iteri : (int -> 'a -> unit) -> 'a array -> unit
val mapi : (int -> 'a -> 'b) -> 'a array -> 'b array
val fold_left : ('a -> 'b -> 'a) -> 'a -> 'b array -> 'a
val fold_right : ('a -> 'b -> 'b) -> 'a array -> 'b -> 'b
```

```
# Array.iter print_int my_array;;
766032781662090488- : unit = ()
# Array.map string_of_int my_array;;
- : string array =
[|"76"; "60"; "32"; "78"; "16"; "62"; "0"; "90"; "4"; "88"|]
```

```
# Array.iteri (fun i x -> Printf.printf "%i at location %i\n" x i) my_array;;
76 at location 0
60 at location 1
32 at location 2
78 at location 3
16 at location 4
62 at location 5
0 at location 6
90 at location 7
4 at location 8
88 at location 9
- : unit = ()
# Array.mapi (fun x y -> (x,y)) my_array;;
- : (int * int) array =
[|(0, 76); (1, 60); (2, 32); (3, 78); (4, 16); (5, 62); (6, 0); (7, 90);
  (8, 4); (9, 88)|]
# Array.fold_left (+) 0 my_array;;
- : int = 506
# Array.fold_right (+) my_array 0;;
- : int = 506
```

Arrays also can be sorted. The result of sorting an array is that the array is modified in place. The comparison function passed to the array sort must follow the same conventions as all comparison functions.

```
val sort : ('a -> 'a -> int) -> 'a array -> unit
```

```
# Array.sort compare my_array;;
- : unit = ()
# my_array;;
- : int array = [|0; 4; 16; 32; 60; 62; 76; 78; 88; 90|]
```

Arrays have access semantics that enable you to bypass the bounds checking. These unsafe actions always succeed, but they might not do what you want. This is one of the (very) few areas in which you can create an unsafe Caml program. It's still much safer than its C or C++ analog, but the results can be unknown. For this reason, the unsafe actions probably shouldn't be used unless you understand all the ramifications.

The actions are there for a purely practical reason: they are faster because they do not have go through the checking that is normally done. They can return wrong results, however, such as those shown in the following example (there is no element 10; arrays are indexed from zero).

```
external unsafe_get : 'a array -> int -> 'a = "%array_unsafe_get"
external unsafe_set : 'a array -> int -> 'a -> unit = "%array_unsafe_set"
```

```
# Array.unsafe_get my_array 10;;
- : int = 1536
# Array.unsafe_get my_array 9;;
- : int = 90
```

```
# Array.unsafe_set my_array 10 20;;
- : unit = ()
# my_array;;
- : int array = [|0; 4; 16; 32; 60; 62; 76; 78; 88; 90|]
```

There are no matrix functions outside of the capability to create them. You have to write your own matrix-manipulation routine or find it on the Internet.

```
  val make_matrix : int -> int -> 'a -> 'a array array
 val create_matrix : int -> int -> 'a -> 'a array array
# let my_matrix = Array.make_matrix 3 5 10;;
val my_matrix : int array array =
  [|[|10; 10; 10; 10; 10|]; [|10; 10; 10; 10; 10|]; [|10; 10; 10; 10; 10|]|]
# my_matrix.(2).(4) <- 999;;
- : unit = ()
# my_matrix;;
- : int array array =
[|[|10; 10; 10; 10; 10|]; [|10; 10; 10; 10; 10|]; [|10; 10; 10; 10; 999|]|]
#
```

Hashtables

A hashtable is basically just a key/value mapping container. You have used hashtables in previous examples (but not all the available functions). Hashtables must be created before they can be used via the create function, which takes an argument that indicates how many slots the table will be created with. Hashtables grow if you put more elements in them, but starting out with a reasonable size helps performance by giving hints to the allocator. You should weigh memory usage with performance and not specify more slots than you will ever need just to be safe.

```
  val create : int -> ('a, 'b) Hashtbl.t
```

```
# let myhash = Hashtbl.create 100;;
val myhash : ('_a, '_b) Hashtbl.t = <abstr>
```

After being created, data can be added to a hashtable by using the add function. The type information must match; otherwise, an error occurs. Many values can be used with one key.

```
  val add : ('a, 'b) Hashtbl.t -> 'a -> 'b -> unit
```

```
# Hashtbl.add myhash "ten" "ten value";;
- : unit = ()
# Hashtbl.add myhash "ten" "ten(1) value";;
- : unit = ()
# Hashtbl.add myhash "ten" "ten(2) value";;
- : unit = ()
# Hashtbl.add myhash "twenty" "twenty value";;
- : unit = ()
```

```
# Hashtbl.add myhash "thirty" "thirty value";;
- : unit = ()
# Hashtbl.add myhash 40 "forty value";;
Characters 19-21:
  Hashtbl.add myhash 40 "forty value";;
                     ^^
```

This expression has type int but is here used with type string

Although many values can be associated with one key, only the last value is returned by the find function. The find_all function returns all values associated with a given key. This information is returned in a list. The find function raises a Not_found exception if the key does not exist, but the find_all function simply returns an empty list.

```
val find : ('a, 'b) Hashtbl.t -> 'a -> 'b
val find_all : ('a, 'b) Hashtbl.t -> 'a -> 'b list
```

```
# Hashtbl.find myhash "ten";;
- : string = "ten(2) value"
# Hashtbl.find_all myhash "ten";;
- : string list = ["ten(2) value"; "ten(1) value"; "ten value"]
```

You can test for membership (that is, whether the given key exists in the hashtable) by using the mem function. It returns true if the key is present and false if not. Keys and values can be removed by using the remove function. If there is more than one value for a given key, only the first key/value pair is removed with the remove function. The replace function replaces only the first key/value pair. If the key does not exist in the hashtable, the effect of the replace function is the same as the add function. The length function returns the number of key/value pairs and is the total number.

```
val mem : ('a, 'b) Hashtbl.t -> 'a -> bool
val remove : ('a, 'b) Hashtbl.t -> 'a -> unit
val length : ('a, 'b) Hashtbl.t -> int
val replace : ('a, 'b) Hashtbl.t -> 'a -> 'b -> unit
```

```
# Hashtbl.mem myhash "not there";;
- : bool = false
# Hashtbl.mem myhash "ten";;
- : bool = true
# Hashtbl.remove myhash "not there";;
- : unit = ()
# Hashtbl.length myhash;;
- : int = 5
# Hashtbl.remove myhash "ten";;
- : unit = ()
# Hashtbl.length myhash;;
- : int = 4
```

```
# Hashtbl.find myhash "ten";;
- : string = "ten(1) value"
# Hashtbl.length myhash;;
- : int = 4
# Hashtbl.add myhash "ten" "ten(1) value";;
- : unit = ()
# Hashtbl.length myhash;;
- : int = 5

# Hashtbl.replace myhash "ten" "this is a new ten value";;
- : unit = ()
# Hashtbl.find myhash "ten";;
- : string = "this is a new ten value"
# Hashtbl.find_all myhash "ten";;
- : string list = ["this is a new ten value"; "ten(1) value"; "ten value"]
# Hashtbl.replace myhash "ten" "eulav net wen a si siht";;
- : unit = ()
# Hashtbl.find_all myhash "ten";;
- : string list = ["eulav net wen a si siht"; "ten(1) value"; "ten value"]
```

The iter function calls the given function on all keys and values in the hashtable. Although all keys and values will be visited, they are not in any order. There is only one fold function because the collection is unordered (the example returns all the keys in the hashtable).

```
val iter : ('a -> 'b -> unit) -> ('a, 'b) Hashtbl.t -> unit
val fold : ('a -> 'b -> 'c -> 'c) -> ('a, 'b) Hashtbl.t -> 'c -> 'c
```

```
# Hashtbl.iter (fun x y -> Printf.printf "%s %s\n" x y) myhash;;
ten eulav net wen a si siht
ten ten(1) value
ten ten value
thirty thirty value
twenty twenty value
- : unit = ()
# Hashtbl.fold (fun x y z -> x :: z) myhash [];;
- : string list = ["twenty"; "thirty"; "ten"; "ten"; "ten"]
# Hashtbl.fold (fun x y z -> y :: z) myhash [];;
- : string list =
["twenty value"; "thirty value"; "ten value"; "ten(1) value";
 "eulav net wen a si siht"]
```

Finally, the hashtable can be cleared, which deletes all keys and values.

```
val clear : ('a, 'b) Hashtbl.t -> unit
```

```
# Hashtbl.clear myhash;;
- : unit = ()
# Hashtbl.length myhash;;
- : int = 0
# myhash;;
- : (string, string) Hashtbl.t = <abstr>
#
```

Any hashable type can be used as a key in a hashtable, and lookups on those keys are very fast. Hashtables are not unique, however, and multiple values for a given key can be stored in a hashtable. If you want a unique key/value pair container, you must use a set or a map. Hashtables are not purely functional in OCaml. Hashtables are unordered (this cannot be said too many times).

Queue

Queues implement a First In/First Out (FIFO) stack for OCaml and can hold any type. Queues are also modifiable in place. Like hashtables, they must be created before they can be used. Unlike hashtables, however, no size specification needs to be made. The Queue module raises an exception if you try to access elements when it is empty.

Queues are not purely functional. This was done for practical reasons, even though purely functional Queue implementations do exist. They are not, however, included in the OCaml standard library.

```
exception Empty
val create : unit -> 'a Queue.t
# let myqueue = Queue.create ();;
val myqueue : '_a Queue.t = <abstr>
```

After creating a new queue, data can be added (add or push) or removed (pop), or you can view the top element on the queue without modifying the queue.

```
val add : 'a -> 'a Queue.t -> unit
val push : 'a -> 'a Queue.t -> unit
val pop : 'a Queue.t -> 'a
val top : 'a Queue.t -> 'a
# Queue.push 10 myqueue;;
- : unit = ()
# Queue.push 20 myqueue;;
- : unit = ()
# Queue.push 30 myqueue;;
- : unit = ()
# Queue.push 40 myqueue;;
- : unit = ()
```

```
# Queue.top myqueue;;
- : int = 10
# Queue.pop myqueue;;
- : int = 10
# Queue.top myqueue;;
- : int = 20
```

Now that you have some sample data in the queue, you can check to see whether it is empty. You also can find the length of the queue, which returns the number of elements in the queue. Queues are not indexed at zero, which means the length function returns the actual number of elements in the queue.

```
val is_empty : 'a Queue.t -> bool
val length : 'a Queue.t -> int
```

```
# Queue.is_empty myqueue;;
- : bool = false
# Queue.length myqueue;;
- : int = 3
```

Queues can be iterated over, folded, and transferred. Iteration and folding do not modify the queue, but transferring does. transfer actually transfers all of the elements from one queue into another.

```
val iter : ('a -> unit) -> 'a Queue.t -> unit
val fold : ('a -> 'b -> 'a) -> 'a -> 'b Queue.t -> 'a
val transfer : 'a Queue.t -> 'a Queue.t -> unit
```

```
# Queue.iter (fun x -> print_int x) myqueue;;
203040- : unit = ()
# Queue.fold (fun x y -> x + y) 0 myqueue;;
- : int =90
# Queue.is_empty myqueue;;
- : bool = false
# Queue.length myqueue;;
- : int = 3
# let newqueue = Queue.create ();;
Val newqueue : '_a Queue.t = <abstr>
# Queue.transfer myqueue newqueue;;
- : unit = ()
# Queue.length myqueue;;
- : int = 0
# Queue.length newqueue;;
- : int = 4
```

The last two queue operations are clearing and copying. Clearing a queue removes all the elements and leaves the queue empty. Copying a queue does not modify the source queue; it creates a new queue with all the elements from the source queue. This is needed because assigning a new name to a queue does not copy it (OCaml passes it by reference).

```
val copy : 'a Queue.t -> 'a Queue.t
val clear : 'a Queue.t -> unit

# let newqueue = Queue.copy myqueue;;
val newqueue : int Queue.t = <abstr>
# Queue.clear myqueue;;
- : unit = ()
# Queue.is_empty myqueue;;
- : bool = true
# Queue.length myqueue;;
- : int = 0
#
```

Stack

Stacks are Last In/First Out (LIFO) stacks for OCaml and are probably the simplest collection in the OCaml standard library. Stacks are much like queues—they are modifiable and are not purely functional. If you look at the queue and stack signatures, you will notice significant overlap. Stacks must be created before they can be used, and they throw an exception if you attempt to operate on them while they are empty. Unlike queues, stacks cannot be folded, mapped, or transferred.

```
exception Empty
  val create : unit -> 'a Stack.t

# let mystack = Stack.create ();;
val mystack : '_a Stack.t = <abstr>
```

Values on the stack are added (push) or removed (pop), or you can view the top of the stack without changing it (via top).

```
  val push : 'a -> 'a Stack.t -> unit
  val pop : 'a Stack.t -> 'a
  val top : 'a Stack.t -> 'a
```

```
# Stack.push 10 mystack;;
- : unit = ()
# Stack.push 20 mystack;;
- : unit = ()
# Stack.push 30 mystack;;
- : unit = ()
# Stack.push 40 mystack;;
- : unit = ()
# Stack.top mystack;;
- : int = 40
# Stack.pop mystack;;
- : int = 40
# Stack.top mystack;;
- : int = 30
```

You can see whether the stack is empty instead of relying on catching the exception. You also can clear it (so you know the stack is empty) or check its length. The length returns the total number of elements and is not indexed at 0 like arrays or lists. Stacks also can be copied. A copied stack is not altered by the copy operation.

```
 val is_empty : 'a Stack.t -> bool
 val clear : 'a Stack.t -> unit
 val length : 'a Stack.t -> int
  val iter : ('a -> unit) -> 'a Stack.t -> unit
val copy: 'a Stack.t -> 'a Stack.t = <fun>
```

```
# Stack.is_empty mystack;;
- : bool = false
# Stack.length mystack;;
- : int = 3
# Stack.iter (fun x -> print_int x) mystack;;
302010- : unit = ()
# Stack.clear mystack;;
- : unit = ()
# Stack.is_empty mystack;;
- : bool = true
# Stack.length mystack;;
- : int = 0
# let newstack = Stack.copy mystack;;
val newstack : int Stack.t = <abstr>
# Stack.length mystack;;
- : int = 4
# Stack.length newstack;;
- : int = 4
#
```

Set

A set is an ordered collection. It is also a functor collection, so you must pass a module to the set as an argument when you create a new module based on the set. Sets are implemented by using balanced binary trees, so they are quite fast. They are also purely functional data structures.

This sounds complicated—and it is. However, just because it is complicated doesn't mean it stays complicated after you understand it. Functors are important because they are higher-order modules. Like higher-order functions, higher-order modules enable you to do computation that would be very difficult without them.

```
# module MySet = Set.Make(String);;
module MySet :
  sig
    type elt = String.t
    type t = Set.Make(String).t
    val empty : t
    val is_empty : t -> bool
    val mem : elt -> t -> bool
    val add : elt -> t -> t
    val singleton : elt -> t
    val remove : elt -> t -> t
    val union : t -> t -> t
    val inter : t -> t -> t
    val diff : t -> t -> t
    val compare : t -> t -> int
    val equal : t -> t -> bool
    val subset : t -> t -> bool
    val iter : (elt -> unit) -> t -> unit
    val fold : (elt -> 'a -> 'a) -> t -> 'a -> 'a
    val for_all : (elt -> bool) -> t -> bool
    val exists : (elt -> bool) -> t -> bool
    val filter : (elt -> bool) -> t -> t
    val partition : (elt -> bool) -> t -> t * t
    val cardinal : t -> int
    val elements : t -> elt list
    val min_elt : t -> elt
    val max_elt : t -> elt
    val choose : t -> elt
    val split : elt -> t -> t * bool * t
  end
```

The signature gives all the operations and types available in the new functorized module. These operations include many of the standard mathematical operations on sets. Because you have created a set based on the String module, you now have a set of strings.

Now you can create new sets of strings. An empty set is provided for you to make creating new sets easier.

```
# let littleset = MySet.add "hello" MySet.empty;;
val littleset : MySet.t = <abstr>
```

New sets can be created by adding new elements to an empty set. You also can assign a value to the presupplied empty set. Keep in mind that you cannot change a set; the functions return a new set with the data you have added or removed.

```
# let littleset = MySet.add "world" littleset;;
val littleset : MySet.t = <abstr>
# MySet.elements littleset;;
- : MySet.elt list = ["hello"; "world"]
```

After you add a few elements to the set, you can look at the elements. The following listing returns a list of the elements that can be manipulated as any list can. Now, if you create another set, you can find unions, intersects, and differences.

```
# let newset = MySet.add "world" MySet.empty;;
val newset : MySet.t = <abstr>
# MySet.union newset littleset;;
- : MySet.t = <abstr>
# let unionof = MySet.union littleset newset;;
val unionof : MySet.t = <abstr>
# MySet.elements unionof;;
- : MySet.elt list = ["hello"; "world"]
# let diffof = MySet.diff littleset newset;;
val diffof : MySet.t = <abstr>
# MySet.elements diffof;;
- : MySet.elt list = ["hello"]
# let intersect = MySet.inter littleset newset;;
val interse : MySet.t = <abstr>
# MySet.elements intersect;;
- : MySet.elt list = ["world"]
```

You also can check for membership in a set, which returns a bool.

```
# MySet.mem "hello" littleset;;
- : bool = true
# MySet.mem "not there" littleset;;
- : bool = false
```

The length of a set is given by the cardinal function.

```
# MySet.cardinal littleset;;
- : int = 2
```

You also can test to see whether one set is a subset of another.

```
# MySet.subset littleset newset;;
- : bool = false
# MySet.subset newset littleset;;
- : bool = true
#
```

There are more functions available, but this gives you the idea. The functoral interface to sets enables sets to operate on any type. If you are familiar with generics from languages such as C++ and C#, you might notice that functors share some of the same concepts. Functors are not generics, but they do solve some of the same problems (for example, allowing collections to contain various types).

Map

A map is essentially a mapping between an element of one type to another element. Maps are also ordered, which is one of the things that distinguishes them from hashtables.

Maps are much less complicated than sets and have fewer operations. Maps are not as fast as hashtables, but they offer a purely functional data structure that can be operated on without side effects. Maps also allow for finer control over how the internals are ordered because you must pass a function that defines the internal ordering. Keep in mind that the word "map" is used by many modules and functions. In fact, there is a map function in the Map module.

```
# module MyMap = Map.Make(String);;
module MyMap :
  sig
    type key = String.t
    type 'a t = 'a Map.Make(String).t
    val empty : 'a t
    val is_empty : 'a t -> bool
    val add : key -> 'a -> 'a t -> 'a t
    val find : key -> 'a t -> 'a
    val remove : key -> 'a t -> 'a t
    val mem : key -> 'a t -> bool
    val iter : (key -> 'a -> unit) -> 'a t -> unit
    val map : ('a -> 'b) -> 'a t -> 'b t
    val mapi : (key -> 'a -> 'b) -> 'a t -> 'b t
    val fold : (key -> 'a -> 'b -> 'b) -> 'a t -> 'b -> 'b
    val compare : ('a -> 'a -> int) -> 'a t -> 'a t -> int
    val equal : ('a -> 'a -> bool) -> 'a t -> 'a t -> bool
  end
#
```

Unlike hashtables, maps can contain only one mapping for a given key. Maps are implemented using balanced binary trees (like sets) and are purely functional data structures.

Maps are created by adding keys and values to a map, or by adding a key and value to an empty map, which is similar to sets.

```
# let littlemap = MyMap.add "hello" 10 MyMap.empty;;
val littlemap : int MyMap.t = <abstr>
# let littlemap = MyMap.add "world" 20 littlemap;;
val littlemap : int MyMap.t = <abstr>
```

Maps can be map'd and mapi'd.

```
# MyMap.map (fun x -> Printf.printf "%i\n" x) littlemap;;
20
10
- : unit MyMap.t = <abstr>
# MyMap.mapi (fun x y -> Printf.printf "%s %i\n" x y) littlemap;;
world 20
hello 10
- : unit MyMap.t = <abstr>
```

Maps also can be fold'd. Maps and lists share some functionality. In fact, you can do assoc lists natively, although they are not as fast, nor can they be forced to be unique.

```
# MyMap.fold (fun x y z -> y + z) littlemap 0;;
- : int = 30
#
```

Although maps are quite useful, they are more complicated to use because of their functoral interface. You used the String module to create these maps, but what if you want to use integers? Because there is no Int module, you would have to create one. You would also have to create the type signature for the module, which you can do with an anonymous module.

```
# module MyIntMap = Map.Make(struct type t = int let compare = compare end);;
module MyIntMap :
  sig
    type key = Int.t
    type 'a t = 'a Map.Make(Int).t
    val empty : 'a t
    val is_empty : 'a t -> bool
    val add : key -> 'a -> 'a t -> 'a t
    val find : key -> 'a t -> 'a
    val remove : key -> 'a t -> 'a t
    val mem : key -> 'a t -> bool
    val iter : (key -> 'a -> unit) -> 'a t -> unit
    val map : ('a -> 'b) -> 'a t -> 'b t
    val mapi : (key -> 'a -> 'b) -> 'a t -> 'b t
    val fold : (key -> 'a -> 'b -> 'b) -> 'a t -> 'b -> 'b
    val compare : ('a -> 'a -> int) -> 'a t -> 'a t -> int
    val equal : ('a -> 'a -> bool) -> 'a t -> 'a t -> bool
  end
#
```

Anonymous modules are discussed further in Chapter 13. For now, try it out to see how it works.

Not Quite Collections

There are also things that are very much like collections in that they are often used to hold data. However, they are not (strictly speaking) collections.

Strings and buffers are often used to store data in OCaml programs. Strings are also useful for storing marshaled data structures for network communications and persistence.

Later chapters go into more detail on strings, but for now you should remember that OCaml is a practical language—if you can use a given module in a way that solves a problem for you, go for it.

Labeled Variants

There are labeled variants of many of the containers, which are often used for porting efforts and internal items. They probably should not be used (the documentation agrees with this assessment).

The comments about these variants are included here for completeness. In OCaml (unlike some other languages), if a feature is labeled Do Not Use, it is probably best to not use it. The language developers are not in the habit of marking useful things out of bounds without good reason. They might not always put that good reason in the documentation, but these warnings should be heeded. Trust me.

Functors

Several of the collections that you have looked at here are functorial. Functors are higher-order modules that provide very powerful ways of attacking certain problems. Functors do not have an analog in other programming styles such as structured or object-oriented programming.

Functors are not covered in depth here for a couple of reasons. First, functors are covered later in Chapter 13. Second, functors are very closely related to the way the module system in OCaml works. Without modules, there can be no functors in OCaml. The reverse is also true. So if you do not feel that you understand functors yet, don't worry—you probably don't.

Finally, functors are moderately difficult to understand. It is unfortunate that you had to be exposed to them so soon.

Conclusion

You should now have a good understanding of the collections available in the OCaml standard library and how they can be used. These collections are very powerful and give you the building blocks to create your own if you want. They also give you well-implemented solutions to often difficult problems.

The next chapter looks at input/output (I/O) and how to get data into and out of programs. You will also look at some of the issues that functional programming has with regard to I/O operations.

■■■

## CHAPTER 9

Files and File I/O

Although pure algorithmic programming can certainly be fun, any programming language would not be very practical without the capability to store and retrieve data from a persistent source. OCaml is a practical language that provides sophisticated methods for storing, retrieving, sending, and receiving data from outside itself.

The most common input/output (I/O) operations are on files. A Unix-dominated history gives an added benefit because sockets and network I/O are also files and are largely indistinguishable from normal disk files in OCaml. With a little care, nearly all your applications can be made network-aware without difficulty.

This chapter will cover both normal file I/O and network I/O. You will also learn about some of the differences between performing I/O in a functional environment and imperative programming.

Channels

Most I/O operations in OCaml are performed by using what OCaml calls *channels*—buffered I/O objects that are either input channels or output channels. Unbuffered I/O does exist, but it is not recommended (although it is covered later on).

The Pervasives module includes many of the primitives for reading from and writing to a given channel. It is the one module that is always open.

Pervasives Module

In previous chapters, you have seen how to use Scanf and Printf to do I/O. There are also built-in functions for performing operations on channels. This table lists a few of them, showing their input/output corresponding functions and a brief description. You'll use all these functions in examples.

Table 9-1. *I/O Functions*

in_channel Function	out_channel Function	Description
open_in	open_out	Opens a channel
open_in_binary	open_out_binary	Opens a channel in binary mode
open_in_gen	open_out_gen	Opens a channel and specifies all the modes
input_char	output_char	Operates on a char
input_line	output_string	Inputs a line or outputs a string
input	output	Operates on a string buffer; partial reads/writes are allowed
really_input	really_output	Operates on a string buffer; partial reads/writes are not allowed
pos_in	pos_out	Determines what position (in characters) the channel is at right now
seek_in	seek_out	Seeks to a given location in the channel
in_channel_length	out_channel_length	Returns the length of the channel (in chars)
close_in	close_out	Closes the channel

Although these functions work with any channel, their output might not make sense with every channel. This is especially true of the position functions. A device that cannot report a location or size cannot report it sensibly, even if the function returns. It is up to you to know whether the channel you're operating on makes sense for these functions.

Using Input Channels

There are three functions for opening input channels from files, which are really just one function with arguments already set. Channels are buffered in OCaml.

Using your favorite text editor, you should create a file containing some text. Remember to note the path to this file; you'll be using it for the following examples. The file will be called c:\temp\testfile and will contain the following:

```
hello
there
world
```

First, you create a function that prints out the contents of a file.

```
let catfile filename =
  let rec print_all_lines in_chan =
    output_string stdout ((input_line in_chan) ^ "\n");
    print_all_lines in_chan
  in
  let in_file = open_in filename in
  try
    print_all_lines in_file
  with End_of_file -> close_in in_file;;
```

This function works, but it is pretty simple. You can write a function that prints out a random part of any given file (you close the file before the function exits).

```
let random_catfile filename =
  let in_file = open_in filename in
  let length = (Unix.stat filename).Unix.st_size in
  let starting_point = Random.int length in
  let segment = Random.int (length - starting_point) in
  let str_buf = String.create segment in
  let actually_input =
    seek_in in_file starting_point;
    input in_file str_buf 0 segment in
  close_in in_file;
  output_string stdout str_buf;;
```

Using Output Channels

Like their input counterparts, there are three functions for creating output channels, which are also really just one function. These channels are buffered. One thing to remember about channels in OCaml is that they must be closed. Even if open files will be garbage collected, the garbage collector does not close files when it collects the channel. In many languages (such as Python), a file is closed when it is garbage collected. OCaml does not do this because the action of closing a file might not succeed. Instead of ignoring this failure, OCaml needs to have open files closed explicitly. When a file is closed, the buffers are flushed to disk, so you don't need to explicitly flush buffers to disk (unless you want to). Although explicit flushing of output channels is often of little benefit, it can be useful for log files or other file actions that you want to ensure get written to disk (there will be a performance penalty paid for this, however).

```
# let file = open_out "testfile.2";;
val file : out_channel = <abstr>
# pos_out file;;
- : int = 0
```

If you open a file without arguments, a file is created if it does not exist and is truncated if the file does exist. You can then put data into the file.

```
# output_string file "hello\n";;
- : unit = ()
# output_string file "world\n";;
- : unit = ()
# close_out file;;
- : unit = ()
```

This file now contains the two lines you just put into it. But if you try it as follows, you find that the file is now empty:

```
# let file = open_out "testfile.2" in output_string file "hello\nworld\n";;
- : unit = ()
```

When a channel is garbage collected, it is not closed, and the buffers are not flushed. If you explicitly close the file, the buffers are flushed. The following example creates a file with the correct contents:

```
# let file = open_out "testfile.2" in output_string file "hello\nworld\n";close_
out file;;
- : unit = ()
```

The standard open command truncates, but you sometimes want to open a file and append to it. This is where the other open commands come into play:

```
# let append_file = open_out_gen [Open_append;Open_binary] 0o644 "testfile.2";;
val append_file : out_channel = <abstr>
```

This command takes a list of flags and a permission integer as well as a filename for opening. The permission integer is for the file permissions if the file needs to be created. The preceding example throws an exception if the file was not found. Table 9-2 shows the available flags for both input and output channels.

Table 9-2. *Open Flags*

Open Flag	Description
Open_rdonly	Opens as read-only
Open_wronly	Opens as write-only
Open_append	Opens for appending (seeks to the end of the file)
Open_creat	Creates the file if it does not exist
Open_trunc	Truncates the file
Open_excl	Raises an exception if the file does not exist
Open_binary	Opens in binary mode (does nothing if binary mode is not supported)
Open_text	Opens in text mode; can perform end-of-line conversions
Open_nonblock	Opens the file in nonblocking mode

You can also move around in channels by using the seeking functions.

```
# let seek_example x =
  let file = open_out x in
  Printf.fprintf file "hello world\n";
   seek_out file 6;
   Printf.fprintf file "INSERTED ";
   close_out file;;
val seek_example : string -> unit = <fun>
```

This function writes some text to a file, goes to a new position in the file, and writes some more:

```
# seek_example "testfile.3";;
- : unit = ()
# catfile "testfile.3";;
hello INSERTED - : unit = ()
#
```

Note that the new text is not inserted into the old text. You should be aware of this issue when doing random access on files.

Information About Files

You can access information about files (disk files, especially) in a few different ways. The most information is found in the stat function in the Unix module. Not all the information contained with the record is valid on all platforms, however. For example, the file owner is not valid on Windows. This function is also the only way in OCaml to get the file owner and permission information.

You often just want to know whether a given file exists. Sys.file_exists returns true if the file exists and false if it doesn't:

```
# Sys.file_exists "testfile";;
- : bool = true
# Sys.file_exists "not there";;
- : bool = false
```

The Unix module contains the stat function that can be used to get information about the size, creation time, modification time, and so on. The times are all given in epoch seconds—the number of seconds since January 1, 1970. (Not all fields of the stat struct are available on all operating systems.)

```
# Unix.stat "file_io.ml";;
- : Unix.stats =
{Unix.st_dev = 2; Unix.st_ino = 0; Unix.st_kind = Unix.S_REG;
 Unix.st_perm = 438; Unix.st_nlink = 1; Unix.st_uid = 0; Unix.st_gid = 0;
 Unix.st_rdev = 2; Unix.st_size = 6; Unix.st_atime = 1145659522.;
 Unix.st_mtime = 1145659522.; Unix.st_ctime = 1145659502.}
```

You must specify filenames correctly for your operating system. The following generates a warning, but still works (the correct escape is provided and the warning goes away):

```
# Unix.stat "C:\Program Files";;
Characters 13-15:
Warning X: illegal backslash escape in string.
  Unix.stat "C:\Program Files";;
              ^^
- : Unix.stats =
{Unix.st_dev = 2; Unix.st_ino = 0; Unix.st_kind = Unix.S_DIR;
 Unix.st_perm = 365; Unix.st_nlink = 1; Unix.st_uid = 0; Unix.st_gid = 0;
 Unix.st_rdev = 2; Unix.st_size = 0; Unix.st_atime = 1145657202.;
 Unix.st_mtime = 1144693438.; Unix.st_ctime = 1135710047.}
```

```
# Unix.stat "C:\\Program Files";;
- : Unix.stats =
{Unix.st_dev = 2; Unix.st_ino = 0; Unix.st_kind = Unix.S_DIR;
 Unix.st_perm = 365; Unix.st_nlink = 1; Unix.st_uid = 0; Unix.st_gid = 0;
 Unix.st_rdev = 2; Unix.st_size = 0; Unix.st_atime = 1145657202.;
 Unix.st_mtime = 1144693438.; Unix.st_ctime = 1135710047.}
#
```

There are no links under Windows. Okay, so Windows has shortcuts, but they are not links like symbolic and hard links under Unix. The functions that operate on links are not supported under Windows.

```
# Unix.symlink "testfile" "test";;
Exception: Invalid_argument "Unix.symlink not implemented".
```

If you find yourself on an operating system in which the functions are supported, you can create links and gather information about them.

Locking Files

File locking presents difficulties for OCaml programmers. It is possible to lock a file descriptor by using the Unix module, but this functionality is not implemented in Windows. So you must either implement your own file locking mechanism or use a database or network storage method to handle your data.

Filenames and Portable Paths

OCaml provides a module for handling portable filenames. This library is not as well-equipped as some languages, but it does enough to make it worthwhile, especially if you need to manipulate filenames in a portable manner.

The Filename module includes a function that enables you to concatenate strings together by using the valid directory separator for the OS that you currently use.

```
# Filename.concat "c:\\" "test"
- : string = "c:\\test"
# Filename.concat (Filename.concat "c:\\" "test") "testfile";;
- : string = "c:\\test\\testfile"
# Filename.basename "c:\\test";;
- : string = "test"
#
```

It also includes a basename function, which again uses the correct separator for the OS you are using. There is also a function to chop the extension from a given filename:

```
# Filename.chop_extension "test.exe";;
- : string = "test"
```

The Filename module includes two functions for dealing with temporary files, which are very useful because they create unique filenames for the OS you are using.

```
# Filename.temp_file "pre" "suff";;
- : string = "c:\\DOCUME~1\\josh\\LOCALS~1\\Temp\\pre895d5asuff"
# let temp = Filename.open_temp_file "pre" "suff";;
val temp : string * out_channel =
  ("c:\\DOCUME~1\\josh\\LOCALS~1\\Temp\\pre86037esuff", <abstr>)
#
```

The temp_file function creates a unique filename that has the prefix and suffix you supply, with the path to where temporary files should go on your OS. The open_temp_file is better because it opens the file for you. It is more secure because the temporary filename it uses is far less likely to be replaced during your operations. The function returns a pair: the first item is the filename, and the last item is an out_channel opened to that filename. This channel can be operated on like any out_channel. This function also takes an optional argument of open_flags, much like the open_out_gen function.

Reading Directories

There are two ways to read directories in OCaml. There is the hard way, which is to write a set of functions using the Unix module. Then there is the easy way, which is using the built-in function to do this. Take a look at an example of the hard way—you'll see which one is better:

```
let is_dir x =
  let dstat = Unix.stat x in
  if dstat.Unix.st_kind = Unix.S_DIR then
    true
  else
    false;;

let ls x =
  match is_dir x with
    false -> [x]
  | true ->
    let udir = Unix.opendir x in
    let rec buildlist d acc =
      try
              buildlist d (acc @ [(Unix.readdir d)])
      with End_of_file -> acc
    in
      buildlist udir [];;
```

The following is a function that uses the built-ins and returns an array of filenames in a given directory:

```
let ls x = Sys.readdir x;;
```

Large File Support

OCaml supports large files (64-bit file sizes). Normally, the maximum file size is a file of size max_int that on most systems comes in at less than 2 GB. The Unix.LargeFile module supplies functions that can return size and position, and also can seek on these larger files. This module should not be used unless you really need to operate on files larger than the built-in maximum.

Sockets

Socket functions are contained with the Unix module. Parts of this module are implemented on Win32, so you will focus on those functions that are available on all platforms.

If you are familiar with socket programming in C, the OCaml functions will look very familiar. They are mostly direct translations of the Portable Operating System Interface (POSIX) functions into OCaml.

Low-level Functions

The following is an example of creating a socket. You can connect that socket to an address, send some data to it, and then receive some data from it. In this case, you have created a very crude http client and are downloading the first 255 characters of a web page.

```
# let address = Unix.ADDR_INET ((Unix.inet_addr_of_string "64.236.24.4"),80);;
val address : Unix.sockaddr = Unix.ADDR_INET (<abstr>, 80)
# let socket = Unix.socket Unix.PF_INET Unix.SOCK_STREAM 0;;
val socket : Unix.file_descr = <abstr>
# Unix.connect socket address;;
- : unit = ()
# let buffer = String.create 255;;
val buffer : string = ""
# let sendstr = "GET / HTTP/1.0\n\n" in Unix.send socket sendstr 0 ➥
        (String.length sendstr) [];;
- : int = 16
# let getstr = Unix.recv socket buffer 0 255 [];;
val getstr : int = 255
# lUnix.shutdown socket Unix.SHUTDOWN_ALL;;
-: unit = ()
# buffer;;
- : string =
"HTTP/1.1 200 OK\013\nDate: Thu, 25 Aug 2005 03:02:09 GMT\013\nServer:
Apache\013\nContent-Type:
 text/html\013\nLast-Modified:
Thu, 25 Aug 2005 03:02:02 GMT\013\nCache-Control: max-age=60,
 private\013\nVary: Accept-Encoding,User-Agent\013\nExpires:
Thu, 25 Aug 2005 03:03:02 GMT\013\nCont"
```

You would have to make multiple calls to recv until it returned 0, indicating that there is nothing more to receive. Although recv can block, you can set the socket to be nonblocking.

You also can use more standard channel functions if you create channels from file descriptors, which the Unix module enables you to do. Thus, you can avoid the problems of send and recv on sockets and deal with the connection just like any other channel in OCaml.

```
# let address = Unix.ADDR_INET ((Unix.inet_addr_of_string "64.236.24.4"),80);;
val address : Unix.sockaddr = Unix.ADDR_INET (<abstr>, 80)
# let socket = Unix.socket Unix.PF_INET Unix.SOCK_STREAM 0;;
val socket : Unix.file_descr = <abstr>
# Unix.connect socket address;;
- : unit = ()
# let inchan = Unix.in_channel_of_descr socket;;
val inchan : in_channel = <abstr>
# let outchan = Unix.out_channel_of_descr socket;;
val outchan : out_channel = <abstr>
# Printf.fprintf outchan "GET / HTTP/1.0\n\n";;
- : unit = ()
# flush outchan;;
- : unit = ()
# Scanf.fscanf inchan "%s %i %s" (fun x y z -> (x,y,z));;
- : string * int * string = ("HTTP/1.1", 200, "OK")
# close_in inchan;;
```

Where did that IP address come from? It happens to be an address from http://www.cnn.com. The Unix module also provides access to name services.

```
# let addr_string x = Unix.string_of_inet_addr
    (Array.get (Unix.gethostbyname x).Unix.h_addr_list 0);;
    val addr_string : string -> string = <fun>
# addr_string "www.cnn.com";;
- : string = "64.236.16.116"
```

This code takes the first entry in the returned array, which is probably not the best way to do it, especially if you want robust code (it doesn't hurt for this example, however). The host record type contains more information than just IP addresses, too; it also includes an array of aliases and the address type.

The PF_INET type is the only type supported under Windows. Unix supports the others, although they are not found as often as they once were.

Good clients should always shut down the socket when they finish. Although simply closing the channel created is good enough for most operations, you should probably still use the Unix.close_socket command. If you are using the low-level operators exclusively, you must shut down the socket, or else your application will leak file descriptors.

```
let shut_socket = Unix.shutdown socket Unix.SHUTDOWN_ALL;;
- : unit = ()
```

This shutdown ensures that you are no longer using that socket, and future operations will raise exceptions. All file descriptors, including sockets, must be closed even if they have been shut down.

High-level Functions

The high-level functions offer a much easier way to create client and server socket connections. The client socket functions are available on all platforms. Good clients should also remember to use the shutdown_connection function when closing down the connection. Sockets have the same issue with garbage collection and closing that normal files do. You must explicitly close sockets or you will leak file descriptors.

The creation of servers is also made much simpler by the high-level functions, although only if you are on a Unix or Unix-like system. The reason it is not implemented on Windows is because it creates a forking server. On Windows you should use threads instead of creating new processes.

So you must use some of the lower-level functions directly. The good news is that you have to write this code only once. (Later chapters cover the creation of servers in much more depth, as well as other network programming topics.)

Unix and Windows

Although most of the functions for I/O work transparently across all platforms that OCaml supports, some do not. The main differences exist between Windows platforms and Unix (and Unix-like) platforms.

One of the biggest things missing from Windows is the capability to run select on files other than sockets. Another issue is that you need to take the file type into consideration via the open_in_binary or open_in_text functions. If you are writing cross-platform code, you need to pay close attention to this issue.

Conclusion

In this chapter, you read from and wrote to files in various ways. You also implemented a very simple http client and demonstrated how easy it is to use network I/O. Armed with this knowledge and an understanding of how to do structured I/O, you have the necessary building blocks for doing all kinds of file I/O. You also learned how to create cross-platform temporary files and to manipulate paths in a cross-platform manner.

The next chapter covers exception handling, which enables you to write code that can handle problems in an effective manner. This facility can be very important because real-world code often runs into exceptional circumstances.

CHAPTER 10

■ ■ ■

Exception Handling

OCaml has exceptions, which are integrated into the language and are basic types. Exceptions cannot be polymorphic. Unlike some languages (such as Java), there is only one kind of exception, and there is no requirement to handle any exception. However, it's often a good idea. Also, exception handling in OCaml is quite fast.

This chapter also discusses OCaml asserts. Although asserts are not really exceptions, an assert violation is an exception by definition. Asserts, like exceptions, are designed to minimize the amount of explicit value testing required by any given function.

Using Exceptions

The basic handling of all exceptions in OCaml is the try … with block. It is important to remember that exceptions do not free your functions from returning the same type. If a function normally returns a string, it cannot return an integer (int) from an exception. The function can raise an exception, however, and you can continue to process things from there.

```
try
  raise Not_found
with Not_found -> Printf.printf "Hello!\n"
    Hello!
- : unit = ()
#
```

The preceding code doesn't really do anything, although it does illustrate how exceptions are raised and dealt with. You used exceptions in previous chapters and now you will understand them more clearly.

Exceptions use pattern matching, too (in fact, the with clause uses pattern matching). However, exceptions are designed for handling exceptional situations, which are situations that should not happen. For example, if you have a function that is designed to divide two numbers, you want to know whether the denominator is a zero. You can check that explicitly by using an if statement or some other control. In OCaml, however, you do not have to—you can wrap the calculation in a try … with block, knowing that an exception will be thrown. Dividing by zero is a pretty simple situation, and often what is or is not exceptional is left to the programmer's discretion.

Many handlers can be assigned using the with statement, although the handlers must return the same type as the function if they return anything. If a handler reraises another exception, it does not need to have any return type at all. The underscore wildcard that works with exceptions matches in the same way it works for pattern matches. In fact, the same mechanism is at work. If an exception is raised, and there is no matching handler for that exception, it behaves as if there were no try … with block.

```
try
  failwith "Bummer, dude!"
w ith Not_found -> Printf.printf "Hello!\n"
    Exception: Failure "Bummer, dude!".
#
```

Exceptions can have arguments, as in the preceding example. These arguments can be any valid OCaml type, although they cannot be polymorphic. These arguments can be accessed via the with pattern matching. Handlers can be any valid OCaml code. If the handlers return a value, it must be the same return type as the function.

```
try
  failwith "Bummer, dude!"
with Failure x -> Printf.printf "%s\n" x
    Bummer, dude!
- : unit = ()
#
```

The pattern matching also can use the wildcard _ to match any exception.

```
try
  raise Not_found
with Failure x -> Printf.printf "%s\n" x
  | _ -> Printf.printf "Found something, don't know...\n"
      Found something, don't know...
- : unit = ()
#
```

Although using the wildcard is almost always a bad idea, there are times when you want to catch any exception that is thrown and emit a message about it (in multithreaded code, for example). An uncaught exception will kill the thread that raised it in OCaml. You must decide whether it is better to kill the program or keep going when a thread catches an exception, and it is almost never a good idea to let a thread silently fail. You can catch and report these exceptions by wrapping each thread in a try .. with block. When it's caught, you can use the Printexc function to report this error and perform some other action. For example, you can do this:

```
# Thread.create (fun () -> try
        Thread.delay 3.;failwith "Help!"
        with ex -> print_string (Printexc.to_string ex)) ();;
- : Thread.t = <abstr>
#
Failure("Help!")
```

You can use the built-in exceptions in your own programs. In fact, unless you need to create a new exception, I recommend using the built-in exceptions. Doing so provides two benefits. First, people who are using your functions already understand the call semantics of the exceptions. And for those who maintain your code, using built-in exceptions reduces the burden of maintenance programming.

Note You should always be thinking about the maintenance programmer—especially if the maintenance programmer might just be you.

Because exceptions are basic types, you can do things with them you might not expect. For example, you can create a set of exceptions.

```
# module Setofexceptions = Set.Make(struct type t = exn let compare =
                                                    Pervasives.compare end);;
  module Setofexceptions :
  sig
  end
# let soe = Setofexceptions.add Not_found Setofexceptions.empty;;
val soe : Setofexceptions.t = <abstr>
# let soe = Setofexceptions.add (Failure "Bummer, dude!") soe;;
val soe : Setofexceptions.t = <abstr>
# Setofexceptions.elements soe;;
- : Setofexceptions.elt list = [Not_found; Failure "Bummer, dude!"]
# Setofexceptions.iter (fun x -> match x with
                                  Not_found -> Printf.printf "Not Found, eh?\n"
                                | Failure m -> Printf.printf "Failed: %s\n" m
                                    | _ -> raise x) soe;;
      Not Found, eh?
Failed: Bummer, dude!
- : unit = ()
#
```

This example shows the creation of a new set type using exceptions and then shows the additions and iteration on that set. Because exceptions are basic types, you can use them as parameters with any function or module.

Would you do this in real life? There are many situations in which you might want to pass exceptions as parameters to functions. Most often, however, this is a really bad idea. Later in this chapter, you'll see one example in which error functions are used for logging and debugging.

Understanding Built-in Exceptions

OCaml comes with built-in exceptions that are designed to handle a variety of runtime conditions and situations. You can use these built-in exceptions in your own code if you choose, and many library writers use these exceptions instead of creating their own for all cases.

```
exception Match_failure of (string * int * int)
```

This exception is raised when a function does not have any pattern-matching rules that apply. A function that has obvious gaps in its pattern matching often generates a warning from the compiler, so you will seldom see it.

You might run into this exception when using many guarded functions. This exception is probably not common enough to merit general catching, although you might want to catch it in your own code when you know a pattern-match failure might occur. The arguments are the location of the match keyword, which is the filename, line number, and column number.

```
exception Assert_failure of (string * int * int)
```

This exception is raised when an assert statement fails. The arguments are the location of the assert keyword, which is the filename, line number, and column number.

```
exception Invalid_argument of string
```

This exception is raised by many libraries. The argument is a string that often includes more detail about the specifics of the failure. This exception is often used by library writers.

```
exception Failure of string
```

This exception is also often used in libraries. It is a general exception, and the string argument often includes more detail about the specifics of the failure.

```
exception Not_found
```

This exception is raised by many libraries and searching functions when the search criteria are not found.

```
exception Out_of_memory
```

This exception is raised by the garbage collector and is not catchable. It indicates that the garbage collector could not allocate memory. This exception is quite rare, and generally you would not try to catch this exception in common code.

```
exception Stack_overflow
```

This exception is raised by the byte-code interpreter and is not fully implemented by the native code compiler. This exception is most often raised by too-deep recursion. This exception is often the result of programmer error and wrongly implemented functions instead of a more typical runtime error.

```
exception Sys_error of string
```

This exception is raised by functions doing system-level actions. The string argument often contains further information and sometimes operating system (OS) error messages.

```
exception End_of_file
```

This exception is raised by functions doing input/output (I/O) when they have reached the end of a file or the end of input. This exception is commonly caught when doing I/O operations.

```
exception Division_by_zero
```

This exception is raised when you are trying to divide integers and integer-like numbers by zero or something zero-like. Floating-point numbers (floats) are divisible by zero because it yields infinity. Integers are not divisible by zero.

```
exception Sys_blocked_io
```

This is a special case of the Sys_error exception. It is raised only when operations are attempted on blocking I/O when the channel is blocked. This exception should be caught if you are using blocking I/O. If you are using blocking I/O, you probably already know this.

```
exception Undefined_recursive_module of (string * int * int)
```

This exception is raised when a recursive module definition is undefined. The arguments are the location of the module definition and include the filename, line number, and column number.

Recursive module definitions are an experimental feature in OCaml. This means that the definition might change in the future (if you are using this, you probably already know that, too).

Creating Custom Exceptions

You can create your own exceptions, and the definitions can include any type available— although they cannot be polymorphic. Exceptions can be defined as being of object types and even function types. You can even define an exception of exceptions and exception lists (although you should make sure you want to do this).

Exceptions are defined (simply enough) by using the exception keyword. To define an exception with no arguments, you can just do this:

```
# exception Myexception;;
exception Myexception
# raise Myexception;;
Exception: Myexception.
#
```

Once defined, this exception can be raised just like built-in exceptions. Exceptions raised must be defined as exceptions and cannot be of any other type. Some languages enable you to raise exceptions of any type (Python and C++ do this), but OCaml does not.

```
# raise Myexception;;
Exception: Myexception.
#
```

If you try to raise an undefined exception, it causes a compiler error.

```
# raise Notdefined;;
Characters 6-16:
  raise Notdefined;;
        ^^^^^^^^^^
Unbound constructor Notdefined
#
```

Exceptions can have arguments of any type. This argument then is passed to the exception when it is raised.

```
# exception Myexception of int;;
exception Myexception of int
# raise (Myexception 10);;
Exception: Myexception 10.
#
```

Exceptions can even have arguments that are functions and objects, although they cannot have module types.

```
# exception Myexception of int;;
exception Myexception of int
# exception Myexception of (int -> string);;
exception Myexception of (int -> string)
#
```

Even if you define the module type, you cannot define an exception of that type. Nor can you create an implementation of that module type and define an exception of that type.

```
# module type T =
sig
  val a: int
end;;
      module type T = sig val a : int end
# exception Myexception of T;;
Characters 26-28:
  exception Myexception of T;;
                          ^^
Syntax error
#
```

Here is the example of attempting to define an exception with a module implementation as the type:

```
# module Q:T =
struct
  let a = 10
end;;
      module Q : T
# exception Myexception of Q;;
Characters 26-28:
  exception Myexception of Q;;
                          ^^
Syntax error
#
```

Although there are a few restrictions on defining an exception, there are no restrictions on raising one. Exceptions can be raised anywhere code can be validly placed. You can't put them just anywhere, but you can put them anywhere valid code can go (they still cannot be polymorphic).

Why Exceptions Cannot Be Polymorphic

This is much more complicated than you might expect because the reason lies in type theory and the calling semantics of exceptions.

If it seems like a nonissue, you probably wonder why it is being covered so closely. It is covered because exceptions cannot be polymorphic, and the error messages the compiler generates are largely unhelpful.

```
# class ['a] pexampl(x:'a) =
object
  val d = x
  method get () = d
end;;
        class ['a] pexampl : 'a -> object val d : 'a method get : unit -> 'a end
# let d = new pexampl(10);;
val d : int pexampl = <obj>
#
```

Now that you have your polymorphic class, you can try to create an exception around it. You cannot do it, however, and the error message is not helpful.

```
# exception Pexp of pexampl;;
Characters 18-25:
  exception Pexp of pexampl;;
                    ^^^^^^^
The type constructor pexampl expects 1 argument(s),
but is here applied to 0 argument(s)
```

It is not helpful because even if you supply an argument, the syntax error remains. The error message also doesn't give you any indication of how to fix it.

```
# exception Pexp of (new pexampl(10));;
Characters 19-22:
  exception Pexp of (new pexampl(10));;
                     ^^^
Syntax error
#
```

Because you know that exceptions cannot be polymorphic, you can use a typed class—and it will work. This exception now works only with integer instances of that class.

```
# exception Pexp of int pexampl;;
exception Pexp of int pexampl
# raise (Pexp (new pexampl(10)));;
Exception: Pexp <obj>.
```

Now that you have defined it, the error message you see if you use the wrong class type is much more helpful.

```
# raise (Pexp (new pexampl("hello")));;
Characters 12-34:
  raise (Pexp (new pexampl("hello")));;
              ^^^^^^^^^^^^^^^^^^^^^^
```

This expression has type string pexampl, but is here used with type:

```
  int pexampl
Types for method get are incompatible
#
```

Example: Some Error Functions

Now that the basics are explained, you can delve into some more complicated examples and theory surrounding exception handling.

Can You Use an Object Instead?

In a word, yes. However, if you use a polymorphic class, you must specify a concrete class for the exception because exceptions cannot be polymorphic.

Thou Shalt and Other Rules for Coding

Okay, I lied. There really are not any "shalts" in the OCaml exception world. It should not be taken to mean that you should do whatever you want. There are best practices associated with exception handling, and many of them are as applicable to OCaml as they are to any other language.

One of the most important of these best practices is that exceptions should cover situations that are errors. You should examine each case in which you are raising an exception and make sure that the exception is being raised because something happened that is wrong. Exceptions should not be used as "final else's" in code.

You should also use exceptions when the error condition is the exception instead of writing checking code. Here is an example. Suppose that you have a hashtable; you want to return a value if it exists or return some default value if it doesn't. You could implement it with checking code like this:

```
# let find xval ht = if (Hashtbl.mem ht xval) then
  Hashtbl.find ht xval
else
  (Hashtbl.add ht xval 0;0);;
      val find : 'a -> ('a, int) Hashtbl.t -> int = <fun>
```

This code works, but the value should be found, so checking for it is wasteful. Instead of checking every time, you can replace the check with a try … with block, yielding a function more like this, which is more efficient:

```
# let betterfind xval ht = try
  Hashtbl.find ht xval
with Not_found -> Hashtbl.add ht xval 0;0;;
    val betterfind : 'a -> ('a, int) Hashtbl.t -> int = <fun>
#
```

This function also demonstrates that the exceptional case is the absence of the value.

Six Simple Rules

Although these rules are not industry standard practices, they are a set of prudent practices that will help keep you out of trouble and regret. They are also generally agreed upon, which is something of a rarity in the coding world.

Use Built-in Exceptions Whenever Appropriate

You don't always have to define your own exceptions. The built-in exceptions cover a lot of common error conditions, and programmers already understand them.

```
# let read_whole_file filename =
  let ichan = open_in filename in
  let ibuffer = Buffer.create 100 in
  try
    while true do
      let line = input_line ichan in
      Buffer.add_string ibuffer (line ^ "\n")
    done;""
  with End_of_file ->
    close_in ichan;Buffer.contents ibuffer;;
                val read_whole_file : string -> string = <fun>
# read_whole_file "examplefile";;
- : string = "hello\nworld\n"
#
```

The preceding example is a short one that shows the use of built-in exceptions. Most of the OCaml I/O files raise an End_of_file exception, so there is no need to define a new one.

Document Exception Use

This can't be stressed enough. The OCamldoc system includes keywords for documenting exceptions, so use them. Not only do people expect your exception use to be documented but you'll also be setting traps for people if you don't document them.

The ocamldoc-generated documentation, along with the code, is shown as follows for a simple function that raises an exception if a token is not found. In this case, the programmer knows that that token should always be there, so it is an exceptional condition if it is not there.

```
(** find an element and return it
    @returns 'a
    @raises Not_found *)
let find_in token lst = List.find token lst;;.
```

Use Exceptions for Exceptional Situations

This one is a little murky. Basically, you are writing the code so you know what is or is not an "exceptional" event or state in your code. Exceptions are for exceptions, not rules. In the previous example, not finding the token is exceptional, which is only something that you would know if you knew the application. This rule is pretty much decided on a case-by-case basis.

Don't Run Code Raising Exceptions in Handlers

You cannot always follow this rule, but most of the time you can. Exception handlers are basically case statements (as discussed), but that doesn't mean you should use them like case statements. Handlers should be trustable code, which means you should not put important code that might itself raise exceptions in those handlers.

This rule is about being careful with your control flow. You should always be thinking about how your handlers will affect control flow and future functionality. This is also something that can bite you very hard. Following is a very simple example that serves to illustrate that you must always scrutinize the code that executes in an exception handler:

```
# let write_log_message filename message = let oc = try
  open_out_gen [Open_append] 0644 filename
with Sys_error n -> open_out_gen [Open_append;Open_creat] 0644 filename
in
  output oc message 0 (String.length message);
  close_out oc;;
        val write_log_message : string -> string -> unit = <fun>
# write_log_message "/tmp/broken" "hello";;
Exception: Sys_error "/tmp/broken: No such file or directory".
#
```

This example shows one of the problems associated with performing actions that can raise exceptions from within exception handlers. This code seems somewhat innocuous; if the file can't be opened, try to open it again in the handler, overlooking problems other than a nonexistent file.

Never Silently Ignore Exceptions

Silently ignoring exceptions is just plain wrong. It also can wreak havoc later on—when your assumptions (or those who come after you) have changed and now that error you thought you could ignore is dangerous to ignore.

Remember the Maintenence Programmer and Your Users

Maybe remembering them isn't so simple, but it is important. How you use exceptions can make a big impact on how usable your code is to other programmers and how easy it is to maintain.

You might be thinking "Well, this code is only prototype that I'll just throw away." But that doesn't happen nearly as often as it should (the actual throwing away part). Often, so much effort is put into the prototype code that programmers are loath to simply start over and reimplement things that have already been implemented, even if the implementation has some flaws.

Just remember: one day I might have to maintain your code, so if you won't do it for yourself, please do it for my sake. After all, you've already gone through all the trouble of reading this book.

Using Asserts

The assert function in OCaml enables you to assert that something should be true. That something can be any valid OCaml code that evaluates to a Boolean value. Asserts are often used to enforce invariants and other assumptions within code. Asserts can often communicate assumptions about code in a very clean manner and make your code more readable than if you tried to validate the data every time.

Asserts also can be a speed improvement. This might sound like a contradiction, but often people write code to validate, checking it for compliance. You can do this by using asserts, which can allow you to test your code for compliance and then turn them off in production code. Assertion checking is on by default, but can be turned off by the compiler using the -noassert compiler option.

Unlike C, assert violations do not cause a program to terminate. The assert function raises an exception, Assert_failure, and enables you to deal with it as you see fit. However, OCaml asserts are runtime instead of compile time. There are many people who feel that asserts should be temporary and should always be turned off in production code. I think the jury is still out on that, and turning off asserts is often highly dependent on the application in question.

```
# let add_ten x = assert(x < 10);x + 1;;
val add_ten : int -> int = <fun>
# add_ten 20;;
Exception: Assert_failure ("", 39, -52).
# add_ten 9;;
- : int = 10
#
```

One important thing to remember is that the Assert_failure exception is rarely trapped, which makes an Assert_failure a de facto exit for the program. However, as mentioned earlier, you should weigh the harm of a program ABEND with the harm of a program running with bad data.

Asserts also can be used to perform the kind of checking that you would do in Design by Contract (DbC). DbC, which was developed by Bertrand Meyer, is implemented in the Eiffel and D programming languages. OCaml does not support DbC natively, although there have been people who have developed DbC modules for OCaml. Asserts can be used to express something similar to an invariant or a precondition because initialization functions are inherited in OCaml. Post conditions can be simulated using the Gc.finalise function; however, this procedure can be quite complicated and is beyond the scope of this book.

Unfortunately, there are no static (also called compile-time) asserts in OCaml. However, much of what you might use compile-time asserts for is taken care of already. You probably could implement this kind of functionality using Camlp4—this is left as an exercise for the reader.

Getting Line Numbers and Function Names

One bit of functionality that is sorely lacking in OCaml is the capability to easily find out what line and function or filename a given piece of code is in. This feat is easily accomplished in C using preprocessor directives such as __LINE__.

OCaml does not have a simple preprocessor like C (although it does have a preprocessor, which will be discussed in later chapters), nor does it have functions to return this information.

If you are on a Unix or Unix-like system, the following will probably work. First, create a file that contains the following and then pass it through the C pr-processor before compiling it.

```
#define Ep(x) Printf.printf "On line %i in file %s: %s\n" __LINE__ __FILE__; x
let _ = Ep("hello world!\n");;
```

If you redirect the output into a new file, it will look like this:

```
# 1 "sa.ml"
# 1 "<built-in>"
# 1 "<command line>"
# 1 "sa.ml"


let _ = Printf.printf "On line %i in file %s: %s\n" 3 "sa.ml" "hello world!\n";;
```

This file will compile just fine, however.

```
josh@sputnik ~
$ ocamlc -o sa.exe -pp cpp sa.ml

josh@sputnik ~
$ ./sa.exe
On line 3 in file sa.ml: hello world!
```

You should see the same results.

Conclusion

You now should be able to effectively use exception handling in OCaml. Exception handling in any programming language is very important, especially in code that is meant to be reliable. Exceptions and proper exception handling are both important for creating robust and reliable code.

You should also have an understanding of asserts in OCaml. Asserts can be very powerful and also can help make your code more understandable by clearly showing assumptions about the data. The compiler cannot check your data, though, and asserts are runtime checks.

■ ■ ■

## CHAPTER 11

Practical: A URI Library

OCaml provides a module for dealing with paths and filenames in an operating system (OS)–independent manner (this applies only to files, not to Uniform Resource Identifiers [URIs]). I have had to convert programs from using files to using other sources of input; during one of those conversions, I wondered how nice it would be if OCaml had functions that worked with URIs such as Java. There is a very comprehensive URI module included in the Netstring library. It is a third-party library that is part of the Ocamlnet package. Written by Gerd Stoplmann, this library can be found at http://www.ocaml-programming.de.

The module described here is not nearly as complete as those available from Java (or from Ocamlnet). However, it provides much of the same functionality as the existing OCaml filename module and offers a clean way to extend that functionality while maintaining a high degree of reuse and compatibility between implementations.

There are a couple of functions in the Filename module that you will explicitly not be implementing—the functions related to temporary files. The Filename module provides several functions for dealing with the creation and manipulation of temporary files. Because you are dealing with URIs, though, bolting on temporary files to that would be quite a job and would not really add much value to the module.

Looking at the URI Signature

Before getting into the implementation details, the module type will be discussed first so that you can see what will be implemented in a clear manner instead of figuring it out from the implementation. When the OCaml module system is discussed in later chapters, you will learn in detail about the relationship between modules and module types. For now, however, it will be glossed over a bit.

The following is the signature for the URI module. This code is what would be put into the .mli file for the module. You haven't defined the name of the module or anything like that because the module name is implicitly derived from the filenames. The .mli file must have the same name as the .ml file, and that filename will be the name of the module. This file would be called first_uri.mli.

```
exception Error of int
exception Unreg_protocol of string * int
type email = Email of string * string
type uri = File of string | Http of string * string | Mailto of email
type t = uri
val get_error: int -> string
val compare: t -> t -> int
val basename: t -> string
val is_relative: t -> bool
val concat: t -> string -> uri
val check_suffix: t -> string -> bool
val chop_suffix: t -> string -> t
val chop_extension: t -> t
val quote: t -> string
val string_of_uri: t -> string
val uri_of_string: string -> t
```

Exceptions

You define two exceptions for this module. The first one is a generic Error exception that takes an integer parameter. The parameter is an errno-like number that you will use later for reporting and information.

The next exception is for handling unregistered protocols. This exception takes two parameters: a string giving the protocol identifier and an int that is suitable for use with the Error exception defined previously.

Why use an error code? Using an error code like this enables you to expand the functionality in the future without fundamentally changing the API. Error codes are very useful for handling situations that are exceptional but not fatal (which is how they are used in this module).

Types

The first type you define is used to describe email addresses. This type, which is named email, is an enumerated type. Some of the URIs you will be handling contain email addresses. This type is pretty simple—it uses a string tuple to contain the username and the domain.

The next type defined is the uri type, which is also an enumerated type and includes all the protocols that the library can handle. Although it includes all the protocols the library can handle, the existence of a protocol in the type does not guarantee that all operations are applicable for it. In fact, there is no indication in the type as to which operations are valid on which uri. For example, a mailto URI cannot be relative, nor does it have a basename. Thanks to the type system, you can ensure that functions are called with the proper type and do not yield bad results.

Notice that there is a definition for a type t. It is a special type in modules that represents the type of the module itself. You do not need to define a type t in your modules, but it is common practice. Having a type t defined also makes it easy to use the module with the functors Set and Map because they require this type to be defined.

Functions

Now you get to the actual "doing stuff" part of the module. The first function you'll define is the error-handling/reporting function. This is a perror-like function taking an integer and returning a message string.

■Note *Perror* is a common error-handling function on Unix systems that enables simple handling of error codes and messages associated with error codes.

The comparator function is a function that provides an OCaml-compatible comparison integer. You can use the compare built-in function or write your own.

The basename function, which returns the basename of the path, should work only on URIs that have a basename. Mailtos, for example, really don't support the basename concept. The signature does not define what happens if you use a type that this operation doesn't support—that is the job of the implementer.

The is_relative function returns true if the path is relative. This function should work only on URIs in which this is relevant, with the same caveats as the basename function.

The concat function concatenates a URI and a string. For URIs in which this is meaningful, it provides the appropriate path separator.

The check suffix function checks to see whether the URI has a suffix matching the supplied string. Although it probably doesn't apply to all URIs, it can be helpful to match suffixes (for example, .html or .php) to pass the URI to a different handler. And although suffixes cannot be relied upon in all contexts, they can be very helpful. The File module also implements this function.

The chop_suffix function removes the suffix supplied from the URI. It returns the given filename without its extension. The extension is the part of the string between the last . after the last directory separator and the end of the string. For example, test/test.html has an extension of .html. The chop_suffix function returns a URI even if there is no modification to the URI. The chop_extension function is just an alias for the chop_suffix function.

The quote function returns a quoted string of the URI, which applies the quotes so that the returned string is a valid OCaml string. This can be important because not all paths and URIs are valid OCaml strings. The last two functions provide the capability to convert URIs to and from normal strings.

First Implementation

Now you can look at the first actual implementation of the code. The code in this section would be placed into a file called first_uri.ml.

```
exception Error of int
exception Unreg_protocol of string * int
```

This list of pairs is to match the error code with the message you want to display.

```
let errors = [
  (1,"This library cannot handle this protocol");
  (2,"This operation unsupported on this protocol");
  (3,"Can't chop this suffix");
  (4,"This is unimplemented")]
type email = Email of string * string
type uri = File of string
  | Http of string * string
  | Mailto of email
type t = uri
```

Here you define your translation functions. Because they are not defined in the signature, they will not be accessible outside this module. There is no requirement that these functions be within the module, but it does simplify maintenance tasks.

```
let trans_file c = match c with
           '/' -> "\\/"
  | ' ' -> "\\ "
  | '"' -> "\\\""
  | _ -> String.make 1 c
let trans_http c = match c with
           ' ' -> "%20c"
  | '~' -> "%30e"
  | _ -> String.make 1 c
let trans_mailto c = match c with
           '&' -> "_"
  | _ -> String.make 1 c
let get_error x = try
  List.assoc x errors
           with Not_found -> "I'm sorry, this is an unidentified error"
let compare (x:t) (y:t) = Pervasives.compare x y
let basename x = match x with
           File n -> Filename.basename n
  | Http (n,m) -> n
  | Mailto (Email (q,r)) -> r
let is_relative x = match x with
           File n -> Filename.is_relative n
  | Http (n,m) -> Filename.is_relative m
  | _ -> raise (Error 2)
let concat x s = match x with
           File n -> File (Filename.concat n s)
  | Http (n,m) -> Http (n,(m ^ "/" ^ s))
  | _ -> raise (Error 2)
let check_suffix x s = match x with
           File n -> let suf =
             (String.sub n ((String.length n) - (String.length s))
                (String.length s)) in
                suf = s
```

```
  | Http (n,m) -> let suf =
            (String.sub m ((String.length m) - (String.length s))
              (String.length s)) in
            suf = s
  | Mailto (Email (q,r)) -> let suf =
            (String.sub r ((String.length r) - (String.length s))
              (String.length s)) in
            suf = s
let chop_suffix x s = match x with
          File n when (check_suffix x s) -> File
            (String.sub n 0 ((String.length n) - (String.length s)))
          | Http (m,n) when (check_suffix x s) -> Http
            (m,(String.sub n 0 ((String.length n) - (String.length s))))
          | _ -> raise (Error 3)

let chop_extension x = match x with
          File n -> File (Filename.chop_extension n)
  | Http (m,n) ->
      (try
          let lastdot = String.rindex n '.' in
          try
            let lastdirsep = String.rindex n '/' in
              if lastdot > lastdirsep then
            Http (m,(String.sub n 0 lastdot))
          else
              Http (m,n)
          with Not_found -> Http (m,(String.sub n 0 lastdot))
        with Not_found -> Http (m,n))
  | _ -> raise (Error 2)
```

The chop_extension code is a little more complicated than you might think. The problem lies in the rule that the extension lies after the last directory separator. You have to find both the last dot and the last directory separator, and the absence of a directory separator does not imply the absence of a last dot. But this is okay because you can nest try … catch blocks.

```
let quote x = match x with
          File n -> let acbuf = Buffer.create (String.length n) in
          let b = Buffer.add_string acbuf "file://" in
          let res = String.iter (fun x ->
                                    Buffer.add_string acbuf (trans_file x)) n in
          Buffer.contents acbuf
  | Http (m,n) ->  let acbuf = Buffer.create (String.length n) in
          let b = Buffer.add_string acbuf "http://" in
          let dom_res = Buffer.add_string acbuf m in
          let res = String.iter (fun x ->
                                    Buffer.add_string acbuf (trans_http x)) n in
          Buffer.contents acbuf
```

```
           | Mailto (Email (p,n)) -> let acbuf = Buffer.create (String.length p) in
                  let b = Buffer.add_string acbuf "mailto://" in
                  let name_res = String.iter (fun x ->
                                Buffer.add_string acbuf (trans_mailto
                                            x)) p
                  in let add_at = Buffer.add_string acbuf "@" in
                  let res = String.iter (fun x ->
                                Buffer.add_string acbuf (trans_mailto
                                            x)) n in
                  Buffer.contents acbuf
```

Quoting is accomplished by using a transform function, which takes a char and returns a string. You used pattern matching in the example, but there is no reason why you couldn't use any technique you want to accomplish this. You could even use this quoter to perform arbitrary substitutions of your URIs.

```
let string_of_uri x = match x with
        File n -> "file://" ^ n
    | Http (m,n) -> "http://" ^ m ^ n
    | Mailto (Email (m,n)) -> "mailto:" ^ m ^ "@" ^ n
Making a string out of a uri is quite straightforward.
```

```
let uri_of_string (m:string) =
  let b = Scanf.Scanning.from_string m in
  Scanf.bscanf b "%s@:" (fun x -> match (String.lowercase x) with
                        "file" -> (
                          let path =
                          String.sub m 7
                            ((String.length m) - 7) in File path
                        )
                        | "http" -> (
                                let web = Scanf.bscanf
                                  b "%s@/" (fun x -> x) in
                                let path = Scanf.bscanf
                                  b "%n" (fun x -> String.sub m (x-1) (
                                            (String.length m) - (x-1))) in
                                Http (web,("/" ^ path))
                                )
                        | "mailto" -> let em = Scanf.bscanf
                                  b "%s@@" (fun x -> x) in
                                let dom = Scanf.bscanf
                                  b "%n" (fun x -> String.sub m (x-1) (
                                            (String.length m) - (x-1))) in
                                Mailto (Email (em,dom))
                        | _ -> raise (Unreg_protocol (x,1)))
```

Using the Module

You can compile the module using ocamlc (assuming that the module signature and implementation are in two different files) like so:

```
# ocamlc -c first_uri.mli
# ocamlc -c first_uri.ml
```

In the OCaml toplevel, you can load the library and it will be available to you.

```
#load "first_uri.cmo";;
```

You can create a new toplevel that incorporates this library using the ocamlmktop command.

```
$ ocamlmktop -o mytop first_uri.cmo
$ ./mytop
```

You can then create URIs from strings.

```
# let b = First_uri.uri_of_string "mailto:josh@apress.com";;
val b : First_uri.t = First_uri.Mailto (First_uri.Email ("josh", "apress.com"))
# let b = First_uri.uri_of_string "file://this/is/a/test";;
val b : First_uri.t = First_uri.File "this/is/a/test"
# First_uri.is_relative b;;
- : bool = true
# let b = First_uri.uri_of_string "file:///this/is/a/test";;
val b : First_uri.t = First_uri.File "/this/is/a/test"
# First_uri.is_relative b;;
- : bool = false
# First_uri.concat b "/another/test";;
- : First_uri.uri = First_uri.File "/this/is/a/test//another/test"
# First_uri.concat b "another/test";;
- : First_uri.uri = First_uri.File "/this/is/a/test/another/test"
# First_uri.quote b;;
- : string = "file://\\/this\\/is\\/a\\/test"
# First_uri.string_of_uri b;;
- : string = "file:///this/is/a/test"
#
```

Improvements and Toys

This module is solid, but more can be done (which seems to always be the case). There are some improvements you can make. There are also some things you can do that fall decidedly into the toy category.

Mythical Rot13 Path Maker

Because you are using a filtering function for the quote generation, you can do all kinds of things with the quoting. You could implement pretty much any filter you want, including a Rot13 quoter. In this example, you can see that character ranges are used in the pattern match:

```
let trans_file c =
  match c with
    'a' .. 'z' ->
      let nc = Char.code c in
      let b = (nc + 13) in
                if (b > 122) then
                    String.make 1 (Char.chr (96 + (b - 122)))
                else
                    String.make 1 (Char.chr b)
  | 'A' .. 'Z' ->
      let nc = Char.code c in
      let b = (nc + 13) in
                if (b > 90) then
                    String.make 1 (Char.chr (64 + (b - 90)))
                else
                    String.make 1 (Char.chr b)
  | _ -> String.make 1 c
```

The preceding example is only the file translation function, but you really only need the one function. The matches were used to translate only the letters and preserve anything not a letter. It would be trivial to implement the reverse function.

Using Regular Expressions

Using Scanf is a difficult and fragile way to implement this module. It does work, but it does not parse the whole range of URIs. Notably absent is the capability to handle and parse URLs with usernames and passwords encoded in them. Also absent is the capability to specify a port in a URL. There is also the issue of adding new URI classes. Adding them by using Scanf codes can be a pain. Scanf is also quite fragile, and errors and poorly formed strings create problems for a library implemented in this way.

To solve most of these problems, you can use regular expressions with one of the supporting libraries such as Str or Pcre (although Pcre increases the number of dependencies the library would then have). You also can use ocamllex and create a lexer for these items.

You might want to not only use regular expressions but also to specify more formal grammars for URIs by using ocamllex and ocamlyacc. This is probably the most complete and robust solution, although it is also the most work. Paradoxically, it probably uses the fewest lines of code of all the listed methods. This code is not covered here because it is discussed in depth in later chapters. The first file is the lexer, which would go into a file named uri_lexer.mll and be compiled with the following:

```
$ ocamllex uri_lexer.mll
$ ocamlc -c uri_lexer.ml

{
 open Uri_parser
}
```

```
rule token = parse
  "http://" { HTTP }
| "mailto://" { MAILTO }
| "file://" { FILE }
| ':' { SEP }
| ['/' '\\'] { PATHSEP }
| '@' { AT }
| eof { EOF }
| (['a'-'z' 'A'-'Z' '0'-'9' '%' '^' '&' '*' '(' ')' '-' '_' '+' '=' '?' '<' '>'
  '|' '{' '}' '[' ']' '!' '.' ',']+ as st) { STRING(st) }

{

  let lb = Lexing.from_string "http://www.slashdot.org/index.html";;
  let _ = let res = Uri_parser.main token lb in
    Printf.printf "[%s %s]" (fst res) (snd res);;
}
```

The next file (uri_parser.mly) is shown as follows. This is an ocamlyacc file that must be processed by ocamlyacc before being compiled (much like the preceding ocamllex file).

```
$ ocamlyacc uri_parser.mly
$ ocamlc -c uri_parser.mli
$ ocamlc -c uri_parser.ml
```

```
%token HTTP MAILTO FILE SEP PATHSEP AT EOF
%token<string> STRING
%start main
%type<string * string> main
%%

main:
http EOF { $1 }
| file EOF { $1 }
  ;

  path:
    STRING { $1 }
| PATHSEP STRING { $2 }
| path PATHSEP { $1 ^ "/" }
| path STRING { $1 ^ "/" ^ $2 }
  ;
```

```
http:
   HTTP STRING path { ($2,$3) }
| HTTP STRING AT STRING path { ($4,$5) }
| HTTP STRING SEP STRING AT STRING path { ($6,$7) }
 ;

file:
   FILE PATHSEP PATHSEP path { ("",$4) }
 ;

mailto:
   MAILTO PATHSEP PATHSEP STRING AT STRING { ($4,$6) }
 ;
```

After you process these two files, you can compile them to a single executable by simply calling the compiler on both of the generated .cmo files.

```
$ ocamlc -o parse_test uri_parser.cmo uri_lexer.cmo
$ ./parse_test
www. slashdot.org /index.html
$
```

Conclusion

With this code under your belt, you should be well on your way to actually solving problems with OCaml. You have created a module to handle URIs in a platform-independent manner, including filenames. A module like this creates the ability to improve code maintenance because you can make changes at the module layer for handling different URIs.

The next chapter discusses the ocamldoc system, which is a Javadoc-like tool that enables you to embed documentation in your code and output HTML, LaTeX, Texinfo, and man pages for your code. ocamldoc is a powerful and very useful tool that is widely used. Nearly all the official documentation comes from ocamldoc sources and was used to format many of the examples used in this book.

CHAPTER 12

###

Using Ocamldoc

Almost everyone can agree that writing proper documentation is very important for programmers, but that this task is often overlooked or done poorly.

Programmers often say that they already comment the code, so creating documentation seems like duplication of effort. This opinion is not totally off-base. In fact, many tools have sprung up over the years that enable documentation to be extracted from the comments in the code. Doxygen and Javadoc are two notable tools that do just that. Ocamldoc is a tool very similar in function to these tools.

Ocamldoc can generate dependency tree graphs by using the GraphViz application set. It also pretty prints code very effectively (it is one of the few pretty printers available for OCaml).

Who Uses Ocamldoc?

Almost everyone who writes OCaml code documents is using ocamldoc. There are some who use literate tools such as Noweb, but they are in the minority. Ocamldoc creates much of the standard OCaml documentation and nearly all web-accessible API documentation.

Probably the main reason why people use ocamldoc is because it works so very well. The markup covers most of what you want to put into API documentation and is very easy to use.

The variety of output formats is also very helpful. Using ocamldoc, you can output HTML, LaTeX, man pages, and even Texinfo pages. You can even add your own custom tags pretty easily.

It does have a few (small) weaknesses. For one, ocamldoc doesn't output to XML in any helpful way. You could probably transform the HTML with work, but it isn't as convenient as real XML output. It doesn't support object-oriented design documentation all that well (it does not have support for UML or the like). You also cannot create tables with ocamldoc.

These small issues are probably too small to consider as "weaknesses." Design documents and their construction are largely a matter of taste and are a hotly debated topic. XML output is a nice-to-have option instead of a requirement. In fact, few programmers use XML documentation formats extensively.

Creating tables can be frustrating. You can create them by using raw LaTeX in the output, but that is not really using ocamldoc. This limitation is arguably a very minor one in terms of using ocamldoc to document your programs. If you really need tables, you can use a custom generator (which is discussed later) to handle their creation.

Using Ocamldoc

The most basic use of ocamldoc is as simple as commenting. In fact, you add one character to your comments to create ocamldoc text. The most basic ocamldoc element is this special comment character:

```
(** this is ocamldoc text *)
(* while this comment is not interpreted as ocamldoc *)
```

Running the Command

The ocamldoc binary, which is a part of the standard distribution, should be in the same path as the OCaml compiler binary. The ocamldoc command is normally run with an output flag and a list of files to process. It supports globing, so *.ml is acceptable.

The default behavior puts the output files in the current directory. You can set this output directory with the -o flag. If you put the preceding basic example lines into a file by themselves and run ocamldoc on that file, it would not produce any files.

```
$ ocamldoc ocamldocstuff.ml
$ echo $?
0
$ ocamldoc ocamldocstuff.ml
File "ocamldocstuff.ml", line 1, characters 0-2:
Comment not terminated
1 error(s) encountered

$ echo $?
1
```

From this example you can see that the first run return code is 0, indicating that the command completed successfully. The second run return code is 1, indicating that it was not successful, and an error message is displayed. The second run is on a modified version of the file, with one of the comment terminators removed. To produce files, you must specify an output type.

Output Types

There are four output types that ocamldoc supports: HTML, LaTeX, Texinfo, and Unix man pages. It also can output dot graph files, which are processed by using the Graphviz set of tools available from http://www.research.att.com/sw/tools/graphviz/. These files are useful for displaying dependency graphs and other network information (mathematical networks, not communication networks).

HTML

HTML output is specified with the -html flag passed to ocamldoc, which generates a collection of linked HTML pages and indexes. These files are ready to be published on a web site, and the defaults look like the official documentation. Most people use the default appearance.

The HTML output also includes a style sheet that can be easily modified. The default name for the style sheet is style.css; you can also provide your own style sheet using the -css-style parameter (it does not do any validation of your style sheet).

Eleven files will be created if you use the HTML output on the previous two-line example. Most of them are index files that are common to all the files you process with ocamldoc. The style sheet is also generated—you can either edit that style sheet or specify one yourself.

```
index_module_types.html
index_modules.html
index_attributes.html
index_class_types.html
index_classes.html
index_methods.html
index.html
index_exceptions.html
index_types.html
index_values.html
Ocamldocstuff.html
style.css
type_Ocamldocstuff.html
```

There is no way to automatically make compressed HTML pages for CHM-compatible help systems. After you have the HTML, you can further process these files, however.

LaTeX

By default, the output of the -latex flag is to create a single LaTeX file called ocamldoc.out. You create a file per toplevel module by using the -sepfiles option. You also can suppress table of contents generation with the -notoc flag. This option, along with the -noheader and -notrailer options, assist you with including generated documentation in your LaTeX documents.

You can include the generated LaTeX in your own documents with the -latextitle option, which enables you to map section numbers with LaTeX section styles. This is also one of the ways to use ocamldoc to generate specific program documentation, but you can use tables and other display methods to include documentation that is maintained outside of the source code.

As with the HTML stylesheet, a LaTeX style sheet is also generated. The ocamldoc.sty file is generated by ocamldoc if it does not exist. You can modify this file if you know how, and it defines the ocamldoc LaTeX package information. The ocamldoc.sty file is the only style file you can use, and there is no way to specify another style file on the command line (as you can with the HTML style file).

Manual Pages

Manual pages (man pages) are generated for each element, type, module, and class. Although many man pages are thus generated, there is a flag, -man-mini, which restricts the generation of man pages to only modules and classes.

You can also change the suffix for the generated man pages. The default is o, but you can set it to whatever you want by using the –man-suffix flag. Man pages are often-overlooked pieces of documentation; if your programs include man pages, you will make (at least) the system administrators happy.

Texinfo Pages

Contrary to popular myth, Texinfo is not dead (if you are an (X)Emacs user, you probably already know this). Ocamldoc can generate info pages. You can specify the dir page with the –info-entry flag. The section can also be specified with the –info-section flag.

The ability to generate info pages is a very nice feature. I use the info pages for the OCaml distribution quite a bit because I use (X)Emacs to edit much of my code.

Dependency Graphs

Dependency graphs can be generated by using the –dot flag. By default, only the modules contained within the files specified are used. However, you can use all dependencies with the –dot-include-all flag.

Transitive dependencies can be reduced before output with the –dot-reduce flag. It can be helpful to reduce clutter, but only if the clutter is the result of transitive dependencies.

The dot graphs that are generated must be processed with the GraphViz package for the graphs to be converted in image files.

Running Ocamldoc Calls the Type Checker

Although it can sometimes be a source of frustration, it is unavoidable because some of the information in the documentation is derived from the compiler. Specifically, type information is unavailable otherwise because type is inferred.

Because you must have type information available, the ocamldoc command supports all the type information and path arguments that the OCaml compiler supports.

Markup

The markup is contained within special comment blocks that can be in either .ml or .mli files. You begin an Ocamldoc block with (** and end it with *). Each block documents the code following the documentation block if there is no blank line or special comment line between them (normal comments are okay).

Judicious use of white space can help your document formatting quite a bit. Also, if you have two functions, types, classes, or modules with the same name in the same module you can create cross-referencing problems. Having name collisions is generally something to be avoided, anyway, so it should not be a problem.

Much of the output formatting is determined by where the comment is in relation to a given function, type definition, or whatever. Blank lines can be significant.

As Simple As Commenting

For most tasks, creating the documentation is as easy as commenting. But there are a few rules governing how the ocamldoc comments need to be placed.

The comments can be located before or after an element. If a comment is located before an element, there cannot be a blank space between the element and the comment (a regular comment can be there, however). The comment is associated with the element if it is not the first comment in the file and if it is not already associated with the previous element.

Basic Formatting

It is easier to look at visual examples than read descriptions. So the following code gets transformed into HTML that looks like Figure 12-1:

```
(** {1 This is a Section Heading}
    {b Here is some Bold Text} with examples of
    {i italics} and {e emphasized} text, too.
    {C We can Center}
    {L and Left and } {R Right Align too}

    We can reference code with links like this: {!Chapter12.Docoff.bar}.
    Notice it has to be fully qualified.

    Source code can be inlined like this:
    [val source_code_style: string -> int]

    Or preformated like this:
    {[  let source_code_string x = String.length x;;  ]}

    {v Verbatim text can be added,  though you
    may still have to escape certain text in verbatim blocks. v}
    {{:http://www.slashdot.org} this text can be a link}

    We can also make L{_a}T{^e}X look (almost) correct.
*)
```

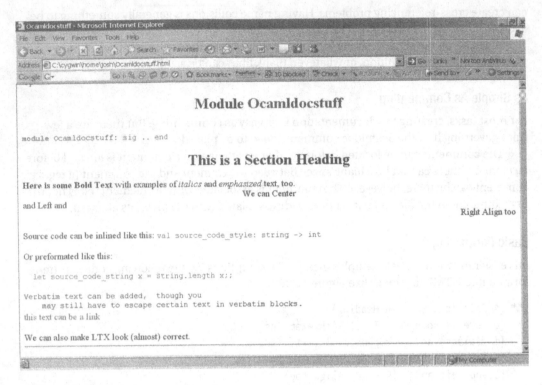

Figure 12-1. *Code transformed into HTML*

Lists

There are shortcuts available, but they should not be used to define nested lists.

```
{ol List} with {li list items}
{ul List with {li list items}
```

Sections and Headings

From the basic formatting example, you can see one example of a section heading. They can be up to the number 6 and can be nested.

Special and Class/Module Specific Tags

Any tag with an @ sign is used to indicate a special tag. There are several predefined special tags that are ignored if the comment is not associated with any element. There are tags for both @deprecated and @version information, which can be at any level (function, module, type, and so on). The @author tag enables a systematic way to indicate the author of any given code item.

The very helpful @raise tag enables you to indicate which exceptions can be raised by a given code segment. Users of your code then know which exceptions can be raised—instead of having to guess.

There are specific rules governing the placement of ocamldoc-formatted comments in module files and around classes. If the ocamldoc comment is on the first line of the file, it is special and applies to the entire module.

If there are ocamldoc comments in both the .mli and the .ml files, they will be merged. However, it is a widespread practice to put the bulk of ocamldoc documentation in .mli files.

Stopping Processing

You can stop processing by using the (**/**) string, which suspends processing of ocamldoc elements until the end of the current class or module. Processing can be turned back on with another (**/**) string.

Using these tags does more than turn off documentation processing, however. A tag means that anything documented past the tag will not show up in the generated documentation.

```
module type Docoff =
sig
  (** document foo *)
  val foo: int -> int -> float

  (** document bar *)
  val bar: int -> unit

  (**/**)

  (** baz will not show up in the docs *)
  val baz: float -> string -> char
end;;
```

Both foo and bar show up in the documentation, but baz does not. It does not show up in the index, either, but it does pop up in the code listing, so you cannot use these tags to hide anything.

A Complete Example

```
(** This is the complete exmaple for Ocamldoc.
    @author Joshua Smith
    @version 1.9
*)

(** Here we have some unassociated documentation.
    {- With a list}
    {- that doesn't}
    {- really add any value}
*)

(***********************************************************************)
(***** these will be ignored. more than one * gets you ignored *********)
(***********************************************************************)
```

```
(** Our module type, Docoff,  shows the turning off of documentation
    processing *)
module type Docoff =
sig

  (** document foo
          @author Joshua Smith
*)
  val foo: int -> int -> float

  (** document bar
@deprecated This had to be deprecated in favor of baz
*)
  val bar: int -> unit

  (**/**)
  (** this will not show up *)
  (**/**)

  (** baz will show up in the docs *)
(* this comment will be in the source but not the docs *)
  val baz: float -> string -> char
end;;

(** {1 This is a Section Heading}
    {b Here is some Bold Text} with examples of
    {i italics} and {e emphasized} text, too.
    {C We can Center}
    {L and Left and } {R Right Align too}

    We can reference code with links like this: {!Chapter12.Docoff.bar}.
    Notice it has to be fully qualified.

    Source code can be inlined like this:
    [val source_code_style: string -> int]

    Or preformated like this:
    {[  let source_code_string x = String.length x;; ]}

    {v Verbatim text can be added,  though you
    may still have to escape certain text in verbatim blocks. v}
    {{:http://www.slashdot.org} this text can be a link}

    We can also make L{_a}T{^e}X look (almost) correct.
*)
```

Which Files to Document?

This is not a trick question. Note that the question asks which files to document, not which files to comment. All files should have comments—that's a given. In fact, all files should be documented as well.

However, just because all files should be documented doesn't mean that they should be documented the same way. Much of the documentation that you see when you are looking at ocamldoc-generated files comes from the .mli files. The documentation of the other files is very important, but the front-end documentation almost always comes from the .mli file instead of the .ml file.

This documentation technique creates some important side effects (one is that OCaml programmers will look to your .mli files for developer documentation). These files serve as the backbone of the API documentation and should be treated accordingly.

Although maintainers are interested in the .ml documentation, users of your code might never look at it. The OCaml source is a good example of this. I often review the documentation that comes from the .mli files of the standard library, although I almost never look at the documentation of the source code itself.

This split is something you can capitalize on. Any given API documentation probably doesn't need to reference internals, and vice versa. This means you can use the ocamldoc-generated documentation for both API users and internal users without being concerned that you will upset your API docs with implementation details that will just muddy the waters. So document all your files—you (and your users) will be happier for it.

Creating Custom Tags and Generators

You don't have to be limited by the built-in tags and output formats. The authors of ocamldoc have created a system that enables you to create your own tags and output format in OCaml.

You can just start adding them. When you run ocamldoc, it gives a warning if a tag is not handled by the selected generator, but it will continue, and you should just ignore it. (They will be included in the pretty printed source, though.)

The easiest way to add your own custom tag is to inherit from one of the existing generators and add it.

```
class cooltag =
object(self)
  inherit Odoc_html.html

    (** this is where we define the member function to handle
            the cool tag.
       @cool Cool, eh?  *)
  method html_of_cool t = Printf.sprintf "<blink>Blink</blink>\n"
  initializer
    tag_functions <- ("cool", self#html_of_cool) :: tag_functions
end
let cooltag = new cooltag
let _ = Odoc_args.set_doc_generator (Some (cooltag :> Odoc_args.doc_generator))
```

You can compile this code using `ocamlc -I +ocamldoc -c cool.ml` and then run it by using `ocamldoc -g cool.cmo -I +ocamldoc cool.ml`. This enables you to see the `cool` tag. Don't pass the command any output flags; otherwise, it uses that flag instead of the custom generator. This generator adds the `cool` tag only to HTML output; if you want to do it for the other outputs, you have to subclass their output classes individually.

More complete custom generators are not this simple—in fact, they can be very complicated (and happen very rarely).

Conclusion

Now that you understand ocamldoc, you should be able to add documentation to your code and produce high-quality output for it. I don't know that it will make you a better programmer, but it will make your code more likely to be used correctly.

Keep in mind that OCaml programmers will look for ocamldoc in your code. Ocamldoc does not, however, replace careful commenting. Think of ocamldoc as comments for the users of your code, whereas comments are often more important for maintainance programming or future extensions.

CHAPTER 13

■■■

Modules and Functors

OCaml provides a very advanced module system. It is based on the meta-language (ML) module system, and it is similar to systems provided in Modula-3 and Ada as well. The module system is basically a small typed language on top of OCaml that enables a programmer to group values, functions, types, classes, and other modules together.

They are also sometimes called libraries, although a library is more often really a collection of modules. These modules help large-scale programming by making programs easier to compile and use. Each module can be a complete grouping of data and functionality, which also makes reuse easier because the functionality each module provides can be as generic as needed. Modules themselves cannot be polymorphic, however.

Using Modules

Modules do not have to be opened in order to be used. Many people do open modules, which can simplify coding and enable you to swap in new modules with only a two-line change. However, many people also avoid opening any modules to minimize the danger of name conflicts.

Modules also provide functionality similar to namespaces, although they are not namespaces. Namespaces cannot be parameterized, whereas modules can. However, modules present a de facto hierarchical namespace, so it might not be an issue for you. These namespaces can be defined at the file level or inside any other module, and can be nested to an arbitrary depth. For example, you have seen the List.map function used in previous chapters. This function is actually a function named map in the List module.

```
# List.map (fun x -> x * x) [1;2;3;4;5;6];;
- : int list = [1; 4; 9; 16; 25; 36]
# open List;;
# map (fun x -> x * x) [1;2;3;4;5;6];;
- : int list = [1; 4; 9; 16; 25; 36]
#
```

From the preceding example, you can see that both List.map and map are the same in function.

Defining Modules

Module names must start with a capital letter. Module interfaces (which are covered later) do not share this restriction, but it is convention to name them the same way. The simplest module is one that does not include any function definitions.

```
# module Simple =
struct
end;;
    module Simple : sig  end
#
```

The Simple module is defined using the module keyword. Modules are also automatically defined at the file level, with the module name being the same as the filename.

Defined at the File Level

Modules are defined implicitly at the file level, and each file has its own module name that is the same as the filename (with the first letter capitalized). The convention is to have the files not capitalized. This default module is in addition to any other modules that might be defined in the file. Filenames should not contain characters other than letters and numbers. Underscores are allowed, but dashes should not be used. For example, the following code is saved into a file called first_module.ml.

```
# module First_module=
  struct
  let addone arg = arg + 1
  module InFirst =
  struct
              type suite = Heart | Spade | Club | Diamond
              type card = One of suite | Two of suite | Three of suite
  end
  end;;
module First_module :
  sig
    val addone : int -> int
    module InFirst :
      sig
        type suite = Heart | Spade | Club | Diamond
        type card = One of suite | Two of suite | Three of suite
      end
  end
# First_module.addone 10;;
- : int = 11
# Heart;;
Characters 0-5:
  Heart;;
  ^^^^^
Unbound constructor Heart
```

```
# First_module.InFirst.Heart;;
- : First_module.InFirst.suite = First_module.InFirst.Heart
# First_module.InFirst.One First_module.InFirst.Heart;;
- : First_module.InFirst.card =
First_module.InFirst.One First_module.InFirst.Heart
# open First_module;;
# addone 10;;
- : int = 11
# InFirst.Heart;;
- : First_module.InFirst.suite = First_module.InFirst.Heart
# open InFirst;;
# Heart;;
- : First_module.InFirst.suite = Heart
# One Heart;;
- : First_module.InFirst.card = One Heart
#
```

Exercise Care When "Open"ing

This can lead to collisions. See the following:

```
# module A =
  struct
    let b x = x * 10
  end;;

module B =
  struct
    let b x = x *. 3.14159
  end;;
      module A : sig val b : int -> int end
#          module B : sig val b : float -> float end
# open B;;
# open A;;
# b 10;;
- : int = 100
# B.b 10.;;
- : float = 31.4159
# A.b 10;;
- : int = 100
#
```

Also Useful for Creating "Private" Modules

Modules defined explicitly enable you to define modules within modules. You can then restrict access to these internal modules using the interface signature.

```
# module type RESTR =
  sig
      val superB: int -> int
  end;;
module type RESTR = sig val superB : int -> int end
# module Test:RESTR =
  struct
      module B =
        struct
          let b x = x * 10
          end
      let superB x = B.b x
  end;;
module Test : RESTR
# Test.B.b 1;;
Characters 0-8:
  Test.B.b 1;;
  ^^^^^^^^
Unbound value Test.B.b
```

If you define the module without the restriction, you can then access the internal module.

```
# Test.superB 10;;
- : int = 100
# module Test =
  struct
      module B =
        struct
          let b x = x * 10
          end
      let superB x = B.b x
  end;;
module Test :
  sig module B : sig val b : int -> int end val superB : int -> int end
# Test.B.b 100;;
- : int = 1000
#
```

Using Interfaces

Interfaces in OCaml are not like interfaces in other languages. An interface is most often contained in a special .mli file. These files have several important properties, the first of which is that they define the publicly accessible functions and types for the module of the same name. Interface files often contain the bulk of the documentation for a given module. Also, interface files must be compiled before the corresponding .ml files because they provide the type specifications that the code file will be validated by.

No Header Files in OCaml

There are no header files in OCaml. In C, header files contain the definition of functions, their parameters, and information important to the construction of functions and variables.

Unlike in C, the signatures of functions can be inferred if you do not define them. Module types are often called signatures because they contain a representation of what the module contains and does. Module types are not often used.

Interfaces are not the same as header files in C or C++. The types and functions defined in the interface are the types and functions available for use outside the module. Any types and functions not defined in the interface can still be used within the module, but they are completely not available outside. This is similar in concept to public and private variables in an object-oriented language such as Java. This privacy is enforced by the compiler.

These functions also must match the module type definition. For example, if a function returns a string in the module type, it must return a string in the implementation.

Users of your code will pay close attention to your signatures. They might even pay more attention to your signatures than your code because the signature defines the visible portion of your module. Regardless, if you rely on your users to understand some particular feature of the implementation, you should try to reflect that in the signature.

A simple example illustrates what this means. In this example, you define a module called Module contained within a file named `module.ml` and an associated `*.mli` interface file. When compiled and loaded, only one function is accessible.

Creating Multiple Views of a Module

You can use module types to create different views of the same module.

```
module type CONTROL_ACCT_NUM =
  sig
    val set_base: string -> unit
    val next: unit -> string
    val reset: unit -> unit
  end;;

module type ACCT_NUM =
  sig
    val next: unit -> string
  end;;

module Cacc_num:CONTROL_ACCT_NUM =
  struct
    type counter = {mutable base:string;mutable count:int }
    let base = {base="base";count=0}
    let set_base x = base.base <- x
    let base_to_string x = Printf.sprintf "%s-%i" x.base x.count
    let next () = (ignore(base.count <- base.count + 1);base_to_string base)
    let reset () = base.count <- 0
  end;;

module Uacc_num = (Cacc_num:ACCT_NUM);;
```

One of the interesting effects is that it creates the same effect of the singleton design pattern. The module system provides a kind of singleton-esque management at a global level. You can see this in action in the following snippet:

```
# Uacc_num.next ();;
- : string = "base-1"
# Uacc_num.next ();;
- : string = "base-2"
# Cacc_num.next ();;
- : string = "base-3"
#
```

You cannot mix signatures that are incompatible, however. For example, a functor and a nonfunctor signature cannot apply to the same code. The code must also match the signatures that you are using. These are all checked at compile time.

What Are Generics?

Generics can be found in many languages. C++ templates are some of the most established generics, although they can be found in languages such as Java and C#, too. A generic is a way of providing parameterized types most commonly used with collections of data. In OCaml, functors provide many of the solutions people use generics for, while not creating more problems (such as type erasure in Java generics).

In many languages, generics are a way to offer type-checked containers that can contain different data types. This is not a problem in OCaml because OCaml already supports polymorphic containers. More-complex collections and operations are more difficult to handle only via polymorphism. An example is creating a module that performs mathematical operations on lists and you want to provide sum, range, and mean functions. However, you do not want to have to write a new module every time you want to use a different type of number (that is, float, integer, and so on). You can use functors to do this.

Understanding Functors

Functors are higher-order modules that are parameterized, and that parameter can be a module or another functor. Functors can even take more than one parameter.

Functors provide the capability to create generic modules, which have effects similar to mix-in inheritance (such as Java's interfaces) as well. Functors can be defined to take only a specific module type as an argument. This module type must be defined and available at compile time. A module can have multiple views of itself, and functors can be defined to take those kinds of modules, too.

Functors can be defined by using the functor keyword or with the parameter syntax. Either syntax is correct; the use of one or the other is a matter of style. I prefer the functor keyword style because of readability.

```
module type EXAMPLE =
  sig
    type maybe
    val plus : int * int -> int * int -> int * int
    val minus : int * int -> int * int -> int * int
  end

module Dbg_E:EXAMPLE =
  struct
    type maybe = X | Y
    let plus x y = Printf.printf "%i %i\n%i %i\n" (fst x) (snd x) (fst y)
      (snd y);((fst x),(fst y))
    let minus x y = Printf.printf "%i %i\n%i %i\n" (fst x) (snd x) (fst y)
      (snd y);((snd y),(snd x))
  end;;


module type F_TOR =
  functor(E: EXAMPLE) ->
sig
  val plus: int -> int -> int -> int -> int * int
  val minus: int -> int -> int -> int -> int * int
end;;

module F_tor: F_TOR =
  functor(E: EXAMPLE) ->
    struct
      let plus x y z m = E.plus (x,y) (z,m)
      let minus x y z m = E.minus (x,y) (z,m)
    end;;

module F = F_tor(struct type maybe = A | B let plus x y = ((fst x),(fst y))
                                           let minus x y = ➡
((snd y),(snd x)) end);;

module F' = F_tor(Dbg_E);;
#                              module type F_TOR =
  functor (E : EXAMPLE) ->
    sig
      val plus : int -> int -> int -> int -> int * int
      val minus : int -> int -> int -> int -> int * int
    end
module F_tor : F_TOR
#     module F :
  sig
    val plus : int -> int -> int -> int -> int * int
    val minus : int -> int -> int -> int -> int * int
  end
```

```
#   module F' :
  sig
    val plus : int -> int -> int -> int -> int * int
    val minus : int -> int -> int -> int -> int * int
  end
# F.plus 10 11 12 13;;
- : int * int = (10, 12)
# F'.plus 10 11 12 13;;
10 11
12 13
- : int * int = (10, 12)
# F.minus 10 11 12 13;;
- : int * int = (13, 11)
# F'.minus 10 11 12 13;;
10 11
12 13
- : int * int = (13, 11)
#
```

Although functors can be difficult, they are really not that hard to understand and can be extremely useful.

When Should You Use Functors?

This question has no simple answer. One of the main reasons to use a functor is when you need to enforce polymorphism across a group of items and functions. For example, the Set module in the standard library is a functor. Two different Sets of any given type have compatible comparison operators. You can also use functors to create generics (especially containers). Again, the Set is an example of this. Remember generics are different from simple polymorphism. There are people who shy away from using functors because they have a mixed reputation. Often, new programmers have trouble understanding functors and their implications. However, they are a fully supported part of the language and offer functionality that is difficult to replicate.

You also might want to use a functor when implementing generic containers. In fact, functors provide functionality similar to generics in languages such as Java or C++. Unlike Java generics, however, functors are completely typesafe.

Although you could replicate much of the runtime functionality with curried functions and careful thought, runtime is not where all the power of functors resides. The ability to create generic code in a highly reusable fashion is powerful. This ability to do generic programming in a fully typesafe way is a strong argument to use functors whenever you think you might want to have a generic module.

If you are in a situation in which you are considering using a functor, you should make sure that a polymorphic function (or a set of polymorphic functions) won't solve the problem just as well. Personally, I do not subscribe to the belief that "hard" sections of any language should be avoided. "Bad" and or "wrong" sections should be avoided, but functors are neither of those. However, functors are more complicated than many other kinds of solutions, so you should add complexity only if it is unavoidable.

Currying Functors

Functors can be curried, which is an interesting side effect of the functor. As you can see in the following example, a new module might be defined from the curried functor in module D.

```
# module type A =
  sig
    val a: int
    val b: int -> int
  end;;

module type B =
  sig
    val a: unit -> unit
  end;;

module C = functor(S: A) -> functor(T: B) ->
  struct
    let q m = S.b m
    let d f = T.a f
  end;;

module D = C(struct let a = 10 let b x = x * a end);;
module E = D(struct let a () = () end);;
module type A = sig val a : int val b : int -> int end
module type B = sig val a : unit -> unit end
module C :
            functor (S : A) ->
            functor (T : B) -> sig val q : int -> int val d : unit -> unit end
module D : functor (T : B) -> sig val q : int -> int val d : unit -> unit end
module E : sig val q : int -> int val d : unit -> unit end
```

A Complete Example

The following example relies on the functions and types defined in the example of multiple views of a module. It does not include curried functors, but that is a small omission. In this example, you create an account management system of limited functionality. However, you use functors to create a module that will work with any back-end store that matches your signature.

```
type account = {id:string;username:string;contact_email:string;};;

module type STORE =
  sig
    val init: unit -> unit
    val get: string -> account
```

```
      val add: account -> unit
      val remove: string -> unit
      val exists: string -> bool
    end;;

module Datastore:STORE =
  struct
    let init () = ()
    let store = ref []
    let get x = List.assoc x store.contents
    let add x = store.contents <- store.contents @ [(x.username,x)]
    let remove x = store.contents <- List.remove_assoc x store.contents
    let exists x = List.mem_assoc x store.contents
  end;;

module type ACCOUNT =
  functor(S:STORE) ->
  sig
    val get_account_id: string -> string
    val get_contact_email: string -> string
  end;;

module type ACCOUNT_priv =
  functor(A:ACCT_NUM) -> functor(S:STORE) ->
  sig
    exception Account_error of string
    val create:string -> string -> unit
    val delete: string -> unit
  end;;

module Account_unp:ACCOUNT =
  functor(S:STORE) ->
  struct
    let get_account_id unme = let acc = S.get unme in acc.id
    let get_contact_email unme = let acc = S.get unme in acc.contact_email
  end;;

module Account_p:ACCOUNT_priv =
  functor(A:ACCT_NUM) -> functor(S:STORE) ->
struct
    exception Account_error of string
    let create x y = let exists = S.exists x in
      if (exists) then
                  raise (Account_error "Username Already Exists")
      else
                  S.add {id=(A.next ());username = x;contact_email = y}
    let delete x = S.remove x
  end;;
```

```
module Account_infomation = Account_unp(Datastore);;
module Account_management = Account_p(Uacc_num)(Datastore);;
```

If you use this code, you see the following:

```
#type account = { id : string; username : string; contact_email : string; }
#module type STORE =
  sig
    val init : unit -> unit
    val get : string -> account
    val add : account -> unit
    val remove : string -> unit
    val exists : string -> bool
  end
# module Datastore : STORE
#module type ACCOUNT =
  functor (S : STORE) ->
    sig
      val get_account_id : string -> string
      val get_contact_email : string -> string
    end
# module type ACCOUNT_priv =
  functor (A : ACCT_NUM) ->
    functor (S : STORE) ->
      sig
        exception Account_error of string
        val create : string -> string -> unit
        val delete : string -> unit
      end
module Account_unp : ACCOUNT
module Account_p : ACCOUNT_priv
#   module Account_information :
  sig
    val get_account_id : string -> string
    val get_contact_email : string -> string
  end
# module Account_management :
  sig
    exception Account_error of string
    val create : string -> string -> unit
    val delete : string -> unit
  end
# Account_management.create "Josh" "josh@apress.com";;
- : unit = ()
# Account_information.get_account_id "Josh";;
- : string = "base-1"
# Account_information.get_contact_email "Josh";;
- : string = "josh@apress.com"
```

```
# Account_management.create "Josh" "josh@apress.com";;
Exception: Account_p(A)(S).Account_error "Username Already Exists".
# Account_management.delete "Josh";;
- : unit = ()
# Account_management.create "Josh" "josh@apress.com";;
- : unit = ()
# Account_infomation.get_contact_email "Josh";;
- : string = "josh@apress.com"
# Account_management.delete "Josh";;
- : unit = ()
# Account_infomation.get_contact_email "Josh";;
Exception: Not_found.
# Account_infomation.get_account_id "Josh";;
Exception: Not_found.
# Account_management.create "Josh" "josh@apress.com";;
- : unit = ()
# Account_infomation.get_account_id "Josh";;
- : string = "base-3"
#
```

Dealing with Dependencies

There are no restrictions on module dependencies. That being said, circular dependencies should be avoided because they can cause problems. You do not need to open modules, and calling modules by their full names enables you to access them. This all gets handled automatically during compilation. You must pass the modules needed to the compiler so that the depended-upon modules are processed before the code that depends on them.

Suppose that you have two modules, A.ml and B.ml, where B.ml has some modules that rely upon code in A.ml. Assume that A.mli and B.mli exist and contain signature information for both modules. To compile this code into one library, all the files (the .mli and .ml files) must be compiled in the correct order.

```
/home/josh $ ocamlc.exe -c A.mli
/home/josh $ ocamlc.exe -c A.ml
/home/josh $ ocamlc.exe -c B.mli
/home/josh $ ocamlc.exe -c B.ml
/home/josh $ ocamlc.exe -a  -o combined.cma A.cmo B.cmo
```

Then you can load the new library, and you do not need to specify the toplevel module because the pack option does away with it.

```
# #load "combined.cma";;
# B.run "hello world\n";;
hello world

- : unit = ()
#
```

Installing Modules

Modules should be installed wherever they are installed in your OCaml distribution (usually in the lib directory). Although that sounds glib, it is the best practice. You probably will not do a lot of installations of single modules. Most third-party packages have installation routines, and you can create these installation routines yourself for your own code.

Library Directory

This directory is usually defined at compile time. The compiler will define it for you in your compiled code. One way to find the library path is to use the OCaml compiler. If you pass the OCaml compiler the -where flag (both the native and byte-code compilers do this), it will print out the library path it uses when compiling. Another way to find this path is via the ocamlfind command. If you are using ocamlfind, you can pass it the query stdlib parameters.

Compiling with Nonstandard Paths

Compiling with nonstandard paths can be helpful if you are building with libraries that have the same name but different functionality.

You can pass these paths to the compiler using the -I flags. These libraries should not have names that conflict with other modules installed in the standard path because adding them does not remove the others from the search path.

Using OCamlMake

If you have findlib installed, you can issue a make libinstall. OCamlMakefile already has routines for installing libraries using findlib. You still have to create a META file (which is discussed in the next section), but that is it.

Using Findlib

Findlib is a widely used OCaml application that simplifies the use and compilation of OCaml code. Findlib does what its name implies: it finds libraries.

There are some limitations in using findlib, although they mostly rest at the operating system (OS) level. For example, if your OS does not support dynamic linking, findlib is not of much use in the toplevel.

Findlib can be very useful—it integrates with OcamlMakefile to make building complex OCaml projects much easier. Findlib is not distributed with the standard release, however. If you are not using godi or a Debian-based Linux distribution, you can download it from http://www.ocaml-programming.de. If you are using godi, it is already installed because godi relies on findlib extensively. If you are using a Debian-based Linux distribution, you can use apt-get to install it. Otherwise, you can download the source and install it manually.

Creating a Findlib META File

Findlib relies upon properly formatted and installed META files. The Make_wizard automates this process quite nicely, but it requires labltk, which is not always available.

The Make_wizard generates a new makefile, and does not use OCamlMakefile. This means that if you are using OCamlMakefile, you cannot use the Make_wizard (and vice versa).

The following shows how to construct a META file by hand. The library has some interfaces in the Test module. You also specify where the library is installed, where the ^ is a placeholder for the default library directory. You must also denote a description, a version, and which other libraries are required. The last part tells findlib what archives to supply to the compiler if you want to use this library.

```
requires = ""
description = "Account Management Example"
version = "From the Apress Book"
directory = "^"
browse_interfaces = " Test "
archive(byte) = "account.cma"
archive(native) = "account.cmxa"
```

Creating a META file is usually done only once in a great while.

Conclusion

Now you should have a grasp of modules and their uses in OCaml. Don't worry if you are having some trouble with functors; they are a concept that often eludes people for awhile.

The module system in OCaml is very powerful. With the existence of functors, you can use modules to (forgive the wording) modularize your code in a way that is very clean and is often difficult to do in other languages.

Although the lack of real namespaces can lead to confusion, proper module construction limits the possibility and damage of name conflicts (for the most part). You should always be on the alert for this, however.

## CHAPTER 14

Practical: A Spam Filter

Everyone knows what spam is, even if they don't know that it refers to unwanted (and usually advertisement-ridden) email instead of the venerable meat product made by the Hormel Corporation.

Unlike Hormel Spam, email spam has been annoying people and reducing productivity since the 1990s. In August 2002, Paul Graham published his essay, "A Plan for Spam," which outlined a new idea in ending the spam problem. Now almost everyone uses a variant of the idea he popularized, but at the time it was the first. Paul Graham, of course, published his code in Lisp.

His "plan" for spam consisted of a Bayesian classifier that put any given email message into one of two buckets: ham or spam. This chapter presents a working OCaml-based classifier and provides for code reuse and modularity.

Naive Bayesian Spam Filtration

Paul Graham knew he was on to something with his seminal essay. The method that he describes comes from Bayes' Theorem, which when applied to spam can be described formally as follows. The equation means that the probability that a given email message is spam is equal to the probability of finding the words contained within that email in other spams divided by the probability of finding those words in any email.

$$P(spam|words)\,spam = \frac{\mathrm{P}(words|spam)\mathrm{P}(spam)}{\mathrm{P}(words)}$$

All this basically translates to the idea that a word such as "Oxycontin" will show up in spam much more often than it will in your normal email (unless you're a doctor or a drug rep). So you can use the probability that words will appear in an email to determine whether it is spam or not.

The one downside of the method is that it requires a corpus of spam and ham to "train" the probabilities. There are also certain implications as to the possible effectiveness of the method in general because it is only as good as the corpus upon which it is trained.

Brief Digression

Probabilities do not add together. If you have two events, both with a 30 percent probability that they will occur individually, the probability that they will both occur simultaneously is not 60 percent. Instead, probabilities are combined for these kinds of problems as shown in the following equation, which yields a probability of about 15.5 percent:

$$P = \frac{ab}{(ab) + (1 - a)(1 - b)}$$

This combination is also why the original Paul Graham article looked at only the first 15 to 20 "interesting" tokens.

The way these probabilities combine makes the probability of a given email being spam decrease at a rapid rate. Sampling (and taking only a few samples) is an effective way to combat this problem. However, how you get the samples is an open problem, and we take the top 20 interesting tokens in our example.

Talking About the Design

Because the algorithm is provided, you do not have to worry about it. You'll use the original Paul Graham algorithm, even though several additions and improvements have been made to it since the paper was published. The original algorithm provides a great example without getting bogged down in the math (remember, this book shows OCaml programming instead of teaching probability theory). You still have to think about how this code will be used. Do you want it to be a stand-alone module so you can use the classifier in other programs? How do you want to store the data, if at all? Is speed an issue? Do you want it to automatically learn?

First, consider speed. Because the goal of this code is to process email, you have to take speed into account. It can't be slow, but it also doesn't have to be super fast. The data-storage choices probably affect speed most. You use an ocamllex-based tokenizer, so the import of the email should be reasonably fast. It also allows the possibility of tokenizer changes in the future without having to deal with complicated Scanf lexers. This should be a module and (as in most projects) you should think about making it as reusable as possible.

Although portability is not normally talked about in terms of code reuse, it should be. Your code should be portable, so you cannot use any module that is not a generally portable module (such as a DBM), which does present a minor obstacle.

Personally, whenever I have a key/value pair situation that requires disk-based persistence, a DBM file is the logical choice. Either the GNU DBM or Berkeley DBM formats enable this kind of operation to be simple and reliable. The problem is that those modules might not work on all operating systems. To avoid this problem, you can use the Marshal module and serialize your data to disk.

Automatic learning of new ham or spam is out for this example. Automatic learning should be part of a production application, but it can be very difficult to implement. Not only is it difficult; implementing it does not add anything to the ultimate goal of this chapter: to teach you more about OCaml code. So, it is left as an exercise for the reader.

Training is something that the module should (and does) support, however.

Code

Now you see some code. There are no comments in this example and no ocamldoc because it's been stripped out of the code listing. (An .mli file that does include ocamldoc is shown at the end of the chapter.) This .mli file, which is optional for you to use, is included to show another example of how powerful the interface files can be. The interface is much shorter than the code and much more comprehensible. It also restricts the library substantially.

The tokenizer is pretty simple—it splits only on new lines and strings and also includes punctuation in the tokens. This is slightly different from Paul Graham's original because he stripped out the punctuation, but makes the tokenizer much easier to write.

```
rule tokens = parse
    ' ' { tokens lexbuf }
  | "the" { tokens lexbuf }
  | "and" { tokens lexbuf }
  | "on" { tokens lexbuf }
  | "a" { tokens lexbuf }
  | ['\n' '\t']+ { tokens lexbuf }
  | ['-']?['0' - '9']+ { tokens lexbuf }
  | [':' ';' '{' '}' '(' ')' '[' ']' '!' '@' '#' '$' '%' '^' '&' '*' '|' '\\' '/' ➥
'?' '<' '>' ',' '.' '+' '=' '~' '`' '\"' '\'']+ { tokens lexbuf }
  | ['a'-'z' 'A'-'Z' '0'-'9' '_' '-']+ { Lexing.lexeme lexbuf }
  | eof { raise End_of_file }
  | _ { tokens lexbuf }
```

Notice that words such as "the" and "a" have been stripped out of the input automatically— and any character that isn't a letter, punctuation mark, or number is discarded. You can modify it to ignore or pick up any regular expression you want. The rest of the code is in the same ocamllex file.

```
module  StringMap =  Map.Make(String);;
```

This (deceptively short) line creates a new module via the Map.Make functor. This is a string -> integer mapping. You use this map as the principal data structure in the module.

```
let (goodmap,badmap) = try
    let ic = open_in (Filename.concat (Sys.getenv "HOME")
                                          ".spamdb") in
    let (g,b) = Marshal.from_channel ic in
    close_in ic;
    g,b
with Sys_error n -> StringMap.empty,StringMap.empty;;
```

This function creates two maps that are global variables in the module: maps of tokens and the historical frequency of occurrence (represented as a simple count) of the token.

```
let goodcount = StringMap.fold (fun _ y z -> y + z) goodmap 0;;
let badcount = StringMap.fold (fun _ y z -> y + z) badmap 0;;
```

These two variables are also module globals. They are the number of tokens in both maps. The next two functions are helper functions. The increment function increments the seen count of a token in a given map. The truncate function truncates a string for you because (at least in English) there are few words more than 15 letters long. In fact, if you have a string that has more than 15 letters, you can be reasonably sure that it is not a word—it is truncated so it is easier to store. The information is lost, but it's not very useful information for your purposes, anyway.

```
let incr_map map str =
  let curval = try StringMap.find str map with Not_found -> 0 in
  StringMap.add str (curval + 1) map;;


let truncate ?(leng=15) str = match str with
    m when (String.length str) > leng -> String.sub str 0 leng
  | _ -> str;;
```

The buildmap function builds up a map of tokens and the frequency count of that token in a given file or string. The function itself takes a lexing buffer as an argument, so any thing that can give a lexing buffer can be used as a source.

```
let rec buildmap startmap lb =
  let next_tok = try Some (truncate (tokens lb)) with End_of_file -> None
  in match next_tok with
            Some n -> buildmap (incr_map startmap n) lb
    | None -> startmap;;
```

The next two functions are there to emulate two Lisp functions that Graham uses in his article. Given two arguments, they return the smaller or the larger.

```
let min x y = match x with
    n when x < y -> x
  | _ -> y;;


let max x y = match x with
    n when x > y -> x
  | _ -> y;;
```

This brings you to the function that does most of the work (named in honor of the programmer who thought of it first). The paul_graham function returns the probability that a given token is a spam token. This number has a range from 0.0 to 1.0. There are several guards for this function because not having any data in either map (ham or spam) yields bad results. There is a final check to make sure that neither the numerator nor denominator of the last calculation is zero. This check is there for two reasons. First, not all implementations of OCaml throw a Divide_by_zero exception all the time. Second, the zero-divided-by-zero situation results in the special Not A Number (or nan) condition, not an exception.

This situation can occur only when the token is in neither the ham nor the spam map. The token then is given a default value (0.5 in this case), and the calculation returns.

```
let paul_graham word goodMap badMap ngood nbad =
  match ngood,nbad with
    0,0 -> raise (Invalid_argument "Database Must Be Trained First!\n")
  | 0,_ -> raise (Invalid_argument "Ham Token count cannot be Zero\n")
  | _,0 -> raise (Invalid_argument "Spam Token count cannot be Zero\n")
  | _,_ -> let g = try
                2 * (StringMap.find word goodMap)
    with Not_found -> 0 in
    let b = try
                StringMap.find word badMap
    with Not_found -> 0 in
    let numerator = try min 1.0 ((float_of_int b) /. (float_of_int nbad))
    with Division_by_zero -> 1.0 in
    let denom = try
                (min 1.0
                  ((float_of_int g) /.
                  (float_of_int ngood)))
    with Division_by_zero -> 1.0 in
    if ((numerator = 0.0) && (denom = 0.0)) then
            0.5
    else
      let targ = min 0.99 (numerator /. (numerator +. denom) ) in
      max 0.01 targ;;
```

The next function is a helper function as well. It returns the first n elements of a sorted list in a somewhat crude way—by converting the list into an array and then taking a subarray.

The function after that actually calculates the probability of a given email being spam by finding the probabilities of each token being spam, taking the top 20 tokens (those with the highest probability of being spam), and combining them. There is no danger of this function returning Not A Number because you ensured that the scoring function (the paul_graham function) always returns some nonzero value.

```
let top_n n lst = try
  let ar = Array.of_list lst in
  Array.to_list (Array.sub ar 0 n)
 with Invalid_argument("Array.sub") -> lst;;


let calc_email_prob lbuf =
  let email = buildmap StringMap.empty lbuf in
  let scored = StringMap.mapi (
    fun x va -> paul_graham x goodmap badmap goodcount badcount
    ) email in
let top_vals =
    top_n 20 (List.rev (List.sort compare (StringMap.fold (fun x y z -> y :: z) ➥
scored []))) in
```

```
let n = List.fold_left (fun x y -> x *. y) 1.0 top_vals in
let dn = List.fold_left (+.) 0.
  (List.map (fun x -> 1.0 -. x) top_vals) in
try
  n /. (n +. dn)
with Division_by_zero -> 0.0;;
```

That is pretty much it for the actual calculating functions. The remaining functions are utility functions and training functions. First look at the three calling functions that enable you to calculate the probability of a channel, string, or file being spam according to the stored data.

```
let spam_prob_of_channel ch = calc_email_prob (Lexing.from_channel ch);;
let spam_prob_of_string st = calc_email_prob (Lexing.from_string st);;
let spam_prob_of_file f =
  let ic = open_in f in
  let sp = spam_prob_of_channel ic in
  close_in ic;
  sp;;
```

The next two functions are the training functions that train the database when given a ham or a spam data file. They write the data file out to the user's home directory. This value, the home directory environment variable, might not work correctly on Windows systems.

```
let train_spam ch =
  let newbad = buildmap badmap (Lexing.from_channel ch) in
  let oc = open_out (Filename.concat (Sys.getenv "HOME")
                                      ".spamdb") in
  Marshal.to_channel oc (goodmap,newbad) [];
  close_out oc;;

let train_ham ch =
  let newgood = buildmap goodmap (Lexing.from_channel ch) in
  let oc = open_out (Filename.concat (Sys.getenv "HOME")
                                      ".spamdb") in
  Marshal.to_channel oc (newgood,badmap) [];
  close_out oc;;
```

Compiling the Code

It is not enough to write the code; now you have to compile it. You can compile it by hand, and in this case it is pretty simple. The following generates a library named spam.cmo that can be linked to other code:

```
/home/josh/projects/de-spam $ ocamllex spam.mll
/home/josh/projects/de-spam $ ocamlc -c spam.ml
/home/josh/projects/de-spam $
```

However, it is much easier to create a makefile to handle this. You have two choices: you can create a makefile yourself or you can use OCamlMakefile.

Makefile

The following examples are for the GNU version of make (they should work with all compliant makes).

Gmake

A simple makefile can be created that looks like this, which enables you to compile a lot of OCaml code:

```
dep:
          ocamldep *.mli *.ml > .depend

-include .depend
%.ml: %.mll
          ocamllex $<
%.cmo: %.ml
          ocamlc -c $<
%.exe: %.cmo
          ocamlc -o $@ $<
```

The ocamldep command automatically figures out dependencies in compilation units.

OCamlMakefile

The OCamlMakefile (written by Markus Mottl and available on his site at http://www.ocaml. info/home/ocaml_sources.html) is a makefile with almost all the hard work done for you. To use this makefile, you include it into your makefile and set a couple of variables.

```
SOURCES = spam.mll
RESULT  = spam
all: byte-code-library
-include /opt/ocaml-3.09.2/share/OCamlMakefile
```

These four lines are all you need. The only real issue with the OCamlMakefile is that you need more than one for multiple results (which is a very small price to pay for such a useful utility).

Running It

You need a very large corpus of email to train a Bayesian classifier like this one. Luckily, the "spamassassin" developers have released a public corpus of email that can be used to develop antispam utilities. (A command-line client for this module is presented at the end of this chapter.)

This corpus, broken up into ham and spam of varying stripes, can be downloaded from http://spamassassin.apache.org/publiccorpus/. Running the code on these corpuses gives results not nearly as good as Paul Graham says he got, but they are still very good. When tested on the files that made up the training corpus, the results are quite effective, especially with regard to false positives (nonspam mail was not flagged as spam). However, testing it against my own email (but not having it trained on that email) yielded what you might expect. This kind of classifier must be trained with data from your own email if you want it to work for your own email. The files "test" and "test2" were my email (spam and ham, respectively); the rest are clearly marked. The more email messages in your training files, the better.

```
# #load "spam.cmo";;
# open Spam;;
# let ic = open_in "hamfile_training.txt" in train_ham ic;close_in ic;;
- : unit = ()
# let ic = open_in "spamfile_training.txt" in train_spam ic;close_in ic;;
- : unit = ()
# paul_graham "sex" goodmap badmap goodcount badcount;;
- : float = 0.216727266836569121
# paul_graham "diet" goodmap badmap goodcount badcount;;
- : float = 0.773374476628347907
# spam_prob_of_file "spam/0250.80b7bd444753246734e015af7b6d2d65";;
- : float = 0.8035183840360689
# spam_prob_of_file "test";;
- : float = 0.00369466636815619486
# spam_prob_of_file "test2";;
- : float = 1.54243567250543923e-06
# spam_prob_of_file "spam/0494.a0865131f55d26362a8efad99c37de01";;
- : float = 0.8035183840360689
# spam_prob_of_file "easy_ham/1954.5e99943978d64989611d5bd4814126ab";;
- : float = 3.79551940380821694e-11
```

Things You Might Want

First, a command-line interface to the preceding module is probably a good thing.

```
(** Command Line Utility for Bayesian Spam Library *)

(** first we set up some variable that can be
    changed *)
  let spamfile = ref "";;
  let hamfile = ref "";;
  let input_file = ref stdin;;
  let training_ham = ref false;;
  let training_spam = ref false;;

  (** our simple usage message *)
  let usage_msg = "spam [-spam <SPAMFILE>|-ham <HAMFILE>] ➥
[-t TESTFILE] [-v (verbose mode)]";;


(** Here we use the arg module to parse the command line and
    set the appropriate variables *)
let _ = Arg.parse [
```

```
  ("-spam",Arg.String (fun a -> spamfile:= a;training_spam := true),➦
"Train with spam from FILE");
  ("-ham",Arg.String (fun a -> hamfile := a;training_ham := true), ➦
"Train with ham from FILE");
  ("-t",Arg.String (fun a -> input_file := open_in a),➦
"Use this file instead of stdin");
] (fun x -> ()) usage_msg;;

(** Then run *)

let _ = if !training_ham then
  let ic = open_in !hamfile in
    Spam.train_ham ic;
    close_in ic;
    print_string "Done Training Ham";
    print_newline ()
else if !training_spam then
  let ic = open_in !spamfile in
    Spam.train_spam ic;
    close_in ic;
    print_string "Done Training Spam";
    print_newline ()
else
  let spamprob = Spam.spam_prob_of_channel !input_file in
    Printf.printf "Probability of Spam: %f\n" spamprob;
```

This can be compiled and run after the library is compiled by using the following commands:

```
/home/josh/projects/de-spam $ ocamlc -o command_line spam.cmo command_line.ml
/home/josh/projects/de-spam $ ./command_line -?
./command_line: unknown option `-?'.
spam [-spam <SPAMFILE>|-ham <HAMFILE>] [-t TESTFILE] [-v (verbose mode)]
  -spam Train with spam from FILE
  -ham Train with ham from FILE
  -t Use this file instead of stdin
  -help  Display this list of options
  --help  Display this list of options
/home/josh/projects/de-spam$ ➦
./command_line -t easy_ham/1954.5e99943978d64989611d5bd4814126ab
Probability of Spam: 0.000000
/home/josh/projects/de-spam$ ➦
./command_line -t spam/0494.a0865131f55d26362a8efad99c37de01
Probability of Spam: 0.803518
```

Finally, there is the interface file, which is very short and limits the capability of module users to call only five functions. In many other programming languages, this level of abstraction and encapsulation would be available only at the object level, if at all.

```
(** This interface file restricts the type information and functions that
    can be accessed from outside the module *)

(** {6 Probability of spam functions} *)

(** returns a probability of spam from a given in_channel*)
val spam_prob_of_channel: in_channel -> float;;

(** returns a probability of spam from a given string *)
val spam_prob_of_string: string -> float;;

(** returns a probability of spam from a given file *)
val spam_prob_of_file: string -> float;;

(** {6 Training Functions} *)
(** All of these functions overwrite the ham/spam
    database. *)

(** trains the database in the given ham *)
val train_ham: in_channel -> unit;;

(** trains the database in the given spam *)
val train_spam: in_channel -> unit;;
```

Deficiencies in the Code

There are many deficiencies in this code. Not only does it not take advantage of new developments in the method but there are also other things that can be improved.

How lucky it is, then, that this code is reusable. You could replace your scoring function and recompile your code with only a one-line change in the application. You could even replace the local scoring function with a network-aware module (as you will do in coming chapters). You could also introduce some of the changes to the algorithm to boot.

Conclusion

Hormel has been remarkably good-natured on the whole Spam/spam issue. I know of few companies who would be so understanding if one of their flagship product names were widely applied to such an odious problem. Having eaten my fair share of Spam/spam (both in canned and email form), I want to say "thank you, Hormel" for behaving like a good corporate citizen instead of responding with a full-on lawyer blitz.

This chapter demonstrates how OCaml shines when faced with mathematical code. Not only is the module short in terms of lines of code but it is also easy to understand what is going on. This clarity is a boon for maintenance programmers and students alike.

In the next chapter, you'll create a network-aware scoring module and plug it into the module presented in this chapter. You will be able to work out some of the issues that exist in this code, all while not requiring downstream changes to the code.

## CHAPTER 15

Practical: A Network-Aware Scoring Function

In the last chapter, you built a simple spam detector (well, a simple text classifier that can be used for spam detection). It used an on-disk storage mechanism, which works fine for one person on one machine. However, what if that person uses multiple machines? What if you want to have many people or processes contributing information to the text storage?

This chapter shows you a client-server application to provide this support. You will learn about OCaml network functions as well as threading support. You will use threads because the fork function is not implemented under Windows, and this code is to be cross-platform. Don't worry; threads are covered in Chapter 24 in depth. For now, the usage is pretty simple (and not exceptionally robust).

Supporting Clients and Servers

OCaml has support for sockets and network programming in the Unix library. Client sockets are easier to deal with than server sockets, as you might expect. Server sockets (often) need to handle many clients, synchronization, and communication.

The Unix library provides high-level functions for creating both servers and clients. The server-creation functions do not work on Windows, but the client functions do. Because not all of the functions are available, only functions that are cross-platform are presented.

Creating a Simple Server

First, have a look at a very simple server. It handles only one request, but it comes with an example echo server. The signature for the module looks like this:

```
module SimpleServer:
  sig
    val echo_server: string -> int -> unit
    val server: string -> int -> (in_channel -> out_channel -> unit) -> unit
  end;;
```

The echo server is a function that takes an IP address string and a port number. The other function takes these arguments and a third argument that is itself a function that takes two channels as arguments. The implementation for this is longer than the signature, but it is still not long. The following 30 lines implement both the echo server and the generic server. The code also sets the REUSEADDR flag on the socket, which is important if you stop and restart the server often.

```
module SimpleServer =
  struct
    let server_setup ip portnum =
      let s = Unix.socket Unix.PF_INET Unix.SOCK_STREAM 0 in
      let sockad =
                Unix.ADDR_INET ((Unix.inet_addr_of_string ip),portnum) in
                (
                  ignore(Unix.bind s sockad);
                  ignore(Unix.listen s 10);
                  ignore(Unix.setsockopt s Unix.SO_REUSEADDR true);
                  s
                ) ;;

    let echo_server i p =
      let s = server_setup i p in
      let a = Unix.accept s in
      let (i,o) = ((Unix.in_channel_of_descr (fst a)),
                   (Unix.out_channel_of_descr (fst a))) in
      try
                while true do
                  Scanf.fscanf i "%c" (fun x -> Printf.fprintf o "%c" x);
                  flush o
                done
      with End_of_file -> Unix.shutdown (fst a) Unix.SHUTDOWN_ALL;;
    let server i p f =
      let s = server_setup i p in
      let a = Unix.accept s in
      let (i,o) = ((Unix.in_channel_of_descr (fst a)),
                   (Unix.out_channel_of_descr (fst a))) in
      f i o
  end;;
```

You can use this code right from the toplevel. The echo server returns only after the socket is closed by the client, so you should expect that.

```
josh@sputnik ~/de-spam
$ ledit ./thr
        Objective Caml version 3.09.0
```

```
# #use "test2.ml";;
module SimpleServer :
  sig
    val server_setup : string -> int -> Unix.file_descr
    val echo_server : string -> int -> unit
    val server : string -> int -> (in_channel -> out_channel -> 'a) -> 'a
  end
# SimpleServer.echo_server "192.168.1.101" 8889;;
- : unit = ()
#
```

To connect to the server socket, you can use telnet if your system has it. On most telnet implementations, you must use ^] to get to the prompt and then type exit to close the connection.

```
josh@sputnik ~/de-spam
$ telnet 192.168.1.101 8889
Trying 192.168.1.101...
Connected to 192.168.1.101.
Escape character is '^]'.
hello
hello
there
there
how are you?
how are you?
?
telnet> quit
Connection closed.
```

You also can use OCaml to make the client connection by using the open_connection function in the Unix library. The client function works on Windows and Unix (and Unix-like) operating systems.

```
josh@sputnik ~/de-spam
$ ledit ./thr
        Objective Caml version 3.09.0

# let b = Unix.open_connection (Unix.ADDR_INET ((Unix.inet_addr_of_string "192.1
68.1.101"),8889));;
Exception: Unix.Unix_error (Unix.ECONNREFUSED, "connect", "").
# let b = Unix.open_connection (Unix.ADDR_INET ((Unix.inet_addr_of_string "192.1
68.1.101"),8889));;
val b : in_channel * out_channel = (<abstr>, <abstr>)
```

```
# Printf.fprintf (snd b) "Hello world\n" ;;
- : unit = ()
# flush (snd b);;
- : unit = ()
# input_line (fst b);;
- : string = "Hello world"
# Unix.shutdown_connection (fst b);;
- : unit = ()
#
```

The server must be running when you try to connect; otherwise, you get a Unix_error exception such as the one shown (ECONNREFUSED). You should also note the use of flush, which can be important for socket communication when using OCaml channels.

Implementing a Spam Server

The server needs a protocol. Line-oriented ASCII protocols are easy to implement and debug, so that is what you will use. The server responds to one of three keywords: Query, Ham, and Spam. These keywords are followed by a word and then, for updates, are followed by an integer indicating the number of times the word has been seen. A query will return a floating point number indicating the spaminess of the token, whereas the updates will simply tell you whether they are okay.

```
Query chess
|0.400000|
Spam lotto 32
OK!
```

Although the signature for this server is not short, it can be made very short because only one function is really available to be called by users of this function. The signature file comes at the end of this chapter, along with changes to the signature presented in the last chapter. (The server needs some information to function, including frequency information.)

The following is the signature for the StringMap module (which is based on the Map standard module). This map is what holds the frequency information about tokens in the emails. The server needs to know about this type so that it can update the ham and spam maps.

```
module StringMap :
  sig
    type key = String.t
    type 'a t = 'a Map.Make(String).t
    val empty : 'a t
    val is_empty : 'a t -> bool
    val add : key -> 'a -> 'a t -> 'a t
    val find : key -> 'a t -> 'a
    val remove : key -> 'a t -> 'a t
    val mem : key -> 'a t -> bool
    val iter : (key -> 'a -> unit) -> 'a t -> unit
    val map : ('a -> 'b) -> 'a t -> 'b t
```

```
  val mapi : (key -> 'a -> 'b) -> 'a t -> 'b t
  val fold : (key -> 'a -> 'b -> 'b) -> 'a t -> 'b -> 'b
  val compare : ('a -> 'a -> int) -> 'a t -> 'a t -> int
  val equal : ('a -> 'a -> bool) -> 'a t -> 'a t -> bool
end
```

The kind of server shown following is a select-based server, which does not use threads or processes to handle new connections. The select function, when given a list of file descriptors, returns only those file descriptors that are ready for some kind of operations (reading, writing, or out-of-band). You won't use the out-of-band stuff, but you will use reading and writing.

What this enables you to do is multiplex connections through a single server. And you do not have to worry about the kind of concurrency issues that would exist if you were using a multithread or multiprocess approach. Select-based servers are very efficient and are often used in high-performance applications.

```
module SelectServer :
  sig
    type token_type =
        Spam of string * int
      | Query of string
      | Ham of string * int
```

The token type is used only inside the module. It is used primarily to be able to perform different actions based on different tokens. The next example shows the connection type, which is used to implement buffering for incoming and outgoing input/output (I/O).

The connection type uses a queue to handle output. Because of the nature of I/O, it can be difficult to sync up the input and the output. By using a buffer for the input and a queue for the output, these concerns are minimized. The queue is a Last/In/First/Out (LIFO) queue, so the responses are always in sequence with the input, without having to write overly complicated serialization code. You also can use the queue to handle the input and then the output, again avoiding problems with concurrent access.

```
    type connection = {
      fd : Unix.file_descr;
      addr : Unix.sockaddr;
      mutable input_buffer : string;
      output_queue : token_type Queue.t;
    }
```

Almost all the functions, other than the run function, are helper functions that make operations easier to perform and easier to debug.

```
    val add_string : connection -> bool
    val server_setup : string -> int -> Unix.file_descr
    val newconn : Unix.file_descr * Unix.sockaddr -> connection
    val get_token : Scanf.Scanning.scanbuf -> string * int
    val get_score : Scanf.Scanning.scanbuf -> string * int * int
    val scan_buffer : Scanf.Scanning.scanbuf -> connection -> int -> unit
    val process_data : ('a * connection) list -> unit
```

```
    val run_results :
      connection ->
      int Spam.StringMap.t ->
      int Spam.StringMap.t ->
      int -> int -> int Spam.StringMap.t * int Spam.StringMap.t * int * int
    val results :
      ('a * connection) list ->
      int Spam.StringMap.t ->
      int Spam.StringMap.t ->
      int -> int -> int Spam.StringMap.t * int Spam.StringMap.t * int * int
    val multiplex_server :
      (Unix.file_descr * connection) list ->
      float ->
      int Spam.StringMap.t ->
      int Spam.StringMap.t ->
      int ->
      int ->
      (Unix.file_descr * connection) list * int Spam.StringMap.t *
      int Spam.StringMap.t * int * int
    val newcon :
      Unix.file_descr ->
      (Unix.file_descr * connection) list ->
      int Spam.StringMap.t -> int Spam.StringMap.t -> int -> int -> 'a
    val run_server : string -> int -> 'a
  end
```

A Working Server

Now you see the code for the library that implements the server. The preceding signature indicates that this library relies upon the Spam library from the previous chapter to supply some things. You can see that this library is also included.

```
module SelectServer =
  struct
    type token_type = Spam of string * int |
                Query of string | Ham of string * int

    type connection = {fd:Unix.file_descr;
                            addr:Unix.sockaddr;
                            mutable input_buffer: string;
                            output_queue: token_type Queue.t};;
```

In the add_string function, reading 0 bytes means that the socket has been closed on the client side. You know it is closed because the select operation returns only sockets that have data ready for reading. If a socket is ready for reading but has no data in it, the client has disconnected, and the connection should be cleaned up. Although the add_string function does not clean up, by returning a Boolean value it is used later to filter the list of connections and remove unconnected sockets.

```
    let add_string conn =
       let strbuf = String.create 32 in
       let res = Unix.read conn.fd strbuf 0 32 in
          match res with
                    0 -> Printf.printf "Failed to get anyting!\n";flush stdout;false
                    | n when res < 32 ->
                    conn.input_buffer <- conn.input_buffer ^ (String.sub strbuf 0 res);➥
true
                    | _ -> conn.input_buffer <- conn.input_buffer ^ strbuf;true
```

The server_setup function takes a string that represents an IP address and a port number.
Two important operations that this function performs include setting the REUSEADDR option
and setting the socket to nonblocking.

By setting the server socket to RESUSEADDR (via the Unix.setsockopt function), you tell the
operating system not to keep the socket unavailable if you shut the server down. This enables
you to restart the server without waiting too long for the socket timeout.

Setting the socket to nonblocking is important when you are implementing select-based
servers. Socket nonblocking means that any operation on that socket does not block (although
it might block through an exception). Because there is no way to unblock an operation after it
gets blocked, using nonblocking I/O can be a big win when writing server applications.

```
    let server_setup ip portnum =
      let s = Unix.socket Unix.PF_INET Unix.SOCK_STREAM 0 in
      let sockad =
            Unix.ADDR_INET ((Unix.inet_addr_of_string ip),portnum) in
                Unix.bind s sockad;
                Unix.listen s 10;
                Unix.setsockopt s Unix.SO_REUSEADDR true;
                Unix.set_nonblock s;
                s
```

The next three functions are just convenience functions designed to make other functions
more readable. Although the scan_buffer function is long for a convenience function, it is that
length because of the way the socket input is being tokenized using Scanf. All the input that
has been buffered (into the input_buffer) is processed at this step. Any action that should be
performed is added to the queue to be acted upon later.

```
    let newconn (fdsc,ad) = {fd=fdsc;
                                addr=ad;
                                input_buffer = "";
                                output_queue = Queue.create ()}


    let get_token sb = Scanf.bscanf sb "%s@\n%n" (fun t count -> (t,count))
    let get_score sb = Scanf.bscanf sb "%s %d@\n%n" (fun t freq count -> ➥
(t,freq,count))
    let rec scan_buffer sb conn taken =
      let total = try
```

```
Scanf.bscanf sb "%s@ %n" (fun q count -> match q with
        "Query" -> let (t,newcount) = get_token sb in
                        Queue.push (Query t) conn.output_queue;
                        (count + newcount)
      | "Ham" -> let (t,freq,newcount) = get_score sb in
                        Queue.push (Ham (t,freq)) conn.output_queue;
                        (count + newcount)
      | "Spam" -> let (t,freq,newcount) = get_score sb in
                        Queue.push (Spam (t,freq)) conn.output_queue;
                        (count + newcount)
      | "" -> raise End_of_file
      | _ -> count)
    with End_of_file -> 0
  in
    match total with
        0 -> (if (taken = 0) then
                  ()
              else
                let strlen = (String.length conn.input_buffer) - total in
                      match strlen with
                          0 -> conn.input_buffer <- ""
                        | _ -> try
                                 conn.input_buffer <- String.sub
                                     conn.input_buffer taken strlen
                               with (Invalid_argument m) ->
                                   Printf.printf "%s %d %d\n"
                                       conn.input_buffer
                                       taken
                                       strlen;
                                   conn.input_buffer <- "")
      | _ -> scan_buffer sb conn total
```

The next function, process_data, makes it easier to call the previous function. After that, the function that is used to process the waiting outputs queue items.

```
let process_data conn_list =
    List.iter (fun (y,conn) -> let sb = Scanf.Scanning.from_string conn.input_buffer
in
    scan_buffer sb conn 0) conn_list


let rec run_results conn goodmap badmap goodcount badcount =
    match conn with
        n when (Queue.is_empty conn.output_queue) ->
                                goodmap, badmap, goodcount, badcount
      | _ -> let nextv = Queue.pop conn.output_queue
            in
                match nextv with
```

```
            Query m -> let outst =
                       Printf.sprintf "|%f|\n"
                       (Spam.paul_graham m goodmap badmap goodcount badcount)
                       in
                              Unix.write conn.fd outst 0 (String.length outst);
                   run_results conn goodmap badmap goodcount badcount
            | Spam (m,f) -> let curval = try
                Spam.StringMap.find m badmap
            with Not_found -> 0 in
            let outst = Printf.sprintf "|%d|\n" (badcount + f) in
                Unix.write conn.fd outst 0 (String.length outst);
                   run_results conn goodmap (Spam.StringMap.add m (f + curval)➥
badmap) goodcount (badcount + f)
                | Ham (m,f) -> let curval = try
                Spam.StringMap.find m goodmap
            with Not_found -> 0 in
            let outst = Printf.sprintf "|%d|\n" (goodcount + f) in
                Unix.write conn.fd outst 0 (String.length outst);
                   run_results conn (Spam.StringMap.add m (f + curval) goodmap) ➥
badmap (goodcount +f) badcount
     let rec results connlist goodmap badmap goodcount badcount =
        match connlist with
                   [] -> goodmap,badmap,goodcount,badcount
          | (f,h) :: t -> let (g,b,gc,bc) = run_results h goodmap badmap ➥
goodcount badcount in
                     results t g b gc bc
```

The select function is called twice: once for file descriptors ready to read and once for descriptors ready to write. The main reason for this double call is that select returns if any of the three sets of descriptors is ready. Because most of the sockets are available to write most of the time, the function goes into a tight loop. To avoid that loop, select is called twice. Although this double call is not the best configuration for high performance, it is the best configuration for efficiency and low overhead.

```
    let multiplex_server conn_list timeout (goodmap: int Spam.StringMap.t) ➥
badmap goodcount badcount =
        let sock_list = List.map (fun (m,y) -> m) conn_list in
        let (r,_,_) = Unix.select sock_list [] [] timeout in
        let (to_shutdown: Unix.file_descr list) = List.filter (fun x -> not ➥
(add_string (List.assoc x conn_list))) r
        in
        let (_,w,_) = Unix.select [] sock_list [] timeout in
                process_data conn_list;
                Printf.printf "Writing to: %d\n" (List.length w);
                Printf.printf "Reading from %d of %d\n" (List.length to_shutdown) ➥
(List.length r);
```

```
                  let (gmap,bmap,gcount,bcount) = results
                  (List.filter (fun (x,y) -> List.mem x w) conn_list) goodmap badmap➡
goodcount badcount in
                  let (bad,good) = List.partition (fun (x,y) -> List.mem x➡
to_shutdown) conn_list in
                     Printf.printf "Shutting down: %d of %d\n" (List.length bad) ➡
(List.length good);
                     flush stdout;
                     List.iter (fun (x,y) ->
                                try
                                    Unix.shutdown x Unix.SHUTDOWN_ALL
                                    with (Unix.Unix_error(Unix.ENOTCONN,_,_)) -> ()) ➡
bad;
                  (good,gmap,bmap,gcount,bcount)
    let rec newcon server_socket connlist goodmap badmap goodcount badcount =➡
 let a = try
      let m = Unix.accept server_socket in
                 Printf.printf "Got Connection from %s\n" (Unix.getnameinfo (snd m) ➡
[Unix.NI_NOFQDN]).Unix.ni_hostname;
                 flush stdout;Some m
    with Unix.Unix_error (Unix.EAGAIN,_,_) -> None
      | Sys.Break -> List.iter (fun (x,y) -> try Unix.shutdown x Unix.SHUTDOWN_ALL ➡
with (Unix.Unix_error(Unix.ENOTCONN,_,_)) -> ()) connlist;➡
Unix.shutdown server_socket Unix.SHUTDOWN_ALL;exit(1)
    in match a with
                  Some nc -> let (clst,gmap,bmap,gcount,bcount) = multiplex_server➡
(((fst nc),(newconn nc)) :: connlist) 12.0 goodmap badmap goodcount badcount in
                  newcon server_socket clst gmap bmap gcount bcount
         | None -> let (clst,gmap,bmap,gcount,bcount) = multiplex_server ➡
connlist 12.0 goodmap badmap goodcount badcount in
                  newcon server_socket clst gmap bmap gcount bcount
```

This run_server function is the main function that developers and users of this library actually call. Normally, this function does not return; it forms the main event loop of the server and loops forever, serving requests.

An uncaught exception can propagate up to this level. If an exception does propagate to this level, the server will probably fail (this server is not particularly robust).

```
let run_server i p =
  let s = server_setup i p in
  newcon s [] Spam.goodmap Spam.badmap Spam.goodcount Spam.badcount
end;;
```

The library is not a working server—there is still some code that needs to be written to make it a working server. There is a check in the main thread that looks for a file and will exit if it finds this file. This is the simplistic way to implement it; you might want to add an administrative port for signaling. You also can use signals or even the Event library (which is covered later in this book).

Building the Server

Using OCamlMakefile, a small makefile can be constructed to build the example command-line server. Note the THREADS variable, which is required for the compilation to succeed (threaded programs need this variable in the OCamlMakefile).

```
SOURCES = spam.mll spam_server.ml server.ml
RESULT  = server
THREADS = yes
PACKS: unix
all: native-code
-include /usr/local/share/OCamlMakefile
```

The server can be run from the command line (remember to supply the correct server IP address and ports for your system). This server should run unmodified on Win32 and Linux. Unfortunately, a server all by itself is of limited usefulness—you'll need a client, too.

Providing Client Functions

You probably want to use client functions instead of making developers develop their own. This is easier than it sounds, and the signature shows that the client module can be kept quite short.

```
type token_type = Spam of string |
    Query of string | Ham of string
module Client:
sig
  val connect: string -> int -> unit
  val query: string -> float
  val ham: string -> int -> int
  val spam: string -> int -> int
  val disconnect: unit -> unit
end;;
```

The implementation is only a little bit longer and is stored in the same file as the server code to make things easier.

```
module Client =
  struct
    let cons = ref (stdin,stdout)
    let connect ip portnum = let sockadd =
      Unix.ADDR_INET((Unix.inet_addr_of_string ip),portnum) in
    let c = Unix.open_connection sockadd in
      cons := c
    let query tok = Printf.fprintf (snd cons.contents) "Query %s\n" tok;flush➥
(snd cons.contents);
      Scanf.fscanf (fst cons.contents) "|%f|\n" (fun x -> x)
    let ham tok count = Printf.fprintf  (snd cons.contents) "Ham %s %d\n" tok➥
count;flush (snd cons.contents);
      Scanf.fscanf (fst cons.contents) "|%d|\n" (fun x -> x)
```

```
    let spam tok count = Printf.fprintf  (snd cons.contents) "Spam %s %d\n" tok➥
count;flush (snd cons.contents);
       Scanf.fscanf (fst cons.contents) "|%d|\n" (fun x -> x)
    let disconnect () = Unix.shutdown_connection (fst cons.contents)
  end;;
```

You can provide a working command-line client. The command-line interface to the
client module is actually longer than the module itself.

```
type action_type = Query of string | Spam of string | Ham of string;;

let usage = "client [-?] [-server IP_ADDRESS] [-port PORT_NUMER] ➥
[-query WORD] (-spam WORD | -ham WORD)] [-count INT] \n";;

let ipadd = ref "192.168.1.26";;
let port = ref 8889;;
let action = ref (Query "chess");;
let count = ref 0

let specs = [
("-server", Arg.String (fun x -> ipadd := x),": IP address of the server");
("-port", Arg.Int (fun x -> port := x),": Port number to use");
("-query",Arg.String (fun x -> action := (Query x)),": Query a word");
("-count",Arg.Int (fun x -> count := x),"What is the count");
("-spam", Arg.String (fun x -> action := (Spam x)),
 ": Update a spam word (requires -score)");
("-ham",Arg.String (fun x -> action := (Ham x)),
 ": Update a ham word (requires -score)");
];;

  let _ = Arg.parse specs (fun x -> ()) usage in
  let _ = Spam_server.Client.connect !ipadd !port in
  let _ = match !action with
      Query m -> Printf.printf "%s is %f spam\n" m (Spam_server.Client.query m)
    | Spam m -> let n = Spam_server.Client.spam m !count in
                Printf.printf "OK!\n"
    | Ham m -> let n = Spam_server.Client.ham m !count in
                Printf.printf "OK!\n"
  in
    Spam_server.Client.disconnect ();;
```

Building the Command-Line Client

Using OCamlMakefile, a small makefile can be constructed to build the example command-
line client. Assuming that you have saved the command-line client in a file called
client_app.ml, the following OcamlMakefile should work for you (you might need to change
the include line and point that to where you have installed the OCamlMakefile):

```
SOURCES = spam.mll spam_server.ml client_app.ml
RESULT  = client
all: native-code
PACKS: unix
-include /opt/godi/share/OCamlMakefile
```

This code builds an executable, which can be used to query and update the server. The command-line client can be used alongside other clients without interfering. It produces the following output (assuming that the server is running):

```
josh@sputnik ~/de-spam
$ ./client -query hello -server 192.168.1.26 -port 8889
hello is 0.010000 spam
```

Conclusion

This chapter covered a lot of ground. It introduced network communication and showed a select-based socket server.

This chapter is also one of the more practical examples of modules and code reuse you have been given. The fact that the scoring function could be integrated so easily is a testament to the power and flexibility of the OCaml module section.

Chapter 16 covers ocamllex and ocamlyacc. These tools give access to regular expressions and a powerful typesafe parsing environment. They can be used to tackle problems as diverse as log file parsing to language construction. In fact, OCaml (and all meta-language [ML] family languages) have a lot of features that make writing compilers easier.

Ocamllex and Ocamlyacc

You might have heard of Lex and Yacc. Lex, the Lexical Analyzer Generator, is a tool that helps you build programs that are built around regular expressions. Yacc, Yet Another Compiler Compiler, is a program for building interpreters and compilers from grammars that you define. Although you do not have to use these tools together (people often use just Lex or Yacc with a custom lexer), but they are often used together.

This chapter presents ocamllex and ocamlyacc. You will see examples of how to build applications with both, including a word counting utility, a Reverse Polish Notation (RPN) calculator, and a configuration file language.

Ocamllex and ocamlyacc both have syntax that is very similar to Lex and Yacc. These two tools have a long history in the Unix world, and there are several books and web sites dedicated to their use. The good news for OCaml users is that many of the examples and discussion are applicable to ocamllex and ocamlyacc.

Lexing Has No Relation to Luthor

Lexing is the process of breaking up a stream of input into a stream of tokens. The difference between input and tokens is that tokens are categorized, and input is not. Consider the following sentence: The Quick Brown Fox is running around the henhouse. One way to tokenize this sentence is to break it up into nonwhitespace tokens, which would yield nine tokens of type string. Another way is to break it up into characters, which would yield 49 tokens of type char. This action of tokenization is what ocamllex is designed to do; it performs this tokenization based on rules that are expressed in regular expressions.

Ocamllex is actually a program generator—it takes an input file that describes a set of regular expressions and a set of actions associated with those regular expressions. The OCaml source code is actually generated by ocamllex from the ocamllex source file.

Lex was created before most programming languages had access to rich regular expression libraries. Even now, when regular expressions are prominent, Lex enables you to tackle problems in ways that other programming languages cannot (even Perl).

One of the advantages is the capability to define actions, called semantic actions, when a given regular expression matches. The following example, which helps to clarify, is an implementation of a program like the wc program commonly found on Unix (and Unix-like) systems. Given an input file, it returns the number of lines, words, and characters in that file.

```
rule tokens = parse
    ['\n' '\013'] { `Line }
  | ([^ ' ' '\t' '\n' '\013']+ as word) { `Word (String.length word)}
  | [' ' '\t'] { `Whitespace }
  | eof { `Eof }
{
  let _ =
    let lb = Lexing.from_channel (open_in Sys.argv.(1)) in
    let rec countemup lbuf words chars lines =
      let tok = tokens lbuf in
        match tok with
              `Line -> countemup lbuf words (chars + 1) (lines + 1)
          | `Whitespace -> countemup lbuf words (chars + 1) lines
          | `Word n -> countemup lbuf (words + 1) (chars + n) lines
          | `Eof -> Printf.printf " %i %i %i %s\n" lines words chars Sys.argv.(1)
      in
      countemup lb 0 0 0;;
}
```

The word count this code produces is identical to the output of the Unix wc command.

Compiling ocamllex programs requires an extra step, which is the processing of the ocamllex file into an .ml file, which is then compiled and used like any other OCaml source code file.

Why Use a Lexer Generator?

Given the fact that most languages (OCaml included) support regular expressions, why would you even want to use a lexer generator at all? There are a couple of reasons to use one. For starters, using a tool such as ocamllex makes maintaining the code very easy (this is especially true when you want to extend the program later).

Anther reason to use a program like Lex is that the code is often much shorter than the hand-coded alternatives (shorter code is code that has fewer bug opportunities).

Suppose that you want to create a multifunction RPN calculator. You could write code to parse input using Scanf or using the OCaml matching functions, but you could also implement it by using ocamllex.

One benefit of using ocamllex is that most of the features you would have to implement are already done in the ocamllex state machine. The following example shows a multifunction calculator implemented in ocamllex. The calculator code automatically converts from and to integers (ints) and floating-point numbers (floats) for you.

```
{
  type number = Int of int | Float of float;;
  let current = Stack.create ()

  let add x y = match x,y with
      Int n,Int m -> Int (n + m)
    | Int n,Float m -> Float ((float_of_int n) +. m)
    | Float n,Int m -> Float ((float_of_int m) +. n)
    | Float n,Float m -> Float ( m +. n);;
```

```
  let subtract x y = match x,y with
      Int n,Int m -> Int (n - m)
    | Int n,Float m -> Float ((float_of_int n) -. m)
    | Float n,Int m -> Float ((float_of_int m) -. n)
    | Float n,Float m -> Float (m -. n);;
  let divide x y = match x,y with
      Int n,Int m -> Int (n / m)
    | Int n,Float m -> Float ((float_of_int n) /. m)
    | Float n,Int m -> Float ((float_of_int m) /. n)
    | Float n,Float m -> Float (m /. n);;
  let multi x y = match x,y with
      Int n,Int m -> Int (n * m)
    | Int n,Float m -> Float ((float_of_int n) *. m)
    | Float n,Int m -> Float ((float_of_int m) *. n)
    | Float n,Float m -> Float (m *. n);;
  let string_of_number x = match x with
      Int n -> Printf.sprintf "%i" n
    | Float n -> Printf.sprintf "%f" n;;

}


rule tokens = parse
    [' ' '\n'] { tokens lexbuf }
  | (['0'-'9']+ as num) { Stack.push (Int (int_of_string num)) current }
  | ['0'-'9']+'.'['0'-'9']* as fl { Stack.push (Float (float_of_string fl))➡
current}
  | '-' { let f = Stack.pop current in let s = Stack.pop current in
                    Stack.push (subtract s f) current}
  | '+' { let f = Stack.pop current in let s = Stack.pop current in
                    Stack.push (add s f) current }
  | '%' { let f = Stack.pop current in let s = Stack.pop current in
                    Stack.push f current;Stack.push s current }
  | '/' { let f = Stack.pop current in let s = Stack.pop current in
                    Stack.push (divide s f) current }
  | '*' { let f = Stack.pop current in let s = Stack.pop current in
                    Stack.push (multi s f) current }
  | 'p' { Printf.printf "%s\n" (string_of_number (Stack.top current));
                    flush stdout}
  | 'q' { exit 0 }


{
  let _ = let lb = Lexing.from_channel stdin in
    while (true) do
      tokens lb
    done;;
}
```

If you want to add a new keyword, it is very easy to do. If you want to add a function for printing out the current stack, you can add it without having to do a lot of work.

Building ocamllex programs requires an extra step. You can build the preceding example with the following commands:

```
/home/josh/$ ocamllex.exe calc.mll
11 states, 279 transitions, table size 1182 bytes
/home/josh/$
/home/josh/$ ocamlc.exe -o calc.exe calc.ml
/home/josh/$ ./calc.exe
23
10+
p
33
q
```

Using Ocamllex

Now that you have seen a couple of examples, you'll get more detail about what is really going on in those examples. You'll learn more about the general lexing commands (which are in the standard library) and the lexing buffers.

Lexbuf

The operations of the lexer are performed on a structure called a lexbuf, which is a structure with fields that have a lot of information about the state of the current buffer. This includes the current position (lex_curr_pos), which is an integer showing the number of characters from the beginning. There is also a field that indicates whether the end of the file has been reached (lex_eof_reached).

```
type lexbuf = {
            refill_buff : lexbuf -> unit;
            mutable lex_buffer : string;
            mutable lex_buffer_len : int;
            mutable lex_abs_pos : int;
            mutable lex_start_pos : int;
            mutable lex_curr_pos : int;
            mutable lex_last_pos : int;
            mutable lex_last_action : int;
            mutable lex_eof_reached : bool;
            mutable lex_mem : int array;
            mutable lex_start_p : position;
            mutable lex_curr_p : position;
}
```

You do not normally interact with a lexbuf yourself (except perhaps for the position fields); instead, you use the functions found in the lexing library, which provides functions that perform operations on lexbuf structures (discussed a bit later).

Creating Lexing Buffers

Lexing buffers can be created from strings using the from_string function and from input channels using the from_channel function.

They also can be created from functions. The from_function creates a buffer that passes a string and an integer to the function when more data should be read. The integer specifies the maximum number of characters that should be put into the string passed, and the function should return the actual number of characters.

Positions

A position is a type that describes a specific location in a source. If there is a filename, it is stored in pos_fname; otherwise, it is blank. The pos_lnum is the line number the position is at, and pos_bol is the position of the beginning of the current line. The pos_cnum is the absolute position (in characters) of the current buffer. The absolute position is indexed from 0.

```
type position = {
                pos_fname : string;
                pos_lnum : int;
                pos_bol : int;
                pos_cnum : int;
}
```

There are functions that return positions from a lexbuf. These functions (Lexing.lexeme_start_p and Lexing.lexeme_end_p) return the position of a match start or end. These functions are normally used in ocamllex semantic actions.

You should understand that only the pos_cnum file is actually updated by the lexer. If you want the other fields to be accurate, you must update them yourself. The fields in the position structure are not mutable, but the fields in the lexbuf are. So if you want to update this information, you must update it in the lexbuf instead of updating the position. This is discussed in more detail in upcoming examples; just keep this information in mind.

Ocamllex Source File

Ocamllex processes a source file (usually named with an .mll extension) into an OCaml source file. The language used in the ocamllex source file is very similar to (but not exactly the same as) an OCaml source file.

An ocamllex source file is divided into three sections: header, body, and trailer. The header and trailer are optional and can contain any valid OCaml code.

Header

The header is the first optional part of an ocamllex file. The code in this section is copied verbatim into the generated OCaml source file. This code must be enclosed in curly braces.

Note Ocamllex generated code can use other OCaml libraries just like normal OCaml source code.

This section of the file is used for code that you want to have implemented before the other two sections. In the preceding calculator example, this section was where the stack used by the program was set up. This section is also where you should open libraries you want to use.

Body

The body of the ocamllex file is the only part of the file that is not optional. The `rule` keyword is used to assign a label to a given entry point.

An entry point is a value that can be called with a `lexbuf` as an argument. Entry points can be thought of as the lexing function. Entry points must be valid OCaml identifiers and they must start with a lowercase letter. Each entry point reads characters from a `lexbuf`, and a match is attempted with the regular expressions in the rule. When a match occurs, the action specified for that regular expression is executed. If there is no match, a `Failure` exception is raised.

The entry point can be of two kinds: `parse` or `shortest`. In the calculator example, you used `parse`. You will probably use `parse` for most of your coding (you'll learn the differences between the two when the chapter discusses how input is actually matched).

Actions associated with each regular expression can contain any valid OCaml code. In the preceding calculator example, all the computation is done in the semantic actions.

These actions are where you would update the `lexbuf` position (if you want to do that).

```
let update_position lex_buf =
  let pos = lex_buf.Lexing.lex_curr_p  in
  lex_buf.Lexing.lex_curr_p <- { pos with
  Lexing.pos_lnum = pos.Lexing.pos_lnum + 1;
  Lexing.pos_bol = pos.Lexing.pos_cnum };;
```

For example, the previous function could be called when a new line is encountered. It would update the unmanaged portions of the position structure, enabling the information to be used.

You also can assign variables that contain regular expressions in the body. They can then be used just like regular expressions in the regexp section. For example, if you often use the following regexp for an IP address, you could assign that regexp to a value and use it instead (which would make your rule cleaner): let ip_addr = "['0'-'9']?['0'-'9']?['0'-'9']'➡ .'['0'-'9']?['0'-'9']?['0'-'9']'.'['0'-'9']?['0'-'9']?['0'-'9']'.'['0'-'9']? ['0'-'9']?['0'-'9']" You can see this technique in the following ocamllex fragment:

```
let ip_addr = "['0'-'9']?['0'-'9']?['0'-'9']'.'['0'-'9']?['0'-'9']?['0'-'9']'➡
  .'['0'-'9']?['0'-'9']?['0'-'9']'.'['0'-'9']?['0'-'9']?['0'-'9']"
```

```
rule tokens = parse
  ip_addr { Printf.printf "%s" (Lexing.lexeme lexbuf) }
| ip_addr as b { Printf.printf "%s" b }
```

The preceding code demonstrates two ways to access the match string. Because they are both the same, only the first one would be called if you actually ran this code.

Regular Expressions   Ocamllex supports regular expressions natively. The format for the regular expressions follows OCaml code restrictions with regard to escaping and formatting. In Table 16-1, you see the most common regular expression codes used in OCaml.

Table 16-1. *Regular Expressions Reference*

Regular Expression	Description
'char'	Char literal; for example, '\t' would match a tab character.
"string"	String literal; matches everything in that string.
_	Underscore; matches any character (including newline).
[set of char]	A character class; can be a range such as ['0'-'9'], which matches any number from 1 to 9. The characters are enclosed in single quotes.
[^ negative set]	A negative character class; matches any character not in the set. For example, [^'0'-'9'] would match any char that is not a number.
eof	Matches the end of file.
#	Matches the difference between two character classes. For example, ['0'-'9'] # ['3"5'] would match numbers from 0 to 9 that are not 3 or 5.
|	Matches one regexp or the other (can be more than two). For example, ['0'-'9'] | ['3"5'] | ['a'-'z'] would match any character from 0 to 9 or from a to z.
*	Matches zero or more of the previous regexp. For example, 'a'* would match "", "a", "aa", "aaa", and even "aaaaaaaaaaaaaaaaaaaaaaaaa".
+	Matches one or more of the previous regexp (basically the same as the previous statement except that there must be at least one of the regexp).
?	Matches zero or one of the previous regexp; 'a'?'b' would match "ab" or "b".
regexp1regexp2	Regexps automatically concatenate. For example, ['a'-'z']+['0'-'9']+ would match one or more lowercase letters followed by one or more numbers.
(regexp)	A grouping operator; often used with the as keyword.
Regexp as ident	Assigns the match to the ident name. For example, (['a'-'z' 'A'-'Z']+ as string) would enable you to use the ID string instead of using Lexing.lexeme to get the information about the match.
ident	Refers to the variable name set to a regexp using a let binding. For example, let myreg = ['0'-'9']+, which can then be used by referring to the ident named myreg. This is a good way to improve the readability of complex regular expressions.

How Input Is Matched   If you are using the parse keyword, expressions are matched longest first, and if an equal-length match is found, the order of precedence is used. (This is the normal case.)

If you use the shortest keyword (instead of parse), the shortest match is used. This has some interesting consequences, including the fact that repetition in regular expressions might not work the way you think it should. For example, using shortest and the following string "hello" with the regexp ['a'-'z']+ would yield each character of the string as a match (because of the one-or-more nature of the +) instead of the whole string.

After input is matched, you can access the matched string by using the as keyword or the Lexing.lexeme functions. The most common function used is Lexing.lexeme lexbuf, which returns the match string from the last match. Following is a short example that shows the difference between the parse and shortest keywords.

```
{

  let example_string = "Hello an example string"
  let print_error msg lbuf  = Printf.eprintf "%s at %i\n" msg ➥
(Lexing.lexeme_start_p lbuf).Lexing.pos_cnum

  let rec all_tokens lxr lbuf = ignore(try
    lxr lbuf
  with x -> raise x);
    all_tokens lxr lbuf


}


rule with_parse = parse
    ['H' 'h'][^ ' ']+ { print_string (Lexing.lexeme lexbuf);
                                             print_newline () }
  | ['a' - 'z' ' ']+ { print_string (Lexing.lexeme lexbuf);
                                             print_newline () }
  | eof { raise End_of_file }
and with_shortest = shortest
    ['H' 'h'][^ ' ']+ { print_string (Lexing.lexeme lexbuf);
                                             print_newline () }
  | ['a' - 'z' ' ']+ { print_string (Lexing.lexeme lexbuf);
                                             print_newline () }
  | eof { raise End_of_file }

{


  let _ = let lb = Lexing.from_string example_string in
    try
      all_tokens with_parse lb
    with Failure(m) -> print_error m lb
      | End_of_file -> ()

  let _ = let lb = Lexing.from_string example_string in
    try
      all_tokens with_shortest lb
    with Failure(m) -> print_error m lb
      | End_of_file -> ()


}
```

Compiling this code and running it yields the following ouput:

```
Hello
 an example string
He
l
l
o

a
n

e
x
a
m
p
l
e

s
t
r
i
n
g
```

Trailer

All code in the trailer is copied verbatim to the generated source code file. In the previous RPN calculator, the main function of the program was in the trailer. Functions in the trailer can be accessed like any other module function.

You can write your own .mli file for the generated code, but it will not be updated automatically by ocamllex (this is why you should consider the code you put in the trailer very carefully).

Generating and Building Code

To compile this code, you need to create the OCaml source file from the ocamllex file. When you generate the OCaml source file, ocamllex will tell you some important information about the generated code.

The output contains information on the size of the automata that is generated.

Error Reporting and Handling

You can use the position information in the lexbuf to tell where you are in a file, which is the only way to know where a given error occurred. Unfortunately, there are no built-in commands that make accessing this information easier.

The lexing functions will throw a `Failure` exception if they encounter problems, but this error is often not as informative as you might hope. You can catch this error and (using the `lexbuf` position commands) try to recover. You can also report what exactly caused the error and treat it like a bug. When you are first writing a lexer (especially if it is complicated), this is probably the best way to handle this situation.

Transition Table Size

There is a limit of 32,767 transitions. If you exceed that limit, you will get an error such as this one: `ocamllex: transition table overflow, automaton is too big`. There are ways of reducing your automaton size, so you are not out of luck if you get this error.

If you have a lexer with a huge number of keywords, you might want to use the following kind of function to handle it. This situation is quite common, and the function presented is the canonical way to handle the problem.

You first must define a lookup table in the header. You can use whatever container you want to use. In this example, a hashtable is used.

```
{
  let keywords = Hashtbl.create 100
  (* load up the keyword table with the keyword to token mapping *)
  let _ =
    List.iter (fun (keyword, token) -> Hashtbl.replace keywords keyword token)
              [ "keyword1", KWD1;
                "keyword2", KWD2;
                                (* all the keywords are not shown *)
                "keywordN", KWDN ]
}

rule token = parse
  ['A'-'Z' 'a'-'z']['A'-'Z' 'a'-'z' '0'-'9' '_']* as id
        {
                try
                  Hashtbl.find keyword_table id
                with Not_found ->
                  STRING(id)
}
```

Know Your Grammar

A grammar is the set of rules that govern a particular language. In natural languages such as English or French, these rules might be very complicated; for artificial languages such as OCaml, the rules are much simpler. And as with natural languages, a mechanism for understanding a given grammar must exist. For artificial languages, it is the parser, which takes a stream of tokens and processes them according to rules.

Ocamlyacc cannot, however, parse any grammar; it can deal only with grammars that are not ambiguous. This means that each sequence of tokens can match only one parse tree. Ocamlyacc also has only one token of look ahead, so grammars that need more than one token of look ahead cannot be parsed.

Understanding grammars can be very difficult. Writing them can be even harder. Writing them so that they actually work is extremely hard, so try not to get discouraged. The benefits of being able to effectively understand and construct parsers can be huge.

Why Use a Parser?

For many applications, a full-blown parser is probably overkill. However, for many applications, using a parser will make your life much easier in the future.

Not only does using a parser mean that your lexer might be simplified, but you can provide for functionality far beyond what you can do with a lexer only.

You might need a parser when you implement a domain-specific language (DSL). DSLs, which are found in a variety of applications, are configuration languages, embedded scripting languages, and data description languages. SQL is probably the most popular DSL in wide use. These kinds of languages can be built using ocamlyacc.

You also can use a parser to handle situations that are too complicated for regular expressions alone. Text mining and log file analysis are two areas in which having a lexer/parser combination can result in better code and easier maintenance.

A Small Discussion of Small Languages

DSLs are programming languages that are focused on one problem domain. That problem domain can be anything: text processing, image manipulation, configuration, page layout, and so on. This focus on a single domain is what separates DSLs from general-purpose programming languages such as OCaml. OCaml is designed to be able to solve problems in a variety of problem domains.

DSLs can be a real boon in complicated programs. These languages are often called "extension" languages because they are designed to extend some core functionality. The Emacs text editor, with its extension language Emacs Lisp, is probably one of the best examples of how powerful having an extension language can be. Another is Microsoft Excel with Visual Basic for Applications. These two applications have a programming language embedded within them that enables a user to extend the functionality of the application in ways that the original programmer did not do.

However, DSLs are not restricted to extension languages. SQL, for example, is a DSL. Many report generators use their own DSL to describe reports. Make is another application that uses a DSL to accomplish its goals.

When writing a complicated application that might have complex customization or actions, consider writing a DSL for it, thus allowing extension to be done this way rather than via code changes. One of the biggest questions to ask when making this decision is this: is it worth it? Writing a small language is not hard to do using tools such as ocamllex and ocamlyacc, but writing a good language is always hard—no matter which tools you use.

Using Ocamlyacc

Like ocamllex, ocamlyacc transforms an input file that is not OCaml code into OCaml code. The input file is writing in a language that is very similar to the original Yacc. Yacc is written in C, and the output files are also C files. Semantic actions in ocamlyacc are written in OCaml code.

One difference between ocamllex and ocamlyacc is that ocamlyacc also generates an interface file for the parser (this adds another step to the build process).

Ocamlyacc File

Note the file structure in the following example. An ocamlyacc file has three sections, delimited with %%. The %% is optional between the body and trailer if the trailer is empty.

```
%{
  (* header: this is copied verbatim *)

%}
%token DEFINITION
%token <string> WORD
%type <string> main /* terminal symbol */
%left DEFINITION /* a precedence definition */
%start main /* where to start at */
%%
/* this is the body */
main:
DEFINITION WORD { $2 }
;
%%


(* Trailer: This code would be copied verbatim also *)
```

Header

The header contains two parts. The first part is contained within the %{ and %} symbols. Any code in this section will be copied verbatim to the OCaml source file. It will not be copied to the associated .mli file that is created by ocamlyacc, so be aware of that.

The second part of the header contains the token definitions and precedence rules. These definitions are how you tell ocamlyacc what type of tokens it will be receiving. Tokens that do not have arguments, such as the preceding DEFINITION token, do not need a type definition. The type of the argument to the WORD token is specified in its definition.

You can also specify precedence rules, which give hints to the parser about when to shift and when to reduce (discussed in more detail in a little while).

The start tag defines the initial entry point into your parser. There is only one of these and it is usually the last item in this list, followed by the %% section delimiter.

Body

Terminal tokens are those that are returned by the lexer and actually appear in the input file. Nonterminal tokens are those that are not returned by the lexer. The body of an ocamlyacc file consists of sequences of terminal and nonterminal tokens and semantic actions.

Both kinds of tokens might be recursive. In fact, this is the way sequences of items are built up. There are two general types of recursion in ocamlyacc tokens: right and left. You see recursion in nearly all ocamlyacc-based programs.

Right recursion, which is not as efficient as left recursion, occurs when the recursion occurs on the right side of a token, as shown in the following example:

```
words:
WORD { [$1] }
| WORD words { $1 :: $2 }
;
```

Left recursion is when the recursion happens to the left of the token. The following example shows left recursion:

```
words:
WORD { [$1] }
| words WORD { $2 :: $1 }
;
```

These semantic actions, just like those in the lexer, can be any valid OCaml code. The return type of the semantic action is something that should be carefully considered. This is especially true if you are building up complex data structures from your ocamlyacc code.

It can be hard to get the grammar right the first time. Sometimes you will have shift/reduce conflicts, which occur when there is some ambiguity to the grammar (it is sometimes something that ocamlyacc can handle automatically).

The if statement is one that often generates this kind of shift/reduce conflict.

```
if:
  IF condition THEN action { Execute action }
| IF condition THEN action ELSE otheraction { Condexec action otheraction }
;
```

As you can see from this example, it can be hard to know whether action is where the parser should stop. Should it keep looking? Luckily, this kind of conflict is handled automatically by ocamlyacc. Basically, the next token is read and becomes the look ahead token. If it is an ELSE, it shifts to the next rule; otherwise, it reduces.

A reduce/reduce conflict is a sign of problems in your grammar. It means that there are two rules that could match a given input. This kind of error is not handled automatically and should be resolved.

Trailer

The trailer is delimited from the body with a %% symbol. All the code in the trailer is copied verbatim to the OCaml source files.

This code is not altered, and errors might show up when it is compiled. Luckily, the compiler will report syntax errors on the line number in the ocamlyacc file instead of the generated source files.

Error Handling and Reporting

Error handling and reporting are the weakest areas in ocamlyacc, but it is not really the fault of ocamlyacc. The error-reporting facilities of most Yacc derivatives are weak, primarily because error conditions are errors. Unlike Yacc or Bison, ocamlyacc does not support the %error=verbose token in the parser file.

The most important thing is to define the parse_error function in the parser file header. The simplest definition can be like this:

```
let parse_error msg = Printf.eprintf "%s\n" msg
```

When it is set, you can use this function to throw exceptions or get information about the current state of the system. Debugging a grammer can often be a trial-and-error process.

To get position information, you have to use the lexing functions. There is an example in the next section.

Generating and Building Code

There is an extra step in building ocamlyacc files because of the creation of an .mli file. The following sections show a lexer and a parser. This parser turns a file with comma-separated tokens into a list of tokens.

Lexer

The lexer is pretty simple. It does not handle any sophisticated comma-separated value (CSV) files, but it will suffice for an example.

```
{

  open Csv_parser
}
rule tokens = parse
    ',' { tokens lexbuf }
  | '\n' { tokens lexbuf }
  | eof { EOF }
  | [^ ',' '\n']+ as words { WORDS(words) }

{

  let run x = let lb = Lexing.from_channel x in
    Csv_parser.main tokens lb

}
```

Parser

This parser shows an example of constructing lists of items from an input file.

```
%{
  let parse_error msg = Printf.eprintf "%s\n" msg
%}
%token EOF
%token <string> WORDS
%type <string list> main
%start main
%%
```

```
main:
words EOF { $1 }
;

words:
WORDS { [$1] }
| words WORDS { $2 :: $1 }
;
```

Building

First, you run the ocamlyacc command on the parser file and then you compile the components of the parser.

```
/home/josh $ ocamlyacc.exe csv_parser.mly
/home/josh $ ocamlc.exe -c csv_parser.mli
/home/josh $ ocamlc.exe -c csv_parser.ml
```

After that, you can run ocamllex on the lexer file. Then you can compile the generated lexer file. You have to do this after the ocamlyacc-generated files are present because the ocamllex-generated file includes the parser-generated file.

```
/home/josh $ ocamllex.exe csv.mll
5 states, 258 transitions, table size 1062 bytes
/home/josh $ ocamlc.exe -c csv.ml
```

After they're all compiled, you can build a new toplevel with these files as part of it. If you are on a system that supports dynamic loading, you can just #load the files.

```
/home/josh $ ocamlmktop -o test.exe csv_parser.cmo csv.cmo
```

You can run the new toplevel. You have a file prepared that contains several lines of comma-separated text.

```
/home/josh $ ./test.exe
        Objective Caml version 3.09.0

# Csv.run (open_in "testfile");;
- : string list =
["worked"; "this"; "hello"; "worked"; "this"; "hello"; "worked"; "this";
 "hello"]
#
stop signal from tty
```

Now you can go on to a more complicated example.

Using Ocamlyacc and Ocamllex

Although you can use ocamllex without using ocamlyacc, the two are often used together. You do not have to use them together, but they are well-suited for applications, and people expect to find them together.

A More Complicated Example

In most literature, the example is a multifunction calculator. There are a huge number of calculator examples in the world, so this example is not a calculator. The example used here is a simple configuration language that enables you to set and unset variables.

Lexer

The lexer for this example is pretty simple. The two keywords (set and unset) have been defined, as well as associated tokens such as = and ;.

```
{  (* this is the header *)
  open Config_parser

  let update_position lex_buf =
    let pos = lex_buf.Lexing.lex_curr_p in
    lex_buf.Lexing.lex_curr_p <- { pos with
    Lexing.pos_lnum = pos.Lexing.pos_lnum + 1;
    Lexing.pos_bol = pos.Lexing.pos_cnum };;
}

(* body comments use a different style than Ocamlyacc *)
rule tokens = parse
    [' ' '\t' ] { tokens lexbuf }
  | '\n' { update_position lexbuf;tokens lexbuf }
  | "set" { SET }
  | "unset" { UNSET }
  | ['a'-'z']['a'-'z' 'A'-'Z' '0'-'9']* as var_name { VAR_NAME(var_name) }
  | '=' { EQUAL }
  | ';' { SEMI }
  | eof { EOF }
  | '#' { comments lexbuf }
and comments = parse
    '\n' { tokens lexbuf }
  | eof { EOF }
  | _ { comments lexbuf }

{

  (* this is the trailer *)
  let load_file f_name = let lb = Lexing.from_channel (open_in f_name) in
    Config_parser.main tokens lb;;
}
```

Parser

The parser builds a list of pairs from the set variables. This parser processes the entire file until a syntax error or the end of the file is encountered.

```
%{
  (* This is the header *)
    (* comments here work like normal *)
(* define the parse error function *)
  let parse_error msg = print_string msg
%}
%token SET UNSET EQUAL EOF SEMI
%token <string> VAR_NAME
%start main
%type< (string * string) list > main
%%
main:
vars EOF { $1 }
;

/** but comments here do not */

vars:
SET VAR_NAME EQUAL VAR_NAME SEMI { [($2,$4)] }
| UNSET VAR_NAME EQUAL VAR_NAME SEMI { [] }
| vars SET VAR_NAME EQUAL VAR_NAME SEMI { ($3,$5) :: $1 }
| vars UNSET VAR_NAME EQUAL VAR_NAME SEMI { List.remove_assoc $3 $1 }
;
%%
(* The trailer is here.  This section is just copied verbatim.
the %% are not required if you don't have anything in here *)
```

Compiling and Running

Just as in the simple example, you need to process the files in a certain order.

```
/home/josh $ ocamlyacc.exe config_parser.mly
/home/josh $ ocamlc.exe -c config_parser.mli
/home/josh $ ocamlc.exe -c config_parser.ml
/home/josh $ ocamllex.exe config_lexer.mll
5 states, 258 transitions, table size 1062 bytes
/home/josh $ ocamlc.exe -c config_lexer.ml
/home/josh $ ocamlmktop -o test.exe config_parser.cmo config_lexer.cmo
/home/josh $ ./test.exe
        Objective Caml version 3.09.0
```

```
# Config_lexer.load_file "config.txt";;
- : string * string list =
[("world","hello");("hello","stuff")]
#
```

Once processed, you now have a library that can load simple configuration files.

BNF and EBNF

Backus-Naur Form (BNF) is a way to describe a given language in a formal and mathematical way. It got its name from John Backus, who used it to describe the Algol 60 language, and from Peter Naur, who popularized the notation (although he is very modest about his role).

It is intended as a way to describe programs so that programs can generate code conforming to the specification. Yacc, the compiler compiler, is the most famous example of this. Yacc (and its derivatives) use BNF to describe their rules, and looking at a BNF is pretty close to looking at the Yacc code to generate a compiler for the language. BNF and its older cousin, Extended Backus-Naur Form (EBNF), are based on the same notation. EBNF includes operators for recursion and globing, so it is far more convenient and popular. Most BNF listings that you see will be EBNF for this reason. In the next chapter, there is an EBNF description of the parser used in the example.

An Example

In the following example, the language contains two tokens. First is a DIGIT, which can be any one of the specified characters. The other token is a NUMBER, which is a sequence of DIGITs (one or more) followed by a '.' and a sequence of zero or more DIGITs.

```
NUMBER := D+ ('.' D*)?
DIGIT := '0' | '1' | '2' | '3' | '4' | '5' | '6' | '7' | '8' | '9'
```

Although this is a pretty simple example, you get the gist of it. You can look at the OCaml documentation for more complex examples. In fact, the lexical conventions are spelled out via a BNF-like notation.

Why Are They Important to Learn?

This question does not have a simple answer. On one hand, it is important to understand BNF notation so that you can understand it when you come across it (which you will). I cannot, however, point to a specific positive outcome that will occur if you understand BNF notation.

If you want to use and create grammars and structured data files, understanding BNF will enable you to communicate and understand definitions. Understanding BNF will also enable you to understand programming languages better (including OCaml). Almost all programming languages have BNF structures available for them.

Conclusion

This chapter gave you an introduction to the ocamllex and ocamlyacc tools, and the best way to gain depth in your understanding is to use them. These tools are very powerful and they help you with many different kinds of problems.

They are, however, also difficult and they require a lot of time and effort to properly master them.

In the next chapter, you will be presented with an implementation of a tool using ocamllex and ocamlyacc. The tool described is a log file parser and analysis tool that displays the power and flexibility of these two tools.

## CHAPTER 17

Practical: Complex
Log File Parsing

Ocamllex and ocamlyacc can be used to build compilers for languages. They also can be used to handle any kind of text file that you might want to parse. Complex log files are places in which ocamllex and ocamlyacc can be used that are not often talked about in the literature.

People often use plain regular expressions to handle these tasks, which can often be a good choice. However, after you get away from simple parsing tasks, the benefit provided by these tools becomes clear. There is also an advantage of runtime speed as well as development speed. Ocamllex and ocamlyacc are well-optimized programs. They both generate code that, on average, is hard to beat with hand-coded alternatives.

A Simple Example

A simple example provides a basic understanding of the kinds of code you will use and some of the pitfalls you might encounter.

You will focus on log file processing in this chapter. Just because the examples are log files doesn't mean that the techniques that are used are useful only for log files. In fact, one of the reasons why log files are being used as examples is that they are often (basically) structured text files and often have few real utilities for dealing with them.

Sample Data

This sample data comes from the syslog file on one of my machines (it's a Linux box named bebop). Syslog is a logging facility found on most Unix and Unix-like systems. It is even available for Microsoft Windows systems, although it is very infrequently found in the wild.

These messages are not particularly interesting, but they represent "normal" messages that you might find in a syslog file.

```
Nov 22 17:38:25 bebop kernel: Kernel logging (proc) stopped.
Nov 22 17:38:25 bebop kernel: Kernel log daemon terminating.
Nov 22 17:38:25 bebop exiting on signal 15
Nov 22 21:04:46 bebop syslogd 1.4.1#17: restart.
Nov 22 21:04:46 bebop kernel: klogd 1.4.1#17, log source = /proc/kmsg started.
```

```
Nov 22 21:04:46 bebop kernel: Inspecting /boot/System.map-2.6.12
Nov 22 21:04:46 bebop kernel: Loaded 29754 symbols from /boot/System.map-2.6.12.
Nov 22 21:04:46 bebop kernel: Symbols match kernel version 2.6.12.
Nov 22 21:04:46 bebop kernel: No module symbols loaded - kernel modules not enabled.
Nov 22 21:04:46 bebop kernel: Linux version 2.6.12 (root@Knoppix)
Nov 22 21:04:46 bebop kernel: BIOS-provided physical RAM map:
```

The format of each message in pseudocode is the following:

DATETIME HOST IDENT COLON MESSAGE

IDENT is a string provided by the application making the log entry. On some systems (Linux included), this string might contain spaces and might even contain special characters (which is everything except NULL characters). Although you could probably use a lexer to handle this particular task, the following example uses both a lexer and a parser to demonstrate the concepts.

Code

The lexer, which is stored in a file called syslog_lexer.mll in the example, is quite short—even though it also includes the main executable code within it. You are basically defining only five tokens to handle the kinds of data found in syslog files.

```
{
open Syslog_parser
}

let time = ['0'-'9']['0'-'9']':'['0'-'9']['0'-'9']':'['0'-'9']['0'-'9']

rule tokens = parse
[' ' '\t']+ { tokens lexbuf }
| (['a'-'z' 'A'-'Z']+[' ']+['0'-'9']+[' ']+time as dt) { DATETIME(dt) }
| ':' { COLON }
| [^ ' ' '\t' '\n']+ { WORD(Lexing.lexeme lexbuf) }
| '\n' { EOL }
| eof { EOF }

{

let tostring (n, m, l, k) = Printf.printf "%s|%s|%s|%s\n" n m l k;;

let _ = let ichan = open_in "messages" in
            let lb = Lexing.from_channel ichan in
    try
      let p = Syslog_parser.main tokens lb in
                match p with
                    [] -> close_in ichan
```

```
              | h :: t -> close_in ichan;tostring h
    with
      Parsing.Parse_error ->
        Printf.printf "Between location %i and %i near '%s'"
          (Lexing.lexeme_start lb) (Lexing.lexeme_end lb) (Lexing.lexeme lb);
        close_in ichan;
        exit(1)
      | Failure(x) ->
        Printf.printf "Between location %i and %i near '%s'" ➥
(Lexing.lexeme_start lb)
          (Lexing.lexeme_end lb) (Lexing.lexeme lb);
      close_in ichan;
      exit(1)


}
```

The parser defined as follows would be saved in a file called syslog_parser.mly (only
because other code you have calls this code with that name).

```
%{
  let print_error msg lbuf  =
    Printf.eprintf "%s at %i\n" msg (Lexing.lexeme_start_p lbuf).Lexing.pos_cnum

  let cond_concat x y = match x with
      "" -> y
    | _ -> x ^ " " ^ y;;

%}
%token COLON EOL EOF
%token <string> WORD DATETIME
%type <(string * string * string * string) list> main
%start main
%%
main:
lines EOF { $1 }
;


lines: { [] }
  | lines line { $2 :: $1 }
;


line:
  DATETIME WORD facility COLON message EOL  { ($1,$2,$3,$5) }
| DATETIME WORD facility EOL { ($1,$2,$3,"") }
```

```
facility: { "" }
| facility word { cond_concat $1 $2 }
;


message: { "" }
| message word { cond_concat $1 $2 }
| message COLON { $1 }
| message DATETIME { cond_concat $1 $2 }
;


word:
WORD { $1 }
;
```

Building and Running

You can use the following OCamlMakefile to build the code:

```
SOURCES = syslog_parser.mly syslog_lexer.mll
RESULT = syslog.exe
OUTPUT = byte-code
include /usr/local/share/OCamlMakefile
The build output should look similar to the following.
/home/josh/doc/OcamlBook/multi-line-log $ make.exe -f makefile.syslog
ocamllex syslog_lexer.mll
18 states, 630 transitions, table size 2628 bytes
make[1]: Entering directory `/cygdrive/c/Documents and ➡
Settings/josh/My Documents/OcamlBook/multi-line-log'
making ._bcdi/syslog_parser.di from syslog_parser.mli
making ._d/syslog_parser.d from syslog_parser.ml
making ._d/syslog_lexer.d from syslog_lexer.ml
make[1]: Leaving directory `/cygdrive/c/Documents and ➡
Settings/josh/My Documents/OcamlBook/multi-line-log'
make[1]: Entering directory `/cygdrive/c/Documents and ➡
Settings/josh/My Documents/OcamlBook/multi-line-log'
ocamlc -c syslog_lexer.ml
ocamlc -o syslog.exe syslog_parser.cmo syslog_lexer.cmo
make[1]: Leaving directory `/cygdrive/c/Documents and ➡
Settings/josh/My Documents/OcamlBook/multi-line-log'
Then, if you run the application, you should see the last line ➡
in the file displayed with the spaces turned into seperators.
/home/josh/doc/OcamlBook/multi-line-log $ ./syslog.exe
Nov 22 21:04:46|bebop|kernel|BIOS-provided physical RAM map
/home/josh/doc/OcamlBook/multi-line-log $
```

A Complex Example

Now you can move on to a more complex example, which is a log file that has various kinds of entries—some of which span multiple lines.

Example Log File with Various Kinds of Entries

This log file has four basic kinds of entries: connection, disconnection, heartbeat, and command. Only clients can issue commands.

Code

To make operations on the data easier, you should first define some types to handle the data. These types encode the different kinds of ports and peer connections/servers that the log file describes.

The types also encode information about each kind of log entry, which enable you to write functions to operate on these various log file entries.

You can write the type definitions in a separate file (named mll_types.ml) to make things easier for you later. If you defined them in the lexer file, you might run into circular dependencies, so you should avoid doing this. The circular dependencies can come into play when you have types defined in the lexer that are needed by the parser. By putting them in their own file, you make sure that the types are available to all code in the order needed.

```
type port = Port of int | Siteport of int * int * string

type date_host = { date:string ; host:string }

type client = { c_id: int; c_port: port }

type other_side = Client of client | Peer of string

type log_entry = Connected of (date_host * other_side * string)
                         | Heartbeat of (date_host * other_side)
                         | Command of (date_host * client * string)
                         | Disconnect of (date_host * other_side * string)
```

The lexer is short and should be put in lexer.mll. It defines the tokens and the keywords that you will be using. Remember the restrictions associated with ocamllex (especially the limitations on keywords). Because you have only a few keywords, you do not have to use a lookup table. However, if you have many (hundreds) of keywords, you probably want to use a lookup table for them.

```
{
  exception Eof
  open Mll_types
  open Parser
}
```

```
rule tokens = parse
    [' ' '\n']+ {tokens lexbuf}
  | '[' { R_BRAKET }
  | ']' { L_BRAKET }
  | '#' { SHARP }
  | ['0'-'9' '-']+[' ']+['0'-'9' ':']+ { TIME(Lexing.lexeme lexbuf) }
  | ['0'-'9']+ { NUMBER(int_of_string(Lexing.lexeme lexbuf)) }
  | "\tBEGIN_MESSAGE:" { messages lexbuf }
  | ":END_MESSAGE" { tokens lexbuf }
  | "\tAUDIT:" { audit lexbuf }
  | "heartbeat received from" { HEARTBEAT }
  | "connected" { CONNECTED }
  | "command" { COMMAND }
  | "disconnected" { DISCONNECTED }
  | "peer" { PEER }
  | "port" { PORT }
  | "client" { CLIENT }
  | ['0'-'9']?['0'-'9']?['0'-'9']'.'['0'-'9']?['0'-'9']?['0'-'9']'.'['0'-'9']➥
?['0'-'9']?['0'-'9']'.'['0'-'9']?['0'-'9']?['0'-'9'] { IP_ADDR➥
(Lexing.lexeme lexbuf) }
  | '/' { SLASH }
  | ['A'-'Z']['A'-'Z'] { ADDR(Lexing.lexeme lexbuf) }
  | ['a'-'z' 'A'-'Z']+ { SERVER(Lexing.lexeme lexbuf) }
  | eof { raise Eof }
and messages = parse
    ":END_MESSAGE" { tokens lexbuf }
  | [' ' 'a'-'z' 'A'-'Z' '0'-'9' '\n']+ { MESSAGE(Lexing.lexeme lexbuf) }
and audit = parse
    '\n' { tokens lexbuf }
  | [^ '\n']+ { audit lexbuf }
```

For this example, you write the application code into the lexer, which saves you from having another file to implement this code. It is not really much of a savings, except that it enables you to edit most of the logic close to the lexer. The only action these functions perform is to print out the data (but you can write any action on these types if you want).

```
{

  let ic = open_in "mll.txt";;
  let lb = Lexing.from_channel ic;;

  let next () = tokens lb;;
```

```
   let _ = try
     while true do
       let m = Parser.main tokens lb in match m with
                   Connected (q,r,s) -> Printf.printf "Connect! %s\n" s
                 | Heartbeat (q,r) -> Printf.printf "Heartbeat! %s\n" q.host
                 | Command (q,r,s) -> Printf.printf "Command %s\n" s
                 | Disconnect (q,r,s) -> Printf.printf "Disconnect %s\n" q.host
     done
   with Eof -> close_in ic
     | Parsing.Parse_error ->
       Printf.printf "Between location %i and %i\n"
         (Lexing.lexeme_start lb) (Lexing.lexeme_end lb);
       close_in ic;
       exit(1)
     | Failure(x) ->
       Printf.printf "Between location %i and %i\n"
         (Lexing.lexeme_start lb) (Lexing.lexeme_end lb);
       close_in ic;
       exit(1);;

}
```

In parser.mly, the parser is where the actual rules for handling the tokens are defined.
Some of the actions look complicated, largely because of the large and complex types you are
using. In this example, the parser passes full formed types to the application. It could just send
a sequence of strings or other built-in types. You will often pass some composite types to your
applications from the parser. The following code might take some time to understand if you
are not familiar with reading ocamlyacc files. The limitations of typography in displaying the
code can also hinder understanding.

Tip Remember to define the parse_error function in the parser header.

```
%{

let parse_error s = print_endline s;;

%}
%token R_BRAKET L_BRAKET SHARP HEARTBEAT CONNECTED
%token PORT CLIENT SLASH COMMAND DISCONNECTED PEER
%token <int> NUMBER
%token<string> ADDR SERVER MESSAGE AUDIT TIME IP_ADDR
%type<Mll_types.log_entry> main
%start main
%%
```

```
main:
heartbeat { $1 }
| connected { $1 }
| disconnected { $1 }
| command { $1 }
;

time_and_server:
  TIME R_BRAKET SERVER L_BRAKET { {Mll_types.date=$1;
                                                Mll_types.host=$3} }

;

heartbeat:
time_and_server HEARTBEAT IP_ADDR { Mll_types.Heartbeat
                                                ($1,(Mll_types.Peer $3)) }

;

connected:
time_and_server CONNECTED CLIENT SHARP NUMBER PORT NUMBER MESSAGE
  { Mll_types.Connected ($1,(Mll_types.Client
                { Mll_types.c_id = $5;
             Mll_types.c_port=(Mll_types.Port $7)}
             ),$8) }
| time_and_server CONNECTED CLIENT SHARP NUMBER PORT NUMBER SLASH ➥
NUMBER ADDR MESSAGE
      { Mll_types.Connected ($1,(Mll_types.Client
                                        { Mll_types.c_id = $5;
                          Mll_types.c_port=(Mll_types.Siteport
                                        ($7,$9,$10))}),$11) }
| time_and_server CONNECTED PEER IP_ADDR {
    Mll_types.Connected ($1,(Mll_types.Peer $4),"") }
;

command:
time_and_server COMMAND CLIENT SHARP NUMBER PORT NUMBER SLASH ➥
NUMBER ADDR MESSAGE
  { Mll_types.Command ($1,
            {Mll_types.c_id = $5;
         Mll_types.c_port = (
          Mll_types.Siteport ($7,$9,$10))},$11) }
| time_and_server COMMAND CLIENT SHARP NUMBER PORT NUMBER MESSAGE
      { Mll_types.Command ($1,
            {Mll_types.c_id = $5;
            Mll_types.c_port = (Mll_types.Port $7)},$8) }
;
```

```
disconnected:
time_and_server DISCONNECTED PEER IP_ADDR MESSAGE
  { Mll_types.Disconnect ($1,(Mll_types.Peer $4),$5) }
| time_and_server DISCONNECTED CLIENT SHARP NUMBER PORT NUMBER MESSAGE
      { Mll_types.Disconnect ($1,

                                     (Mll_types.Client
                                        {Mll_types.c_id = $5;
                                         Mll_types.c_port = ➥
(Mll_types.Port $7)}),$8)}
| time_and_server DISCONNECTED CLIENT SHARP NUMBER PORT NUMBER SLASH NUMBER ADDR ➥
MESSAGE
            { Mll_types.Disconnect ($1,

                                      (Mll_types.Client
                                         {Mll_types.c_id = $5;
                                          Mll_types.c_port = (
                                           Mll_types.Siteport ➥
($7,$9,$10))}),$11)}
;
```

The following sample from the input file is short and was put into a file called mll.txt. It is often easier to test with shorter segments and then verify with the longer ones. You don't have to do this, however (the following segment was chosen as much to save pages as it was to keep things manageable).

```
2004-10-11 10:14:00 [ Quillen ] connected client #1142345 port 23
            BEGIN_MESSAGE: client clear :END_MESSAGE
2004-10-11 10:14:00 [ Quillen ] connected peer 10.10.10.20
2004-10-11 10:14:30 [ Quillen ] heartbeat received from 10.10.10.1
2004-10-11 10:14:31 [ Adams ] command client #1132423 port 23/9 US
            BEGIN_MESSAGE: client not clear :END_MESSAGE
            AUDIT: level 1
2004-10-11 10:14:38 [ Quillen ] disconnected peer 10.10.10.42
            BEGIN_MESSAGE: abend disconnect :END_MESSAGE
2004-10-11 10:20:24 [ Sampson ] disconnected peer 10.10.10.25
            BEGIN_MESSAGE: abend disconnect
Development Server :END_MESSAGE
2004-10-11 10:14:30 [ Adams ] heartbeat received from 10.10.10.1
2004-10-11 10:14:31 [ Adams ] disconnected client #1142345 port 23
            BEGIN_MESSAGE: logged out :END_MESSAGE
```

You can see from these entries that some of the entries span multiple lines. These kinds of entries can be very difficult to parse using regular expressions alone.

Building and Running

You can use the following OCamlMakefile to build the code:

```
SOURCES = parser.mly lexer.mll
RESULT = complex.exe
OUTPUT = byte-code
include /usr/local/share/OCamlMakefile
```

The build output should look similar to the following. You can then run the command and view the output.

```
/home/josh/doc/OcamlBook/multi-line-log $ make.exe
ocamllex lexer.mll
139 states, 3586 transitions, table size 15178 bytes
ocamlyacc  parser.mly
make[1]: Entering directory `./multi-line-log'
making ._bcdi/parser.di from parser.mli
making ._d/parser.d from parser.ml
making ._d/lexer.d from lexer.ml
making ._d/mll_types.d from mll_types.ml
make[1]: Leaving directory `./multi-line-log'
make[1]: Entering directory `./multi-line-log'
ocamlc -c mll_types.ml
ocamlc -c parser.mli
ocamlc -c parser.ml
ocamlc -c lexer.ml
ocamlc  -o test.exe mll_types.cmo parser.cmo lexer.cmo
make[1]: Leaving directory `./multi-line-log'

josh@sputnik ~/doc/OcamlBook/multi-line-log
$ ./test
Connect!  client clear
Connect!
Heartbeat! Quillen
Command  client not clear
Disconnect Quillen
Disconnect Sampson
Heartbeat! Adams
Disconnect Adams

josh@sputnik ~/doc/OcamlBook/multi-line-log
$
```

Discussion

So now you can build complex text parsing applications using ocamllex and ocamlyacc. Would you ever want to? It depends.

Not everyone does text processing. However, if you do any amount of text processing in OCaml, you should know ocamllex and ocamlyacc. People sometimes shy away from these tools because of unfortunate associations with Lex and Yacc.

I say unfortunate because the rise of easy regular expressions has lulled many people into a false sense of programming. Regular expressions are powerful—without a doubt. In fact, without regular expressions, ocamllex could not function. However, regular expressions are tools, and all tools have their strengths and weaknesses.

Advantages of Using the Tools

One of the biggest advantages is that you know that the file will be processed correctly. There are times when you want to know, for sure, that the processing was correct. Ocamllex and ocamlyacc enable you to have that confidence.

You might also want to abort when a file is poorly formed, especially when dealing with data that is interdependent. If some part of the data depends on other parts, you don't want to load only some of it (especially if you might not know which "some of it" you have).

You can also identify poorly formed files before operating on them. If you have a functioning parser, you can create actions that verify the data structure. This can be especially helpful for situations in which the data must be correct.

These tools also create applications that are easier to maintain than a spaghetti mass of regular expressions. As the data gets more complicated, these tools do not (this is in stark contrast with regexp-only strategies that increase in complexity as the data does).

These tools are also fast. I processed a slightly-more-than 500,000 line log file (containing 294,912 log entries) with the preceding code in about 13 seconds with my laptop (including the time required to write the output to a file).

These tools are highly optimized and generate efficient code. The code is often shorter. Shorter is always less buggy, so using these tools gives you fewer bugs, faster code, and easier maintenance. What more could you ask for?

Shortcomings of the Approach

These tools are not silver bullets. There are no silver bullets, even in the OCaml world. For one, messy data can be a real problem. You might have to preprocess it to get it into a form that can be described by a nonambiguous grammar. If the data cannot be represented by an unambiguous grammar, you cannot use ocamlyacc.

Finally, these tools do require a larger effort (in smaller cases) than just writing some regexps. If you are just looking for a glorified grep, a lexer/parser combo is probably not for you. However, as in the example given here, when you are looking for detailed ways to analyze files, using these tools can help a lot.

Conclusion

This example shows how the text analysis tools associated with OCaml can be used in very powerful ways. You don't have to be a total compiler junkie to use them or be interested in writing your own languages.

These tools can help you solve problems that you might have had with other tools. They also help you to understand how languages are constructed (even if you're not very interested in knowing about that).

## CHAPTER 18

The Objective Part of Caml

Objective Caml includes very powerful object-oriented features. Although that might seem somewhat obvious given that "objective" is in the language name, the extent and focus of the object system in OCaml is different from many other object-oriented languages currently in use.

OCaml provides an object system that is primarily focused on being a tool for software reuse and encapsulation.

Many programmers find that the OCaml module system provides much (if not all) of the functionality commonly found in object systems. Features such as data hiding and code reuse are definitely an important part of the module system. However, modules cannot be inherited and extended in the way that objects can. It is often easier to use objects to describe data relationships that are actually objective instead of trying to manipulate your data model in a way that is compatible with the OCaml module system. Modules also lack the capability to be polymorphic in the way that objects can.

This chapter is not meant to be an introduction to object-oriented programming (OOP). If you have no prior experience with OOP, there are topics in this chapter that might be confusing. If you have had experience with it, you should take special care. OCaml uses terminology found in other object-based languages, but these terms might not mean the same thing. Objects in OCaml still must obey the rules of the type system and follow other syntax restrictions. As in other aspects of OCaml development, you should never assume that a keyword in OCaml means the same thing as a keyword in another language.

Note This chapter does not discuss patterns. Although design patterns are indispensable when doing and understanding object-oriented design, they are not required for understanding the object features of OCaml (and vice versa).

Basics

OCaml supports OOP. This is what the *Objective* part of the OCaml name means. Saying this, however, does little to describe what that actually means.

OCaml has rich support for programming with objects. An *object* is a "thing" that can also have functions associated with it. Unlike data types, which are just data, objects can include both data and functions. Functions in an object are also called *methods*. Classes in OCaml are not data types, although they do have data types associated with them (for many programs and programmers, the difference is irrelevant). Objects can be inherited by other objects and extend their functionality. OCaml supports multiple inheritance and virtual objects.

You will learn more about classes not being data types later in the chapter. For now, you should understand that classes have an associated type, but they are not types themselves. You can make class types independently of objects, which is a way of creating type information independent of the object in the same way that Java's interfaces and abstract classes in C++ do.

Note A virtual object cannot be instantiated. An object must be declared virtual if it has any methods that are virtual. Virtual methods do not have an implementation in the virtual object. Virtual objects exist so that they can be inherited from and they often play an important role in complex object designs.

Simple Example

Although OCaml has a random number library called Random, sometimes I want the initialization of the random number generator to be more automatic than it is with the library.

Tip What is the difference between classes and objects? A desk is a class of object. The desk you are sitting in front of is an instance of the desk class. It is the instance of a desk that is actually an object.

I can create a simple class to create the functions that I use most often. A class is created by using the class and object keywords.

```
class random =
object
  method int x = Random.int x
  method float x = Random.float x
  method rand () = Random.float 1.
  initializer Random.self_init ();Printf.printf "Random Constructor\n"
end
```

The preceding code creates a new class, called random, that provides three method functions and an initializer. The initializer prints a message and performs the initialization of the Random library's pseudo-random number generator.

Note Methods do not need to have an empty unit argument the way I've written the rand method. There is an implicitly empty argument for methods (implied by the method keyword), but Jacques Garrigues (who implemented the object system in OCaml) uses both. In many of his libraries (the lablgtk library in particular), he uses the added empty unit argument when the method alters the object's state or must be called from a callback function. In the callback function, the argument is specified to distinguish the method from the application of the method. These are conventions of programmers instead of rules of the language.

I can create a new instance of the class and always initialize the library properly.

```
# class random =
object
  method int x = Random.int x
  method float x = Random.float x
  method rand () = Random.float 1.
  initializer Random.self_init ();Printf.printf "Random Constructor\n"
end;;
  class random :
  object
    method float : float -> float
    method int : int -> int
    method rand : unit -> float
  end
# let rnum = new random;;
Random Constructor
val rnum : random = <obj>
# rnum#int 6;;
- : int = 4
# rnum#float 100.;;
- : float = 82.8656205913089678
# rnum#rand ();;
- : float = 0.0700932072180878579
#
```

Caution Initializers are inherited and cannot be overridden.

Why Use Classes and Objects?

There are several reasons why you should use objects. The first one is to hide code from the user. The users of the preceding class do not even have to know that there is some kind of initialization going on. They also do not have to know anything about the underlying implementation of the class.

Users of the class are insulated from the implementation, which provides the programmer with the ability to change the underlying implementation without affecting users of that code. This idea, known as data hiding and encapsulation, is an important feature of OOP.

Note A class is the definition, and an object is an instantiation.

This encapsulation promotes code reuse. Users of the preceding class do not have to worry if I change the implementation as long as the methods stay the same. I could rewrite the class to use a hardware random number generator, if available; the users of the class will not be affected. Object-based encapsulation is conceptually the same as the OCaml module system's capability to hide data and functions.

Another way that OOP promotes code reuse is via the inheritance mechanism. *Inheritance* is when a class inherits the methods and values of a parent class. You will learn about this in much greater depth later in this chapter.

Finally, OOP should be used when objects are the best way to express a solution. There are times when you are working with "things" that might have data attributes and actions that they can perform. Problems in which you are working with objects are sometimes best solved by using objects.

It is important to remember that much of the functionality provided by objects in more traditional object-oriented languages can be implemented by using the OCaml module system. OCaml enables you to make methods and data members private, although privacy is also available via the module system. In OCaml, it is not an either/or situation with regard to modules and objects. You can use objects within modules. As always, you should use the tool that enables you to accomplish your goals.

Object and Class Keywords

The class keyword behaves much like the function keyword; it tells the compiler that the next segment of code describes a class. The object keyword marks the beginning of the class definition. The object keyword can take an argument, which is the name of this class (similar to the this keyword in Python or C++).

```
# class showingthis =
          object(self)
                      val a = 10
                      method print_a = Printf.printf "%i\n" a
                      method call_method = self#print_a
          end;;
class showingthis :
  object val a : int method call_method : unit method print_a : unit end
```

This is a pretty simple class having one data member and two methods (a function in a class is called a method). The signature indicates that it is an object and shows the type information for the internal data. You create an object (commonly referred to as instantiating an object) by using the new keyword.

```
# let b = new showingthis;;
val b : showingthis = <obj>
# b#call_method ();;
Characters 0-13:
  b#call_method ();;
  ^^^^^^^^^^^^^
This expression is not a function, it cannot be applied
# b#call_method;;
10
- : unit = ()
```

■**Caution** The methods you defined did not specify an argument, so passing an argument to them results in an error. Methods have an implicit empty argument.

Classes can have arguments, which are listed after the name of the class. These arguments can be any valid OCaml type. Constructor arguments are available even after the object has been constructed.

```
# class livingargs x y =
            object
                      method print_sum_of_args = Printf.printf "%i\n" (x + y)
            end;;
class livingargs : int -> int -> object method print_sum_of_args : unit end
# let l = new livingargs 10 20;;
val l : livingargs = <obj>
# l#print_sum_of_args;;
30
- : unit = ()
#
```

Methods May Not Be Polymorphic

This is a very important subject. Methods in OCaml classes can not be polymorphic, so the types must be known for all methods. This does not mean that methods cannot operate on polymorphic types like lists; it means that polymorphic type information must be specified in a different way for objects than for regular functions. The type information is specified via a type parameter.

The word *polymorphic* has a very large number of meanings and applications in programming, which is unfortunate because it can really make some things complicated. Parametric polymorphism in OCaml objects (say that five times quickly!) is one of those areas.

```
# let polyfunc x = match x with
              Some m -> m
            | None -> raise Not_found;;
val polyfunc : 'a option -> 'a = <fun>
# polyfunc (Some 10);;
- : int = 10
# polyfunc (Some "hello");;
- : string = "hello"
# polyfunc (Some 10.0);;
- : float = 10.
# class nonpoly = object
            method polyfunc x = match x with
                          Some m -> m
                        | None -> raise Not_found
  end;;
Characters 5-110:
  ..... nonpoly = object
            method polyfunc x = match x with
                          Some m -> m
                        | None -> raise Not_found
    end..
Some type variables are unbound in this type:
  class nonpoly : object method polyfunc : 'a option -> 'a end
The method polyfunc has type 'a option -> 'a where 'a is unbound
#
```

The error message says some type variables are unbound because classes and objects do not escape the type checker. All the type information about a class must be known at compile time, including the methods and data members.

Classes can be polymorphic (via parameterization), which is how you can have methods that operate on known types and be (effectively) polymorphic. This topic is discussed in detail later in the chapter, although you can see a quick example following (implementing correctly the preceding example that failed).

```
# class ['a] polyclass =
            object
              method polyfunc (x: 'a option) = match x with
                                      Some m -> m
                                    | None -> raise Not_found
            end;;
class ['a] polyclass : object method polyfunc : 'a option -> 'a end
```

When you use this new class in the toplevel, it does not become concrete until you use it on a defined type. After that, it is concrete and can be used only on that type. In compiled code, the type inference occurs automatically.

```
# let np = new polyclass;;
val np : '_a polyclass = <obj>
# np#polyfunc (Some 10);;
- : int = 10
# np;;
- : int polyclass = <obj>
#
```

Direct Objects

In OCaml, objects can be created directly (they are called *direct objects* in the OCaml documentation). This direction creation is often referred to as *duck typing* (a play on the phrase "if it walks like a duck and quacks like a duck, it is a duck"). Although direct objects do not have to be classes or need to be instantiated, there are some restrictions. One of the most prominent restrictions on direct objects is that they cannot be inherited from.

Direct objects can be useful for prototyping. In fact, there are programming languages (often called *prototyping languages*) that support direct-object creation to achieve the ability to rapidly prototype objects and types.

Direct objects (sometimes called *immediate objects*) can be defined anywhere. Unlike classes, direct objects can be created inside of other functions and methods. Direct objects support everything else that classes do. In fact, a direct object that takes arguments can even be thought of as an object factory.

One concrete benefit of using immediate objects is that they can be used in situations in which classes cannot be used. An example is when the self type might escape the class in which it is being used, which can happen when using a class to update a reference.

```
let living_objects = ref [];;
val living_objects : '_a list ref = {contents = []}
# class myobject =
object(self)
method register_object = living_objects := self :: living_objects.contents
method unregister_object = living_objects := List.filter (x != self) living_objects
end;;
Characters 79-83:
method register_object = living_objects := self :: living_objects.contents
                                           ^^^^
This expression has type < register_object : 'a; unregister_object : 'b; .. >
but is here used with type 'c
Self type cannot escape its class
```

The previous error message tells you that the self type escapes the class, which is a no-no. However, because direct objects are themselves a type (they are objects, not classes), you can escape this restriction and provide the global registration functions.

```
# let myobject =
object(self)
method register_object = living_objects := ➡
self :: living_objects.contents
method unregister_object = living_objects := ➡
List.filter (fun x -> x!= self) living_objects.contents
end;;
val myobject : < register_object : unit; unregister_object : unit > = <obj>
# living_objects;;
- : < register_object : unit; unregister_object : unit > list ref
```

The array defined earlier now has a concrete type thanks to the definition of the previous direct object. Although the limitations on direct objects make them unsuitable for many applications (especially applications that require inheritance), direct objects can be used to solve problems that are otherwise very difficult.

Initializers and Finalizers

Initializers, known as constructors in some languages, are defined by using the `initializer` keyword, which executes the code specified when an object is instantiated. In some languages, constructors are used to allocate resources for the object. OCaml uses automatic memory management, so this kind of allocation is not necessary. The functions called by the initializer must return `unit`.

There can be many initializers for any given class. They are also inherited and cannot be overridden. Initializers are used to perform setup operations in the class. For example, if you have a class that provides database methods, you might have an initializer that creates the connection to the database automatically. In the first example, the initializer was used to set up the random number generator. Initializers can also be used to enforce preconditions. The following example demonstrates a finalizer used to enforce a precondition with a direct object:

```
# let precond x y = object
val first = x
val second = y
method adder () = x + y
initializer assert(x > y)
end;;
val precond : int -> int -> < adder : unit -> int > = <fun>
# let d = precond 11 10;;
val d : < adder : unit -> int > = <obj>
# d#adder ();;
- : int = 21
# let d = precond 10 11;;
Exception: Assert_failure ("", 31, 12).
#
```

Finalizers, known as destructors in some languages, are not supported by OCaml. Finalizers in other languages are used to perform tear-down functions or memory and resource deallocation.

There is no `finalize` keyword for OCaml objects. Because the garbage collection facility in OCaml handles the destruction of objects in OCaml, there is no way to tell when this will happen. There is a function in the Gc library to provide a function that is called when an item is garbage collected, which should be used only if you understand the ramifications of doing it. If you need to provide cleanup operations, a method to do this should be provided. You need to be aware of your object lifetimes because the garbage collector cannot read your intentions.

Privacy and Data Member Access

The data in OCaml objects is private, so data values cannot be accessed outside of the class. If you want to access data values, you must provide accessor methods for this data. Ensure that your accessor methods do not allow for data that should be hidden within your object to escape. There is something of a standard for the definition of accessor functions in OCaml. The convention is to name the accessor methods after the variable accessed. If a set method for value X exists, it should be named set_X.

Keeping this data private creates better encapsulation and keeps users from the underlying representation in your classes.

OCaml objects have no friends. Before you weep for the friendlessness, consider that the whole concept of friends in objects breaks strong encapsulation. There is no friend keyword, however. In some programming languages (notably C++) you can define a class as a friend of another class. This designation enables that class to access the private data in the class it is a friend of. Some languages, such as Python, do not have private data, so friendship is not even needed.

By strictly enforcing the privacy of data members, OCaml provides strong encapsulation by default. It also encourages programmers to keep their class data private, which is enforced by the compiler.

Methods might use the `private` keyword to make them private (that is, accessible only within the class) when you have methods defined that you do not want users to be able to access. This is similar to restricting functions in the module system. When a class with private methods is inherited, private methods retain their private status.

Internal Classes

Classes might not be defined within other classes. If you need private classes, you can define classes within modules and then use the module system to prevent access to these classes.

The functionality of friend classes should also be implemented the same way. There is no friend keyword in OCaml, and accessor functions that reveal the internals of a class should be avoided. You can provide those methods, but use the module system to make them not accessible outside of that module.

Virtual Classes and Methods

You do not have to define all the methods in a given class. The virtual keyword provides a way to describe a class without implementing it. If a class has virtual methods, it must be declared virtual. A virtual class might not be instantiated.

```
# class virtual v_random =
object
  method virtual int: int -> int
  method virtual float: float -> float
  method virtual rand: unit -> float
end;;
class virtual v_random :
  object
    method virtual float : float -> float
    method virtual int : int -> int
    method virtual rand : unit -> float
  end
# let vr = new v_random;;
Characters 9-21:
  let vr = new v_random;;
           ^^^^^^^^^^^^
One cannot create instances of the virtual class v_random
#
```

You create virtual classes when you know you want only to inherit from them. A class with only virtual methods can be referred to as a pure virtual class. These kinds of classes are useful to describe and restrict an inheritance hierarchy.

Most virtual classes have a mix of virtual and nonvirtual methods. Private virtual methods do not retain their private status when they are inherited. Virtual classes have very important ramifications for inheritance, as will be discussed later.

Parameterized Objects

Classes might be polymorphic via parameterization, but these parameterized classes still cannot have methods that are polymorphic. However, it is via this parameterization that type information can be stated in a way that satisfies the compiler.

Constraints

Constraints are generated when a parameterized class is restricted to which types it can take as a parameter. Constraints are important to understand because the error messages they generate can be confusing.

Constraints affect only parameterized classes. They often occur when some operation requiring a given type is used in conjunction with the parameterized type. For example, the following (largely not useful) class exhibits a constraint:

```
# class ['a] constrained x =
object
val f = (x: 'a)
method adder y = f + y
end;;
        class ['a] constrained :
  'a -> object constraint 'a = int val f : 'a method adder : int -> int end
#
```

The constraint listed indicates that the type can be only an integer. In the following examples, in which you try to instantiate the class, you can see the error when a type other than integer is used.

```
# let wontwork = new constrained "hello";;
Characters 31-38:
  let wontwork = new constrained "hello";;
                                 ^^^^^^^
This expression has type string but is here used with type int
# let willwork = new constrained 10;;
val willwork : int constrained = <obj>
```

The constraint is passed on when you inherit from the class. In this example, the inheritance removes the constraint because the argument must be an integer:

```
# class constrained_in x =
object
  inherit ['a] constrained x
  method printer () = Printf.printf "%i\n" f
end;;
        class constrained_in :
  int ->
  object
    val f : int
    method adder : int -> int
    method printer : unit -> unit
  end
# let willwork = new constrained_in 20;;
val willwork : constrained_in = <obj>
```

However, if you try to make the class work with a string, it fails because the constraint is there waiting for you.

```
# class constrained_in x =
object
  inherit ['a] constrained x
  method printer () = Printf.printf "%s\n" f
end;;
```

```
        Characters 104-105:
    method printer () = Printf.printf "%s\n" f
                                             ^
```

This expression has type int but is here used with type string
#

Constraints are important to understand and notice (especially complex constraints). One way to avoid constraints is to make the parameterized object virtual.

Virtual methods can make use of the type parameter; then your implementation can create the kinds of methods you need.

Inheritance

Inheritance occurs when a class gains all the methods and values of a parent class. It enables developers to extend the functionality already in a class without changing the parent class.

This can be a major win in long-lived applications because new features can be added without requiring old applications to change.

Simple Inherit

Earlier in this chapter, you defined a random number class. If you want to extend that class, you could copy the code and add the feature. You could also inherit from the class and add a new method.

```
class extended_random =
object
  inherit random
  method between x y = let range = y - x in
    (Random.int (range + 1) + x)
  initializer Printf.printf "Extended Random Constructor\n"
end;;
```

The preceding code creates a new class that has all the values and methods of the superclass. The following signature shows that the methods from the superclass are there and have the same signature as the parent class:

```
class extended_random :
  object
    method between : int -> int -> int
    method float : float -> float
    method int : int -> int
    method rand : unit -> float
  end
```

Now you can use this new class. When you instantiate a new object, you see that both of the initialization messages are displayed. There is, in fact, no way to stop the initialization methods of base classes from executing.

```
# let erand = new extended_random;;
Random Constructor
Extended Random Constructor
val erand : extended_random = <obj>
```

You can also inherit as LABEL (the next example shows this), which gives you access to the superclass via the label that you assigned. Be careful when doing this, however, because you can cause information about the underlying implementation to leak out by abusing your access to the superclass. The following is basically the same as the previous example, except you have given a name to the superclass and added a method that calls a method from the superclass:

```
# class extended_random =
object
  inherit random as superclass
  method between x y = let range = y - x in
    (Random.int (range + 1) + x)
  method super_int x = superclass#int x

  initializer Printf.printf "Extended Random Constructor\n"
end;;
class extended_random :
  object
    method between : int -> int -> int
    method float : float -> float
    method int : int -> int
    method rand : unit -> float
    method super_int : int -> int
  end
# let nerand = new extended_random;;
Random Constructor
Extended Random Constructor
val nerand : extended_random = <obj>
# nerand#super_int 20;;
- : int = 6
#
```

Parametric Inherit

You can inherit from a parameterized class; you just have to specify a type argument.

```
# class ['a] get_demo x =
object
  val element = ref (x: 'a)
  method get () = element.contents
end;;
```

```
class ['a] get_demo :
  'a -> object val element : 'a ref method get : unit -> 'a end
# class strings x =
object
  inherit ['a] get_demo x
  method appender x = element:= !element ^ x
end;;
class strings :
  string ->
  object
    val element : string ref
    method appender : string -> unit
    method get : unit -> string
  end
#
```

The type parameter enables this class to be definable. If this class were not parametric, the compiler would issue an error because not all type information can be determined from the code provided (as you can see from the following compiler errors).

```
# class get_demo x =
object
  val element = ref x
  method get () = element.contents
end;;
        Characters 5-86:
  ..... get_demo x =
  object
    val element = ref x
    method get () = element.contents
  end..
Some type variables are unbound in this type:
  class get_demo :
    'a -> object val element : 'a ref method get : unit -> 'a end
The method get has type unit -> 'a where 'a is unbound
#
```

Composition vs. Inheritance

Inheritance isn't the only way to provide functionality in a class; you can also use composition. Composition is when you have a class that has some feature (instead of being some feature). If you refer to the extended_random number class from the inheritance examples, there is an example of composition. You will define a new class that uses composition instead of inheritance to provide functionality.

The extended_random class provides a new method that mimics a single die with an arbitrary number of sides. The new class (using composition) uses this class to provide a craps simulation.

```
# class craps =
object
  val rand = new extended_random
  method roll () = ((rand#between 1 6),(rand#between 1 6))
end;;
        class craps :
  object val rand : extended_random method roll : unit -> int * int end
# let cr = new craps;;
Random Constructor
Extended Random Constructor
val cr : craps = <obj>
# cr#roll ();;
- : int * int = (6, 6)
# cr#roll ();;
- : int * int = (4, 3)
#
```

Although these two rolls were not very lucky, composition can be used exclusively—you do not need to use inheritance to use objects.

Multiple Inheritance

Multiple inheritance is one of those features that cause controversy. OCaml fully supports multiple inheritance, as do languages such as Python and C++. Java, however, does not. Even in languages that support it, its use is rare.

Multiple inheritance occurs when a class inherits from two classes that share a common ancestor. Demonstrating multiple inheritance requires a few classes to be created. These classes do not really do anything, but they serve as good examples of what multiple inheritance is, what problems it solves, and why people think it is a bad idea.

Suppose that you are designing an HR system. You start to work on the parts that deal with employees, so you start with an employee base class. This class has hire and fire methods, and holds information common to all employees.

```
class employee =
object
  val mutable hiredate = ""
  val mutable isactive = false
  val mutable firedate = ""
  method hireDate () = hiredate
  method isActive () = isactive
  method terminationDate () = firedate
  method hire x = hiredate <- x;isactive <- true
  method fire x = firedate <- x;isactive <- false
end;;
```

The company is a trading firm, so you also have to create a specific class for employees who are traders. Traders have limits on the quantities they can trade and should have those limits eliminated when they are fired.

```
class trader =
object(s)
  inherit employee as super
  val mutable limit_quant = 0
  method canTrade () = (limit_quant > 0) && isactive
  method setLimit x = limit_quant <- x
  method fire x = super#fire x;s#setLimit 0
end;;
```

The company employs researchers who cannot trade, but they can study things. So researchers also inherit from the employee base class and extend that class with new methods.

```
class researcher =
object(r)
  inherit employee
  val mutable studies: string list = []
  method studies x = List.mem x studies
  method addStudies x = studies <- x :: studies
end;;
```

This class looks pretty good. Then the head of HR tells you that the company also has trader-researchers who can trade and have the same activities as both a trader and a researcher. To solve the problem of needing a hybrid type of employee, use a new class that implements methods from traders and researchers.

```
class traderresearcher_first =
object(s)
  inherit employee
  val mutable limit_quant = 0
  method canTrade () = (limit_quant > 0) && isactive
  method setLimit x = limit_quant <- x
  val mutable studies: string list = []
  method studies x = List.mem x studies
  method addStudies x = studies <- x :: studies
end;;
```

The problem with this method is that it duplicates code. If you make a change to the trader class, you have to make changes to this one, too, which can introduce errors or (worse) create a situation in which they are out of sync. What you want to be able to do is inherit from both the trader class and the researcher class—this is called multiple inheritance.

```
class traderresearcher_second =
object(trs)
  inherit trader as strade
  inherit researcher
  method fire x = strade#fire x
end;;
```

This new class will change if you change the underlying classes. The inheritance diagram in Figure 18-1 shows one problem that is confirmed when you compile the code.

Figure 18-1. *Inheritance diagram showing the dreaded diamond.*

This diamond-shaped inheritance diagram is sometimes referred to as the *dreaded diamond*. It is so named because of the problem the compiler warns you about when you compile the class:

```
Warning V: this definition of an instance variable isactive hides a previously ➡
defined instance variable of the same name.
```

The new class has two copies of the isactive value. It has two copies of several values, too, and the compiler will tell you about all of them. But which copy is the correct one? Is it the one from the trader class or the one from the researcher class? OCaml solves this problem by picking the last one. You can also use the superclass to explicitly manipulate both copies, but that can lead to serious confusion later.

Although not always practical, you should use only pure virtual classes when you use multiple inheritance. That way, you cannot hide variables. As long as you are aware of this functionality, the diamond does not need to be dreaded.

Functional Objects and Object Cloning

You do not have to keep state within your objects; you can create functional objects by using the {< >} notation.

```
# class funcobj (x: int) =
          object
                      val data = x
                      method get_data = data
                method set_data newdata = {< data = newdata >}
          end;;
```

You define the class by using the {< >} construct, which returns a copy of self, leaving the original intact. You can see this class instantiated and run here, creating two instances of the object:

```
class funcobj :
  int ->
  object ('a)
    val data : int
    method get_data : int
    method set_data : int -> 'a
  end
# let b = new funcobj 30;;
val b : funcobj = <obj>
# b#get_data;;
- : int = 30
# let q = b#set_data 35;;
val q : funcobj = <obj>
# q#get_data;;
- : int = 35
# b#get_data;;
- : int = 30
#
```

· You can use this construct to copy objects without chaining variables by specifying no arguments between the braces. This is equivalent to using the Oo.copy function directly. Using this construct is not the same as having a function that returns a new object. For example, if you rewrote the preceding code using new, it would look like this:

```
# class nonfuncobj (x: int) =
            object
                       val data = x
                       method get_data = data
                   method set_data newdata = new nonfuncobj newdata
            end;;
class nonfuncobj :
  int ->
  object
    val data : int
    method get_data : int
    method set_data : int -> nonfuncobj
  end
```

Although the instances of nonfuncobj behave the same as the previous example, classes that derive from it will not (because the method explicitly returns a new object instead of a copy of self).

```
# let f = new nonfuncobj 10;;
val f : nonfuncobj = <obj>
# let q = f#set_data 20;;
val q : nonfuncobj = <obj>
# q#get_data;;
- : int = 20
```

```
# class inherit_nonfuncobj x =
          object
              inherit nonfuncobj x
          end;;
class inherit_nonfuncobj :
  int ->
  object
    val data : int
    method get_data : int
    method set_data : int -> nonfuncobj
  end
# let f = new inherit_nonfuncobj 20;;
val f : inherit_nonfuncobj = <obj>
# let q = f#set_data 30;;
val q : nonfuncobj = <obj>
#
```

This difference is important. Using 0o.copy avoids this problem, as does using the {< >} construct. You should always be mindful of the consequences of your design decisions when using objects; you never know whether they will be inherited from (unless you use only direct objects).

Larger Example

Now you can put (almost) everything together in a larger example. The edit distance (or Levenshtein distance) describes how close two strings are to one another. It describes the number of transformations or substitutions required to turn one string into another. The calculation uses a two-dimensional matrix and is iterative.

The two dimensions of the matrix are determined by the length of the strings. Each letter in the first string is compared with each letter in the second; if it is the same, the cost is 0. If it is not the same, the cost is 1. The value of each element i.(x).(y) in the matrix is set equal to the lesser of the elements in location i.(x – 1).(y) or i.(x).(y – 1) or i.(x – 1).(y – 1). You can see a representation of the matrix in Figure 18-2.

		t	o	s	s	e	d
	0	1	2	3	4	5	6
t	1	0	1	2	3	4	5
o	2	1	0	1	2	3	4
a	3	2	1	2	2	3	4
s	4	3	2	1	1	2	3
t	5	3	3	2	2	2	3
e	6	4	4	3	3	2	3
d	7	5	5	4	4	3	2

Figure 18-2. *Matrix*

The solution is in the lower-right corner of the matrix. In this example, you turn one s into an a and insert one t (you get "toasted" from "tossed"). Although you can do this calculation by hand, it is much easier to use a computer to do it. (The following code describes a set of classes to do this.)

The base class is a parametric virtual class. It is parametric because you cannot have polymorphic methods or data in a given class. It is virtual because the calculation method is left unimplemented. This next class has been created to calculate edit distances of data types other than strings.

```
class virtual ['a] edit_distance first_item  second_item =
object(ed)
  val f = (first_item: 'a)
  val s = (second_item: 'a)
  val mutable calced = false
  val mutable matrix = ([|[|||]|] : int array array)
  method private gen_matrix f_size s_size = let matri =
    Array.create_matrix (s_size + 1) (f_size + 1) 0 in
    Array.iteri (fun x y -> match x with
                            0 -> Array.iteri (fun n m -> matri.(x).(n) <- n) y
                          | _ -> matri.(x).(0) <- x ) matri;matri
  method private trimin x y z = match x,y,z with
      m,n,o when (m > n) -> if (n < o) then n else o
    | m,n,o when (m < n) -> if (m < o) then m else o
    | m,n,o -> if (n < o) then n else o
  method private update_matrix m d d' cost = let fval = m.(d).((d' - 1)) + 1 in
  let sec = m.((d - 1)).((d')) + 1 in let third = m.((d - 1)).((d' - 1)) + cost in
  let newval = ed#trimin fval sec third in
    m.(d).(d') <- newval
  method virtual private calc: unit -> unit
  method distance () = ed#calc ();matrix.((Array.length ➥
 matrix)-1).((Array.length matrix.(0)) - 1)
end;;
```

The signature for this class looks like this:

```
class virtual ['a] edit_distance :
  'a ->
  'a ->
  object
    val mutable calced : bool
    val f : 'a
    val mutable matrix : int array array
    val s : 'a
    method private virtual calc : unit -> unit
    method distance : unit -> int
    method private gen_matrix : int -> int -> int array array
    method private trimin : int -> int -> int -> int
    method private update_matrix :
       int array array -> int -> int -> int -> unit
  end
```

I wanted to encapsulate this into a class so that the users of the class do not have to know that it is not a purely functional solution. I am modifying data and using imperative techniques to generate the solution. However, because I encapsulated it into a class, the users will be unaffected if I change it in the future.

To calculate the edit distance for strings, I inherit from the preceding and create a new class. This new class implements the calculation for strings and provides an initializer. The initializer prepares the matrix for the calculation that is done. Notice that the calculation function is private because users of the class can call only the distance method, which returns the edit distance. This method (the distance method) is public in the base class.

```
# class string_edit_distance x y =
    object(sed)
    inherit ['a] edit_distance x y
    method next m n =
       {< matrix = sed#gen_matrix (String.length m) (String.length n);
          f=m;
          s=n;
          calced = false >}
method private calc () =
       if (not calced) then
          (Array.iteri (fun ind x -> match ind with
                      0 -> ()
                    | dex -> Array.iteri (fun ind' x' -> match ind' with
                             0 -> ()
                           | dex' -> if (f.[(dex' - 1)] = s.[(dex - 1)])
                                   then
                                      sed#update_matrix matrix dex dex' 0
                                   else
                                      sed#update_matrix matrix dex dex' 1
                    ) x) matrix;
          calced <- true )
initializer matrix <- sed#gen_matrix (String.length x) (String.length y)
end;;

# class string_edit_distance :
  string ->
  string ->
  object ('a)
    val mutable calced : bool
    val f : string
    val mutable matrix : int array array
    val s : string
    method private calc : unit -> unit
    method distance : unit -> int
    method private gen_matrix : int -> int -> int array array
    method next : string -> string -> 'a
    method private trimin : int -> int -> int -> int
```

```
    method private update_matrix :
        int array array -> int -> int -> int -> unit
  end
```

Using this class is simple.

```
# let ed_string = new string_edit_distance "toasted" "tossed";;
val ed_string : string_edit_distance = <obj>
# ed_string#distance ();;
- : int = 2
#
```

However, the calculation required is somewhat labor-intensive. What if you want to do this for thousands of words with many repeats? You need a memorized version of the class. Lucky for you, this class was created, and inheritance can help you add this feature.

```
class sed_memoized x y =
object(sm)
  inherit string_edit_distance x y as sed
  val memo = Hashtbl.create 100
  method distance () = try
    Hashtbl.find memo (f,s)
  with Not_found ->
    let d = sed#distance () in
    Hashtbl.add memo (f,s) d;
    d
  method keys = Hashtbl.fold (fun key hval arr ->
                                        if (List.mem key arr) then
                                                arr
                                        else
                                            (key :: arr)) memo []
  method memo_size () = Hashtbl.length memo
end;;
```

In this case, you just add a new data value, add a hashtable to store the results of the calculation, and change the distance function. (A function to return the current size of the memorization store was added for display purposes.) If there is a lot of duplication of data, and the data strings are long, this memorized version of the class can yield a great performance improvement.

```
class sed_memoized :
  string ->
  string ->
  object ('a)
    val mutable calced : bool
    val f : string
    val mutable matrix : int array array
    val memo : (string * string, int) Hashtbl.t
    val s : string
    method private calc : unit -> unit
```

```
      method distance : unit -> int
      method private gen_matrix : int -> int -> int array array
      method keys : (string * string) list
      method memo_size: unit -> int
      method next : string -> string -> 'a
      method private trimin : int -> int -> int -> int
      method private update_matrix :
          int array array -> int -> int -> int -> unit
   end
#
# let s = new sed_memoized "groused" "greased";;
val s : sed_memoized = <obj>
# s#distance ();;
- : int = 2
# let s = s#next "toasted" "tossed";;
val s : sed_memoized = <obj>
# s#distance ();;
- : int = 2
# s#memo_size ();;
- : int = 2
# let s = s#next "grandmother" "grandfather";;
val s : sed_memoized = <obj>
# s#distance ();;
- : int = 2
# s#memo_size ();;
- : int = 3
# let s = s#next "incompetent" "competent";;
val s : sed_memoized = <obj>
# s#distance ();;
- : int = 2
# s#memo_size ();;
- : int = 4
#
```

These classes work only on strings. What if you want a class that works on lists? The algorithm is equally applicable to lists of arbitrary items as it is to strings, so it should be possible (and the base class has been parameterized to support it). The next class, list_edit_distance, does just this. It creates a class that can return the edit distance of any list of comparable elements. The compare function from the Pervasives module was used, so it should work on just about anything. The following example shows the code and a usage example using integer lists:

```
# class list_edit_distance x y =
object(led)
  inherit ['a] edit_distance x y
  method calc () = Array.iteri (fun ind x -> match ind with
                          0 -> ()
```

```
                                | dex -> Array.iteri (fun ind' x' -> match ind' with
                                                               0 -> ()
                       | dex' -> if ((List.nth f (dex' - 1))= (List.nth s (dex - 1)))
                                 then
                                  led#update_matrix matrix dex dex' 0
                                 else
                                  led#update_matrix matrix dex dex' 1) x) matrix
initializer matrix <- led#gen_matrix (List.length x) (List.length y)
end;;
class list_edit_distance :
  'a list ->
  'a list ->
  object
    val mutable calced : bool
    val f : 'a list
    val mutable matrix : int array array
    val s : 'a list
    method calc : unit -> unit
    method distance : unit -> int
    method private gen_matrix : int -> int -> int array array
    method private trimin : int -> int -> int -> int
    method private update_matrix :
        int array array -> int -> int -> int -> unit
  end
# let led = new list_edit_distance [1;2;3;4;5] [1;2;4;5];;
val led : list_edit_distance = <obj>
# led#distance ();;
- : int = 1
#
```

Conclusion

The object-oriented features in OCaml give the programmer access to advanced features to help with reuse and encapsulation. Although understanding OOP helps you use the OCaml object system, you don't need to be an OOP guru to use it to provide encapsulation for your own applications.

OCaml is a practical language. It seeks to provide the programmer with the tools to solve problems, even if those tools use a methodology and practice that is not neatly contained within functional programming. The object model for OCaml is one of these tools. It is a mature and powerful framework for solving real problems.

The next chapter is a bit of a digression. You'll find a discussion about the nature of OCaml and how it is (or is not) pure in the functional programming sense. Although not a strictly technical chapter, I encourage you not to skip over it. Understanding the thought behind things can help you use all aspects of the language.

CHAPTER 19

■ ■ ■

Digression: OCaml Is Not Pure

A purely functional function has no side effects. A purely functional programming language would not allow functions with side effects to be defined. But wait, there's more! Because functions and algorithms cannot have side effects, variables are immutable and persistent. This persistence is not the same as disk storage or serialization; it means that previous versions of a given value can be retained by the language.

OCaml is not a purely functional programming language, but it does implement many things that make a "pure-er" language than a strictly imperative language such as C. Persistence and immutability, for example, are something OCaml uses quite effectively. Consider the following example:

```
# let mystring = "First Value\n";;
val mystring : string = "First Value\n"
# let printer () = print_string mystring;;
val printer : unit -> unit = <fun>
# let mystring = "Second Value\n";;
val mystring : string = "Second Value\n"
# let second_printer () = print_string mystring;;
val second_printer : unit -> unit = <fun>
# printer ();;
First Value
- : unit = ()
# second_printer ();;
Second Value
- : unit = ()
# mystring;;
- : string = "Second Value\n"
#
```

The printer function prints the original value, not the current value because that function was defined using the original value. This is different from a language like Python because values in Python are really variables, which are just names for bits of data. These variables are mutable, unlike the values in OCaml.

```
>>> mystring = "First Value"
>>> def printer():
...      print mystring
...
>>> mystring = "Second Value"
>>> def second_printer():
...      print mystring
...
>>> printer()
Second Value
>>> second_printer()
Second Value
>>>
```

Functional programming has not been as popular as other styles of programming. Object oriented programming (OOP), for example, has pretty much won the language style popularity contest (a title it stole away from C and other structured programming languages that were once very popular).

One reason why functional programming has lagged behind is that, historically, functional programming languages could not match the speed of imperative languages. This has changed with the advent of modern compilers and processors, and OCaml is often as fast as imperative languages. Sometimes even faster.

Speed alone is not the only reason why programmers have chosen imperative methods over functional ones, however. If only it were a simple matter of execution speed, converts could be made easily with benchmarks and tests. No, one of the reasons why programmers have stayed away from functional languages is that expressing solutions to some problems is much easier in an imperative manner. The presence of modifiable variables and data structures can simplify the writing of code.

In the OCaml code, there is no way to change the output of the first printer function without redefining it. The Python code, however, enables you to change the output of both functions simply by changing one variable. You can even change that variable, as opposed to the OCaml, where we cannot.

However, OCaml is not a pure language; you can use the impure parts of OCaml to write the same code as the Python code. You can use mutable references, which are more akin to Python variables than OCaml values. The following OCaml code now behaves in an imperative way.

```
# let mystring = ref "First Value\n";;
val mystring : string ref = {contents = "First Value\n"}
# let printer () = print_string !mystring;;
val printer : unit -> unit = <fun>
# mystring := "Second Value\n";;
- : unit = ()
# let second_printer () = print_string !mystring;;
val second_printer : unit -> unit = <fun>
```

```
# printer ();;
Second Value
- : unit = ()
# second_printer ();;
Second Value
- : unit = ()
```

This ability to choose between functional and imperative programming styles means that you can choose the best way to solve whatever problem you are trying to solve. Solving problems is why programming languages were invented in the first place.

Functional Programming

A functional programming language is (sometimes) referred to as pure if it performs computation via functions without side effects. Any manipulation, outside of returned information, of data or state is a side effect.

The kind of purity discussed here is relevant only in the world of functional programming. There is no universally accepted definition of what is (or is not) a purely functional language. A common definition is that a language is pure if it does not allow side effects. However, a language can also be referred to as pure if it does not allow its functions to have side effects. This looser definition enables languages that implement monadic computation to be considered pure. Monadic computation and monads in general are creations that open up a small loophole for purely functional languages. Although a purely functional language cannot have functions with side effects, it can have values that describe and contain side effects. This boils down to computational sleight-of-hand that comes with a cool-sounding name. OCaml avoids this kind of situation by enabling functions to have side effects, but not relying on them.

This distinction between pure and impure is largely an academic one, which revolves around whether the evaluation of an expression is separate from its execution. This separation enables code evaluation without mixing up the properties of functions and expressions. Separating evaluation from execution means that the code is evaluated into the set of operations to be performed before these operations are executed. This has nothing to do with the code or the compiler: this evaluation and execution are at the semantic (or the meaning of the program) level.

This kind of purity enables a programming language to have input/output (I/O) operations that include state information and still be considered purely functional. This is something that Haskell uses extensively (see later sections in this chapter).

Really, Why Should You Care?

I cannot answer that question for you. However, I can tell you that the effects of a purely functional language include a fully explicit data flow within the program. In and of itself, that is not a very interesting item of discussion. However, one of the effects of a fully explicit data flow is that it makes the order of execution of functions within a program irrelevant.

You might want to think about that for a moment before moving on because it is a pretty profound statement. Not only does it mean that the program is always (and maybe automatically) parallelizable but it also means that you can optimize the program in ways that are impossible with other languages.

One major problem with the previous statement is that life doesn't always enable it to come to reality. I/O, for example, can be a real serious problem for real, true, purely functional languages. In fact, statefulness in general creates a problem because statefulness is often tied with order of execution.

This juncture is an area in which real life and mathematical cleanliness collide, much to everyone's dismay. Most useful programs do have some sort of input and some sort of output. To return to the original question of why you should care about this purity, you will find that the answer lies with you. If you are interested in these issues, you will care; if not, you will not.

I can give you one reason to care, though: understanding functional programming will make you a better programmer. Functional programming requires you to think about problems in a way you might not have done before. Although you might consider this expansion negligible, don't discount it so quickly. Functional programs make heavy use of recursion, interesting problems of state, and program flow that can make you a better programmer when going back to an imperative language because you are now armed with new tools.

Purely Functional Data Structures

A purely functional data structure is a data structure that does not allow destructive modification. Updates to this data structure preserve the old values (in some way) and allow for multiple versions of that data structure to exist. This persistence can be very beneficial for some applications.

Purely functional data structures have not been as popular as imperative data structures because imperative data structures have been around longer (and there are more examples of them). The definitive guide to purely functional data structures is the (aptly named) book *Purely Functional Data Structures*, by Chris Okasaki (Cambridge University Press, 1999).

OCaml lists are examples of purely functional data structures. After a list is allocated, individual elements cannot be modified, removed, or added to. A new list can be created, but the old list is preserved, even though you may not be able to access the old list.

Purely functional data structures work best when you are working in a language that supports automatic garbage collection because of the problems associated with managing data structures that cannot be modified. In the list example, one of the problems isn't a problem if you have garbage collection.

```
# let a = [1;2;3;4];;
val a : int list = [1; 2; 3; 4]
# let b = [10;12;14];;
val b : int list = [10; 12; 14]
# let c = List.rev_append a b;;
val c : int list = [4; 3; 2; 1; 10; 12; 14]
# let c = List.rev_append a c;;
val c : int list = [4; 3; 2; 1; 4; 3; 2; 1; 10; 12; 14]
#
```

The second definition of the list named C is the problem. The list that was originally named C is preserved, but you can no longer access it. Without automatic garbage collection, you would have created a memory leak. Discarding previous versions of data structures is common when dealing with purely functional data structures.

Another benefit of using purely functional data structures is that they have properties that make it easier to reason about programs that use them. This ability to reason about programs makes optimization and analysis much easier (in some cases, even possible). As programs get more and more complicated, it will be increasingly important to be able to use other programs to analyze computer programs.

OCaml offers a variety of the purely functional (lists, maps, and sets) and the impure (arrays, hashtables, and queues) that enable you to decide which style of data structure is better for your application. This gives you the flexibility to use the best solution to the problem in practical terms, instead of theoretical terms.

Languages Like OCaml

OCaml is not pure. Like many other meta-language (ML)–derived languages, OCaml includes imperative programming operators and references that enable a programmer to write functions that have side effects.

I/O operations are excellent examples of this kind of function. The Scanf.bscanf function modifies the scanning buffer when it operates on it. This fact is one of the things that make I/O operations less painful in OCaml. The state information that is updated in the scan buffer is a side effect of the bscanf function. Without the capability to perform these kinds of updates, state information would have to be handled in a very different (and certainly more difficult) manner.

I/O isn't the only place in which OCaml shows its impurity. The OCaml object system also enables functions that have side effects.

Note Side effects do not have to be obvious or even visible to qualify as side effects. A side effect is any change of data as a result of a function call.

OCaml is strongly and statically typed and it also throws away all the type information at compile time. These facts have a whole series of implications, including the fact that Java style reflection is impossible.

All the type information must be present and accounted for at compile time; you cannot create a new type on-the-fly. Direct objects and variant types are not dynamically created, even though they might feel as if they are. Both of them provide their type information at compile time, even if those types are never used.

Languages Like Haskell

Haskell is a purely functional language. Like Miranda, it is one of the few purely functional languages in common use, but it is dissimilar in every other way. Purely functional programming languages are rare in common practice. One of the common reasons their opponents give for not using purely functional languages is that the box you must remain in when using a purely functional language is too small. The proponents of purely functional languages often have equally unflattering reasons why the world has not adopted them.

Haskell is the most well-known of the "non-Lisp-y" functional programming languages. It is taught in many university programs, probably even more often than Scheme (even more so as many computer science programs in the United States move to teaching Java instead of Scheme).

Haskell uses a *monad* to accomplish many of the concepts discussed in this chapter. A monad is purely functional, is difficult to fully understand, and is way, way beyond the scope of this discussion and this book.

Benefits of Impurity

Solving problems is often easier if you use an imperative approach. Chapter 18 showed an example of a class that calculated the edit distance of a string. The class used a mostly imperative algorithm to do this.

Although this algorithm could be expressed by using a purely functional approach, it would be much more difficult to describe. I have tried to do this in the past and have always stopped because of the difficulty and because I had an existing solution.

This existing solution is another of the benefits of impurity. You often have the description of an algorithm that will solve a problem you are working on, and that description is probably not in a functional style. Sometimes the conversion into a function style is easy. Sometimes it is not.

I assume that because you are reading this book you are more interested in practical solutions to problems that you have now (or will have soon). Given that assumption, I can tell you that this ability to implement solutions in whatever style the solution exists is a Good Thing.

Hiding the Impure

If a variable is changed in the woods, and no one is around to hear, does it make any difference? The short answer is "No, with a but;" the long answer is "Yes, with a set of caveats."

Either way, hiding side effects in functions is a good idea—no matter what style of programming you are using. Information hiding like this is a central tool in OOP.

You do not have to hide the impure in your code. There is no standard for this sort of thing, and within your own code you can do pretty much whatever you want. However, you will probably want to hide most function side effects from your users (to make maintenance programming easier, at least).

Preventing Information Leaks

Really, what side effects come down to are information leaks. Information about the specifics of your implementation of a given function "leak" out when you use side effects.

It means that programmers using your functions must be aware of these side effects and account for them. This is a problem even if you are the programmer using it because it makes your future changes more difficult.

The example used to discuss encapsulation is the creation of a circular list, which is a list that doesn't have a beginning or an end. The beginning of the list is linked to the end of the list. One way to implement and hide the imperative side of this is to use objects. Although this example uses objects to encapsulate the imperative operations, you also can use the module system to do it.

The signature for the class follows. This is a parameterized class because you will be dealing with different types of lists, and methods cannot be polymorphic. This implementation is an imperative implementation and is not pure in a functional sense.

```
class ['a] imperative_cerc :
  object
    val mutable data_array : 'a array
    val mutable index : int
    method add_item : 'a -> unit
    method empty : unit
    method item : 'a
    method iter : ('a -> unit) -> unit
    method map : ('a -> 'b) -> 'b array
    method next : unit
    method prev : unit
  end
```

Following is the implementation code for the imperative_cerc class. Note the mutable data values.

```
class ['a] imperative_cerc =
  object(s)
    val mutable data_array = [||]
    val mutable index = 0
    method item = try
      data_array.(index)
    with Invalid_argument "index out of bounds" -> raise Not_found
    method add_item (x: 'a) = data_array <- Array.concat [data_array;[|x|]]
    method next =
      let newindex = index + 1 in
      match newindex with
              n when n < Array.length data_array -> index <- newindex
            | _ -> index <- 0
    method prev = let newindex = index - 1 in
      match newindex with
              n when n > 0 -> index <- newindex
            | _ -> index <- (Array.length data_array) - 1
    method iter (x:('a -> unit)) = Array.iter x data_array
    method map : 'b . ('a -> 'b) -> 'b array = fun f -> Array.map f data_array
    method empty = data_array <- [||];index <- 0
end
```

When you now use this code from the toplevel, after you create the instance of this class, the types are not concrete yet (denoted by the '_a type in response).

```
# let c = new imperative_cerc;;
val c : '_a imperative_cerc = <obj>
# c#add_item 10;;
- : unit = ()
# c#add_item 11;;
- : unit = ()
# c#add_item 12;;
- : unit = ()
# c#item;;
- : int = 10
# c#next;;
- : unit = ()
# c#next;;
- : unit = ()
# c#item;;
- : int = 12
# c#next;;
- : unit = ()
# c#item;;
- : int = 10
# c;;
- : int imperative_cerc = <obj>
#
```

You have taken an impure set of operations and data and encapsulated it into a class. This class is easy to use, especially for programmers who are more comfortable in an imperative context. Encapsulation doesn't have to be imperative.

You can recode this class into a more purely functional form using the functional objects semantics available in the object system. The following signature shows one of the biggest differences between the imperative and the functional example: many methods in the functional example return an object of the same type as itself.

```
class ['a] functional_cerc :
  object ('b)
    val data_array : 'a array
    val index : int
    method add_item : 'a -> 'b
    method empty : 'b
    method item : 'a
    method iter : ('a -> unit) -> unit
    method map : ('a -> 'c) -> 'c array
    method next : 'b
    method prev : 'b
  end
```

The preceding signature shows the implementation code. There are no mutable data values in this implementation. None of the methods changes the state of the object.

```
class ['a] functional_cerc =
  object(s)
    val data_array = [|||]
    val index = 0
    method item = try
      data_array.(index)
    with Invalid_argument "index out of bounds" -> raise Not_found
    method add_item (x: 'a) =
      {< data_array = Array.concat [data_array;[|x|]] >}
    method next = let newindex = index + 1 in
      match newindex with
              n when n < Array.length data_array -> {< index = newindex >}
            | _ -> {< index = 0 >}
    method prev = let newindex = index - 1 in
      match newindex with
            n when n > 0 -> {< index = newindex >}
          | _ -> {< index = (Array.length data_array) - 1 >}
    method iter (x:('a -> unit)) = Array.iter x data_array
    method map: 'b . ('a -> 'b) -> 'b array = fun f -> Array.map f data_array
    method empty = {< data_array = [|||];index = 0 >}
end

# let c = new functional_cerc;;
val c : '_a functional_cerc = <obj>
# let c = c#add_item 10;;
val c : int functional_cerc = <obj>
# let c = c#add_item 11;;
val c : int functional_cerc = <obj>
# let c = c#add_item 12;;
val c : int functional_cerc = <obj>
# c#item;;
- : int = 10
# let c = c#next;;
val c : int functional_cerc = <obj>
# let c = c#next;;
val c : int functional_cerc = <obj>
# c#item;;
- : int = 12
# let c = c#next;;
val c : int functional_cerc = <obj>
# c#item;;
- : int = 10
# c;;
- : int functional_cerc = <obj>
#
```

Both of these classes can be used to create a specific type of circular list, which also can have only a specific type of map function. This means that although each instance of the class is concrete for a specific type, you can have multiple instances of the class operating on many different types.

```
# let c = new imperative_cerc;;
val c : '_a imperative_cerc = <obj>
# c#add_item "hello";;
- : unit = ()
# let d = new imperative_cerc;;
val d : '_a imperative_cerc = <obj>
# d#add_item 10.;;
- : unit = ()
# c;;
- : string imperative_cerc = <obj>
# d;;
- : float imperative_cerc = <obj>
#
```

Objects are not the only way impurity can be hidden; the OCaml module system provides another way to accomplish it. If you are familiar with patterns, the OCaml module system can be described as a singleton pattern.

```
module type Cerc =
  sig
    val implist : 'a list ref
    val implist_index : int ref
    val safe_incr : int ref -> unit
    val safe_decr : int ref -> unit
    val add_item : 'a -> unit
    val next : unit -> 'a
    val prev : unit -> 'a
    val first : unit -> 'a
    val last : unit -> 'a
    val map : ('a -> 'b) -> 'b list
    val empty : unit -> unit
  end
```

The preceding signature shows that although the map function type is polymorphic, the other functions are not. The implementation follows:

```
module Cerc =
struct
  let data_array = ref [||]
  let index = ref 0
  let item () = try
    !data_array.(!index)
```

```
with Invalid_argument "index out of bounds" -> raise Not_found
let add_item (x: 'a) = data_array := Array.concat [!data_array;[|x|]]
let next () = let newindex = !index + 1 in
  match newindex with
            n when n < Array.length !data_array -> index := newindex
      | _ -> index := 0
let prev () = let newindex = !index - 1 in
  match newindex with
            n when n > 0 -> index := newindex
      | _ -> index := (Array.length !data_array) - 1
let iter (x:('a -> unit)) = Array.iter x !data_array
let map (x:('a -> 'b)) = Array.map x !data_array
let  empty () = data_array := [||];index := 0
end;;
```

This module behaves similarly to the imperative class version shown before. There are some major differences, though, because of the OCaml type system. Module functions can be polymorphic, so the module does not have to be parameterized. The module system also does not have an instance the way classes do.

Not being able to create multiple instances of a module means that after you use the module with a given type, you cannot change types. Because it is polymorphic, the map function is not affected by this restriction. The add_item function is not polymorphic, however, so the type is retained even after you empty the list.

```
# Cerc.add_item "hello";;
- : unit = ()
# Cerc.add_item "world";;
- : unit = ()
# Cerc.empty ();;
- : unit = ()
# Cerc.add_item 10;;
Characters 14-16:
  Cerc.add_item 10;;
              ^^
This expression has type int but is here used with type string
# Cerc.add_item;;
- : string -> unit = <fun>
#
```

You can see the effect in the error message generated when you try to put an integer into the circular list.

You can encapsulate impure operations within functions or closures. Doing this does hide the operation from the user of that function, but it taints that function because it does have side effects (you just have to look harder to see them). This is true unless, of course, the side effects do not escape that function.

```
# let freq item lst =
    let newlst =
      List.map (fun x -> item = x) lst in
    let counter = ref 0 in
    List.iter (fun x -> if x then
                    incr counter
                ) newlst;
    !counter;;
val freq : 'a -> 'a list -> int = <fun>
# freq 'e' ['a';'e';'i';'o';'u';'e'];;
- : int = 2
```

Just for the sake of completeness, the previous example can be rewritten in a pure style quite simply:

```
# let freq item lst =
    let newlist = List.filter (fun x -> x = item) lst in
    List.length newlist;;
val freq : 'a -> 'a list -> int = <fun>
# freq 'e' ['a';'e';'i';'o';'u';'e'];;
- : int = 2
```

The functional implementation is, arguably, more elegant than the imperative one.

Conclusion

You should approach the impurity of OCaml the same way you approach any feature in the language: use it if it works for you. The imperative features of OCaml are there to help you solve problems. There are other features to make using these features maintainable and workable for the programmer, but they sometimes require more thought than they do in other languages.

This chapter covers one of the more fuzzy areas of OCaml. The fact that OCaml comes from the wrong side of the tracks, as it were, of the programming community makes it important to talk about these things. For now, OOP rules the popular programming languages. OOP stole the crown from the structured programming community, who stole it from the one before, and so on. There is nothing in the OOP world to indicate why it will not lose its dominance some day, too.

That day might not belong to functional programming languages, but it is likely that functional programming will continue to affect the programming world. It will most certainly affect the programmers of the world, which is more important, anyway.

Chapter 20 discusses functional programming in particular. You have seen that OCaml is not purely functional; in the next chapter you will see that OCaml is quite functional.

■■■

Digression: Functional Programming

At various points in this book, I noted that OCaml is a functional programming language. Chapter 19 told you that OCaml is not a purely functional programming language and what that lack of purity is about.

Functional programming has been the "Next New Thing" longer than most of the current crop of object-oriented languages has been around. This fact often leads people to ask whether functional programming is actually relevant. If you're reading this book, you haven't (hopefully) made up your mind about that topic yet. Although I can tell you that it is still relevant, simply asserting something doesn't make it true (in much the same way that declaring yourself a fish does not stop you from drowning).

A program, once written, should perform a given task. That is pretty obvious, but what is not obvious about that statement is that there is an implicit verification. How can you know the task has been accomplished? Simple tasks are easy to verify, but complex ones are, well, more complex. This is especially true in programming languages and computation. If you have a 10,000-line program, how do you verify that it does what you think it does? What about a 100,000-line program? What about 1,000,000 lines?

Overview of Programming Styles

Functional preprogramming (FP) is only one of several programming styles that are currently in widespread use. Each of these programming styles seeks to maximize programmer efficiency and minimize bugs. Programming has always tried to do these things, even before Grace Hopper created the first useful compiler.

■Note Back in the days before assembly language, programmers had to program in machine code directly or hard-wire the logic directly.

For these purposes, programming styles can be divided into three groups: structured, object-oriented, and functional. They are not strong divisions, and often a given programming language supports features of all three. Most of the time, a given programming language does have more strength in one of the three groups.

Structured Programming

Structured programming is sometimes also referred to as imperative programming. The term *structured* is mostly historical and refers to the way a given program is organized. The structured programming languages rose when programs were often just sequences of instructions (often using GOTOs). Perl, Pascal, and C are examples of structured programming languages.

Structured programs can have subsections with restricted entry points. The restriction on entry points is different from using GOTOs (in which there is no restriction on where the program flow can go). These subsections are often referred to as *functions* and are different from the functions of functional programming because they can have side effects. In fact, side effects are an important feature of the language in languages such as C.

When you are writing a structured program, you should break larger code segments into smaller ones that are simple enough to be easily understood and managed. Features such as global variables should not be used often. Many languages provide support for structure with local variables, functions, and procedures; as well as the capability to pass variables by reference rather than copying the value each time.

Structured programming encourages a "top-down" design, which means that the large-scale aspects of a program must be engineered first. They are then broken down into smaller components, which are then integrated into the larger program.

Top-down design requires that the initial design be correct. If it is not correct, the entire program could be created incorrectly. Structured programming does not, however, require that design be top-down. There are many programming methodologies in existence that attempt to address this particular shortcoming of structured programming.

It has been a long time since there was any debate surrounding the benefits of modular programming. Structured languages allow for modularity of function, although in an importantly different way from functional programming languages.

Object-Oriented Programming

Object-oriented programming (OOP) is a relative newcomer to the programming world. Although the ideas behind OOP have been around for some time, it wasn't adopted by the wider programming community until popular languages such as C++ and Java were formalized in the late 1980s and early 1990s. Smalltalk, arguably the precursor to all modern OOP languages, saw wide use but was never adopted to the extent that C++ and Java have been.

The central idea behind OOP is that a given program is a collection of objects. These objects interact with each other, pass information (or messages), and perform computations. The program itself is then just the interaction of these objects.

This solves several problems for programmers, not the least of which is that many items that programmers try to model are really objects. Hierarchies of objects can model real-world objects and enable flexibility in design.

Proponents of OOP claim that objects make the creation of large applications easier. Not only do objects provide the benefits of structured programming but they also take it further and provide data hiding and polymorphism (as well as other concepts).

It is argued that hierarchies created by inheritance do not accurately represent real-world objects. This complaint is often addressed by the use of composition of objects rather than inheritance.

Objects can also free the program designer from the top-down methodology. Because objects can be freely reused, both within a given program and between programs, a developer can use them as components. These components, which can be taken from a toolbox of components, provide a way for code to be reused and bug fixes to be easily propagated within code bases.

Functional Programming

Functional programming is an old concept, having been created originally in the form of the Lambda Calculus by Alonzo Church in the 1930s. Church's calculus was not a programming language itself. Instead, it was a way to describe calculation (that is, function evaluation—which is why it was called a calculus instead of a language). The concepts behind functional programming are closer in age to structured programming concepts than OOP. Lisp, the first functional programming language, was developed in the 1950s. Languages such as Miranda and Prolog are also in the family of functional languages, as is Haskell. The meta-language (ML) family of languages, from which OCaml is derived, was created in the 1970s. The first ML compilers were written in Lisp.

There are concepts that are easier to implement in a functional style than in an alternative one. An example is the MapReduce concept, which is a function that takes two functions as arguments. The first function is mapped to a container of data; the second reduces the data returned from the map application. This method is used widely in parallel applications and has recently been touted by Google as part of its internal applications in several published papers. This concept is easy to describe using a functional style because functions are treated like other types. Following is an example of a MapReduce program written using ocamllex as the tokenizer. The first example returns the average number of words in all the normal files in a given directory.

```
rule tokens = parse
    ['\n' '\013'] { `Line }
  | ([^ ' ' '\t' '\n' '\013']+ as word) { `Word (String.length word)}
  | [' ' '\t'] { `Whitespace }
  | eof { `Eof }
and words = parse
    ['\n' '\013'] { `Line }
  | ([^ ' ' '\t' '\n' '\013']+ as word) { `Word word}
  | [' ' '\t'] { `Whitespace }
  | eof { `Eof }
```

The preceding lexer is quite simple. There are two entry points: the first one is for the first example, and the second is for the second example. There are variant types with two types in the argument (the `Word type is a `Word of int and a `Word of string).

The countemup function simply counts the number of words, lines, and characters in a given file (you'll see more examples later in the chapter).

```
{
  let rec countemup lbuf words chars lines =
    let tok = tokens lbuf in match tok with
                `Line -> countemup lbuf words (chars + 1) (lines + 1)
      | `Whitespace -> countemup lbuf words (chars + 1) lines
      | `Word n -> countemup lbuf (words + 1) (chars + n) lines
      | `Eof -> lines,words,chars;;
```

The word_count_map_reduce function implements the map and the reduce. It actually implements two MapReduces; the first one is the filter function. List.filter can actually be thought of as a simple form of the MapReduce concept. It is somewhat limited in the fact that the map calculation must return a Boolean, and the input data is not modified.

In this case, the result is the normal files (by name) in a given directory. The function then counts the number of words in each file. This list of word counts is then reduced to a total using the fold_left operation, and the result is the total number of words divided by the number of files.

```
let word_count_map_reduce directory =
  let files = List.filter
    (fun x -> let ftype =
                (Unix.stat (Filename.concat directory x)).Unix.st_kind in
            match ftype with
                Unix.S_REG -> true
                | _ -> false) (Array.to_list (Sys.readdir directory)) in
    let counts = List.map fun x -> let ic = open_in (Filename.concat directory x)
in
    let lb = Lexing.from_channel ic in
    let l,w,c = countemup lb 0 0 0 in
      close_in ic;
      w
) files in
    let numfiles = List.length counts in
      (List.fold_left (+) 0 counts) / numfiles;;
```

This example doesn't provide very much useful code, though. There are other ways to get the average number of words in a given set of files. What if you want to know the most frequent words in a given group of files? Also, the single function used previously is probably best broken into smaller chunks. Following is the get_files function, which gets the normal files in a given directory.

```
let get_files directory = List.filter
    (fun x -> let ftype =
                (Unix.stat (Filename.concat directory x)).Unix.st_kind in
            match ftype with
              Unix.S_REG -> true
              | _ -> false) (Array.to_list (Sys.readdir directory));;
```

Now you need to use the tokenizer to get the words in each file.

```
let rec getwords lbuf wordlst =
  let tok = words lbuf in match tok with
                `Line -> getwords lbuf wordlst
      | `Whitespace -> getwords lbuf wordlst
      | `Word n -> getwords lbuf (n :: wordlst)
      | `Eof -> wordlst;;
```

The count_instances function makes use of the partition function to count the number of instances of a given item in a list of items. It returns a list of pairs of each item and the number of occurrences of that item in the original list. This function, combined with the function that follows it, enables you to choose the top *N* items, by frequency of occurrence, from any given list.

```
let rec count_instances lst acc = match lst with
  [] -> acc
| h :: t -> let instances,rest = List.partition (fun x -> x = h) t in
    let instance_count = (List.length instances) + 1 in
      count_instances rest ((h,instance_count) :: acc);;

let top_n_elements ?(compfunc=compare) count lst = let sorted =
  List.sort compfunc lst in
List.fold_left (fun acc elt -> if ((List.length acc) >= count) then
                                  acc
                                else
                                  elt :: acc) [] sorted;;
```

Finally, the actual function that returns the top *N* items from a given directory is a MapReduce function with a function to return only a subset of the reduced list.

```
let top_n_words_map_reduce count directory =
    let files - get_files directory
    in
    let wordlist =
      List.concat
        (List.map
          (fun x -> let ic = open_in (Filename.concat directory x)
                    in
                    let lb = Lexing.from_channel ic
                    in
                    let words = getwords lb []
                    in
                    close_in ic;
                    words)
        files)
    in
    let reduced = count_instances wordlist []
    in
    top_n_elements ~compfunc:(fun x y -> compare (snd y) (snd x)) count reduced;;
```

This code can be built and used as follows:

```
$ ocamllex map_reduce.mll
7 states, 266 transitions, table size 1106 bytes
$ ocamlc -c map_reduce.ml
$ ocamlmktop -o mr.exe unix.cma map_reduce.cmo
$ ledit mr
        Objective Caml version 3.09.0
```

```
# Map_reduce.word_count_map_reduce "./musepages/";;
- : int = 166
# Map_reduce.top_n_words_map_reduce 10 "./musepages/";;
- : (string * int) list =
[("in", 34); ("for", 34); ("that", 46); ("I", 50); ("a", 63); ("is", 68);
 ("and", 79); ("of", 92); ("to", 95); ("the", 146)]
```

These functions might take some time to complete, especially in directories with many files. Running the code on a directory of text files reveals that there is an average of 166 words in each file and that the word *the* is the most commonly found word, showing up 146 times. The word *in* is the tenth most common word, showing up a scant 34 times.

The preceding code could be implemented in any programming language. However, it is the expressive power of functional programming that enables it to be expressed easily in OCaml—and in only 87 lines of code.

The last point to make about important aspects of functional programming is the idea of lazy evaluation of data. Haskell, for example, is a lazy language and it does not evaluate all function arguments before the function is evaluated. ML and its derivates are strict—all function arguments are evaluated before the function. Lazy evaluation is not, strictly speaking, a requirement for functional programming even though it is often a part of it. OCaml, like the other ML languages, does not support lazy evaluation.

Advantages of Functional Programming

In short: less code and fewer bugs. This may seem like a very strong statement to make, so hold on a moment before rushing to judgment. Functional programs are often shorter in terms of lines of code (LoC) than either structured or OOP implementations. As shown at the Win32 Shootout (found at http://dada.perl.it/shootout), there were a total of 640 lines of OCaml code versus 1068 lines of C and 798 lines of Java (which translates to roughly 40 percent and 20 percent shorter, respectively). If you can agree that the number of bugs in any given program is proportional to the number of LoC, you can argue that a shorter program is (by definition) a less-buggy program.

Note The Win32 Shootout was inspired by the original Shootout created by Doug Bagley. He took a set of problems (the Sieve of Erasthenes, word count, and so on) and tested implementations of many programming languages. He reported their sizes, execution speed, and other variables in an attempt to provide an unbiased comparison between languages. The results achieved are still hotly debated.

Having fewer bugs is not the only reason to use functional programming. With languages such as OCaml, there are functional languages that strive to be correct (discussed in more detail later on). Functional programming also supports and encourages reductionism to solve the problem. By reducing a problem to its component parts, you have modular programs that are often easier to maintain than their structured counterparts (even though they might also be modular). Although there is no short example I can show to demonstrate this, John Hughes and Paul Graham (two highly influential programmers) have published papers on the subject.

You can find them at `http://www.cs.chalmers.se/~rjmh/Papers/whyfp.html`. Graham even credits his ability to produce Viaweb (a product later sold to Yahoo) with the flexibility, modularity, and overall "goodness" provided by the functional language he used (which is Lisp). The modularity of functional languages can be achieved in structured languages, but it is often achieved via policy rather than being enforced by the language. This difference can be very important in terms of maintenance, especially when the maintenance is not done by the original author.

Functional languages are also often easier to analyze programmatically. In many functional programming languages, a given function can have only one entry point and one exit point. OCaml, for example, allows only one entry point and one exit point. This language-level enforcement of Single Entry, Single Exit simplifies creating tools for analyzing the code. Programmatic validation of code is a topic that is gaining a lot of interest in the programming world, especially regarding the creation of more robust systems.

Sometimes, OCaml programmers decry the absence of a return statement in OCaml as a Bad Thing. One of the important things to remember is that mathematical functions do not have multiple points of exit. This kind of conditional result requires two functions, each applied in the domain of the problem. The lack of multiple points of exit results in smaller, more numerous functions—each with a given output on each given input. In turn, these smaller components are less complicated, and (theoretically) easier to debug.

Less Code

There are several reasons why this is true, and one of the biggest is that functional languages are often more terse than their structured counterparts. This terseness does not hamper their expressiveness, and because functional languages are just as Turing-complete as their structured brethren. Expressiveness is more than simple Turing completeness; the functional programming style encourages short functions that perform simple actions.

Less code is also a direct result of more general modularity. The ability to decompose problems into smaller parts is dependent on the ability to utilize those parts. Higher-order functions are a very powerful way in which those parts can be used (often referred to as "bottom-up" programming). Paul Graham pointedly notes in the introduction of his book, *On Lisp*, that bottom-up programming doesn't mean that you are simply writing your program in a different order from top-down methods. When you write programs from the bottom up, you write the program in a different way entirely. Top-down design and programming encourage a more monolithic construction that is often more complex than the equivalent bottom-up design. One of the biggest effects is that bottom-up programming encourages programmers to find patterns in their code.

Bottom-up programming also encourages reuse. When you write many programs, the utilities and functions that are useful in one program are often useful in others. This enables you to (hopefully) use already-debugged functions and routines in new programs, reducing the number of defects in those newly created programs.

Higher-order functions can allow for fewer lines of code and enable programmers to modularize code in ways not available in other styles and languages. Although modularization and bottom-up programming can be done in any language, functional programming languages such as OCaml are designed with this in mind. The features and function of a language often play a subtle role in the way programs written in that language are designed.

Fewer Bugs

The number of defects in a given program is proportional to the number of lines, which is a statistical fact instead of an objective one. Writing defect-free programs is like driving without accidents. Statistically speaking, you have a non-zero probability of getting into an auto accident no matter how good a driver you are. The probability remains non-zero even if you never get into an accident. Couple this with the fact that defects are always more likely to occur in complex code than in simple code, and you have motivation to make your programs as short as possible.

Large functional programs are made up of much smaller functional programs (as a result of the bottom-up design). These smaller programs (the functions themselves) are easier to debug and therefore easier to make defect-free. A program is more than the sum of its parts. That being true, it means that a collection of defect-free parts can be assembled into a defect-containing whole. However, it is easier to build a defect-free whole when you start with defect-free parts.

The central push toward modularity of code also reduces the number of possible bugs. If a segment of code is messy, it probably needs to be modularized. The resulting modules might be useful in other sections of the code or might even have been created in the code already, which eliminates that part of the messy code. This modularity also allows for more thorough checking and validation of each component. That fact that most functional languages do not allow side effects makes this validation easier and more accurate.

If you look at three programs that do the same thing, written in three different languages, you can see an example of OCaml programs requiring less code (and that code being more flexible). The first example is the lowly word count program, often seen as wc on Unix systems. The other two examples are written in plain C and Java.

```
rule tokens = parse
    ['\n' '\013'] { `Line }
  | ([^ ' ' '\t' '\n' '\013']+ as word) { `Word (String.length word)}
  | [' ' '\t'] { `Whitespace }
  | eof { `Eof }
{
  let _ = let lb = Lexing.from_channel (open_in Sys.argv.(1)) in
  let rec countemup lbuf words chars lines =
    let tok = tokens lbuf in match tok with
                `Line -> countemup lbuf words (chars + 1) (lines + 1)
      | `Whitespace -> countemup lbuf words (chars + 1) lines
      | `Word n -> countemup lbuf (words + 1) (chars + n) lines
      | `Eof -> Printf.printf " %i %i %i %s\n" lines words chars Sys.argv.(1)
  in
    countemup lb 0 0 0;;
}
```

This code is 16 lines long and it even uses ocamllex to provide a flexible tokenizer. The next example is the one in C. It is nearly twice as long, coming in at 30 LoC.

```c
#include <stdio.h>
int main(int argc,char **argv) {
  FILE* fd = fopen(argv[1],"r");
  int lines = 0;
  int chars = 0;
  int words = 0;
  int ch = 0;
  while (1) {
    int lastchar = ch;
    ch = fgetc(fd);
    if (ch == EOF) {
      printf(" %d %d %d %s\n",lines,words,chars,argv[1]);
      return(0);
    }
    switch(ch) {
    case '\n':
      lines++;
      chars++;
      break;
    case ' ':
      chars++;
      if (lastchar != ' ') {
              words++;
      }
      break;
    default:
      chars++;
    }
  }
}
```

The last example is the one in Java. At 20 lines, the length of this example is on par with the OCaml example program because of the extensive Java standard library, which has built-in string operations that are sophisticated and easy to use.

```java
import java.io.*;
import java.util.*;
class Wc {
    public static void main(String[] args) throws FileNotFoundException {
              Scanner sc = new Scanner(new File(args[0]));
              int lines = 0;
              int words = 0;
              int chars = 0;
```

```java
        while (sc.hasNext()) {
          String ch = sc.nextLine();
          lines++;
          chars += (ch.length() - 1);
          Scanner wds = new Scanner(ch);
          while (wds.hasNext()) {
                      String discarded = wds.next();
                      words++;
          }
        }
        System.out.printf(" %d %d %d %s\n",lines,words,chars,args[0]);
    }
}
```

Not looked at with these examples are speed of execution and development, which are often insignificant when compared with ease of maintenance. Shorter, more modular code is easier to maintain and easier to extend in the future. If you want to change the program so that it also counts the number of lines containing a given expression, which do you think is easier to modify? For me, the OCaml code is much more flexible in this regard (because of its use of ocamllex). The Java example is probably second on that list, with the C example coming in a distant third.

Programming in the Large

In his famous (and near-mythic) paper, "Why Functional Programming Matters," John Hughes noted the following:

> *Since modularity is the key to successful programming, functional languages are vitally important to the real world.*

The modularity that functional languages are capable of is far greater than just collections of subroutines by which structured languages are characterized. Some people refer to bottom-up versus top-down development. Functional languages are very much bottom-up languages.

In a functional language, a function can be created, tested, and debugged independently of a larger program. That function can be used as a modular component in the composition of larger and more-complicated functions. These modular components can be built up from small parts, like bricks in a house, until the structure of the program is complete.

Because these small components are easy to understand (at least they are easier to understand than the entire program), it is easier for a programmer to create and maintain them. Also, because only the inputs and outputs are important, they are much more useful for composing more-complicated functions. The underlying functions can be changed without disrupting the higher-level functions as long as the inputs and outputs are the same type.

Hughes believed that the modularity provided by functional programming was so important that he wrote his entire paper based on that concept.

Correctness of Programs

Languages such as SPARK Ada from Praxis software embody the idea of "Correctness by Construction" or CbyC. This methodology has arisen because certain very large programming projects (such as air traffic control systems) need to have defect rates that are lower than tolerable from more mainstream programming methodologies.

Correctness, however, is something that is important even in systems that probably will not cause widespread destruction if they fail. Users of consumer products have learned to tolerate defect rates that are very high, higher even than the 7 to 8 defects per 1000 lines of code outlined by the Capability Maturity Model (CMM) Level 1.

Several of the fundamental principles of CbyC are shared by functional programming. These shared principles are as follows:

- Using strong, tool-supported methods to validate each deliverable

- Carrying out small steps and validating the deliverable from each step

- Designing software that is easy to validate

Languages such as OCaml are designed to have very strong methods of validating the code. These strong methods go beyond static checking tools such as Lint for C. The small steps and subsequent validation of those steps is standard practice when designing programs with functional languages. The last point is more than a restatement of the first. Designing software that is easy to validate is concerned more with the language used than with the tools or methodology. The language used and its output must be able to be validated. The ability to reason about programs in the language is a great step toward making these principles practical.

Concurrency

As computer systems require more and more computing power, programmers have had to turn to concurrent computing. Concurrency is a difficult concept for people to deal with because they are serial by nature.

Concurrency is also a real problem for programming styles that are highly dependent upon state (as in structured programs that rely on side effects). Functional programs that do not have side effects are often much easier to make concurrent than other styles because of the referential transparency that side effect–free programming has.

Theoretic ease is quite different from actual ease when implementations are concerned. Some functions are inherently parallelizable, such as the MapReduce function mentioned previously; others are not. Whether a function is inherently parallelizable is often linked very closely with I/O operations and is something outside the functional programmer's control.

All things being equal, though, functional programs are often much more amenable to concurrent versions than other styles because of side effect–free functions and the nature of functional evaluation.

Concurrency is an issue that will become only more important as time goes on. Functional programs are easier to think about for humans than other styles in concurrent environments, which is a major factor in being able to produce defect-free code that actually does what it is supposed to do. If the programmer cannot intellectually process the problem effectively, that programmer has little hope of producing code to create a solution effectively.

The optimizations of function calls that are possible in functional languages also have an effect on concurrency. This is an area that is very active in research and something that will hopefully yield some very interesting parallelizing compilers in the future.

Reasoning About Programs

Being able to reason about programs is a very important idea. It is also an idea that is sometimes difficult to explain. Small and medium-sized programming projects can often be understood by a single programmer (they can be held within one person's brain).

Large projects, however, cannot be contained in the head of one person, which is a major problem because it is very difficult for people to solve problems that they cannot perceive completely. These large projects are often composed of many smaller projects that can be understood by a single person.

Functional programming (mostly) does not allow for side effects in functions, so functions are referentially transparent. This means that the result of a given function for a given set of arguments will have the same result. Having real referential transparency makes the automatic verification of correctness much easier.

For very large programs, the capability to perform programmatic verification of functions and types is a major win. People are very good at figuring out how to do certain things; they are often not so good at verification. Computers, on the other hand, are fantastic at verification, but not so good at the figuring-out part. This is even truer for highly concurrent programs that might be impossible for a human being to adequately understand in any way.

Conclusion

Although functional programming is not the only style of programming that can solve problems, it does have specific merits. Functional programs can be shorter than OOP programs and easier to understand. They also make writing defect-free programs easier because the code is shorter and the components are modular. Functional programming encourages a bottom-up design that can be flexible and enables you to create programs that can adapt to changing requirements and environments. Functional programming is not the only style of programming available, but because this book is about a functional programming language, it is biased toward functional programming solutions.

Remember that there is no silver bullet when it comes to programming. Although functional programming is a very strong style and associated methodology, it is not without warts of its own. When making your design, it is important to not be blind to these weaknesses.

This chapter is not a substitute for more study on the subject. Although I tried to provide a reasonable overview, it is still only an overview.

This chapter focused on some of the more political aspects of OCaml programming. I do not use the word "political" in a pejorative way. On the contrary, I think programmers often do not give things that are not purely technical enough consideration when choosing a given technology.

This chapter also gave you information that can be helpful when discussing the relative merits of one programming style versus another. If you are reading this book, you obviously have an interest in OCaml. Let me assure you that I also have a great interest in OCaml and hope that this book (and the other books on the subject) help the OCaml community grow and thrive.

## CHAPTER 21

Practical: Web Programming

Web programming is one of the best ways for a language to gain visibility. Ever since the web gained widespread popularity, developing for web targets has been important for a wide variety of programmers.

Web front ends have provided many developers an easy way to allow for multiplatform access. In today's world of mobile devices, an application must be web-accessible. In many ways, OCaml is an excellent programming language for web programming.

Because nearly every platform has a web browser (even many cell phones), it makes sense to target the web as a platform when designing applications (this is easier said than done.) How do you handle state? What about security? This chapter will give you some of these answers.

Note Most of the code shown here works only on Unix and Unix-like platforms. Specifically, the third-party Common Gateway Interface (CGI) and FastCGI libraries are for Unix only. The Apache-specific items probably work on Windows, but for the most part this chapter should be considered to be for Unix only.

The focus on security and safety makes OCaml an excellent choice for web programming. There are also a few existing libraries that help take some of the tediousness out of writing web code (especially processes such as parsing query strings and cookie management).

What Does Web Programming Mean?

Many people talk about web programming, and it can mean many different things. Java developers often talk about web programming in the context of Java Server Pages or application frameworks such as Apache Tomcat.

When I talk about web programming, I am talking about CGI and CGI-like programming. OCaml is not designed to be a web programming language like PHP. Because PHP was designed originally to be a web programming language, it includes many features and functions that provide webcentric functionality (for example, the way PHP allows HTML to be intermingled with PHP code).

OCaml was designed to be a general-purpose programming language. As such, it does not focus on one area of deployment, like the web. That doesn't make it less effective for web programming, but it does mean that the approach to web development taken by the language is different. OCaml programs can be run as CGI programs, or you can even write a web server in OCaml and execute web-based applications that way.

CGI

CGI is probably the oldest method of providing abstracted web programming. Most major web servers support CGI, and many web programmers got their start writing CGI scripts.

Note This chapter uses the term *script* to mean any program or fragment.

CGI is the most mature framework for writing web-enabled code. For many applications, it is more than good enough to support the needs of the users.

Benefits of CGI

CGI is the simplest way of doing web programming (in terms of how the program interacts with the web).

When using native code (which OCaml is fully capable of doing), CGI programming can be lightweight. (It is a common misconception that CGI is a heavyweight programming method because the web server serving CGI requests must execute the CGI program every time it is called.)

Drawbacks of CGI

One of the biggest drawbacks of using CGI is that it does not easily support stateful applications. The CGI standard does not define a way for preserving state from one call of a CGI program to another. Each execution of a CGI program is just that: the execution of that program with the input and output redirected by the server. This execution is often done via a fork/exec on the server side (which can be somewhat costly in terms of CPU cycles). This lack of statefulness creates a situation in which a developer must think in pages instead of implicitly having state information available.

Note *State* is all the information about what's going on with a given application. In normal desktop applications, such as a word processor, you know about text that is entered, mouse clicks, and so on. In a CGI application, you have only the data that is sent when the CGI is executed. After the CGI application finishes, it exits and is no longer running. Every time a CGI is called, it is as if it is starting for the first time, which can present interesting challenges for complex applications.

This absence of state information is not an insurmountable problem. There are many ways of handling it, especially because most information is stored in a database. Statefulness is more a help for the programmer than a hindrance for the user.

The most problematic aspect of CGI is that it requires the web server to execute the script every time it is called. On many web servers, the fork/exec carries certain performance and resource penalties that can be a large burden for heavily used applications.

Note the term *fork/exec* is a Unixism that describes the way many applications first fork a child process and then use the exec system command to start another process. This duo is a very convenient mechanism, but it has performance implications.

This fork/exec is not a performance problem in and of itself. However, for applications that expect to get a moderate amount of use, it can create a situation in which a web server can easily be swamped. This is especially true of applications that tend to be peaky (for example, when a press release causes many visitors to rush to a site, all hitting dynamic content). Forking can slow the site down and reduce the number of visitors a given server can handle. OCaml can be compiled to native code, so the startup time required for a given application can be minimized when compared with interpreted code.

For long-running processes, the fork/exec is great. But the performance trade-offs might be higher than is acceptable for many short-lived processes. The programmer must always keep in mind the unique performance characteristics of running applications via CGI.

FastCGI

FastCGI, which was created to address the shortcomings of CGI, started out as a proprietary extension to the CGI spec. It was then released and became a standard.

FastCGI scripts are started only once. They then go into an event loop in which each call to the URL passes the data to an already running script. This eliminates the fork/exec and provides a way to maintain state information.

FastCGI is really a different way of writing web applications than CGI or integrated methods. In FastCGI, your application is running the whole time. FastCGI uses more traditional IPC (Unix domain sockets or IP sockets) to handle the interprocess communication. This IPC mechanism also enables FastCGI programs to be located on more than one machine, which can be important for performance—especially in a language such as OCaml that does not support SMP. Because FastCGI is not a very popular way of writing web applications, it will not be covered in any more detail in this chapter.

Integrated Approaches

Integrated approaches seek to pull the logic of web-based applications closer into the web server to provide better application performance. They also can provide a better way of allowing for state management and interprocess communication.

ASP

Although it might be possible to program ASP (and ASP.NET) with F# (Microsoft Research's port of OCaml to the .NET platform), it is not really a practical suggestion. As noted, most of the web programming resources for OCaml focus on the Unix environment.

Mod_caml

Fashioned after the wildly successful mod_perl library, the mod_caml library enables direct access to the Apache web server, as well as the capability to cache data and substantial performance improvements.

There is also a library (confusingly) called mod_ocaml. Although both libraries were created to solve the same set of problems, the mod_caml library is more mature.

Other Frameworks

There are other frameworks, too. Typesafe programming and secure-by-design programming have become new in web design. Frameworks such as Ex-nunc and Ocsigen are two frameworks that provide typesafe environments for building web applications.

Ex-nunc can be downloaded from http://ex-nunc.sourceforge.net. (At the time of this writing, you can also find sample code and a limited amount of documentation.) Ocsigen (found at http://www.ocsigen.org) is also under active development. Ex-nunc supports CGI and FastCGI, whereas Ocsigen uses its own http server.

Chapter Focus

Now that you know what can be, you can learn about what is. It is possible to fill a set of books on all the fine nuances of web programming with OCaml, but all that reading is probably not the best use of your time.

This chapter focuses on a single simple application and enables you to see how it works under CGI (both hand-rolled and a library) and mod_caml.

CGI

You can roll your own library for handling CGI requests. This process has some advantages, especially if you are trying to integrate your code into an existing code base. The disadvantages of this track are more apparent for complicated apps than for simple ones.

I have found it convenient to embed miniweb servers in applications to provide easy access for clients and users. Although having your application as its own web server is probably not appropriate for every application, it is something to keep in mind because it can be a boon for control panels and for configuration of an application. Having the application as its own web server also reduces the external requirements for the application because they don't need to already be running a web server to use the functionality.

Ocamlnet

Ocamlnet is a third-party library that provides a number of features (CGI functions are only one part). Ocamlnet provides a class-based interface to CGI, FastCGI, the Jserv protocol, an embedded web server, and the Post Office Protocol (POP).

Mod_caml

Capitalizing on the Apache web server, mod_caml provides a robust and functional environment in which to create web services. It also supports a templating mechanism, which enables you to separate your logic from presentation.

Rolling Your Own CGI Functions

The best place to start is with your own-rolled version of the application. The CGI environment is well-documented, and it is easy to access the query string from any language. The query string is just a specially formatted key/value pair string, and each key/value pair is separated from the others by the & char. Many web clients transpose characters into UTF-8 for you if you use restricted chars in your data (such as the ? char, which separates the end of the CGI filename from the beginning of the key/value pairs). You can check this by examining the Content-type: header, looking for the charset parameter (for UTF-8, it is Content-type: text/html; charset=utf-8).

Benefits

One of the biggest benefits of rolling your own code is that you are not tied to the dependencies of another package. Many packages have dependencies on other libraries. Ocamlnet depends on several other libraries that you might not want your code to be dependent upon.

Anther benefit of rolling your own CGI functions is that you can even write your own embedded web server and process CGI calls through it. (Although this approach works fine for a small number of static handlers, if you are planning to deliver an application to a user community of any size, you probably do not want to maintain a web server in addition to the application code itself.) This approach might not be scalable, but it is very powerful. Having an embedded web server in your applications means that you can access the applications from any web client.

Another benefit of rolling your own CGI functions is that you can process the query string any way you want. The query string (the actual data passed to the CGI script in the form of a GET request) is basically a key/value pair list delimited by the & character. POST data is in the same format, but is not passed via an environment variable. This data is passed via standard input. Following is a short example that uses ocamllex to provide a lexer for data passed to a CGI script that prints out the keys and values passed to it:

```
rule tokens = parse
    ([^ '=']+ as key)'='([^ '&']+ as value)['&']? { `Key (key,value) }
  | eof { `Eof }

{
  let rec builder lbuf acc =
    let nextok = try
      tokens lbuf
      with m ->
              Printf.printf "Status: 400 Bad request\n";
              raise m in
    match nextok with
      `Key (m,n) -> builder lbuf ((m,n) :: acc)
    | `Eof -> acc;;
```

```
let get_cgi_data () = let qs = Sys.getenv "QUERY_STRING" in match qs with
            "" -> (let clen = try
                            int_of_string (Sys.getenv "CONTENT_LENGTH")
                        with Not_found -> 0 in match clen with
                            0 -> ""
                            | _ -> let strbuf = String.create clen in
                                let res = input stdin strbuf 0 clen in
                                    strbuf)
            | _ -> qs;;

let parse_cgi () =
  let qs = get_cgi_data () in
  let lb = Lexing.from_string qs in
  builder lb [];;

let _ =
  let items = parse_cgi () in
  print_string "Content-Type: text/html; charset=iso-8859-1\n\n";
  List.iter (fun (x,y) -> Printf.printf "<b>%s</b> %s<br/>\n" x y) items;;
}
```

Drawbacks

Fine control over the code and the data can be a significant drawback to rolling your own CGI functions. You have to maintain all the code you write (unless you are very, very lucky), and more code means more maintenance. You must also implement any feature you want. Some features, such as multipart file downloads, are not simple feature adds—and aren't even supported in mature and robust libraries such as Ocamlnet.

Tip You can specify an HTTP response code from CGI scripts by sending a `Status:` header instead of a `Content-type:` header. For example, if you want a script to return a 301 status because a script has been moved, you can use `print_string "Status: 301 Document Moved\n\n";;`.

The preceding example does not support multipart file downloads. Although the example is flexible, you still have to do the programming to implement any features you want to put into place. One big shortcoming of this code is that it does not handle UUEncoded data.

Longer Examples

For the examples in this section and in the sections to come, you will look at a simple blog-like server. Although it might not seem all that impressive (okay, it really is not all that impressive), it does provide a good way to understand the good, the bad, and the ugly of OCaml web programming.

The Blog

In fewer than 100 lines of code, you can see the code that provides much of what you see on the screen. This is a simple, file-based web log such as CGI. It creates the disk files named by using an MD5 hash of the data within the file, which makes the likelihood of collision so small as to be a nonissue. If I were more concerned, I would add the time to the string used to calculate the MD5 hash, but I haven't done that.

```
exception Short_read;;

let replace_pluses st =
  let buf = Buffer.create (String.length st) in
  String.iter (fun x -> match x with
                    '+' -> Buffer.add_char buf ' '
                  | _ -> Buffer.add_char buf x) st;
                              Buffer.contents buf;;


let compr (_,x) (_,y) = compare y.Unix.st_mtime x.Unix.st_mtime;;

let read_file x = let inf = open_in x in let size =
    (Unix.stat x).Unix.st_size in
let str = String.create size in
let res = input inf str 0 size in
              close_in x;
          (if (res != size) then
              raise Short_read);
          str

let print_header () = Printf.printf "Content-type: text/html\r\n\r\n\n
<!DOCTYPE HTML PUBLIC \"-//W3C//DTD HTML 4.0 Transitional//EN\"
  \"http://www.w3.org/TR/REC-html40/loose.dtd\">
<HTML>
<HEAD>
<TITLE>Simple Blog</TITLE>
<LINK rel=\"stylesheet\" type=\"text/css\" href=\"blog.css\">
</HEAD>
<BODY>
<H1>Simple Blog</H1>
<hr>
<a href=\"blog.cgi?action=main\">Home</a> |
<a href=\"blog.cgi?action=addnew\">New Entry</a> |
<a href=\"blog.cgi?action=about\">About</a> <br>
<hr>
<br>
";;


let print_footer () = print_string "</body></html>";;
```

```ocaml
let print_timestamp x = let st = Unix.stat x in
let utm = Unix.localtime (st.Unix.st_mtime) in
  Printf.printf "<pre>Entry Written: %i/%i/%i %i:%i:%i<pre><br>\n" utm.Unix.tm_mon➥
 utm.Unix.tm_mday
    (utm.Unix.tm_year + 1900) utm.Unix.tm_hour utm.Unix.tm_min utm.Unix.tm_sec;;

let display_all_entries dir = let dirs = Sys.readdir dir in
let sorted = Array.map (fun x -> let fn = Filename.concat dir x in ➥
(fn,Unix.stat fn)) dirs in
  Array.sort compr sorted;
  print_header ();
  Array.iter (fun x -> Printf.printf "%s<br>" (read_file (fst x));➥
print_timestamp (fst x);Printf.printf "<hr>\n") sorted;
  print_footer ();;

let display_entry dir id = print_header ();
Printf.printf "%s\n" (read_file (Filename.concat dir id));
print_footer ();;

let display_about () = print_header ();
Printf.printf "OcamlBlog v.1 2006, by Joshua Smith";
print_footer ();;

let display_posting_form () = print_header ();
  Printf.printf "<form method=\"POST\" action=\"blog.cgi\">
      <input type=\"hidden\" name=\"action\" value=\"newpost\">
      Author: <input type=\"text\" name=\"author\"><br>
      Author Email: <input type=\"text\" name=\"author_email\"><br>
      Title: <input type=\"text\" name=\"title\"><br>
      Entry:<br> <textarea name=\"entry\" rows=\"10\" cols=\"40\"></textarea><br>
      <input type=\"submit\" text=\"Post!\">
    </textarea>
    </form>";
  print_footer ();;

let post_entry dhash outf =
  try
    Printf.fprintf outf "<div class=\"post\">";
    Printf.fprintf outf "<div class=\"author\">Written by: %s</div>\n "
      (replace_pluses (Hashtbl.find dhash "author"));
    Printf.fprintf outf "<div class=\"author_email\"><a ➥
href=\"mailto:%s\">%s</a></div>\n<br>"
      (replace_pluses (Hashtbl.find dhash "author_email")) ➥
(replace_pluses (Hashtbl.find dhash "author"));
    Printf.fprintf outf "<div class=\"title\">%s</div><br></div>" ➥
(replace_pluses (Hashtbl.find dhash "title"));
```

```
      Printf.fprintf outf "<div class=\"entry\">%s</div><br></div></div>" ➡
(replace_pluses (Hashtbl.find dhash "entry"));
      close_out outf
  with Not_found -> Hashtbl.iter (fun x y -> Printf.fprintf ➡
stderr "%s %s\n" x y) dhash;;

let choose_action what dhash qstr = match what with
      "about" -> display_about ()
  | "addnew" -> display_posting_form ()
  | "newpost" -> post_entry dhash (open_out (Filename.concat "/var/tmp/blog" ➡
 (Digest.to_hex (Digest.string qstr))));display_all_entries "/var/tmp/blog"
  | _ -> display_all_entries "/var/tmp/blog";;


let _ = try
  (let qstr = Parse_query_string.get_query_string () in
    match qstr with
                "" -> display_all_entries "/var/tmp/blog"
      | _ -> let dhash = Parse_query_string.parse_query_string qstr in
                choose_action (Hashtbl.find dhash "action") dhash qstr)
with (Parse_query_string.Bad_query_string x) -> display_all_entries "/var/tmp/blog"
  | Parse_query_string.Empty_query_string -> display_all_entries "/var/tmp/blog";;
```

This code does not do the actual CGI part of the program, however. That can be found here (the code should be put into a file called parse_query_string.ml):

```
type tokens = Mainsep | Pairsep | Equal | Normal
exception Bad_query_string of string
exception Empty_query_string

let append x buf = match x with
      '?' -> Mainsep
  | '&' -> Pairsep
  | '=' -> Equal
  | _ -> Buffer.add_char buf x;Normal

let get_query_string () = let reqtype = Unix.getenv "REQUEST_METHOD" in
  match reqtype with
      "POST" -> let qstr = String.create (int_of_string ➡
(Unix.getenv "CONTENT_LENGTH")) in
    let res = input stdin qstr 0 (int_of_string (Unix.getenv "CONTENT_LENGTH")) in
      if (res != (int_of_string (Unix.getenv "CONTENT_LENGTH"))) then
                raise (Bad_query_string qstr)
      else
                qstr
    | "GET" -> let qs = Unix.getenv "QUERY_STRING" in
                qs
    | _ -> raise (Bad_query_string (Unix.getenv "QUERY_STRING"))
```

```ocaml
let get_id qstr_buf = let rec gid sb idbuf lastcall = match lastcall with
    Mainsep -> raise Not_found
  | Pairsep -> raise Not_found
  | Equal -> Buffer.contents idbuf
  | Normal -> let res = Scanf.bscanf sb "%c" (fun x -> append x idbuf) in
      gid qstr_buf idbuf res
in
  gid qstr_buf (Buffer.create 10) Normal

let get_value qstr_buf = let rec gval sb idbuf lastcall = match lastcall with
    Mainsep -> raise Not_found
  | Pairsep -> Buffer.contents idbuf
  | Equal -> raise Not_found
  | Normal -> try
      let res = Scanf.bscanf sb "%c" (fun x -> append x idbuf) in
                gval qstr_buf idbuf res
    with End_of_file -> Buffer.contents idbuf
in
  gval qstr_buf (Buffer.create 10) Normal

let rec parquerstr qstrbuf acc = let id = get_id qstrbuf in
let qval = get_value qstrbuf in
  Hashtbl.replace acc id qval;
  parquerstr qstrbuf acc;;

let print_query_string qst =
  Printf.printf "Content-type: text/plain\r\n\r\n";
  Array.iter (fun x -> Printf.printf "%s\n" x) (Unix.environment ());
  Printf.printf "%s\n" qst;;

let parse_query_string qst = match qst with
    "" -> raise Empty_query_string
  | _ -> let qstrb = Scanf.Scanning.from_string qst in
  let info_hash = Hashtbl.create 10 in
    try
      parquerstr qstrb info_hash
    with End_of_file -> info_hash;;
```

This code is pretty straightforward and to the point. It uses a pretty simple Scanf-based approach to parsing the query strings, either from a GET or a POST operation. It is not very robust, especially because it relies on the CONTENT_LENGTH being set correctly. The CONTENT_LENGTH should be set properly, but it doesn't provide much protection from someone deliberately trying to be sneaky.

This is where OCaml itself comes in. If you fail to handle CONTENT_LENGTH properly, this failure will, at worst, lead to an application crash instead of a buffer overrun or something more sinister. Although that might sound serious, it is definitely preferable to having code that can allow a remote exploit.

But I Want to Add Cookies!

Here is where the drawbacks of rolling your own become apparent. You have your blog application running, but now you want to add authentication. To add support for it, you have to add it myself.

The password code is written (which also gets used in several of the examples), but adding passwords and accounts into the code means you have to write the handlers for it. Not only that, but these features are not trivial (especially if you want to make them robust). The signature for the Password module is much easier to figure out than adding the cookie support will be.

```
val set_file_location: string -> unit
val init: unit -> unit
val full_init: unit -> unit
val change: string -> string -> unit
val check: string -> string -> bool
val add: string -> string -> unit
```

Even the implementation, complete with file locking and caching of information, is easier to write.

```
exception Password_file of string;;

type passwordfile = {location:string;last_loaded:float;➥
data: (string,string) Hashtbl.t};;

let file_location = ref "/var/tmp/passfle";;

let passfile = ref {location=file_location.contents;last_loaded=0.;➥
data=Hashtbl.create 10};;

let load_pwfile pwf = let org_mtime = (Unix.stat pwf.location).Unix.st_mtime in
  if (org_mtime > pwf.last_loaded) then
    let fle = Unix.openfile pwf.location [Unix.O_RDONLY] 0o640 in
    Unix.lockf fle Unix.F_RLOCK 0;
      let ic = Unix.in_channel_of_descr fle in
      let ht = Hashtbl.create 10 in
              try
                while (true) do
                  let line = input_line ic in
                  let splitter = String.index line ':' in
                    Hashtbl.replace ht (String.sub line 0 splitter) ➥
(String.sub line (splitter+1) ((String.length line) - (splitter + 1)))
                done;
              {location=pwf.location;last_loaded=org_mtime;data=ht}
            with End_of_file -> Unix.lockf fle Unix.F_ULOCK 0;Unix.close fle;
              {location=pwf.location;last_loaded=org_mtime;data=ht}
  else
    pwf;;
```

```
let pw_hash_to_string pwf = let buf = Buffer.create 100 in
  Hashtbl.iter (fun x y -> Buffer.add_string buf (x ^ ":" ^ y ^ "\n")) pwf.data;
  Buffer.contents buf;;

let save_pwfile pwf = let fle = Unix.openfile pwf.location➥
[Unix.O_CREAT;Unix.O_TRUNC;Unix.O_SYNC;Unix.O_WRONLY] 0o640 in
  Unix.lockf fle Unix.F_LOCK 0;
  let pwfs = pw_hash_to_string pwf in
  let i = Unix.write fle pwfs 0 (String.length pwfs) in
    if (i = (String.length pwfs)) then
      (Unix.lockf fle Unix.F_ULOCK 0;
       Unix.close fle)
    else
      raise (Password_file "Failed to save");;

let add_password uname pass pwf = Hashtbl.replace pwf.data ➥
uname pass;save_pwfile pwf;;

let verify uname pass passwordfile = let pwf = load_pwfile passwordfile in
  if (Hashtbl.mem pwf.data uname) then
    let pa = Hashtbl.find pwf.data uname in
      pa = pass
  else
    false;;

let set_file_location x = file_location := x
let init () = passfile := load_pwfile passfile.contents
let full_init () = passfile := load_pwfile {location=file_location.contents;➥
last_loaded=0.;data=Hashtbl.create 10};;
let change uname pass = add_password uname pass passfile.contents;;
let check uname pass = verify uname pass passfile.contents;;
let add uname pass = change uname pass;;
```

This Password module is designed to work in a multiuser environment. It uses Unix flock-style file locking to prevent different processes from stomping on one another. The use of these locks is reasonably safe. These locks are only advisory, though, which means that they can be ignored. This fact is important to remember when using flock in your own programs.

Generalized cookie support is not trivial to implement. Fortunately, someone has already done the hard work for you. To take advantage of this library, the code needs to be switched to using the Ocamlnet CGI library.

Ocamlnet

The authors of Ocamlnet have already provided the OCaml world with a library that can handle the parsing of CGI requests, cookies, and pretty much everything else you might want to do with regard to CGI.

It is built on top of the netstream library. It also requires the Perl-compatible, regular expressions library, which you can download from http://www.ocaml.info.

Tip Markus Mottl has written many great OCaml libraries, all of which can be found at http://www.ocaml.info.

Although Ocamlnet has support for many protocols (and even includes an embeddable web server), this chapter focuses on the CGI classes. If you want to do FastCGI programming, Ocamlnet also supports it.

Blog with Authentication

The changes you need to make are pretty minor. While these changes are made, the code can also be modified so that it uses a cookie and has some authentication for posts. That way, only authenticated people can post, but everyone can read all the posts.

The web server's authentication can be used for this, but I wrote a simple cookie-based authentication instead. This code is probably not robust enough for electronic banking, but it demonstrates the basics of using cookies. Much of the following code is the same as the first example, but the code that is unchanged from the first example is bold. The rest of the code is either added or slightly modified from the previous (nonauthenticating) example.

```
open Netcgi;;
open Netcgi_types;;
open Netcgi_env;;
open Netchannels;;

exception Short_read;;

let replace_pluses st =
  let buf = Buffer.create (String.length st) in
  String.iter (fun x -> match x with
                                '+' -> Buffer.add_char buf ' '
                              | _ -> Buffer.add_char buf x) ➥
st;Buffer.contents buf;;

let compr x y = Pervasives.compare (snd y).Unix.st_mtime (snd x).Unix.st_mtime;;

let read_file x = let inf = open_in x in let size =
    (Unix.stat x).Unix.st_size in
let str = String.create size in
let res = input inf str 0 size in
  (if (res != size) then
    raise Short_read);
  str
```

```ocaml
let print_header cgi = let printf = cgi#output#output_string in
  printf "<!DOCTYPE HTML PUBLIC \"-//W3C//DTD HTML 4.0 Transitional//EN\"";
  printf "\"http://www.w3.org/TR/REC-html40/loose.dtd\">";
  printf "<HTML>";
  printf "<HEAD>";
  printf "<TITLE>Simple Blog</TITLE>";
  printf "<LINK rel=\"stylesheet\" type=\"text/css\" href=\"blog.css\">";
  printf "</HEAD>";
  printf "<BODY>";
  printf "<H1>Simple Blog</H1>";
  printf "<hr>";
  printf "<a href=\"blog_cgi_with_auth.cgi?action=main\">Home</a> | ";
  printf "<a href=\"blog_cgi_with_auth.cgi?action=addnew\">New Entry</a> | ";
  printf "<a href=\"blog_cgi_with_auth.cgi?action=about\">About</a> <br> ";
  printf "<hr>";
  printf "<br>";;

let print_footer cgi = cgi#output#output_string "</body></html>";;

let print_timestamp x = let st = Unix.stat x in
let utm = Unix.localtime (st.Unix.st_mtime) in
  Printf.sprintf "<pre>Entry Written:  %i/%i/%i %i:%i:%i<pre><br>\n" ➥
utm.Unix.tm_mon utm.Unix.tm_mday
    (utm.Unix.tm_year + 1900) utm.Unix.tm_hour utm.Unix.tm_min utm.Unix.tm_sec;;

let display_all_entries dir cgi = let dirs = Sys.readdir dir in
let sorted = Array.map (fun x -> let fn = Filename.concat dir x in ➥
 (fn,Unix.stat fn)) dirs in
  Array.sort compr sorted;
  print_header cgi;
  Array.iter (fun x ->  cgi#output#output_string ((read_file (fst x)) ^ "\n");
                        cgi#output#output_string (print_timestamp (fst x));
                        cgi#output#output_string "<hr>\n";()) sorted;
  print_footer cgi;;

let display_about cgi = print_header cgi;
  cgi#output#output_string "OcamlBlog v.1 2006, by Joshua Smith";
  print_footer cgi;;

let check_auth () = let cgi = new std_environment () in
  try
    let has_auth_cookie = List.assoc "blogauth" (cgi#cookies)
    in
      true
  with Not_found -> false;;
```

```
let display_login_form cgi = print_header cgi;
  cgi#output#output_string "<form method=\"POST\" ➥
action=\"blog_cgi_with_auth.cgi\">";
  cgi#output#output_string "<input type=\"hidden\" ➥
name=\"action\" value=\"login\">";
  cgi#output#output_string "Username: <input type=\"text\" name=\"uname\"><br>";
cgi#output#output_string "Password: <input type=\"password\" name=\"pass\"><br>";
  cgi#output#output_string "<input type=\"submit\" text=\"Post!\">";
  cgi#output#output_string "</form>";
  print_footer cgi;;

let display_posting_form cgi = print_header cgi;
  cgi#output#output_string "<form method=\"POST\" ➥
action=\"blog_cgi_with_auth.cgi\">";
  cgi#output#output_string "<input type=\"hidden\" ➥
name=\"action\" value=\"newpost\">";

  cgi#output#output_string "Author Email: <input type=\"text\" ➥
name=\"author_email\"><br>";
  cgi#output#output_string "Title: <input type=\"text\" name=\"title\"><br>";
  cgi#output#output_string "Entry:<br> <textarea name=\"entry\" rows=\"10\" ➥
cols=\"40\"></textarea><br>";
  cgi#output#output_string "<input type=\"submit\" text=\"Post!\">";
  cgi#output#output_string "</textarea>";
  cgi#output#output_string "</form>";
  print_footer cgi;;

let authed_posting_form cgi =
  if (check_auth ()) then
    display_posting_form cgi
  else
    display_login_form cgi

let post_entry (author:string) (author_email:string) (title:string) ➥
(entry:string) outf cgi =
  if (check_auth ()) then
    (try
      Printf.fprintf outf "<div class=\"post\">";
      Printf.fprintf outf "<div class=\"author\">Written by: %s</div>\n " author;
      Printf.fprintf outf "<div class=\"author_email\"><a ➥
href=\"mailto:%s\">%s</a></div>\n<br>" author_email author;
      Printf.fprintf outf "<div class=\"title\">%s</div><br></div>" title;
      Printf.fprintf outf "<div class=\"entry\">%s</div><br></div></div>" entry;
      close_out outf
    with Not_found -> ())
```

```
    else
      display_login_form cgi

let verify_login uname pass = Web_passwords.init ();
  (Web_passwords.check uname (Digest.to_hex (Digest.string pass)));;


let _ =
  let main_cgi =
    new std_activation () in
    let act = main_cgi#argument_value ~default:"show" "action" in
      match act with
                  "about" -> main_cgi#set_header ();display_about main_cgi
                | "addnew" -> main_cgi#set_header ();authed_posting_form main_cgi
                | "login" -> if (verify_login (main_cgi#argument_value
~default:"author" ➡
"uname") (main_cgi#argument_value ~default:"author" "pass")) then
(
                main_cgi#set_header ~set_cookie:[{cookie_name="blogauth";
                cookie_value = (main_cgi#argument_value ~default:"author" "uname");
                cookie_expires = None;
                cookie_domain = None;
                cookie_path = None;
                cookie_secure = false}] ());
                    authed_posting_form main_cgi
                  | "newpost" -> main_cgi#set_header ();➡
post_entry (main_cgi#argument_value ~default:"author" "author")
              (main_cgi#argument_value ~default:"email" "author_email")
                (main_cgi#argument_value ~default:"title" "title")
                (main_cgi#argument_value ~default:"entry" "entry")
                    (open_out (Filename.concat "/var/tmp/blog" ➡
(Digest.to_hex (Digest.string (main_cgi#argument_value ~default:"title" "title")))))
➡main_cgi;display_all_entries "/var/tmp/blog" main_cgi
                    | _ -> main_cgi#set_header ();➡
display_all_entries "/var/tmp/blog" main_cgi;;
```

Even if it looks like there were many changes, most of the code changes were very slight—
they focused mostly on changing the output methods. The application also now supports
cookies.

Mod_caml Library

The mod_caml library provides a way for scripts to be compiled and linked into the web server (these scripts avoid the fork/exec overhead by running inside the web server process). It also enables caching of database connections and template code. Scripts must be registered with the web server before they can be used, which is different from normal CGI programs, which require no registration of any kind. This registration is accomplished by using the Registry class and a run function, which is called every time the script is activated by the web server.

The mod_caml library provides a high-level, class-based interface to CGI calls and templates for generating HTML. Routines are also provided for escaping strings in HTML documents. These interfaces enable you to access the parameters passed to a CGI script from the GET and POST methods.

One benefit of using mod_caml is that it uses Dynalink, which enables the module to reload .cmo files if they change on disk. This means you do not have to restart the web server to roll out changes to a given application. It also means that mod_caml works only on systems that support Dynalink (Microsoft Windows is not one of those systems).

The mod_caml library provides a convenient templating mechanism (it is the only library covered in this chapter that supports it). Templates are great way to separate code from presentation. This is a very important concept because having your logic and presentation intertwined can create problems. The template handling is integrated with the mod_caml library. You can download the code from http://merjis.com/developers, and (assuming that you have the Apache source code downloaded, too) building the code for Apache 1.x is very simple.

There are, however, some issues with using Apache 2.x. The examples used here are from Apache 1.3, but you can read about what needs to be done for Apache 2.x at http://sandbox.merjis.com/developers.

Examples

```
open Apache
open Registry
open Cgi

exception Short_read;;

let replace_pluses st = let buf = Buffer.create (String.length st) in
  String.iter (fun x -> match x with
                             '+' -> Buffer.add_char buf ' '
                           | _ -> Buffer.add_char buf x) st;➡
                        Buffer.contents
 buf;;

let compr x y = Pervasives.compare (snd y).Unix.st_mtime (snd x).Unix.st_mtime;;
```

```
let read_file x = let inf = open_in x in let size =
    (Unix.stat x).Unix.st_size in
let str = String.create size in
let res = input inf str 0 size in
  (if (res != size) then
    raise Short_read);
  str
let viewing_template = "
<!DOCTYPE HTML PUBLIC \"-//W3C//DTD HTML 4.0 Transitional//EN\"
  \"http://www.w3.org/TR/REC-html40/loose.dtd\">
<HTML>
<HEAD>
<TITLE>Simple Blog</TITLE>
<LINK rel=\"stylesheet\" type=\"text/css\" href=\"blog.css\">
</HEAD>
<BODY>
<H1>Simple Blog</H1>
<hr>
<a href=\"blog_mod_caml.cmo?action=main\">Home</a>
<hr>
<br>
::table(entries)::
::entry::
Entry Written: ::timestamp::
::end::
</body>
</html>";;

let get_timestamp x = let st = Unix.stat x in
let utm = Unix.localtime (st.Unix.st_mtime) in
  Printf.sprintf "%i/%i/%i %i:%i:%i" utm.Unix.tm_mon utm.Unix.tm_mday
    (utm.Unix.tm_year + 1900) utm.Unix.tm_hour utm.Unix.tm_min utm.Unix.tm_sec;;

let display_all_entries dir = let dirs = Sys.readdir dir in
let sorted = Array.map (fun x -> let fn = Filename.concat dir x in ➥
 (fn,Unix.stat fn)) dirs in
  Array.sort compr sorted;
  Array.map (fun entry -> ["entry", Template.VarString (read_file (fst entry));
                                        "timestamp",Template.VarString ➥
(get_timestamp (fst entry))]) sorted;;

let run req = let request = new cgi req in
let entrytable = Array.to_list (display_all_entries "/var/tmp/blog") in
let disp_template = Template.template_from_string viewing_template in
  disp_template#table "entries" entrytable;
  request#template disp_template

let () = register_script run
```

Cocanwiki

If you are interested in a large web application that uses OCaml, look at Cocanwiki. You can download the source from http://www.merjis.com (the same site that hosts the mod_caml pages).

Cocanwiki is an excellent wiki. It currently is part of how development on mod_caml and Cocanwiki get paid for.

If You Are Not Using Apache

If you are not using Apache, you are probably stuck with using CGI. Luckily, OCaml supports being compiled to native code, which will mostly eliminate the slow startup times that are often a problem with CGI-based applications.

Being "stuck" with CGI isn't as bad as it sounds. One enormous benefit from targeting CGI is that it is widely supported. Nearly all web servers support it, which means that you can run your code on the widest possible assortment of web servers this way.

You might be able to use FastCGI, but it is unlikely. At this point, FastCGI is fading out of the mainstream of developers. You can also use sockets (as FastCGI does) to run your process and communicate with applications run by the web server that way.

Conclusion

People have written many applications that interact with the web; there are even libraries that support specific web services (Google AdWords is one example). Now that you have seen that OCaml can be used for web programming, I encourage you to explore it more fully. Web enabling existing applications is a great way to increase their usefulness and utility. Web enabling also does not have to be a pure-port of the functionality; you can offer subsets of functionality to different device classes and people.

Chapter 22 continues in the network programming vein and demonstrates a shoutcast server written in OCaml. A shoutcast (streaming MP3 server) is much like data servers of any stripe: they push data to clients. You will see fragments of code from this chapter pop up in the next one.

CHAPTER 22

■■■

Practical: A Shoutcast Server

Shoutcast is a product from Nullsoft (which is also the creator of the WinAMP MP3 player for Windows) to enable audio broadcasting over a network. Nullsoft's Shoutcast server enables clients to stream MP3 data from one client to a server, which is the server that clients connect to in order to listen to that data stream. It is, in effect, a multiplexer of audio streams. Shoutcast was one of the first applications of its kind to become popular. Although streaming network audio predates Shoutcast, it was Nullsoft's product that had the power and flexibility that enabled it to take off.

Shoutcast is also the protocol used by Shoutcast servers to stream data to the client. This protocol defines the information about the data being streamed, as well as the stream itself and how client requests are handled.

The Shoutcast protocol is, in some ways, similar to HTTP. The client request is much like an HTTP GET request (using Icy headers instead of URLs).

■**Caution** A protocol called Icecast has features similar to Shoutcast, but with a completely different implementation. This chapter covers only Shoutcast.

Shoutcast Protocol

When a client makes a request to a Shoutcast server, it sends a specially formatted request to the server that looks like this:

```
GET path/to/the/file HTTP/1.0 <CRLF>
Icy-MetaData:1 <CRLF>
<CRLF>
```

This is pretty much a normal HTTP GET request, except for the inclusion of Icy-MetaData:1, which tells the server that it should send metadata with the stream. The server defined in this chapter always sends the metadata and ignores the specifics of the request.

You can ignore the specifics of the request because the server has only one stream. Many full-featured Shoutcast servers enable you to create multiple streams from the same server. If you want multiple streams from the server, you have to run them on different ports.

After getting a request, the server sends the header information followed by the stream data. The headers will look something like this:

```
ICY 200 OK <CRLF>
icy-name:Ocaml Rocks! <CRLF>
icy-metaint:1024 <CRLF>
Content-Type:audio/mpeg <CRLF>
icy-pub:1 <CRLF>
```

These headers tell the client some very important things. They tell the client that the request was successful; they also tell the client what the name of the stream is (icy-name), how many bytes will pass between metadata updates (icy-metaint), what content type is being streamed (in this case, mpeg audio data), and whether the server is public or private (icy-pub).

The metadata updates in the stream are very important. One major shortcoming of the MP3 standard is that it does not include any way of encoding information about the data (for example, the name of the song being played, the artist, and so on).

Tip The creators of the Shoutcast protocol decided that the metadata would simply be transmitted along with the stream, so the client is responsible for figuring out what part of the stream is metadata and what part of the stream is data-data. To enable the client to do this, the server tells the client how many bytes will pass before the next metadata block. In this case, the client is being told that there will be a metadata block every 1024 bytes of stream data.

A metadata block is a length byte followed by the metadata itself. The length byte is a single byte that represents the length of the metadata divided by 16. Because you know that a byte has a maximum value of 255, you know that the maximum size of the metadata block is 4 KB (or 4096 bytes). The metadata itself is (most often) the title of the current stream, which is sent as the string StreamTitle='ACTUALSTREAMTITLE'; with ACTUALSTREAMTITLE as the name of the current streaming audio. This string must not contain any single quotes ('). The entire length of the metadata block must be at least 16 bytes long (because that is the smallest non-zero value the length byte can hold). The length can also be zero, which also means that the metadata should be zero length as well.

This is important: Metadata must show up where you say it will. You can send a zero, which means a zero length metadata block. If you do not, the client will try to read metadata where there is only real data, which can cause your playback to be choppy.

A big problem occurs when the client mishandles the metadata—the audio will skip. There is also the problem of bandwidth usage. Because you are sending 16 bytes with each metadata block in which you have data, the metadata blocks then occur along with the stream. You can waste a lot of bandwidth with metadata if your update frequency is high.

Note Why is the minimum size for the metadata block 16 bytes? Because the size of the block is specified in multiples of 16.

Handling metadata this way is probably the best solution given the requirements. The client is responsible for catching the metadata in the stream and extracting it. Lucky for you, this works pretty well, and most clients can handle it, too.

Parsing MP3 Files

Because the Shoutcast server serves up MP3 files, you need to be able to find out information about MP3 files. Although the MP3 format does not allow for storage and retrieval of metadata, this shortcoming has been addressed by the ID3 tag standard.

The ID3 standard comes in three flavors: v1, v1.1, and v2. The most common of the three is the v1.1 tag, and the v2 tag is not widely used. MP3 is not the only file in which you can find ID3 tags. Many audio files also use ID3 tags, including Ogg Vorbis and Windows Media files.

Binary Files

OCaml has native support for parsing binary files. When the operating system treats binary files differently from nonbinary files, OCaml provides functions to open these files.

Even on systems that treat binary files differently, the seek and position operators function the same as on systems that do not treat binary files differently. This is very handy if you intend to do binary file processing in OCaml. Scanf and Printf also work the same on binary and nonbinary files. In fact, the only thing you really need to be aware of is that a binary file might contain characters that need to be escaped when concatenating them or they might contain characters that you are not expecting. This is a problem only if you are treating binary data just like text, however. Under normal circumstances, even this isn't really a problem.

Getting the ID3 Tag

As we talked about, the ID3 v1.1 tag is actually not part of the MP3 data at all. Although not all MP3 files will have an ID3 tag, if one does, it is tacked onto the end of the MP3 file. This means that you do not have to actually parse binary data to read the tag. To read the data, you just have to seek to the end of the file and then back up 128 bytes. This is an elegant solution to the problem of providing metadata in a file without changing the file format in a fundamental way. The problem with this kind of tag, though, is that the data is structured within the tag in fixed-length fields, which makes it difficult to extend for future functionality. It does make it easier to process the structure of the tag, however, because you know exactly where the fields will be, how long they are, and what they contain.

Structure of the Tag

The data is encoded in fixed-length fields, all contained within the 128-byte block at the end of any MP3 file that has ID3 data. The first three bytes of this block are just TAG. If you get to the point in an MP3 file 128 bytes before the end of the file, and the next three bytes are not TAG, there is no ID3 tag.

In the v1 standard, the fields are as follows:

Table 22-1. *ID3 v1 Fields*

Field	Length
Song Title	30
Artist Name	30
Album Name	30
Year	4
Comment	30
Genre	1

The field lengths add up to 125 bytes, with the TAG from the beginning adding the last 3 bytes—for a total of 128. If the data in any of these tags (except the Genre field) doesn't require the whole length, it is padded with char 0 (\000). Some tagging software pads the fields with strings, however. The Genre tag is a special field that contains a single byte that represents a genre. There are 255 possible genres, but there were only 79 defined originally—although that has risen to 149 (and possibly more).

There are a few problems with this system, not the least of which is that there is no way to extend it. The fields are fixed length, so if you want to add a new type of information (a track number, for example), you can't. However, v1.1 of the ID3 tag addresses this in a novel fashion. Because the Comment field is really too small to include much information, a small part of it is carved out to encode the track number for a given file. The change is pretty simple and it takes only the last byte out of the Comment field to encode the information.

Table 22-2. *ID3 v1.1 Fields*

Field	Length
Song Title	30
Artist Name	30
Album Name	30
Year	4
Comment	28
Track Number	1
Genre	1

These fields add up to 124, with TAG adding 3, and a single-byte delimiter (char 0 or \000) adding up to 128. This also is fully compatible with v1 readers, which will just discard the tail end of the Comment field because those readers would stop at the first \000 they find.

Now look at the code. The first part is just the genre mapping. You won't be using this in the server, but it is handy to have.

```
let genre_map = [
  (0,"Blues");  (1,"Classic Rock");  (2,"Country");  (3,"Dance");
  (4,"Disco");  (5,"Funk");  (6,"Grunge");  (7,"Hip-Hop");
  (8,"Jazz");  (9,"Metal");  (10,"New Age");  (11,"Oldies");
  (12,"Other");  (13,"Pop");  (14,"R&B");  (15,"Rap");  (16,"Reggae");
  (17,"Rock");  (18,"Techno");  (19,"Industrial");  (20,"Alternative");
  (21,"Ska");  (22,"Death Metal");  (23,"Pranks");  (24,"Soundtrack");
  (25,"Euro-Techno");  (26,"Ambient");  (27,"Trip-Hop");  (28,"Vocal");
  (29,"Jazz+Funk");  (30,"Fusion");  (31,"Trance");  (32,"Classical");
  (33,"Instrumental");  (34,"Acid");  (35,"House");  (36,"Game");
  (37,"Sound Clip");  (38,"Gospel");  (39,"Noise");  (40,"Alternative Rock");
  (41,"Bass");  (43,"Punk");  (44,"Space");  (45,"Meditative");
  (46,"Instrumental Pop");  (47,"Instrumental Rock");  (48,"Ethnic");
  (49,"Gothic");  (50,"Darkwave");  (51,"Techno-Industrial");
  (52,"Electronic");  (53,"Pop-Folk");  (54,"Eurodance");  (55,"Dream");
  (56,"Southern Rock");  (57,"Comedy");  (58,"Cult");  (59,"Gangsta");
  (60,"Top 40");  (61,"Christian Rap");  (62,"Pop/Funk");  (63,"Jungle");
  (64,"Native US");  (65,"Cabaret");  (66,"New Wave");  (67,"Psychadelic");
  (68,"Rave");  (69,"Showtunes");  (70,"Trailer");  (71,"Lo-Fi");
  (72,"Tribal");  (73,"Acid Punk");  (74,"Acid Jazz");  (75,"Polka");
  (76,"Retro");  (77,"Musical");  (78,"Rock & Roll");  (79,"Hard Rock");
  (80,"Folk");  (81,"Folk-Rock");  (82,"National Folk");  (83,"Swing");
  (84,"Fast Fusion");  (85,"Bebob");  (86,"Latin");  (87,"Revival");
  (88,"Celtic");  (89,"Bluegrass");  (90,"Avantgarde");  (91,"Gothic Rock");
  (92,"Progressive Rock");  (93,"Psychedelic Rock");  (94,"Symphonic Rock");
  (95,"Slow Rock");  (96,"Big Band");  (97,"Chorus");  (98,"Easy Listening");
  (99,"Acoustic");  (100,"Humour");  (101,"Speech");  (102,"Chanson");
  (103,"Opera");  (104,"Chamber Music");  (105,"Sonata");
  (106,"Symphony");  (107,"Booty Bass");  (108,"Primus");  (109,"Porn Groove");
  (110,"Satire");  (111,"Slow Jam");  (112,"Club");  (113,"Tango");
  (114,"Samba");  (115,"Folklore");  (116,"Ballad");  (117,"Power Ballad");
  (118,"Rhytmic Soul");  (119,"Freestyle");  (120,"Duet");  (121,"Punk Rock");
  (122,"Drum Solo");  (123,"Acapella");  (124,"Euro-House");
  (125,"Dance Hall");  (126,"Goa");  (127,"Drum & Bass");  (128,"Club-House");
  (129,"Hardcore");  (130,"Terror");  (131,"Indie");  (132,"BritPop");
  (133,"Negerpunk");  (134,"Polsk Punk");  (135,"Beat");
  (136,"Christian Gangsta");  (137,"Heavy Metal");  (138,"Black Metal");
  (139,"Crossover");  (140,"Contemporary C");  (141,"Christian Rock");
  (142,"Merengue");  (143,"Salsa");  (144,"Thrash Metal");
  (145,"Anime");  (146,"JPop");  (147,"SynthPop")];;

let string_of_genre g = try
  List.assoc g genre_map
with Not_found -> "Unknown";;
```

The next part defines a record type to hold ID3 tags, followed by an empty tag value. This empty tag is a convenience value for this code.

```
type ID3tag = {song_title:string;
                        artist:string;
                        album: string;
                        year: int;
                        comment: string;
                        track: int;
                        genre: char };;

let empty_tag = {song_title = "";
                        artist="";
                        album="";
                        year=0;
                        comment="";
                        track=0;
                        genre='\000'};;
```

Next you define an exception for the case of a BadTag, which will contain the 128 bytes
where the tag should be. It could be binary data where there is no tag in the file. It could also
hold a tag that is improperly formed (although this is an unlikely event because the fields are
fixed length) or is too short.

Following the exception, there is the definition of a function to strip the whitespace and/
or \000 from a given field. This type of function does not exist in the String library, so it had to
be defined. The pad function can be thought of as the inverse of the rstrip function. The pad-
ding relies on a function that creates a string filled with only char 0.

```
exception BadTag of string;;

let rstrip str =
  let rec rs sb accbuf =
  let sb_res = try
    Scanf.bscanf sb "%c" (fun x -> match x with
                                        '\000' -> None
                                      | _ -> Buffer.add_char accbuf x;None)
  with End_of_file -> Some (Buffer.contents accbuf)
  in match sb_res with
      None -> rs sb accbuf
    | Some n -> n
in
let scanbuf = Scanf.Scanning.from_string str in
let buf = Buffer.create (String.length str) in
  rs scanbuf buf;;

let zero_string len =
  let q = String.create len in
  let idx = ref 0 in
  String.iter (fun x -> q.[!idx] <- '\000';incr idx) q;
  q;;
```

```
let pad str len =
  let z = zero_string len in match str with
    n when ((String.length str) <= len) ->
      String.blit str 0 z 0 (String.length str);z
  | _ -> (String.sub str 0 len);;
```

The next function, parse_ID3tag, actually does the parsing. Because the fields are fixed length taken from a 128-byte string, you can use substrings instead of a more complicated parser. The next function actually pulls the 128-byte string out of a given file. Notice that the open function used is not one you have used before. Some operating systems treat binary files differently from text files, supported via the open_in_bin function. This is safe to do because the function behaves in the same way as the normal open_in function on systems that do not distinguish between binary and nonbinary files.

```
let parse_ID3tag x = let tagdata = String.sub x 0 3 in
  match tagdata with
      "TAG" -> { song_title = rstrip (String.sub x 3 29);
                          artist = rstrip (String.sub x 33 29);
                          album = rstrip (String.sub x 63 29);
                          year = ( try
                          Scanf.sscanf (String.sub x 93 4) "%i" (fun x -> x)
                                      with _ -> 0);
                          comment = rstrip (String.sub x 97 27);
                             track = int_of_char x.[126];
                             genre = x.[127] }
    | _ -> raise (BadTag x);;

let findtag fname =
  let ic = open_in_bin fname in
  let sz = in_channel_length ic in
  let s = String.create 128 in
  seek_in ic (sz - 128);
  really_input ic s 0 128;
  close_in ic;
  s;;

let getID3 file = parse_ID3tag (findtag file);;
```

The last function provides a convenient calling interface for this ID3 tag library. Following are two calls of the function: one on a file that has a valid ID3 tag, and one that doesn't.

```
# getID3 "./violent_femmes/02 Kiss Off.mp3";;
- : ID3tag =
{song_title = "Kiss Off"; artist = "Violent Femmes";
 album = "Violent Femmes"; year = 0; comment = "Created by Grip"; track = 2;
 genre = '\017'}
```

```
# getID3 "./violent_femmes/01 Blister In The Sun.mp3";;
Exception:
BadTag
  "\255\255\255\255\255\255\255\255\255\255\255\255\255\255\255\255\255\255\255\➡
255\255\255\255\255\255\255\255\255\255\255\255\255\255\255\255\255\255\255\➡
255\255\255\255\255\255\255\255\255\255\255\255\255\255\255\255\255\255\255\➡
255\255\255\255\255\255\255\255\255\255\255\255\255\255\255\255\255\255\255\➡
255\255\255\255\255\255\255\255\255\255\255\255\255\255\255\255\255\255\255\➡
255\255\255\255\255\255\255\255\255\255\255\255\255\255\255\255\255\255\255\➡
255\255\255\255\255\255\255\255\255\255\n".
```

The signature for this library (from its interface file) is shown following.

```
type ID3tag = {song_title:string;
                artist:string;
                album: string;
                year: int;
                comment: string;
                track: int;
                genre: char };;


exception BadTag of string

val genre_map: (int * string) list
val string_of_genre: int -> string
val emtpy_tag: ID3tag
val pad: string -> int -> string
val getID3: string -> ID3tag
```

This library provides a complete framework for getting the metadata from the files you want.

Server Framework

Before you can implement the Shoutcast protocol, you need to provide a server first. There are a few goals that you want for a streaming server. The first is the capability to stream the same data to an arbitrary number of clients. Second, the server should be efficient. Third, the server should be able to handle clients that connect and disconnect as often as they like. The server should run on all platforms supported by the OCaml language, which you can do in slightly fewer than 70 lines of OCaml code.

First, create a record type to describe each connection. This type includes OCaml channels, as well as the raw socket, to provide buffering. Although you could write your own buffering, it is easier to take advantage of the fact that OCaml channels are already buffered.

```
type connection = { sock :Unix.file_descr;
                    adr :Unix.sockaddr;
                    oc :out_channel ;
                    ic: in_channel };;
```

The next function, makeserversocket, creates a server socket and sets the REUSEADDR flag, which is important for servers. This flag enables you to rebind to a socket immediately after someone lets it go. This is helpful for when you restart the server; otherwise, you would have to wait for a timeout.

It is also helpful to wrap up the shutdown of a socket, which enables the clean shutdown of a socket and traps the exception raised if the socket has been disconnected by the client. The code also provides a convenience function to get the hostname from a given address if it exists (if it doesn't, the hostname is just the IP address).

```
let makeserversocket x y =
  let s = Unix.socket Unix.PF_INET Unix.SOCK_STREAM 0 in
  let h = Unix.gethostbyname x in
  Unix.bind s (Unix.ADDR_INET (h.Unix.h_addr_list.(0),y));
  Unix.listen s 10;
  Unix.setsockopt s Unix.SO_REUSEADDR true;
  s;;

let shutdown_socket sock = try
                      Unix.close sock
                      with (Unix.Unix_error (n,m,o)) ->
                  (match n with
                      Unix.ENOTCONN -> ()
                    | _ -> Printf.printf "%s %s\n" m o);;

let get_hostname saddr = (Unix.getnameinfo saddr ➥
[Unix.NI_NOFQDN]).Unix.ni_hostname;;
```

To allow for the connections to be indexed and randomly accessible, they are stored in a hashtable. Connections are often stored in a list or an array, but you want to be able to easily unregister connections from the server. Because this server is multithreaded, a Mutex to control access to the store of connections is created for later use (more on this in a little bit).

```
let hash_mutex = Mutex.create ();;
let (master_hash: (Unix.sockaddr , connection) Hashtbl.t) = Hashtbl.create 100;;
```

The next function, info_messages, is provided so that information about the number of connections can be displayed on the host running the server.

```
let info_messages () = while (true) do
  Printf.printf "Currently, %i threads in system\n"
    (Hashtbl.length master_hash);
  flush stdout;
  Thread.delay 5.
done;;
```

The next function, minder, uses the OCaml Event library to unregister and shut down connections that are no longer active. The Event library is described in depth in Chapter 23; for now you just need to know that the Event library provides a synchronous interthread communication. When the function receives an event that means a connection has been closed, it performs some cleanup and removes that connection from the index of connections. This function also displays a message about the disconnect that tells who disconnected—and why. This function is designed to be run in its own thread.

```
let rec minder dt = let tid = (Event.sync (Event.receive dt))
in
  (try
    (let to_remove = Hashtbl.find master_hash tid in
      Mutex.lock hash_mutex;
      Hashtbl.remove master_hash tid;
    Mutex.unlock hash_mutex;
    try
                    close_out to_remove.oc;
                    close_in to_remove.ic;
      with (Sys_error m) -> Printf.printf "%s\n" m;
                    shutdown_socket to_remove.sock;
                Printf.printf "Disconnect from %s\n" (get_hostname to_remove.adr)
    )
  with Not_found -> Printf.printf "Strange, %s was not found\n" ➥
(get_hostname tid) );
    minder dt;;
```

Finally, there is the event loop that handles all incoming connections. It creates the server thread, the channel for event-based communication, and starts the worker threads. The event loop also handles the acceptance of each new connection.

It takes five arguments. The first two are the hostname and port the server should run on. The third argument is a function that is called first on each connection. The fourth argument is the function that defines the actions on all the connections (the streaming protocol will be defined later). The last argument is the argument that is passed to the worker function. This function does not return; it runs in a loop handling all the connection events, which is why it is called the event loop.

```
let event_loop host port connect_function lfunc args =
  let death_channel = Event.new_channel () in
  let mreader = Thread.create lfunc (args,death_channel,master_hash)
  in
  let minder_thread = Thread.create minder death_channel in
  let sock = makeserversocket host port in
    while (true) do
      let a_sock = Unix.accept sock in
                Printf.printf "Got connection from %s\n" ➥
(get_hostname (snd a_sock));
                let noc = Unix.out_channel_of_descr (fst a_sock) in
                let ioc = Unix.in_channel_of_descr (fst a_sock) in
```

```
            let conn = { sock = (fst a_sock);
                         adr = (snd a_sock);
                         oc = noc;
                         ic = ioc } in
         connect_function conn;
         Mutex.lock hash_mutex;
             Hashtbl.replace master_hash (snd a_sock) conn;
         Mutex.unlock hash_mutex
     done;;
```

Note that the Mutex locks around additions and removals from the hashtable, which stores the connection information. This is done to ensure that operations on the hashtable do not stop on other actions.

The connection function doesn't have to do anything. Any function used in this capacity should also be written carefully because an uncaught exception or block could crash the server. This function is provided so that the server can send header information or other data to the client before it begins to receive the data stream. The connection function is also called only once for each connection.

A very simple streaming server that you could write using this framework just sends the time to all the clients that connect.

```
open Server

let rec curtime ((),death_channel,hash_table) =
  while (true) do
    let ct = Unix.time () in
      Hashtbl.iter (fun x y -> try
                              Printf.fprintf y.oc "%f\n" ct;
                                flush y.oc
                              with _ -> Event.sync (Event.send ➡
death_channel x)) hash_table;
        Thread.delay 1.
  done;;


let _ = let t = Thread.create info_messages () in
  event_loop "localhost" 9988 (fun x -> ()) curtime ();;
```

This example passes a connection function that does nothing and iterates over the hashtable of connections sending epoch seconds every second. The explicit flush of the output channel is there because of the small amount of data you are sending (otherwise, the output will be buffered more than is convenient for a server like this).

Because this code uses threads, you have to pass some extra arguments to the compiler. You might have to change the /usr/local/lib/ocaml (following) to match where the OCaml libraries are installed on your system.

```
$ ocamlc -I /usr/local/lib/ocaml/threads unix.cma ➥
threads/threads.cma Server.ml time.ml
```

If you were using OCamlMakefile, you would create a Makefile that looked similar to this:

```
SOURCES = Server.ml time.ml
RESULT= timeserver
PACKS = threads,unix
All: byte-code
Include /usr/local/lib/Ocaml/OCamlMakefile
```

OCamlMakefile knows how to compile code that depends on any package that uses find-lib (which all the standard libraries do). If you want to run this code, you have to change the hostname (currently listed as sputnik, which is my laptop) to whatever host you are using. After you compile it, if you connect to port 9988 on that host, you will start seeing the time displayed every second. On the screen where you started the server, you will also see connect and disconnect messages displayed, as well as a current count of how many connections are active.

The server window will look something like this:

```
$ ./timeserver.exe
Currently, 0 threads in system
Currently, 0 threads in system
Got connection from sputnik
Connection reset by peer
Disconnect from sputnik
Currently, 0 threads in system
Got connection from sputnik
Currently, 1 threads in system
Connection reset by peer
Disconnect from sputnik
Currently, 0 threads in system
```

The client window will look something like this (assuming you connect via telnet):

```
$ telnet sputnik 9988
Trying 192.168.1.100...
Connected to sputnik.
Escape character is '^]'.
1138793835.000000
1138793836.000000
1138793837.000000
telnet> quit
Connection closed.
```

Now that you have a server framework, you can implement the specific protocol for this Shoutcast server.

Using the High-Level Connection Functions

This framework does not use the high-level socket functions in the Unix library because the high-level server function works only on a Unix or Unix-like host.

Although these functions are very handy for creating servers, it is often just as easy to define your own higher-level function to handle the socket options you want. This is especially true when you are using a multithreaded server instead of a forking server. The high-level functions in OCaml create forking servers. Both methods are valid, but it is important to weigh the advantages and disadvantages of each before choosing one for your own projects.

Implementing the Shoutcast Protocol

The goal here is to implement a Shoutcast server, not a time server. In the implementation, first open the Server module, which makes accessing functions, types, and variables easier because you do not have to prefix them with Server. After that, you define your connection function.

The connection function doesn't even look at the request because the output is the same, no matter what the client requests. The headers are sent to the client and then the buffer is flushed. You are using the OCaml-provided buffering so that you do not have to write your own for this server.

```
open Server;;

let shoutcast_headers sock =
  Printf.fprintf sock.oc "ICY 200 OK\r\n";
  Printf.fprintf sock.oc "icy-name:Ocaml Rocks!\r\n";
  Printf.fprintf sock.oc "icy-metaint:1024\r\n";
  Printf.fprintf sock.oc "Content-Type:audio/mpeg\r\n";
  Printf.fprintf sock.oc "icy-pub:1\r\n";
  flush sock.oc;;
```

The next three functions are convenience functions. They enable you to get the metadata string, complete with length byte properly calculated and set up. This works even if the MP3 file does not have any metadata, which means that zero metadata is sent.

```
let metadata_string id = match id.Id3.song_title with
    "" -> Printf.sprintf "%c" '\000'
  | _ -> let metastr = Printf.sprintf "StreamTitle=\'%s\';"
      id.Id3.song_title in
    let metalen = ((String.length metastr) / 16) + 1 in
      Printf.sprintf "%c%s" (Char.chr metalen) (Id3.pad metastr (metalen * 16));;

let get_input ich str len = let res = input ich str 0 len in match res with
    0 -> raise End_of_file
  | n when (res < len) -> Id3.pad (String.sub str 0 res) len
  | _ -> str;;
```

```
let get_tag file = try
  let id = Id3.getID3 file in id
with (Id3.BadTag m) -> Id3.empty_tag;;
```

You then define your worker thread. You open each MP3 file only once and read each 1024-byte block only once before it is sent to each connection. Because you are sending the metadata every 1024 bytes, you just send it after each read. Notice that a small delay is introduced for times when there are no connections because the server will be in a very tight loop when there are no clients, resulting in high CPU utilization only when the server is actually idle. This delay means that some clients will see a quarter-second pause before they get data if they are the first clients. This seems a small price to pay for the efficiency.

The buffer size was chosen somewhat arbitrarily. I experimented a bit before I found that any value higher than 128 and less than 8128 worked pretty well on my hardware. A buffer that is too small can lead to audio skipping because the buffers aren't big enough; a buffer that is too large can tax your server. This is a producer-subscriber server that is a very common design when writing servers that expect to have many clients.

Whenever an exception is raised when writing to a client, that client is disconnected. This is accomplished by sending a message to the minder thread, which shuts that connection down. This communication is achieved using the Event library, which will be discussed at length in Chapter 23.

```
let rec master_reader file dc mhash = let ic = open_in_bin file in
try
    let id = get_tag file in
      let buf = String.create 1024 in
            while (true) do
                if ((Hashtbl.length mhash) < 1) then
                      Thread.delay 0.25
                else
                    let onebuf = get_input ic buf 1024 in
                        Hashtbl.iter (fun x y ->
                          try
                            Printf.fprintf y.oc "%s" onebuf;
                            Printf.fprintf y.oc "%s" (metadata_string id);
                          with _ -> Event.sync (Event.send dc x)) mhash;
          done
with End_of_file -> close_in ic;;
```

The preceding master reader handles only one file, though. You want to loop over a directory of files, playing until the server is shut off. To accomplish that, you define two more functions. The first iterates over all the files in a given directory, whereas the second loops infinitely—restarting the first every time it finishes. Although this task could be accomplished in one function, it is split up for clarity.

```
let multi_reader dir dc mhash = let rdir = Sys.readdir dir in
  Array.iter (fun file -> master_reader (Filename.concat dir file) dc mhash) rdir;;

let rec loop_reader (dir,dc,mhash) = multi_reader dir dc mhash;
  loop_reader (dir,dc,mhash);;
```

The last function is the wrapup. First, a thread is created to start the information messages being displayed (this is optional). Then the event loop is entered, and the server is actually started. In this case, I happen to have a directory filled with the Violent Femmes quintessential album (I removed some of the metadata from some of the files to test). You can use any MP3 files you have (this protocol works only with MP3 files).

```
let _ = let t = Thread.create info_messages () in
  event_loop "localhost" 9998 shoutcast_headers loop_reader "./violent_femmes";;
```

This code is compiled much like the previous trivial example, although you need to include the ID3 library file as well.

```
$ ocamlc -I /usr/local/lib/ocaml/threads unix.cma ➥
threads/threads.cma ID3.ml Server.ml shoutcast.ml
```

Again, if you are using OCamlMakefile, your Makefile would look a lot like this:

```
SOURCES = ID3.ml Server.ml shoutcast.ml
RESULT= shoutcast
PACKS = threads,unix
All: byte-code
Include /usr/local/lib/Ocaml/OCamlMakefile
```

This code can be run on any operating system that supports OCaml. It is reasonably efficient, too—it uses less than five percent of the CPU on my laptop while serving three clients. This server is very similar to a select-based server.

Connecting to Your Server

If you are using iTunes, you can connect to your server by pressing Ctl+U and entering the URL (with the port) of the host that is running the server. XMMS can take a URL as an argument, although it is important to remember to specify the port.

The server plays all the files in the directory you specify until you turn off the server. The server will try to play all files, even if they are not MP3 files (it really doesn't know to look only for MP3 files).

Conclusion

This chapter created a framework for streaming servers and implemented a Shoutcast server, complete with metadata and efficient streaming. This server can be extended easily to play multiple directories of MP3 files, too.

The next chapter looks at the multithreading aspects of OCaml, which enables you to understand more clearly what was really going on with the Event channels used here. It also gives you the ability to write (and debug) concurrent programs in OCaml.

CHAPTER 23

■■■

Using Threads

As you are reading this, you are performing multiple tasks simultaneously. You are thinking about the words on the page, moving your eyes, hearing sounds in your environment, interpreting these sounds, and more. This ability to perform concurrent actions makes things like walking, talking, and pretty much everything else a living being does possible. Most computer programs, however, do not have the capability to perform concurrent actions.

Threads are one way of enabling a program to perform concurrent actions (they are not the only way, but they are a very common method). OCaml supports threads natively and has an excellent set of libraries for dealing with interthread communication and synchronization. OCaml's threads, however, do not support symmetric multiprocessing (SMP).

Concurrency opens up new doors for the programmer. On one hand, you no longer have to worry about long-running computations or input/output (I/O) operations halting your program. Concurrency can make debugging more difficult and can introduce unexpected complexity into your programs. You should also know that threads can make debugging impossible. Threads can create frustrations that are unthinkable in a nonthreaded world. Threads are sometimes the cause of (and solution to) all the problems in the (programming) world.

Knowing how to create a thread does not mean that you can effectively use threads. A thread of execution is only one component of a concurrent application or environment. A concurrent program also needs ways of handling synchronization, communication, and other tasks that are unique to a threaded program. You also need ways of managing the threads themselves. Threads, like any other construct in your programs, cannot manage themselves. The OCaml distribution provides libraries for handling synchronization (via mutexes and condition variables), interthread communication (via the Event library), and handling threads themselves. OCaml also provides thread-safe versions of libraries, which enables you to use the same libraries in threaded or nonthreaded code.

Why Do You Need Concurrency?

You might not need concurrency. Not all applications require (or can benefit from) concurrency. However, there are two general reasons for using it:

- For parallelism in Shared-Memory-Processor (SMP) systems

- To handle overlapping I/O or user input and computation

For the first reason, you would do this to take advantage of multiple CPUs in a given system. Many servers (and quite a few desktop machines) now are multi-CPU machines. Having multiple threads enables you to spread computation across processors.

The second reason is much more common. Often, graphical user interface (GUI) applications are multithreaded to enable the user to interact with the GUI while other computation is occurring. Network servers and clients are another common situation in which I/O overlap helps with performance and application response.

What Kinds of Concurrency Does OCaml Support?

The main type of concurrency that OCaml supports is via lightweight threads. OCaml's threads are designed for situations of overlapping I/O and the like. Symmetric multiprocessing support is not available in OCaml and this support is not likely to be available in the future. Neither the vmthreads nor the POSIX threads libraries support SMP. If you need SMP concurrency, you need to use a message-passing library (such as MPI) or interface with C. This kind of concurrency is well outside the scope of this chapter.

The OCaml standard library complicates matters somewhat by offering a vmthreads library and a system threads library. In the examples given in this chapter, system threads are used. The choice is made by a compile-time flag (-thread in this case). The vmthreads library operates at the OCaml virtual machine level (the byte-code interpreter). Because it works at the byte-code–interpreter level, this library cannot be used with native code programs. The system threads library can be used with both native code and byte-code and is available on most systems (you should check the distribution docs to see whether your particular distribution is supported). The same OCaml code constructs are used with both libraries, so you don't have to change your code to work with either library.

If you avoid programming with side effects, you do not have to worry about making libraries you write threadsafe. If, however, you do rely upon side effects and updating data structures, you might have to redesign your libraries to make them threadsafe. Most of the distributed OCaml libraries are threadsafe; the ones that are not (several in the Unix module) have threaded variants. In most cases (for example, the ones in the Unix module) you do not have to change how you call those threaded variants—this is taken care of for you at compile time.

Creating and Using a Thread

You might need to create a new toplevel for these examples if you are not using an operating system that supports dynamic loading. If you are on a system that supports dynamic loading of modules, you can just load the modules using the #load directive. Either way, you still must pass more arguments to the toplevel to actually use the threading libraries:

threaded_toplevel -I +threads.

```
        Objective Caml version 3.09.0

# #load "unix.cma";;
# #load "threads.cma";;
#
```

Even if you load the libraries (or have them in your toplevel) they will not be accessible without the command-line flags. Newer versions of findlib provide a #thread pragma that enables you to use threads without command-line flags.

If, however, you are not on a system that supports dynamic loading, you will have to build a new toplevel. This is not difficult, and we covered it in previous chapters. There can sometimes be a problem finding the OCaml libraries, though, and you might need to pass the whole path when building the toplevel.

```
ocamlmktop -o threaded_toplevel -I <PATH_TO_OCAML_LIBRARIES> ➥
unix.cma threads/threads.cma
```

This new toplevel (when called with the –I +threads) will enable you to access the thread libraries at the toplevel. So, now that you can do that, we will create a thread. Our first, very simple example uses three functions from the Thread library: create, delay, and join.

```
let t = Thread.create (fun () -> Thread.delay (Random.float 3.);
                                     Printf.printf "%.2f is the new value\n" ➥
(Random.float 10.)) () in Thread.join t;;
```

The create function takes two arguments. The first argument is a function that is run in the new thread, and the second argument is the argument for the function. The bad news is that the function arguments must be passed as a data structure rather than as normal function arguments. This can have consequences if you are using curried functions for threads.

```
# Thread.create (fun a b c -> ()) (1 10 11);;
This expression is not a function, it cannot be applied
# Thread.create (fun (a,b,c) -> ()) (1,10,11);;
- : Thread.t = <abstr>
```

Return to the first example—you can see that this function also uses the Thread.delay function. This function takes a float and sleeps for that number of seconds (fractional seconds are allowed).

The last Thread function is the join function, which simply blocks the current thread until the thread passed as an argument exits. Although threads do not have to be joined, it is a good practice. The join function is also an effective control-flow operator, enabling you to wait for threads to complete.

Now that you can create threads, look at an example program that works, but is not quite correct. This program simulates doing actual work by doing a random wait. (This program is used to simplify understanding and debugging because the random wait always succeeds.)

```
# let f () =
    let rnum = ref 0. in
    let t = Thread.create (fun float_r ->
                                     Thread.delay (Random.float 3.);
                                     float_r := 90.) rnum in
    let t' = Thread.create (fun float_r ->
                                 Thread.delay (Random.float 3.);
                                 float_r := Random.float 10.) rnum in
```

```
    Thread.join t;
    Thread.join t';
    Printf.printf "The Value is: %.2f" !rnum;;
val f : unit -> unit = <fun>
# f ();;
The Value is: 4.40- : unit = ()
# f ();;
The Value is: 1.49- : unit = ()
# f ();;
The Value is: 90.00- : unit = ()
```

The first thread sets the data structure (in this case, a float reference) to a set value, whereas the second thread sets it to a random value. The problem is that there is a chance (albeit small) that both threads will try to access the variable at the same time. That would be a bad situation, and it is never a good idea to access a shared value without a mutex. The other problem with this code is that sometimes the output variable is set to the specified variable, and sometimes it is a random variable.

The fix for the first issue (only one access at a time) is to use a mutual exclusion (mutex). A mutex is used to avoid concurrent access to any resource that should not be accessed concurrently. Code that should be protected by a mutex is often called a critical section. In this case, the critical section is the actual modification of the reference.

```
# let f () =
    let mutex = Mutex.create () in
    let rnum = ref 0. in
    let t = Thread.create (fun (float_r,m) ->
                                              Thread.delay (Random.float 3.);
                                              Mutex.lock m;
                                              float_r := 90.;
                                              Mutex.unlock m) (rnum,mutex) in
    let t' = Thread.create (fun (float_r,m) ->
                                    Thread.delay (Random.float 3.);
                                     Mutex.lock m;
                                     float_r := (Random.float 10.);
                                    Mutex.unlock m) (rnum,mutex) in
  Thread.join t;
  Thread.join t';
  Printf.printf "The Value is: %.2f" !rnum;;
                          val f : unit -> unit = <fun>
# f ();;
The Value is: 90.00- : unit = ()
# f ();;
The Value is: 8.97- : unit = ()
#
```

Although a mutex solves the problem of concurrent access to parts of the code that should not have concurrent access, it doesn't solve the issue that the output is still random: it could be correct (90) or it could be some other value. What you really want is some way to be able to signal the first thread that the second thread is done modifying the value.

You are in luck; OCaml supports condition variables to accomplish this. A condition variable is an element that can be used to signal conditions to other threads. These variables allow asynchronous communication to threads and provide a mechanism for one thread to wait until another thread satisfies some condition. Although condition variables are simple in their function, they can present some very complex (and problematic) behavior, as shown in the following:

```
let f () =
  let cvar = Condition.create () in
  let mutex = Mutex.create () in
  let rnum = ref 0. in
  let t = Thread.create (fun (float_r,m,c) ->
                                        Thread.delay (Random.float 3.);
                                        Mutex.lock m;
                                        Condition.wait c m;
                                        float_r := 90.;
                                        Mutex.unlock m) (rnum,mutex,cvar) in
  let t' = Thread.create (fun (float_r,m,c) ->
                                        Thread.delay (Random.float 3.);
                                        Mutex.lock m;
                                        float_r := (Random.float 10.);
                                        Mutex.unlock m;
                                      Condition.signal c) (rnum,mutex,cvar) in
  Thread.join t;
  Thread.join t';
  Printf.printf "The Value is: %.2f" !rnum;;
```

The preceding code might never print out a response. This situation can occur because condition variables are asynchronous. If the first thread is not in a wait state (which is possible because the delay is random), it will wait forever because the condition variable is signaled only once.

This situation is very similar to a deadlock, in which two threads are holding resources that the other needs to access. You can see an example of deadlock following:

```
let f () =
  let mutex = Mutex.create () in
  let mutex' = Mutex.create () in
  let rnum = ref 0. in
  let t = Thread.create (fun (float_r,m,m') ->
                                          Mutex.lock m;
                                          Thread.delay (Random.float 3.);
                                          Mutex.lock m';
                                          float_r := 10.;
                                          Mutex.unlock m;
                                          Mutex.unlock m') ➥
(rnum,mutex,mutex') in
  let t' = Thread.create (fun (float_r,m,m') ->
```

```
                                                 Mutex.lock m';
                                                 Thread.delay (Random.float 3.);
                                                 Mutex.lock m;
                                                 float_r := 20.;
                                                 Mutex.unlock m;
                                     Mutex.unlock m') (rnum,mutex,mutex') in
   Thread.join t;
   Thread.join t';
   Printf.printf "The Value is: %.2f" !rnum;;
```

Although it is easy to see the cause of the deadlock in the preceding example, it might be much more difficult in real code. Deadlocks in real code often lurk for a long time before they are discovered.

If you return to the earlier example and the discussion about the problems with condition variables, you can fix the problem with locking a couple of different ways. The easiest in this case is to move the wait to before the work starts (the delay is your work here). It might also be an option to move the work into another thread. This is an example of how designing a program to run with multiple threads presents different design challenges.

```
# let f () =
   let cvar = Condition.create () in
   let mutex = Mutex.create () in
   let rnum = ref 0. in
   let t = Thread.create (fun (float_r,m,c) ->
                                       Mutex.lock m;
                                       Condition.wait c m;
                                       Thread.delay (Random.float 3.);
                                       float_r := 90.;
                                       Mutex.unlock m) (rnum,mutex,cvar) in
     let t' = Thread.create (fun (float_r,m,c) ->
                                       Thread.delay (Random.float 3.);
                                       Mutex.lock m;
                                       float_r := (Random.float 10.);
                                       Mutex.unlock m;
                                   Condition.signal c) (rnum,mutex,cvar) in
   Thread.join t;
   Thread.join t';
   Printf.printf "The Value is: %.2f" !rnum;;
                                   val f : unit -> unit = <fun>
# f ();;
The Value is: 90.00- : unit = ()
# f ();;
The Value is: 90.00- : unit = ()
#
```

This solution still doesn't really solve the problem. You really want synchronous communication between the threads, which can be accomplished by using the Event module.

The Event module is one of the more interesting modules in the OCaml library. It provides channels and events that threads can use to communicate in a producer/consumer kind of way. These channels are synchronous, which means they can block. There are nonblocking functions, but the blocking nature of the Event module is what you are looking for right now.

```
# let f () =
    let ch = Event.new_channel () in
    let mutex = Mutex.create () in
    let rnum = ref 0. in
    let t = Thread.create (fun (float_r,m,chan) ->
                                Event.sync (Event.receive chan);
                                Thread.delay (Random.float 3.);
                                Mutex.lock m;
                                float_r := 90.;
                                Mutex.unlock m) (rnum,mutex,ch) in
    let t' = Thread.create (fun (float_r,m,c) ->
                                Thread.delay (Random.float 3.);
                                Event.sync (Event.send ch true);
                                Mutex.lock m;
                                float_r := (Random.float 10.);
                                Mutex.unlock m) (rnum,mutex,ch) in
    Thread.join t;
    Thread.join t';
    Printf.printf "The Value is: %.2f" !rnum;;
                            val f : unit -> unit = <fun>
# f ();;
The Value is: 90.00- : unit = ()
# f ();;
The Value is: 90.00- : unit = ()
```

The Event module makes this program do what you want it to. The Event.sync function blocks until an event is actually received or sent. Calling either the send or receive function without syncing (or some variant) does not actually perform that action (this strange behavior is covered in depth later on). Now that you have seen a brief overview of using threads, it is time to look closely at the libraries that supply these functions.

One last point about the previous code: a very small change introduces a race condition. This is a shining example of a subtle bug that can creep into your code when you are doing multithreaded applications. Changing the first code segment from this:

```
Event.sync (Event.receive chan);
Thread.delay (Random.float 3.);
```

To this:

```
Thread.delay (Random.float 3.);
 Event.sync (Event.receive chan);
```

This change creates a race condition on the mutex lock, which creates an error (the value is random, not 90) when the second thread delay is shorter than the first. The error is created because when the second delay is shorter than the first, the send and receive happen at the same time; then there is a race to lock the mutex.

Details About the Modules

There are actually four modules that provide all the thread capabilities for OCaml; each provides different functions and none is required (except the Thread library) for using threads.

Of these four modules, the Thread module is (by far) the largest. The others are much smaller and provide very specific functionality.

Thread

The Thread library handles all the functions relating to thread management, as well as thread-safe Unix module calls.

```
val create : ('a -> 'b) -> 'a -> t
external self : unit -> t = "caml_thread_self"
external id : t -> int = "caml_thread_id"
```

The create function has been discussed. It is important to remember that you can pass only one argument to the created function. The next two functions are important for creating indexed data structures of threads. The id function returns a unique integer that is the thread ID. The self function enables you to get a reference to the current thread. So, if you wanted to know the thread ID of the currently running thread you would call Thread.id (Thread.self ()). These two functions are "external," meaning they are not written in OCaml.

A thread will exit if it receives an uncaught exception. This exit is the same as if the thread exited normally. This situation can leave your application in a problematic state, especially if the dead thread was supposed to be doing something important. It is, therefore, very important to make sure that your exception-handling code is correct. Programmers often enclose all threads within a try .. with block to catch exceptions and display a message.

The next two functions deal with killing and exiting threads. The exit function causes the currently running thread to exit; the kill function kills a running thread.

```
val exit : unit -> unit
val kill : t -> unit
```

The kill function might not be implemented for your operating system (OS). Even if it is, you should probably think carefully about using this function (the OCaml maintainers have written that the use of this function should be avoided). One of the biggest problems associated with using the kill function is that killing a thread at an arbitrary time is not a safe operation.

It is inherently unsafe because the killing thread does not know whether the killed thread is holding locks on resources. The killing thread really doesn't know anything about the killed thread, in fact. It is probably a better strategy to write your thread processes so that they can be signaled if they should stop running. This can be done using condition variables, events, or some other method of interthread communication. Having your threads be cooperative in shutting down will help make your threaded code more reliable than if you used the kill function.

```
val delay: float -> unit
val yield : unit -> unit
external join : t -> unit = "caml_thread_join"
```

Use the delay function to have a thread wait for some predetermined amount of time. The argument passed to the delay function is a floating-point number of seconds to wait. While a thread is delayed, other threads are free to run. The yield function gives hints to the scheduler that now is a good time to switch to another thread. Use of the yield function is not required, but it can be beneficial for some applications. The join function waits until the passed thread has finished. This function is a blocking function, so it could cause your program to stop running.

The select function is a Unix function that takes three lists of file descriptors and a float. The lists of file descriptors are descriptors that are to be checked to see whether they are ready for reading, writing, or exceptional events (in that order). The floating-point number is the timeout, which is the longest the function will take to complete. This function works only on sockets under Windows, but works for any file descriptor on Unix-like systems.

```
val select :
  Unix.file_descr list -> Unix.file_descr list ->
  Unix.file_descr list -> float ->
    Unix.file_descr list * Unix.file_descr list * Unix.file_descr list
```

The select function can tell you whether a given I/O operation will block on a given file descriptor. This is very useful for multithreaded programs because you often do not want to do blocking operations (you shouldn't use the kill function) and want to make sure that the operations you perform succeed. The example at the end of this chapter shows how the select function can be used.

Mutex

Mutexes are provided by the Mutex module. This module has four functions, which provide for pretty much everything you want. Although I have sometimes wished for attributes for locks, these four functions are really all you need for mutexes.

```
val create : unit -> t
val lock : t -> unit
val try_lock : t -> bool
val unlock : t -> unit
```

The create function is used to create new mutexes (a mutex must be created before it can be used). The lock and unlock functions enable you to acquire an exclusive lock (or wait until an exclusive lock can be acquired) or unlock a mutex. If you call the lock function on a mutex that is locked by another thread, the call will block until it can acquire the lock.

The try_lock function can be used when you do not want to block if you cannot acquire a lock. The try_lock function tries to acquire a lock and returns true (and locks the mutex) if you can, but returns false if you cannot. Either way, this function does not block.

```
let rec example_rand (acc,m) =
  match acc with
  | m when m > 20 -> ()
  | _ ->
    Mutex.lock m;
    Thread.delay (Random.float 3.);
    Mutex.unlock m;
    example_rand ((acc + (Random.int 5)),m);;

let _ =
  let m = Mutex.create () in
  let t = Thread.create example_rand (0,m) in
  while (true) do
    if Mutex.try_lock m then
      (Printf.printf "The Mutex is unlocked!\n%!";
      Mutex.unlock m;
      Thread.delay 1.)
  done;;
```

This example loops tightly trying to acquire the lock. Because the try_lock does not block, other computation can be done. There is a short delay in this loop, primarily because without it the process runs away after the example thread exits.

Condition

Like the Mutex module, the Condition module has only a few functions. As you saw in the early examples, condition variables can be very powerful when you want to do asynchronous signaling between threads.

The create function creates a condition variable. Condition variables, like mutexes, must be created before they can be used. The wait function suspends the calling thread, unlocks the mutex passed as an argument, and waits for a signal on the condition variable passed as an argument. The mutex is then locked after the signal is received, but before wait returns.

```
val create : unit -> t
val wait : t -> Mutex.t -> unit
```

The signal function sends a signal to one thread waiting on the condition variable. You have no control over which thread is signaled. The thread that receives the signal is then restarted.

```
val signal : t -> unit
val broadcast : t -> unit
```

If you want to signal all threads that are waiting on that variable, you can use the broadcast function, which restarts all functions waiting on the variable.

```
let gotit (mut,cvar) =
  Mutex.lock mut;
  Condition.wait cvar mut;
  Printf.printf "Thread %i got the signal!\n" (Thread.id (Thread.self ()));
  Mutex.unlock mut;;

let _ =
  let m = Mutex.create () in
  let c = Condition.create () in
  let t = Thread.create gotit (m,c) in
  let t1 = Thread.create gotit (m,c) in
  let t2 = Thread.create gotit (m,c) in
Thread.delay (Random.float 1.0);
  Condition.broadcast c;
  Thread.join t;
  Thread.join t1;
  Thread.join t2;;
```

If you run this on my system, you get the following message:

```
$ ./trylock
Thread 1 got the signal!
Thread 2 got the signal!
Thread 3 got the signal!
```

Caution The delay in the preceding example is there to prevent timing problems in the example. Many rapid and nested thread creations can sometimes cause timing problems in the toplevel.

You should see something similar. The broadcast should be used only when you want to wake up all threads that are waiting. Otherwise, you can just call the signal function as many times as you need to. It can even be called from functions that have just been woken up by the signal.

Event

The Event system in OCaml is often misunderstood. It came from the Concurrent Caml-Light system, which is no longer maintained. It is a system that enables you to create synchronous message channels between two threads.

The event channels do not allow one-to-many or many-to-many simultaneous communication. Any given message can come from only one thread and go to only one thread. If you have many threads to send a message to, you need to send it multiple times.

OCaml's event channels are not high-performance channels. In my experience, I have found them to be quite slow compared with other kinds of interprocess communication (IPC) (especially sockets). However, they have their place, especially considering the fact that they are synchronous. When you send or receive a message using event channels, you know it got there and is complete.

The new_channel function creates a new event channel. Each channel can handle only one type of event, so if you want to send integer and float events you need two channels or you have to define a union type. It might help if you think of channels as LILO stacks instead of actual message channels. As each process places another event on the stack, it can be taken off the stack only once.

The new_channel function creates a new channel and returns it. A channel must be created before it can be used.

```
val new_channel : unit -> 'a channel
val send : 'a channel -> 'a -> unit event
val receive : 'a channel -> 'a event
```

The send and receive functions either send an event on a given channel or receive one. These actions, in themselves, do not actually do anything. Each event needs to be synchronized first. There are three functions that can do this. The first two, sync and select, are blocking functions. This means they will block until they complete. The poll function is a nonblocking version of sync, only it returns an option (either None or Some 'a) for a given 'a Event.

```
val sync : 'a event -> 'a
val select : 'a event list -> 'a
val poll : 'a event -> 'a option
```

These three functions each serve a specific purpose. Following are three examples, one of each for these functions. The last two have two channels, though only one is actually used.

```
# let a = Event.new_channel () in
let t = Thread.create (fun ch -> Event.sync (Event.send ch 10)) a in
  Event.sync (Event.receive a);;
    - : int = 10
# let a = Event.new_channel () in
let b = Event.new_channel () in
let t = Thread.create (fun ch -> Event.sync (Event.send ch 10)) a in
  Event.select [(Event.receive a);(Event.receive b)];;
    - : int = 10
# let a = Event.new_channel () in
let b = Event.new_channel () in
let t = Thread.create (fun ch -> Event.sync (Event.send ch 10)) a in
  (Event.poll (Event.receive a)),  (Event.poll (Event.receive b));;
    - : int option * 'a option = (None, None)
#
```

These three functions are important because they enable you to handle single events as well as lists of events (the same with single channels or many channels). The next two functions are, in some ways, not as useful. The always function returns an event that is always ready for synchronization. The choose function returns an event that is ready for synchronization from a list of events. The choose and select functions offer similar functionality—select does the synchronizing step for you.

```
val always : 'a -> 'a event
val choose : 'a event list -> 'a event
```

The next three functions enable you to call functions on events (or events from functions). This can be useful if you need to provide additional computation along with events, or translate an event into another type of event. The wrap function enables you to translate one type of event into another, whereas the wrap_abort function calls the function only if the event is not selected (by the Event.select function).

```
val wrap : 'a event -> ('a -> 'b) -> 'b event
val wrap_abort : 'a event -> (unit -> unit) -> 'a event
val guard : (unit -> 'a event) -> 'a event
```

It might be hard to understand when (or even how) you might use these functions. The following demonstrates each function. The first, wrap, is the easiest to understand. You can see from the second example that the event that is not selected prints out the message. The called function takes a unit argument and must return unit. It is not advisable to use a function that could throw an exception here. The last function, guard, enables you to pass a function that returns an event. This enables you to create functions that perform computation resulting in events and still use them for synchronization. The result is 10 because you sync'd the event.

```
# Event.sync (let a = Event.always "hello" in Event.wrap a
                        (fun m -> String.length m));;
- : int = 5

# let a = Event.new_channel () in
      let b = Event.new_channel () in
          let t = Thread.create (fun ch -> Event.sync (Event.send ch 10)) a
            in
              Event.select [ (Event.receive a);
                             (Event.wrap_abort (Event.receive b) (fun () ->
                                      Printf.printf "I wasn't ready for syncing\n"))];;
I wasn't ready for syncing
- : int = 10
# let a = Event.new_channel () in
    let b = Event.new_channel () in
      let t = Thread.create (fun ch -> Event.sync (Event.send ch 10)) a
        in Event.sync (Event.choose [(Event.receive b);
                                     (Event.guard (fun () -> (Event.receive a)))]);;
- : int = 10

# let a = Event.new_channel () in
  let b = Event.new_channel () in
  let t = Thread.create (fun ch ->Event.sync (Event.send ch 10)) a
  in
    Event.sync (Event.choose [(Event.receive b);
                              (Event.guard (fun () -> (Event.receive a)))]);;
- : int = 10
```

Remember that the Event module is not a high-performance interthread communication system. You should experiment with the Event module and become familiar with it if you intend to use it.

Some Code from the Last Chapter

Now that you've gone through these libraries, if you have a look at one function from the last chapter—the minder function—you can better understand exactly what is going on.

The minder function uses events to remove a thread from that hashtable of active threads and shut down sockets and channels used by that thread.

```
let rec minder dt =
  let tid = Event.sync (Event.receive dt) in
  (try
    let to_remove =
        Hashtbl.find master_hash tid in
    Mutex.lock hash_mutex;
    Hashtbl.remove master_hash tid;
    Mutex.unlock hash_mutex;
    try
              close_out to_remove.oc;
              close_in to_remove.ic;
    with Sys_error m -> Printf.printf "%s\n" m;
              shutdown_socket to_remove.sock;
                  Printf.printf "Disconnect from %s\n" (get_hostname to_remove.adr)
  with Not_found ->
              Printf.printf "Strange, %s was not found\n" (get_hostname tid);
            Mutex.unlock hash_mutex
  );
  minder dt;;
```

This section of code, which is not performance-critical, is an example of the kind of solutions the Event module provides. After a given thread signals the minder that it is no longer connected, the minder synchronizes the event, deletes the thread, and shuts it down. The minder then blocks until another message is ready for synchronization. If an exception is thrown, but not caught, the minder exits, leaving threads lying around. Exception handling with threads is very important because a thread will exit on an uncaught exception, and there might be no way to recover.

A More Complex Example

The example code presents a simple POP3 client that saves messages using multiple threads. POP3 is a very simple protocol, consisting of a few commands, listed in Table 23-1, and fewer responses. It uses the same socket for input and output operations because many POP3 servers allow only one connection at a time. This is important to remember because you might get errors from the class if you attempt multiple connections with the same username on the server you are using.

Table 23-1. *POP3 Commands*

Command	Action
USER <username>	Sends the username
PASS <password>	Sends the password (in plain text)
LIST	Shows the messages and their sizes
TOP <MESSAGE ID> <NUMBER OF LINES>	Shows the top *n* lines of a message, including the headers
RETR <MESSAGE ID>	Retrieves the given message
QUIT	Exits

The response to each command is +OK, followed by an informational message and a new-line, which is followed by the data. It is terminated by a . (period) on a single line. Some servers display a header when a client first connects, but many do not.

This code does not make modifications to a POP mailbox. It is, in my opinion, a bad idea to give demonstration code that can delete a user's mailbox. The following code presents a class to retrieve messages from a POP3 server and store them in a file. The download and stor-age of each message occurs in a separate thread.

```
let make_connection host port =
  let sock = Unix.socket Unix.PF_INET Unix.SOCK_STREAM 0 in
  let server_address = (Unix.gethostbyname host).Unix.h_addr_list.(0) in
  Unix.connect sock (Unix.ADDR_INET (server_address,port));
  sock;;
```

The first function is a helper function that returns a fully connected socket. The next two functions are actually one complete function that enable buffered reading from a socket. This was a design choice to enable the code to run on any platform supported by OCaml. The time-out for the select is three seconds. For heavily loaded servers, this timeout might not be long enough. The buffer size of 128 was chosen because it is an easy number to work with. You can change the buffer size to any number you feel is appropriate.

```
let rec read_data stringbuf buf (m,n,o) = match m with
    [] -> Buffer.contents buf
  | h :: t -> let n = Unix.recv h stringbuf 0
       (String.length stringbuf) [] in match n with
                 p when (n = (String.length stringbuf)) ->
                    Buffer.add_string buf stringbuf;
                    read_data stringbuf buf (Thread.select [h] [] [] 3.)
                | _ -> Buffer.add_string buf (String.sub stringbuf 0 n);
                    read_data stringbuf buf (Thread.select [h] [] [] 3.);;

let reader sock = let st = String.create 128 in
let b = Buffer.create 128 in
  read_data st b (Thread.select [sock] [] [] 3.);;
```

Next, you see the two writing functions, which are similar to the preceding buffered read-ing functions. Again, the timeout might be too short for heavily loaded servers.

```
let rec write_data stringbuf total (m,n,o) = match n with
    [] -> total
  | h :: t -> let amount = (String.length stringbuf) - total in
    let n = Unix.send h (String.sub stringbuf total amount) 0 amount [] in
      match n with
                  p when (n < (String.length stringbuf)) -> write_data stringbuf n
                  (Thread.select [] [h] [] 3.)
              | _ -> n;;

let writer sock str =
  let wrote = write_data str 0 (Thread.select [] [sock] [] 3.) in
    match wrote with
                  p when (wrote = (String.length str)) -> true
        | _ -> false;;
```

The build_list function is a helper function to create a list of pairs from the message list returned by the POP3 server. The list of messages returned consists of the message id (a sequential integer) and the size of the message in octets. Sometimes this message size is reported incorrectly, so this client ignores it.

```
let rec build_list sb acc = let n =
  try
    Scanf.bscanf sb "%i %i\013\n" (fun x y -> (x,y))
  with End_of_file -> (-1,-1)
    | (Scanf.Scan_failure m) -> (-1,-1)
in match n with
    (-1,-1) -> acc
  | _ -> build_list sb (n :: acc);;
```

Finally, you see the class itself. It takes a hostname as an argument and has an optional argument of a port number. This class does not support SSL, POP3, or MD5 authentication. It also does not make any changes to the mailbox.

```
class pop3 ?(prt=110) host_name =
object(so)
  val host = host_name
  val port = prt
  val mutable message_list = []
  val socket_mutex = Mutex.create ()
  val threads = Stack.create ()
  val connection = make_connection host_name prt
  method login user_name passwd =
    Mutex.lock socket_mutex;
    let n = reader connection  in
    let login_string = "USER " ^ user_name ^ "\nPASS " ^ passwd ^ "\n" in
    let sent = writer connection login_string  in
    let sb = Scanf.Scanning.from_string (reader connection) in
```

```
        try
                        Mutex.unlock socket_mutex;
                        Scanf.bscanf sb "+OK%s@\013\n" (fun x -> true);
                with Scanf.Scan_failure m -> false
method logout () = Mutex.lock socket_mutex;
                        ignore(writer connection "QUIT\n");
                        Unix.shutdown connection Unix.SHUTDOWN_ALL;
                        Mutex.unlock socket_mutex;
                        Stack.iter (fun x -> Thread.join x) threads
method list () =Mutex.lock socket_mutex;
                if writer connection "LIST\n" then
                        let sb = Scanf.Scanning.from_string (reader connection) in
                        try
                            Scanf.bscanf sb "+OK%s@\013\n" (fun x -> ());
                            message_list <- build_list sb [];
                            Mutex.unlock socket_mutex;
                            true
                        with Scanf.Scan_failure m -> Mutex.unlock socket_mutex;
                                                     false
                else
                    false
method get_num_messages () = List.length message_list
method save_message id file = match List.mem_assoc id message_list
        with
    | true -> let fchan = open_out file in
                Stack.push (Thread.create
                                (fun x -> Mutex.lock socket_mutex;
                                    if writer connection
                                        (Printf.sprintf "TOP %i 100\n" id)
                                    then
                                    let is = reader connection in
                                    let sub = Scanf.sscanf is "+OK%s@\013\n"
                                        (fun rest ->(String.length rest)+5)
                                    in
                                        output x is sub
                                        ((String.length is) - sub);
                                        close_out x;
                                        Mutex.unlock socket_mutex;
                                        ) fchan) threads
    | false -> raise Not_found
method save_all_messages file = let ofl = open_out file
    in
      Stack.push (Thread.create
                    (fun fl -> Mutex.lock socket_mutex;
                        List.iter (fun (messid,len) ->
```

```
                                if writer connection
                                    (Printf.sprintf "TOP %i 100\n" messid)
                                then
                                  let is = reader connection in
                                      let sub = Scanf.sscanf is "+OK%s@\013\n"
                                          (fun rest -> (String.length rest)+5)
                             in
                        output fl is sub ((String.length is) - sub)) message_list;
                        close_out fl;
                        Mutex.unlock socket_mutex) ofl) threads
end;;
```

Then you can look at the signatures of the following functions, including the signature of the class:

```
# val make_connection : string -> int -> Unix.file_descr = <fun>
# val read_data : string -> Buffer.t ->
          Unix.file_descr list * Unix.file_descr list * Unix.file_descr list ->
                                                              string = <fun>
# val reader : Unix.file_descr -> string = <fun>
# val write_data : string -> int ->
Unix.file_descr list * Unix.file_descr list * Unix.file_descr list -> int = <fun>
# val writer : Unix.file_descr -> string -> bool = <fun>
# val build_list : Scanf.Scanning.scanbuf -> (int * int) list ->
                                                (int * int) list = <fun>


#class pop3 :
  ?prt:int ->
  string ->
  object
    val connection : Unix.file_descr
    val host : string
    val mutable message_list : (int * int) list
    val port : int
    val socket_mutex : Mutex.t
    val threads : Thread.t Stack.t
    method get_num_messages : unit -> int
    method list : unit -> bool
    method login : string -> string -> bool
    method logout : unit -> unit
    method save_all_messages : string -> unit
    method save_message : int -> string -> unit
  end
```

You can now use this class. Using the class is much easier than looking at the code, as you can see from the following example. (The username and password have been changed to protect the innocent.)

```
# let p = new pop3 "bebop";;
val p : pop3 = <obj>
# p#login "USERNAME" "PASSWORD";;
- : bool = true
# p#list ();;
- : bool = true
# p#save_message 1 "test1";;
- : unit = ()
# p#save_all_messages "test2";;
- : unit = ()
# p#logout ();;
- : unit = ()
```

Conclusion

This chapter discussed the threading capabilities of OCaml. The examples in this chapter, combined with the last chapter, should give you an understanding of multithreading I/O and how to write clients and servers.

Although OCaml fully supports threads, it does not support SMP (and probably never will). For many applications, this will not be a problem. This is especially true with I/O-bound applications that spend much of their user time in I/O operations.

An application with multiple threads of control can be difficult to debug. It can also present strange behavior, making careful consideration of what should or should not be threaded important. Having multiple threads of control might not solve any performance problems, either.

■ ■ ■

## CHAPTER 24

Practical: A Concurrent Web Crawler

This chapter introduces a concurrent web crawler written in OCaml, which traverses a web server and finds all the local href links. It then outputs information about which pages link together. A web crawler is different from a web browser in that the web crawler is automated. Both are web (or HTTP) clients and are quite similar, but this automation versus interactivity is the important distinction.

Because crawlers are noninteractive, they are often much simpler than their browser cousins. They can, however, do things that browsers often cannot do. For example, if you want to write an application that operates on the web pages, a web browser probably does not have this functionality.

Web crawlers are often not used alone. The most commonly seen web crawlers are written and run by search engine companies to support their web indexing operations. Spiders and crawlers are also often used in research. The web has become a popular data source for social network researchers and general network theory researchers as well.

Deceptively Simple Application

Writing a web crawler is a deceptively simple problem because you can describe what you want to do quite easily; the problem begins to creep in with the implementation.

One of the big problems is finding pages to crawl. Many search engine companies (such as Yahoo and Google) encourage people to use sitemaps, which are special documents that enumerate all the pages of a particular site. The crawlers' tasks are much simpler because they do not have to discover which links should be traversed. Another major problem is that links in web pages are often not very well formatted. The full definition of what this means can be found in RFC 2396 (it makes for scintillating reading).

So the crawler must do a lot of processing on each link to figure it out. Add in things such as JavaScript and the like, and the whole idea of what is or is not a local link becomes problematic. (The crawler outlined here does not handle JavaScript pages.)

One of the reasons why this application is being used is that it provides a good analog for things that many clients (especially multithreaded clients) must do: process existing information and respond to new information.

Design Goals

Some design goals were set for this application. The first one is that it should crawl only one domain (the little robot should not wander off and try to crawl the entire web).

The robot will crawl only HTTP links. It will get all hrefs in given page, but writing a Secure Sockets Layer (SSL)–capable robot is similar enough to a non-SSL–capable robot that it has been left out in this example. If you understand one, you understand the other, so it isn't really a big loss. The robot cannot support authentication. Although doing basic authentication is not terribly complicated, many web sites that require authentication use state-maintenance techniques that can be problematic to handle for a robot.

This robot will be simple, but it should support future expansion. One of the primary reasons to write your own robot is to customize it in your own way.

This robot can pull one kind of tag out of a page, which does not require a full-on HTML parser. Because you are making it expandable, a parser can be added later. However, this kind of functionality is probably better left to an indexer that operates on the pages retrieved by the crawler.

Although you want the crawler to be concurrent, you also need to make sure that it doesn't put too high a burden on the sites that it crawls. This requires some sort of throttling of the number of connections allowed at any given time.

Regular Expressions

You can use the OCaml implementation of regular expressions to accomplish many of these goals. These regular expressions are different from those found in ocamllex or in languages such as Python or Java. Although they are not substantially different, they do differ in some significant ways.

Regular expression support in OCaml is found in the Str module, which includes functions for creating and operating on regular expressions, as well as the functions needed for using regular expressions. If you have an understanding of regular expressions, you can use the Str module effectively. The syntax for OCaml Regex is found in Table 24-1.

Table 24-1. *Regex Syntax*

Expression	Description
.	Matches any character (except newline).
*	Matches zero or more of the previous regular expression. For example a* matches a, aa, aaa, and aaaaaaaaaaaaa; and also matches nothing.
+	Matches the preceding expression one or more times. Like the previous, but must match at least one time so it will not match nothing.
?	Matches the preceding expression zero or one time. For example, ab? matches a or ab.
[set of char]	Can be a range or group of characters. A range uses a hyphen, as in [a-z]. You don't have to escape a] if you want to include it; you just include it as the first character. You can also include a - in your set by including it last.
^	Matches the beginning of a line.
$	Matches the end of a line.

Expression	Description
|	Matches one regexp or the other (and can be more than two). For example, [a-z] | [0-9] | [A-H] matches any one of the three character classes.
\(..\)	Creates a match group.
\b	Matches a word boundary.

You need to use a \ to quote special characters such as $^.*+?[]. These regular expressions are compiled by using the Str.regexp function and can then be used by the other functions in the library.

The code in this chapter uses string_match, search_forward, matched_string, and matched_group. (They are not the only functions in the Str module, but they are the only ones covered here.)

To use the Str module, you need to load the library or link it into your code or toplevel. The Str module is not available by default. The function used to compile regular expressions takes a string and converts it into a regular expression.

```
# #load "str.cma";;
# Str.regexp;;
- : string -> Str.regexp = <fun>
# let reg = Str.regexp "a+";;
val reg : Str.regexp = <abstr>
```

The string_match function takes a string, a regular expression, and a start location. It returns true if a match is found, or false if not. The start location must be less than the length of the string you intend to search.

```
# Str.string_match;;
- : Str.regexp -> string -> int -> bool = <fun>
# Str.string_match reg "a quick brown fox" 0;;
- : bool = true
```

The matching elements of the string can then be accessed by using the matched_string function. This function takes the same string used in the string_match function and returns only the portion of the string that matches the regexp used. This substring is available only until the next time a search or match function is called. If there is no match, and if the matched_string function is called, an Invalid_argument exception is raised.

```
# Str.matched_string "a quick brown fox";;
- : string = "a"
# Str.string_match reg "a quick brown fox" 1;;
- : bool = false
# Str.matched_string "a quick brown fox";;
Exception: Invalid_argument "Str.matched_group".
```

The search_forward function is like the string_match function, except it returns the location of the match instead of a Boolean. This function raises a Not_found exception if there is no match in the string.

```
# Str.search_forward;;
-: Str.regexp -> string -> int -> int = <fun>
# Str.search_forward reg "a quick brown fox" 0;;
- : int = 0
# Str.matched_string "a quick brown fox";;
- : string = "a"
```

You can access specific segments of a matched string by using the matched_group function. You must, however, supply the grouping expressions within your regular expression. If you request a matched group that does not exist, an Invalid_argument is raised.

```
# let mat = "a quick brown fox";;
val mat : string = "a quick brown fox"
# Str.search_forward (Str.regexp "brown \\(f[a-z][a-z]\\)") mat 0;;
- : int = 8
# Str.matched_string mat;;
- : string = "brown fox"
# Str.matched_group 1 mat;;
- : string = "fox"
# Str.matched_group 2 mat;;
Exception: Invalid_argument "Str.matched_group".
#
```

Understanding the Code

First, you'll see the interface file, which should be saved into a file called crawler.mli. The interface defines the exposed classes and the exposed modules, as well as the Set and Map types that the module uses for managing the links.

```
module StringSet :
  sig
    type elt = String.t
    type t = Set.Make(String).t
    val empty : t
    val is_empty : t -> bool
    val mem : elt -> t -> bool
    val add : elt -> t -> t
    val singleton : elt -> t
    val remove : elt -> t -> t
    val union : t -> t -> t
    val inter : t -> t -> t
    val diff : t -> t -> t
    val compare : t -> t -> int
    val equal : t -> t -> bool
    val subset : t -> t -> bool
    val iter : (elt -> unit) -> t -> unit
    val fold : (elt -> 'a -> 'a) -> t -> 'a -> 'a
```

```
    val for_all : (elt -> bool) -> t -> bool
    val exists : (elt -> bool) -> t -> bool
    val filter : (elt -> bool) -> t -> t
    val partition : (elt -> bool) -> t -> t * t
    val cardinal : t -> int
    val elements : t -> elt list
    val min_elt : t -> elt
    val max_elt : t -> elt
    val choose : t -> elt
    val split : elt -> t -> t * bool * t
  end

module StringMap :
  sig
    type key = String.t
    type 'a t = 'a Map.Make(String).t
    val empty : 'a t
    val is_empty : 'a t -> bool
    val add : key -> 'a -> 'a t -> 'a t
    val find : key -> 'a t -> 'a
    val remove : key -> 'a t -> 'a t
    val mem : key -> 'a t -> bool
    val iter : (key -> 'a -> unit) -> 'a t -> unit
    val map : ('a -> 'b) -> 'a t -> 'b t
    val mapi : (key -> 'a -> 'b) -> 'a t -> 'b t
    val fold : (key -> 'a -> 'b -> 'b) -> 'a t -> 'b -> 'b
    val compare : ('a -> 'a -> int) -> 'a t -> 'a t -> int
    val equal : ('a -> 'a -> bool) -> 'a t -> 'a t -> bool
  end
```

The preceding modules are from the Set and Map functors. They both use the String module, which is the type you will use to describe the paths for URLs. The following module is a nonthreaded web crawler. This code demonstrates the added complexity of making a threaded version of this code. Nonthreaded code is often much, much simpler than the corresponding threaded versions. There is only one exposed function in the module: the mainloop function. Then comes the more complicated (and threaded) crawler, which has only one exposed function.

This example shows that complicated code does not (always) require a complicated API for others to use. All the complexity is hidden behind the module signature, which also enables the programmer to make modifications to the code without worrying about affecting users of that library—as long as she makes sure that the new code conforms to the existing interface.

```
module SimpleCrawler :
  sig
    val mainloop : string -> StringSet.elt -> StringSet.t StringMap.t
  end
```

The first class defined here is the client class, which will become the base class of all future HTTP client classes. This class defines methods that enable you to easily connect and disconnect a socket and then read and write data on that socket. The default socket timeout might be a little too slow for some web servers, so you might want to increase it if you run into timeout problems. Now you go into the file crawler.ml that has the implementation code for this application.

```
class client ?(timeout=10.0) port host =
object(c)
  val mutable socket = Unix.socket Unix.PF_INET Unix.SOCK_STREAM 0
  val input_buffer = Buffer.create 1024
  method connect =
    let server_address =
      (Unix.gethostbyname host).Unix.h_addr_list.(0) in
    Unix.connect socket (Unix.ADDR_INET (server_address,port));
    let (n,m,o) = Unix.select [] [socket] [] timeout in match m with
                [] -> failwith "Failed to connect!"
                 | h :: t -> ()
  method disconnect =
    Unix.close socket;
    socket <- Unix.socket Unix.PF_INET
      Unix.SOCK_STREAM 0
  method read =
    let rec read_all (r,w,x) tmpstr =
    List.iter (fun x ->
                let res = Unix.read socket tmpstr 0 (String.length tmpstr)
                in
                match res with
                 0 -> ()
                | n when n < (String.length tmpstr) ->
                        Buffer.add_string input_buffer (String.sub tmpstr 0 n);
                        read_all (Unix.select [socket] [] [] timeout) tmpstr
                | _ -> Buffer.add_string input_buffer tmpstr;
                        read_all (Unix.select [socket] [] [] timeout) tmpstr) r
    in
    read_all (Unix.select [socket] [] [] timeout) (String.create 1024);
    let info = Buffer.contents input_buffer in
        Buffer.clear input_buffer;
        info
  method write str =
    let rec write_all (r,w,x) output_str startidx len =
    List.iter (fun x ->
                let res = Unix.write socket output_str startidx len
            in
            match res with
              0 -> invalid_arg "Zero write length"
            | n when n < len ->
```

```
              write_all (Unix.select [] [socket] [] timeout) output_str n (len - n)
            | _ -> () ) w
    in
    write_all (Unix.select [] [socket] [] timeout) str 0 (String.length str)
end
```

Because you have a basic client class, you can extend that class via inheritance and create a simple_http class that handles fetching a given path from a web server. The class identifies itself and supports a very limited set of functions.

This class does not process the HTML page returned in any way. It also does not verify that the page returned 400 and returns the error page just as if it were the page originally requested. The recognition of return codes was not implemented in an effort to keep the code short enough to be understandable.

```
class simple_http ?(timeout=10.0) ?(port=80) host =
object(h)
  inherit client port host
  method fetch path = let reqbuf = Buffer.create 40 in
    Buffer.add_string reqbuf "GET ";
    Buffer.add_string reqbuf path;
    Buffer.add_string reqbuf " HTTP/1.1\nHost: ";
    Buffer.add_string reqbuf host;
    Buffer.add_string reqbuf "\nUser-Agent: OcamlClient/0.91 (X11; U; ";
    Buffer.add_string reqbuf "Linux i686; en-US;)\nConnection: close\n\n";
    h#write (Buffer.contents reqbuf);
    h#read
end
```

The next class handles link normalization. This class does not do complete normalization of the URI, but it does enough processing to avoid trying to read JavaScript pages, pages that are not local to the web server, and so on. This class is the one that you might want to extend if you want to add support for the robots.txt on a given web server.

After this class are the functor definitions for the StringSet and the StringMap modules. They enable you to define sets of strings and maps of strings as keys to StringSets of values. Sets are used here for two reasons. First, they are the perfect container for this task because you want unique, ordered strings and functions for comparing two containers and detecting differences. The other reason is that this code is almost purely functional, so you'll use a purely functional data structure to keep that up. This is handy in multithreaded situations because you don't have to worry about mutexes or changing data structures. These are the same reasons for using the StringMap module instead of a HashMap or something similar.

```
class normalize_link host =
object
  method is_local_to link =
    Str.string_match
    (Str.regexp ("http://" ^ host ^ "\\|/[/]?\\|[a-zA-Z0-9_/]+.html")) link 0
  method normalize base link =
    if (Str.string_match (Str.regexp ("[a-zA-Z0-9_]+.html")) link 0)
```

```
        then
            base ^ "/" ^ link
        else if (Str.string_match (Str.regexp ("[^ /][a-zA-Z0-9_/]+.html")) link 0)
        then
            base ^ "/" ^ link
        else
            link
    method dirname path = try
        let idx = String.rindex path '/' in match idx with
                      0 -> "/"
            | _ -> String.sub path 0 idx
      with Not_found -> "/"
end

module StringSet = Set.Make(String);;
module StringMap = Map.Make(String);;
```

You now define the SimpleCrawler. This code is a nonthreaded web crawler. You have implanted it to display the difference in code size and complexity of a nonthreaded versus a threaded implementation of the same functionality.

The link_harvest class does most of the work in the SimpleCrawler. This class implements the methods and data for retrieving HTML documents from web servers and extracting links from those pages.

The link_harvest class also has the capability to filter the extracted links so that only links that point to local documents are accepted. This is important because it allows the crawler to traverse only local links and not spin out of control and try to harvest the entire web. This class inherits from the simple_http class and the normalize_link class.

```
module SimpleCrawler =
  struct
    class link_harvest ?(timeout=10.0) ?(port=80) host =
    object(h)
      inherit simple_http ~port:port host as c
      inherit normalize_link host
      method private get_link_tag str lpos =
                let reg = Str.regexp "<[aA] [^>]+>" in
                let pos = Str.search_forward reg str lpos in
                    (pos,Str.matched_string str)
      method private get_link str lpos =
                let (tpos,tagstr) = h#get_link_tag str lpos in
                  let reg = Str.regexp "[hH][rR][eE][fF]=\"\\([^ \"#]+\\)" in
                let pos = try
                  Some (Str.search_forward reg tagstr 0)
                with Not_found -> None
                in match pos with
```

```
                    Some hpos -> ((tpos+String.length tagstr),
                                           (Str.matched_group 1 tagstr))
                     | None -> h#get_link str (tpos+String.length tagstr)
  method private get_all_links linkbase str lpos acc =
          let nextlink = try
            Some (h#get_link str lpos)
          with Not_found -> None
          in
            match nextlink with
              None -> acc
            | Some (pos,newlink) ->
              if (h#is_local_to newlink) then
                      let newset = StringSet.add
                              (h#normalize linkbase newlink) acc
                    in
                          h#get_all_links linkbase str pos newset
              else
                          h#get_all_links linkbase str pos acc
  method link_fetch path = let res = c#fetch path in
          h#get_all_links (h#dirname path) res 0 StringSet.empty
end
```

There is a labeled argument for a delay in this function. This delay is important because you do not want your crawler to be an assault on the target web server. This delay enables you to throttle the number of requests that are made. For example, on my somewhat slow server, this code can make 25 HTTP requests per second. That is pretty aggressive for a client, so the delay enables you to slow that number down.

The runner function really does most of the work. It is a simple loop that chooses an item from the set, fetches it, and then processes the links to start the loop over again. This is a linear sequence of actions, and it is quite simple compared with the following threaded version.

```
let rec runner ?(delay=0.3) lh links seenlinks linkmap =
  match links with
          n when StringSet.is_empty links -> linkmap
    | _ -> let nextlink = StringSet.choose links in
            Printf.printf "Fetching %s\n" nextlink;flush_all ();
          lh#connect;
          let newlinks = lh#link_fetch nextlink in
          lh#disconnect;
          let combined_links = StringSet.fold
                (fun el targ -> StringSet.add el targ)
                (StringSet.diff newlinks seenlinks) links
            in
            Thread.delay delay;
              runner lh (StringSet.remove nextlink combined_links)
                      (StringSet.add nextlink seenlinks)
                      (StringMap.add nextlink newlinks linkmap)
```

```
      let mainloop host startpath =
        let nlh = new link_harvest host in
        nlh#connect;
        let newlinks = nlh#link_fetch startpath in
        nlh#disconnect;
        runner nlh newlinks (StringSet.add startpath StringSet.empty)
                (StringMap.add startpath newlinks StringMap.empty)
  End
```

After this code is compiled, you can use it in the mainloop function (as shown in the following short example). Also shown is how to compile the code. The example used in running the code is on a platform that supports dynamic loading, so the #load directives are used. If your platform does not support dynamic loading, you have to create a custom toplevel, which means you do not have to use the #load directives.

```
$ ocamlc -I +threads unix.cma threads.cma str.cma crawler.mli
$ ocamlc -I +threads unix.cma threads.cma str.cma crawler.ml

$ ocaml -I +threads
        Objective Caml version 3.09.0

# #load "unix.cma";;
# #load "threads.cma";;
# #load "str.cma";;
# #load "crawler.cmo";;
# let links = Crawler.SimpleCrawler.mainloop "bebop" "/";;
Fetching http://bebop/apache2-default/
Fetching /manual/
val links : Crawler.StringSet.t Crawler.StringMap.t = <abstr>
#
```

Now that you have seen the single-threaded version, you can move on to the multi-threaded version. There are two new types you need to define. The two types in the Crawler module are used to communicate between threads. The code uses Event channels to communicate between threads. After that is the threaded version of the link_harvest class. This class inherits from the link_harvest class and implements some new functionality via the Event channels it takes as arguments.

```
module Crawler :
  sig
    val mainloop : ?nthreads:int -> ?delay:float -> string ->
      StringSet.elt -> StringSet.t StringMap.t
  end
```

The signature for the module defined is shown above (it should be added to the crawler. mli file). Figure 24-1 shows a graph of the class inheritances for the classes defined in the Crawler module.

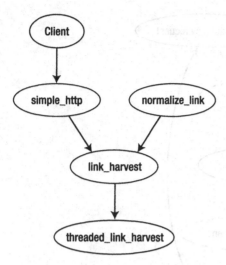

Figure 24-1. *Class inheritence graph for classes defined in the Crawler module*

Now we move into the implementation of the multi-threaded Crawler module. The actiontype type is used to send information to threads, which are instances of the threaded_link_harvest. The responsetype type is used by threads to send information back to the main loop.

```
module Crawler =
struct
  type actiontype = Fetch of string | Shutdown;;
  type responsetype = Returned of string * StringSet.t
                               | Thread_shutdown of int;;
```

The code for this class is somewhat complex because of its multithreadedness. Handling asynchronous communication requires a lot more code than simply processing a sequential set of actions. This class inherits from the class defined in the SimpleCrawler. It is designed to be run as a separate thread of execution, and all the logic is contained within the run method. Figure 24-2 shows a directed graph describing the sequence of actions that this class performs.

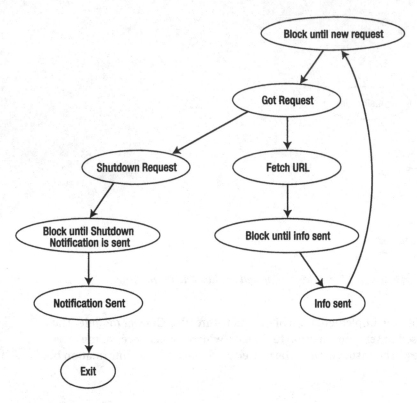

Figure 24-2. *Actions performed by the threaded_link_harvest class*

Luckily, the Events module provides functions for polling channels, which enables you to write a master loop that scatters the requests and gathers the responses without blocking. The clients, however, do block on the communication. This client blocking makes sure that they send and receive the messages correctly, and makes sure that the whole system doesn't spin out of control (looping with many threads can be a problem if you are not careful).

```
class threaded_link_harvest host notification request =
object(tlh)
inherit SimpleCrawler.link_harvest host
method run = while (true) do
            let action = Event.sync (Event.receive request)
            in
             match action with
                Fetch url -> (try
                                tlh#connect;
                                let links = try
                                              tlh#link_fetch url
                                            with ex -> Printf.eprintf
                                                    "Exception: %s\n"
                                                    (Printexc.to_string ex);
                                            StringSet.empty
```

```
                                                in
                              Printf.printf "(%d) Fetching %s\n"
                                        (Thread.id (Thread.self ())) ➥
url; flush_all ();
                                        Event.sync
                                          (Event.send notification
                                              (Returned (url,links)));
                                      tlh#disconnect
                                    with ex -> Printf.eprintf "Exception: ➥
%s\n"
                                        (Printexc.to_string ex))
                    Shutdown -> Printf.printf "(%d) Got Shutdown!\n"
                     (Thread.id (Thread.self ()));
                     (try
                            tlh#disconnect
                      with ex -> Printf.eprintf "Exception: %s\n"
                            (Printexc.to_string ex));
                      Event.sync (Event.send notification
                                        (Thread_shutdown (Thread.id (Thread. ➥
self ()))));
                      Thread.exit ()
        done
      end
```

These two channels are the ones used to communicate with all the threads and the mainloop. The sender function is a helper function that enables you to send out links to as many threads as can listen and then return. Figure 24-3 shows a graph of the actions performed in the module. As you can see, it is often much easier to see the sequence of actions in a graph than it is to see it in the code.

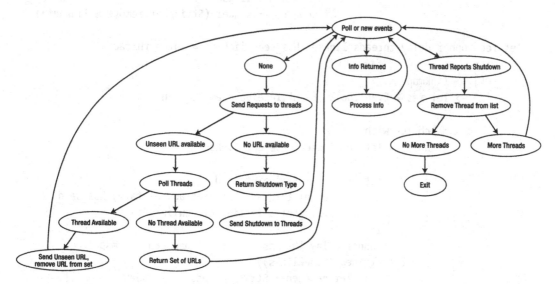

Figure 24-3. *Graph of actions performed in the Crawler mainloop*

The runner function does most of the work. Figure 24-3 shows the sequence of what happens within this looping function. This network of action is significantly more complicated than the straight-line action of the nonthreaded crawler shown first. This runner function also has a delay, for the same reasons that the SimpleCrawler has one: your crawler should not be an unwelcome client for a web server.

There is a risk of thread starvation here, though. Threads are starved when there are many threads waiting for action while previous actions are being processed. For example, if conditions are right, some of the threads created will never perform any action (or perform them very infrequently) because one (or more) of the running threads is faster. It is not a big risk here, but thread starvation is something you should always be on guard for in multithreaded programs. Having threads around that do nothing is also a sign of poor design and can signal a need to rethink the whole thing.

```
let crawler_chan = Event.new_channel ()
let request_chan = Event.new_channel ()
let rec sender linkset =
 let nextitem = try
    let ni = StringSet.choose linkset in (Fetch ni)
  with Not_found -> Shutdown
 in match nextitem with
        Shutdown -> (let res = Event.poll (Event.send request_chan Shutdown)
                     in
                     match res with
                       None -> StringSet.empty
                     | Some () -> sender StringSet.empty)
                     | Fetch m -> (let res =
                              Event.poll (Event.send request_chan nextitem)
                          in
                          match res with
                            None -> linkset
                          | Some () -> sender (StringSet.remove m linkset))

let rec runner delay threads linkset has_seen linkmap = match threads
    with
      [] -> linkmap
    | _ -> let res = Event.poll (Event.receive crawler_chan)
          in
          match res with
             None -> let newlinkset = sender linkset
                     in
                     let newseen = StringSet.fold
                           (fun el targ -> StringSet.add el targ) has_seen
                           (StringSet.diff linkset newlinkset)
                     in
                     runner delay threads newlinkset newseen linkmap
           | Some (Returned (n,newlinks)) ->
                     let newseen = StringSet.add n has_seen
```

```
                                in
                let combined_links =
                    StringSet.fold (fun el targ -> StringSet.add el targ)
                    linkset (StringSet.diff newlinks newseen)
                in
                    Thread.delay delay;
                    runner delay threads combined_links newseen
                        (StringMap.add n newlinks linkmap)
        | Some (Thread_shutdown m) -> Thread.join (List.assoc m threads);
                                runner delay
                                    (List.remove_assoc m threads) linkset
                                    has_seen linkmap
```

The `mainloop` function is the only exposed function in this module. Contrary to its name, this function does not actually loop; it does call the `runner` function, however, which does loop. The `mainloop` function also places the first URL into the set and starts the whole ball rolling. This function returns when the program runs out of URLs to search. This can happen by thread starvation if there are few links between pages.

```
let mainloop ?(nthreads=5) ?(delay=0.3) host startpath =
  let threads = Array.to_list
    ( Array.init nthreads
            (fun x ->
              let newthread = Thread.create
                (fun y ->
                  let ntl =
                      new threaded_link_harvest host crawler_chan request_chan
                  in
                    ntl#run) ()
                in
                  ((Thread.id newthread),newthread)
            ))
  in
      Printf.printf "Sending First Fetch\n";flush_all ();
      Event.sync (Event.send request_chan (Fetch startpath));
      let resp = Event.sync (Event.receive crawler_chan) in
              match resp with
                | Thread_shutdown _ -> assert(false)
                | Returned (n,newlinks) ->
                Printf.printf "Sent First Fetch\n";flush_all ();
                let newseen = StringSet.add n StringSet.empty in
                 let combined_links = StringSet.remove startpath newlinks in
                 Printf.printf "Starting mainloop\n";flush_all ();
                 runner delay threads combined_links newseen
                  (StringMap.add n newlinks StringMap.empty)
end;;
```

And that's it—merely 200 or so lines of code to implement a nonthreaded and a multi-threaded web crawler. This code can be compiled and used in your own code, or you can use the command-line client described in the next section.

One of the reasons why multithreaded programming is so hard is that people don't think that way. People tend to think in one or two streams of actions—not 10 or 100. Although people do multitask (otherwise, you could not read this page and breathe at the same time), it can be a difficult intellectual challenge to think about the multiple threads in a given program.

Building and Running the Code

Although this module relies upon the Unix, Str, and Thread modules, you do not have to compile those modules in. You should use the –thread flag, or you can use the –I +threads flag and make sure to link the threads.cma library.

```
$ ocamlc -c -thread crawler.mli
$ ocamlc -c -thread crawler.ml
$ ocamlc -a -thread -custom -o crawler.cma  crawler.cmo
```

Once compiled, this module can be loaded into a toplevel or compiled into an application, as long as you include the other required modules. This module would be well-served by having an example client (one follows). By default, this client outputs a log of what it has seen and a graphviz file describing the network of nodes it has found.

The output type is used to simplify the processing of filenames and channels within the class. The client class, named run, is used to provide mutable data to handle the information from the Arg library's parsing of command-line parameters. The following code should be saved into a file called crawler_client.ml.

```
type output = Filename of string | Channel of out_channel

class run =
object(r)
  val mutable num_threads = 10
  val mutable host = "localhost"
  val mutable path = "/"
  val mutable do_report = true
  val mutable report_out = (Channel stdout)
  val mutable output_dot = true
  val mutable dot_out = (Filename "docmap.dot")
  method set_num_threads x = num_threads <- x
  method set_host x = host <- x
  method set_path x = path <- x
  method set_do_report = do_report <- true
  method set_dont_report = do_report <- false
  method set_do_dot = output_dot <- true
  method set_dont_dot = output_dot <- false
  method set_dot_file x = dot_out <- (Filename x)
  method set_report_file x = report_out <- (Filename x)
  method private report_action report_channel linkassoc = Crawler.StringMap.iter
    (fun x y ->
```

```
          Printf.fprintf report_channel "%s links to:\n" x;
        Crawler.StringSet.iter
                    (fun el -> Printf.fprintf report_channel "\t%s\n" el)
                    y) linkassoc
  method private dot_action dot_channel linkassoc =
    Printf.fprintf dot_channel "digraph G {\n";
    Crawler.StringMap.iter
        (fun  x y ->
          Crawler.StringSet.iter
           (fun el ->
              Printf.fprintf dot_channel "\"%s\" -> \"%s\";\n" x el) y) linkassoc;
              Printf.fprintf dot_channel "}";
  method private do_output which_out linkassoc func =
     match which_out with
          Filename fname -> let oc = open_out fname in
                             func oc linkassoc;
                             close_out oc
        | Channel oc -> func oc linkassoc
  method run =
    let res = Crawler.Crawler.mainloop ~nthreads:num_threads host path in
      match do_report,output_dot with
                  (true,true) -> r#do_output report_out res (r#report_action);
                   r#do_output dot_out res (r#dot_action);res
                | (true,false) -> r#do_output report_out res (r#report_action);
                                  res
                | (false,false) -> res
                | (false,true) -> r#do_output dot_out res (r#dot_action);
                                  res
end

let usage = Printf.sprintf "%s : Crawl a website and construct ➥
a dotfile of links" Sys.argv.(0)

let _ = let runner = new run in
Arg.parse [
  ("--host",(Arg.String (fun x -> runner#set_host x)),("Set the host to crawl"));
  ("--path",(Arg.String (fun x -> runner#set_path x)),("Set the initial path"));
  ("--threads",(Arg.Int (fun x -> runner#set_num_threads x)),("Set the ➥
 number of threads"));
  ("--dotfile",(Arg.String (fun x-> runner#set_do_dot;runner#set_dot_file x)),
   ("Set the filename for the dot output, implies -d"));
  ("--reportfile",(Arg.String (fun x-> runner#set_do_report;
                                       runner#set_report_file x)),
                    ("Set the filename for the report output, implies -v"));
  ("-d",(Arg.Unit (fun x -> runner#set_do_dot)), ➥
                       ("Output dot graph (defaults to \"docmap.dot\")"));
  ("-v",(Arg.Unit (fun x -> runner#set_do_report)),
                       ("Output report (defaults to standard out)"))
```

```
    ] (fun x -> ()) usage;
  let res = runner#run in
    res;
```

The crawler_client can be compiled and run like so:

```
$ ocamlc -o crawler_client unix.cma -thread threads.cma str.cma ➡
crawler.cma crawler_client.ml
$ ./crawler_client -?
```

```
./crawler_client: unknown option `-?'.
./crawler_client : Crawl a website and construct a dotfile of links
  --host Set the host to crawl
  --path Set the initial path
  --threads Set the number of threads
  --dotfile Set the filename for the dot output, implies -d
  --reportfile Set the filename for the report output, implies -v
  -d Output dot graph (defaults to "docmap.dot")
  -v Output report (defaults to stdandard out)
  -help  Display this list of options
  --help  Display this list of options
```

```
$ ./crawler_client --host bebop --path /htmlman/index.html --dotfile docum.dot
```

```
Sending First Fetch
(1) Fetching /htmlman/index.html
Sent First Fetch
Starting mainloop
(3) Fetching /htmlman/libref/index_module_types.html
(2) Fetching /htmlman/libref/index_exceptions.html
(5) Fetching /htmlman/libref/index_types.html
```

The preceding output shows a sample output from the crawler client. Following is a segment of the text report that this program generates. It shows a link path and the links that the page contains.

```
/htmlman/manual043.html links to:
        /htmlman/index.html
        /htmlman/libref/Array.html
        /htmlman/libref/Bigarray.html
        /htmlman/manual032.html
        /htmlman/manual042.html
        /htmlman/manual044.html
```

Generating a Graph of a Site

The graphs that are used to describe web sites are directed graphs. This means that the links between nodes are one way, which is true of web sites because an HTML link takes you from one page to another but is not bidirectional.

This graph is not a full graph from the documentation web site (it would be very large). Instead, shown is a segment of those links, contained within a dot file that looks like the following code.

```
digraph G {
"/htmlman/index.html" -> "/htmlman/manual043.html";
"/htmlman/manual001.html" -> "/htmlman/manual043.html";
"/htmlman/manual042.html" -> "/htmlman/manual043.html";
"/htmlman/manual043.html" -> "/htmlman/index.html";
"/htmlman/manual043.html" -> "/htmlman/libref/Array.html";
"/htmlman/manual043.html" -> "/htmlman/libref/Bigarray.html";
"/htmlman/manual043.html" -> "/htmlman/manual032.html";
"/htmlman/manual043.html" -> "/htmlman/manual042.html";
"/htmlman/manual043.html" -> "/htmlman/manual044.html";
"/htmlman/manual044.html" -> "/htmlman/manual043.html";
}
```

To display these graphs, a graphviz-compatible file was written that can be used by the GraphViz utility to generate images from these files. Generating an image from a large graph can take a considerable amount of time. The resulting image file is also likely to be quite large. The full graph of the documentation, with options that make it so the nodes don't overlap, is more than 24 MB in size. Figure 24-4 shows a graph generated from the programs output, although it was edited and shows only one page from the output. The dot command was used to generate this graph.

```
$ dot -Tpng -o man43.png man43.dot
```

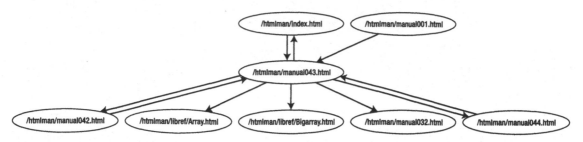

Figure 24-4. *Example output from dot file generated by the crawler*

The GraphViz utility and associated utilities can be downloaded from http://www. graphviz.org/. It was originally a project at AT&T and is an outstanding open-source project that has many features and capabilities beyond what is used for this code.

Conclusion

Writing multithreaded programs is difficult and requires a lot more code than singlethreaded versions do. However, the added throughput and concurrent handling of data and connections provided by multithreaded programs can be a big win for certain applications. The web crawler shown here, although not a search-engine-company-in-a-box, is also not a toy application.

You should have an understanding of Event channels and how they can be used to provide interthread communication. These channels are a very good way to provide reliable communication and can be used without a lot of additional work because they are built in.

■ ■ ■

## CHAPTER 25

Interfacing with OCaml

No language is an island. There are situations in which a programmer wants to interface code with existing code, or system calls, or a new library that is not written in OCaml. Sometimes this can be accomplished using sockets or some other Remote Procedure Call (RPC) mechanism. Sometimes, though, she will need to interface her OCaml code with foreign functions.

A foreign function is not a nationalistic term. Instead, it refers to functions that are not written in the same programming languages they are being called in. Many of OCaml's built-in functions are really calls to C library functions.

OCaml does not have a foreign function interface the way some programming languages do. For example, Java has native methods that enable a programmer to write code in Java while still calling native libraries (with certain caveats). Some languages have the capability to compile to libraries and then have them called from other languages.

In theory, technologies such as CORBA, SOAP, and XML-RPC have eliminated the need to do the kind of programmatic interfacing discussed here. In theory. However, there are still many situations in which you do not want to deal with any kind of RPC.

Although great strides have been made, RPC calls are often much slower than library calls. Even if you are not concerned about speed, RPC adds a layer of complexity to your application that you might not want to add. This is especially true if you have to consider support of your application. This complexity can also be a problem from the debugging perspective; when you have a whole bunch of moving parts it can be difficult to figure out which one is the culprit if it breaks.

There are tools, notably `camlidl`, which make interfacing C code with OCaml much simpler. This chapter discusses both the "native" C OCaml interface and `camlidl`.

This chapter does assume that you are familiar with C and C programming in the Unix environment. You might be able to understand the examples if you are not skilled in C, but you will get more out of it if you are.

Foreign Function Interface

Foreign Function Interfaces (FFIs) are utilities and tools that enable a given programming language to interface with libraries written in another language. They are often focused on interoperating with C because C is the lingua franca of computers (even now).

A language such as C++ does not need an FFI for C because they share the same definitions of types and data. C data is C++ data, and vice versa (for the most part). OCaml, however, does not share the same ideas about data and types as C. For example, in C (and on a 32-bit OS) an int is a 32-bit word. However, OCaml uses the least-significant bit for its own purposes, making OCaml's ints only 31 bits. There are other type-boxing issues, and strings are not understood the same way between these languages.

OCaml pushes the complexity of the C interface out of the OCaml code itself and into C language files. Headers are provided to enable you to write code that interfaces with the OCaml system and the OCaml garbage collector. It is also possible to call OCaml functions from C code, and vice versa. Most of the time, the interface will be calling C code from OCaml instead of the other way around.

There are two ways to directly interface non-OCaml libraries and code with your programs. The first is by implementing new OCaml primitives in C; the second is by using a utility that does this for you.

There are advantages and disadvantages of each method. One of the important disadvantages of either approach is that the code you access this way does not have many of the advantages of OCaml code and can be harder to debug.

These external functions can also be built into a custom runtime for byte-code programs that can be used for deploying and developing OCaml code. This is accomplished via the –make-runtime flag to the ocamlc program.

When compiling a custom runtime, you must specify the byte-code libraries needed both when building the runtime and when building the executable. You must do this so the runtime knows which C primitives are needed and so they are actually linked into the program.

First, you must create the runtime.

```
ocamlc -make-runtime -o /path/to/runtime unix.cma threads.cma
```

Then you can compile programs using the runtime.

```
ocamlc -use-runtime /path/to/runtime -o myprog unix.cma
threads.cma the_files.cmo you_need.cmo
```

The executable `myprog` can be launched by calling `myprog` arguments or `/path/to/runtime` `myprog` arguments.

Implementing Your Own Primitives

You can implement your own primitives (or functions) in C that can be called from OCaml code transparently. These primitives are no different from other functions in OCaml.

These functions are declared in OCaml code using the `external` keyword.

```
external OCAMLFUNCTIONNAME : type = "C FUNCTION NAME"
```

The OCaml function name (`OCAMLFUNCTIONNAME`) does not have to be the same as the function named in the C code (`"C FUNCTION NAME"`).

Writing the primitives in C requires more code than just defining the external value in the OCaml code. First, a set of header files must be included that define all the functions and macros needed to interact with the OCaml system.

Table 25-1. *Include Files*

File	Description
caml/mlvalues.h	Type definition and conversion macros
caml/alloc.h	Memory and object allocation functions
caml/memory.h	Other memory-related functions
caml/fail.h	Exception handling functions
caml/callback.h	Callback functions (from C to OCaml)
caml/custom.h	Functions for handling custom blocks
caml/intext.h	Serialization functions for custom blocks

The value type, which is the most common type used in C code that interfaces with OCaml, is defined in the caml/value.h header file. A value can refer to an unboxed integer (of 31 bits on a 32-bit architecture or 63 bits on a 64-bit architecture) or to some other pointer.

Pointers to other types are referred to as blocks, which can be in the heap or not. If they are in the heap, they are garbage collected. If they are not in the heap, you might need to perform other operations.

Integers and chars can both be represented by unboxed integer values. Most other primitive data types have functions for accessing their information and returning a compatible representation (such as char * for OCaml strings).

Accessing Value Elements

Getting data from a value argument into a C type is done via macros and functions provided in the OCaml header files.

Two logical functions to detect what a given value are Is_long(x) and Is_block(x). These functions return true if a value is a long int or a block; they return false otherwise. However (and this is a pretty big however), you should know what type each of your parameters is because this type is defined in the "external" declaration in your corresponding OCaml code.

The pattern for the access and return functions is Val_TYPE(x) and TYPE_val(v). So, to access the long data from a value that holds a long, you would call Long_val(value). To then return a value from a C long, you would call Val_long(long).

Integers and Boolean values are handled the same way. These functions, Val_int(int) and Int_val(val), handle integers. Boolean values can be handled via Val_bool(b) and Bool_val(v) or via Val_true and Val_false.

You can find the length of a string using the string_length(v) function. You can access the C string from a given value using the String_val(v). This function returns a pointer to the first byte of the string (just like a normal string in C). This string is really a pointer, so if you want to keep this data you must copy the string via a function such as strcopy (because OCaml could garbage collect the string and your pointer would probably be bad). Caml strings can contain embedded nulls, so OCaml strings can confuse C string functions. Strings are different from other values in that you can use the caml_alloc_string(length) function to create a new string in C. This created string contains random data, but conforms to C string semantics (i.e., no embedded nulls).

Double_val(v) returns a floating-point double. To create a value that contains a double, you can use caml_copy_double(d), which returns a value initialized to the double value d. Int32s, int64s, and Nativeints can be accessed via the functions Int32_val(v), Int64_val(v), and Nativeint_val(v). These functions have corresponding caml_copy_ functions as well (such as the caml_copy_double) function.

The preceding functions (when used with the following) enable the conversion of OCaml record types into C structs (and back again). The following functions are used to access blocks (which can be arbitrary data items).

Accessing record elements and structs is done via Field(val,index), where the index is the index of the field of the record and val is the block. Fields are numbered from 0 to Wosize_val(v) - 1. Storing values is done via Store_field(block,index,val). Wosize_val(v) returns the size of the given block (in words). This size excludes the size of the header.

Allocation and the Garbage Collector

You should not mix malloc data with caml_alloc data without care. Often, when you want to allocate a data item, you can use the allocation functions. The following functions are the simple interface functions for allocation. (There is also a low-level interface, but it is not covered in this chapter.)

Using Atom(tag) is the correct way to allocate zero-sized blocks. Atom(0), for example, allocates an empty array. Tuples and strings can be allocated using caml_alloc_tuple(n) and caml_alloc_string(n), respectively, with the argument specifying the length in characters.

There are also functions for copying items, following the pattern of caml_copy_N. For example, caml_copy_string(str) copies a string str, returning a string value that contains a copy of the string str. Doubles can be copied using caml_copy_double(initial_value); this function also sets the double to the initial_value provided.

Exceptions

Exceptions can be raised in C code that will propagate to the OCaml code. There are two functions for handling simple exceptions. The caml_failwith(argument_string) function raises the OCaml Failwith exception with the null-terminated string argument argument_string. The caml_invalid_argument(argument_string) function raises the OCaml Invalid_argument exception with the null-terminated C string argument_string. You can also use the caml_raise_not_found (void) and caml_raise_end_of_file (void).

Although it is possible to raise other exceptions, it is significantly more complicated. The exception identifier is dynamically allocated, and so the C function must be registered via the registration facility. This facility is not discussed in this book.

Defining Functions

There are several macros in the header files that are required when defining C functions that will be called from OCaml. Almost all the C functions you write begin with a call to the CAMLparam macro.

The number of arguments a given function has is called its arity. A function with an arity less than 5 can be implemented as a normal C function (with value arguments). However, if you have more than five arguments, you need to do a lot more work to process them (consult the OCaml manual for more information). All the examples in this book include functions having arity less than 5.

The function defined is a simple mathematical function that calculates the hypotenuse of a triangle using the Pythagorean Theorem. There is a function that always fails, raising an OCaml exception. There is one type defined and some example functions that operate on this type. This example also demonstrates that the C functions do not have to have the same name as their OCaml counterparts. This code should be saved in a file called example_prim.c.

```c
#include <stdio.h>
#include <caml/mlvalues.h>
#include <caml/alloc.h>
#include <caml/memory.h>
#include <caml/fail.h>
#include <caml/callback.h>

// the math headers are needed for the sqrt function
#include <math.h>

CAMLprim value pythag(value _m,value _n)
{
  CAMLparam2(_m,_n);
  int m = Int_val(_m);
  int n = Int_val(_n);
  CAMLreturn(Val_int(sqrt((m*m)+(n*n))));
}

void throws_exception()
{
  CAMLparam0();
  caml_failwith("I can't succeed");
  CAMLreturn0;
}

CAMLprim value example_new_prim(value strval,value intval, value floatval)
{
  CAMLparam3(strval,intval,floatval);
  CAMLlocal1(res);
  res = alloc_small(3,0);
  Store_field(res,0,strval);
  Store_field(res,1,intval);
  Store_field(res,2,floatval);
  CAMLreturn(res);
}
```

```
CAMLprim value example_add_prim(value primval,value intval,value floatval)
{
  CAMLparam3(intval,floatval,primval);
  CAMLlocal4(res,newstringval,newintval,newfloatval);
  res = alloc_small(3,0);
  int int_from_struct = Int_val(Field(primval,1));
  int int_from_val = Int_val(intval);
  double float_from_struct = Double_val(Field(primval,2));
  double float_from_val = Double_val(floatval);
  char *stringval = String_val(Field(primval,0));
  newstringval = caml_copy_string(stringval);
  newintval = Val_int((int_from_struct + int_from_val));
  newfloatval = caml_copy_double((float_from_struct + float_from_val));
  Store_field(res,0,newstringval);
  Store_field(res,1,newintval);
  Store_field(res,2,newfloatval);
  CAMLreturn(res);
}
```

The following code should be saved in a file named example_prim.ml. This code defines the OCaml interface to the C code. In this case, the OCaml function has the same name as the C function, although it is not a requirement.

```
type prim = {name:string;number:int;other_number:float };;
```

```
external pythag : int -> int -> int = "pythag";;
external throws : unit -> unit = "throws_exception"
external new_prim : string -> int -> float -> prim = "example_new_prim"
external add_prim : prim -> int -> float -> prim = "example_add_prim"
```

You can then compile the code and link it into an OCaml library. The ocamlmklib handles a lot of the linking options that are required. In this case, note the -lm at the end. This flag links the math library (which is required for the sqrt function used).

```
josh@bebop:~/OcamlBook$ gcc -c -Wall -fPIC -I/usr/lib/ocaml/3.09.1 example_prim.c
josh@bebop:~/OcamlBook$ ocamlc -c example_prim.ml
josh@bebop:~/OcamlBook$ ocamlmklib -o example_prim ➥
example_prim.cmo example_prim.o -lm
```

You can add the following line to a file called usage.ml.

```
let _ = Printf.printf "%d\n" (Example_prim.pythag 10 20);;
```

You then compile that code, linking in the library you created previously. This application just prints out the hypotenuse of a triangle with sizes of length 10 and 20.

```
josh@bebop:~/$ ocamlc -o usage usage.ml example_prim.cma
josh@bebop:~/$ LD_LIBRARY_PATH=. ./usage
```

You can also import the library into the OCaml toplevel (if your operating system supports this). You can then use this function and the module created as if it were any other OCaml module.

```
josh@bebop:~/OcamlBook$ ledit ocaml
        Objective Caml version 3.09.1

# #load "example_prim.cma";;
# Example_prim.pythag 20 30;;
- : int = 36
# Example_prim.throws ();;
Exception: Failure "I can't succeed".
# let a = Example_prim.new_prim "hello" 10 20.;;
val a : Example_prim.prim =
  {Example_prim.name = "hello"; Example_prim.number = 10;
   Example_prim.other_number = 20.}
# let b = Example_prim.add_prim a 30 40.;;
val b : Example_prim.prim =
  {Example_prim.name = "hello"; Example_prim.number = 40;
   Example_prim.other_number = 60.}
#
```

Using a Tool

Writing your own primitives can be fine when you are writing new code. Most programming, however, is done on existing code. If you want to wrap existing libraries so that they can be used from OCaml, wouldn't it be much easier if there were a tool to write all the boilerplate code for you? Well, there is.

IDL and camlidl

The camlidl distribution can be downloaded from http://caml.inria.fr/pub/old_caml_site/ camlidl/. This site also has documentation and more information about the specifics of the Interface Definition Language (IDL) syntax. (Although this section presents a (very) brief overview of IDL syntax, it is in no way a complete introduction to IDL.)

IDL syntax is very similar to C, with brackets ([and]) used to specify type information when needed. Type information and direction are indicated within the brackets and provide important information to the stub generator.

IDL also understands that some variables are passed to functions with the implicit assumption of direction. These directions, in and out, can be included with the type definition and separated with a comma. For example, if you have a function foo that takes a float and changes its value in the function, you can indicate that. This is helpful when wrapping functions that have side effects.

```
void foo([in,out] double changed);
```

The generated OCaml interface reflects the change by having a return value other than void.

```
external foo : float -> float
      = "camlidl_generated_foo"
```

The IDL describes languages that enable interfaces between programming languages to be defined. For example, the following shows a simple C program that includes a function you want to call from an OCaml program. This code is from a file called example.c.

```
#include <stdio.h>
#include <math.h>

int pythag (int m,int n)
{
  return sqrt (m*m + n*n);
}
```

You can use the camlidl utility to create this interface. The IDL file we might use follows. In this case, the IDL file is called example.idl. There are only two lines in the file: the first adds the math.h header file for inclusion; the other line describes the function we want to call. You do not have to define interfaces for all functions from a given C file.

```
quote(C,"#include <math.h>");
int pythag(int m,int n);
```

You then generate the C stubs and OCaml files.

```
josh@bebop:~/$ camlidl example.idl
josh@bebop:~/$ ls example*
example.ml example_stubs.c example.c example.idl example.mli
josh@bebop:~/$
```

Running the camlidl command on the IDL file generates three files: example_stubs.c, example.mli, and example.ml.

Caution If you do a web search for IDL, you will come across references to the Interactive Data Language. This is something else entirely, and is in no way related to the IDL we describe here.

Understanding Linking Options

Assuming that your host operating system supports it, you have a choice between static and dynamic linking of your code. There are pros and cons of each type of linking (and dynamic linking is not supported on all platforms).

Dynamic linking has an advantage that the byte code produced is platform-independent. The byte-code executable produced does not contain any machine code, so it does not have to be compiled on the same architecture and operating system as the target machine as long as the shared libraries are there. Dynamically linked executables are also smaller because they do not include the platform-specific code.

Statically linked libraries, on the other hand, embed a platform-specific runtime. They require the final users to have access to a C compiler, a linker, and runtime libraries, which can be a major hurdle on platforms that do not have a freely and readily available compiler suite (such as Microsoft Windows). However, deployment of statically linked executables is easier because they can be deployed stand-alone.

Dynamic linking is not without problems, though. The biggest is that the shared libraries along with the OCaml runtime must be installed and available. Dynamic linking can also create dependency problems on the target system, requiring the final user to ensure that the correct versions of the libraries and runtimes are installed.

Readline Example

The lack of readline support is something that is often asked about by new OCaml coders. The problem lies with the licensing between the two code bases. However, that shouldn't stop you from using camlidl to create a quick binding to the readline library for OCaml.

This example shows one benefit from using camlidl: it can be easy to bind existing libraries. The IDL file is pretty short, but this does not interface to the entirety of the readline library. Interfaces for the history functions, for the readline function itself, and for the variable binding function are provided. That last function is the one that allows you to change from VI to Emacs bindings (among other things). If you want to use the history functions, you must call the using_history function before doing so.

```
quote(C,"#include <readline/readline.h>");
quote(C,"#include <readline/history.h>");

[string] char *readline([string] char *prompt);
void using_history();
void add_history([string] const char * line);
void clear_history();
int read_history([string] const char *file);
int write_history([string] const char *file);
int rl_variable_bind([string] const char *var,[string] const char
*val);
```

You then compile the code by using the following commands. (The location of the camlidl library on your system might be different.)

```
josh@bebop:~/$ camlidl -no-include readline.idl
josh@bebop:~/$ gcc -fPIC -c readline_stubs.c
josh@bebop:~/$ ocamlc -c readline.mli
josh@bebop:~/$ ocamlc -c readline.ml
josh@bebop:~/$ ocamlmklib -o readline readline_stubs.o readline.cmo -lreadline
josh@bebop:~/$ ocaml
        Objective Caml version 3.09.1
```

```
# #load "readline.cma";;
# Readline.readline "PROMPT: ";;
PROMPT: hello
- : string = "hello"
#
```

You now have readline support in a few lines of code.

Other Tools

The camlidl tool is not the only tool designed to help you integrate code into OCaml. The Simplified Wrapper Interface Generator (SWIG) also has an OCaml output option.

SWIG is a pretty complicated topic in and of itself. You can download SWIG, including the OCaml portions, from http://www.swig.org. The site also has a tutorial and lots of helpful examples.

Conclusion

Interfacing C with OCaml is a very complex task. Although this chapter gives a brief overview of what is available to help, it is not a complete tutorial on the subject. You should now understand how to implement simple primitives in C and interface them with OCaml code. You should also have a baseline understanding of the camlidl program and how to use it.

One of the reasons why interfacing OCaml with C is so difficult is that it is often hard to integrate libraries and code from two distinct languages. The next chapter provides a much more detailed and complete example on interfacing OCaml code with C.

CHAPTER 26

■ ■ ■

Practical: Time and Logging Libraries

The OCaml standard library is big, but it still could be more complete. Two areas in which it is lacking include time functions and logging. If you are used to a programming language (such as Java or Python) that has an absolutely huge standard library that includes everything you could ever want in the world, you might be disappointed by OCaml's standard library.

However, you learned in the last chapter how to interface external languages and systems with OCaml, which opens up the door to enabling you to write libraries that include pretty much anything you could ever want.

The first things you will look at are time functions, and most of the time functions in the OCaml library are defined in the Unix module. There are some notable omissions in what functions this library provides. We will provide a CamlIDL-based implementation of those missing time functions. We will also present an implementation using the OCaml primitive code in C.

Next is a logging library, which uses the same log levels as syslog. This code is designed to provide flexibility for where log messages go and behave as a sophisticated logging library. Because the main module is a functor, it is possible to define logging methods to databases or sockets, although a file-based logger is presented in this chapter.

This chapter does assume a pretty fair understanding of C programming. If you do not have a good grasp of C and want to get one, I recommend picking up a good book (perhaps *Beginning C*, by Ivor Horton [Apress, 2004]).

Time Library

The following section describes two libraries that do (basically) the same thing, but are implemented in different ways. The first library is implemented using CamlIDL, which is a utility that makes it easy to wrap existing libraries and use them from Ocaml code (it does more than that, but you are using only this functionality). The second library is implemented using OCaml primitives. These libraries add a few time functions that are not present in the Unix standard library.

The time functions you will be defining are strftime, strptime, asctime, and difftime. These functions are commonly used on Unix and Unix-like systems. These four functions are not found in the OCaml standard library, but they are present in various third-party libraries (for example, Julien Signoles' excellent Calendar module: http://www.lri.fr/~signoles/prog.en.html).

The strftime function enables the creation of formatted time strings. It uses scan codes similar to Scanf to represent the different parts of the time struct (hours, minutes, and so on). The exact strftime codes vary somewhat between operating systems, but you can check your system for specifics. The strptime function takes a string and parses it into a time value. It uses strftime scan codes, which are passed to the function and determine how the input string is parsed. The asctime function returns a string that shows the ISO standard time representation. The difftime function returns the number of seconds between two time structs.

Time Library via IDL

The first time library you will see is implemented via CamlIDL, which has the main benefit of having the least amount of code to write. Really, you don't have to write any code—just an Interface Definition Language (IDL) file for the functions you want.

There are two shortcomings to this approach that are addressed by the next library: CamlIDL cannot reuse the existing Unix.tm struct definition, and CamlIDL makes heavy use of option types to represent pointers.

The use of option types isn't really a problem, but it does make your code more convoluted than it would be otherwise. It can also add some complexity to the OCaml code because sometimes you must convert values to and from option types. CamlIDL also retains a mapping that is not idiomatically OCaml by doing this. In other words, the new library doesn't feel like a native OCaml library.

The benefits, though, are more than just less code. You can write an IDL spec file for functions for which you might not understand the internals. This file can be especially useful when writing interfaces for third-party libraries. The IDL file is much easier to maintain than the OCaml code because of the difference in code length.

The complete IDL code for the library follows. You should note the __USE_XOPEN definition at the top; it is for the strptime function. You also have to include the <time.h> header file. Then you define the structure you will use for the time information. There are also two type-defs for the return types of some of the time functions.

```
quote(C,"#define __USE_XOPEN");
quote(C,"#include <time.h>");
struct tm {
    int     tm_sec;         /* seconds */
    int     tm_min;         /* minutes */
    int     tm_hour;        /* hours */
    int     tm_mday;        /* day of the month */
    int     tm_mon;         /* month */
    int     tm_year;        /* year */
    int     tm_wday;        /* day of the week */
    int     tm_yday;        /* day in the year */
    int     tm_isdst;       /* daylight saving time */
};
```

```
typedef double time_t;
typedef int size_t;

time_t time(time_t * t);
struct tm *localtime(const time_t *timep);
struct tm *gmtime(const time_t *timep);
[string] const char *asctime([in] const struct tm *t);
time_t mktime(struct tm *tm);

double difftime(time_t time1,time_t time2);

int strftime([in,out,string] char *s, size_t max, [string] const char *format,
                            const struct tm *tm);

[string] char *strptime([string] const char *s,[string] const ➥
char *format, [in,out] struct tm *tm);
```

This can then be compiled into a library.

```
josh@bebop:$ camlidl -no-include timelib.idl
josh@bebop:$ gcc -c timelib_stubs.c
josh@bebop:$ ocamlc -c timelib.mli
josh@bebop:$ ocamlc -c timelib.ml
josh@bebop:$ ocamlmklib -L/usr/lib/ocaml/3.09.1/ -o timelib ➥
timelib_stubs.o timelib.cmo -lcamlidl
```

Note There is no dynamic CamlIDL library on Linux for AMD64. If you are on that platform, you need
to build a custom toplevel to use this code (for example, ocamlmktop -custom -o timelib
timelib_stubs.o teimlib.cmo -cclib -lcamlidl).

This library can be used without the Unix library because it contains all the required functions and data types for handling time.

```
liar@bebop:~/writing/OcamlBook/code/time$ ledit ocaml
        Objective Caml version 3.09.1

# #load "timelib.cma";;
# let a = Timelib.time None;;
val a : Timelib.time_t = 1153799383.
# let b = Timelib.localtime (Some a);;
val b : Timelib.tm option =
  Some
   {Timelib.tm_sec = 43; Timelib.tm_min = 49; Timelib.tm_hour = 23;
    Timelib.tm_mday = 24; Timelib.tm_mon = 6; Timelib.tm_year = 106;
    Timelib.tm_wday = 1; Timelib.tm_yday = 204; Timelib.tm_isdst = 1}
```

```
# Timelib.strftime;;
- : string -> Timelib.size_t -> string -> Timelib.tm option -> int = <fun>
# let str = String.create 10 in let res = Timelib.strftime
        str 11 "%m/%d/%Y" b in (res,str);;
- : int * string = (10, "07/24/2006")
# Timelib.strptime;;
- : string -> string -> Timelib.tm -> string * Timelib.tm = <fun>
#
```

Time Library via CAMLprim

First, you define the interface file (time.mli) that contains the definitions for the functions you will be using. Although the definition of this interface file is not strictly required, it is usually a good idea to create one (for documentation, if for no other reason).

The four main functions are C functions (which you know because they are designated external) and one OCaml function. The OCaml function is a utility function that demonstrates how easy it is to mix external and OCaml native functions. The following code would go into the time.ml file:

```
external strftime: string -> Unix.tm -> string = "caml_strftime"
external strptime: string -> string -> Unix.tm = "caml_strptime"
external asctime: Unix.tm -> string = "caml_asctime"
external difftime: Unix.tm -> Unix.tm -> float = "caml_difftime"

val now: unit -> string
```

Next is the C code for the library. This code is much longer than the required OCaml code. The __USE_XOPEN definition is defined so that you can use the strptime function. The strptime function is not a standard function, so this implementation might not work with your system. It has been verified to work on Linux and Windows (cygwin).

```
#include <stdio.h>
#include <caml/mlvalues.h>
#include <caml/alloc.h>
#include <caml/memory.h>
#include <caml/fail.h>
#include <caml/callback.h>
#define __USE_XOPEN
#include <time.h>
#include <string.h>

#define TIMEBUF_LEN 40

void alloc_tm(value tm,struct tm *timestruct) {
  timestruct->tm_sec = Int_val(Field(tm, 0));
  timestruct->tm_min = Int_val(Field(tm, 1));
  timestruct->tm_hour = Int_val(Field(tm, 2));
```

```
  timestruct->tm_mday = Int_val(Field(tm, 3));
  timestruct->tm_mon = Int_val(Field(tm, 4));
  timestruct->tm_year = Int_val(Field(tm, 5));
  timestruct->tm_wday = Int_val(Field(tm, 6));
  timestruct->tm_yday = Int_val(Field(tm, 7));
  timestruct->tm_isdst = Bool_val(Field(tm, 8));
}

CAMLprim value caml_strftime(value timefmt,value tm)
{
  CAMLparam2(timefmt,tm);
  CAMLlocal1(formated_time);

  char *time_format = String_val(timefmt);
  char *strbuf = (char *)malloc(sizeof(' ')*TIMEBUF_LEN);
  struct tm timestruct;
  alloc_tm(tm,&timestruct);

  if ((strftime(strbuf,TIMEBUF_LEN,time_format,&timestruct)) == 0) {
   free(strbuf);
    caml_failwith("strftime returned 0!");
  }

  formated_time = caml_copy_string(strbuf);
  free(strbuf);
  CAMLreturn(formated_time);
}

CAMLprim value caml_strptime(value timedata,value timefmt)
{
  CAMLparam2(timedata,timefmt);
  CAMLlocal1(res);

  char *data = String_val(timedata);
  char *fmt = String_val(timefmt);
  char *err;

  struct tm timestruct;

  err = strptime(data,fmt,&timestruct);
  if (err == NULL) caml_failwith("stprtime failed");

  mktime(&timestruct);
```

```
        res = alloc_small(9, 0);
        Field(res,0) = Val_int(timestruct.tm_sec);
        Field(res,1) = Val_int(timestruct.tm_min);
        Field(res,2) = Val_int(timestruct.tm_hour);
        Field(res,3) = Val_int(timestruct.tm_mday);
        Field(res,4) = Val_int(timestruct.tm_mon);
        Field(res,5) = Val_int(timestruct.tm_year);
        Field(res,6) = Val_int(timestruct.tm_wday);
        Field(res,7) = Val_int(timestruct.tm_yday);
        Field(res,8) = timestruct.tm_isdst ? Val_true : Val_false;

        CAMLreturn(res);
}
```

In the asctime function that follows, you are using the threadsafe version of asctime because the nonthreadsafe version returns a statically allocated string that could cause problems for us with the OCaml garbage collector. Because you are not using the statically allocated string, it isn't a problem for this implementation.

```
CAMLprim value caml_asctime(value tm) {

    CAMLparam1(tm);
    CAMLlocal1(res);
     char *strbuf = (char *)malloc(sizeof(' ')*TIMEBUF_LEN);
    struct tm timestruct;
    alloc_tm(tm,&timestruct);

    char *ignore = asctime_r(&timestruct,strbuf);
    if ((strcmp(ignore,strbuf)) != 0) {
      free(strbuf);
}
      caml_failwith("stprtime failed");
    res = caml_copy_string(strbuf);
    free(strbuf);
    CAMLreturn(res);
}

CAMLprim value caml_difftime(value tm,value tm2)
{
    CAMLparam2(tm,tm2);
    CAMLlocal1(res);

    struct tm timestruct;
    alloc_tm(tm,&timestruct);
    struct tm timestruct2;
    alloc_tm(tm2,&timestruct2);
```

```
    double diff = difftime(mktime(&timestruct),mktime(&timestruct2));
    res = caml_copy_double(diff);
    CAMLreturn(res);
}
```

This code can then be compiled, imported, and run. In the following example, a custom toplevel is built adding the libraries. If you are on a system that supports dynamic loading, you could just use the #load directives and load the Unix and time libraries without creating the new toplevel.

```
$ gcc -fPIC -c -O -Wall -I/usr/local/lib/ocaml timefunctions.c
$ ocamlc -c time.mli
$ ocamlc -c time.ml
$ ocamlmklib -o time timefunctions.o time.cmo
$ ocamlmktop -o mytop -cclib -L. unix.cma time.cma
$ ledit ./mytop
        Objective Caml version 3.09.0

# Time.now ();;
- : string = "07/24/2006 21:42:43"
# Time.strptime "07/22/2006 20:30:30" "%m/%d/%Y %H:%M:%S";;
- : Unix.tm =
{Unix.tm_sec = 30; Unix.tm_min = 30; Unix.tm_hour = 20; Unix.tm_mday = 22;
 Unix.tm_mon = 6; Unix.tm_year = 106; Unix.tm_wday = 6; Unix.tm_yday = 202;
 Unix.tm_isdst = true}
# let a = Time.strptime "07/22/2006 20:30:30" "%m/%d/%Y %H:%M:%S";;
val a : Unix.tm =
  {Unix.tm_sec = 30; Unix.tm_min = 30; Unix.tm_hour = 20; Unix.tm_mday = 22;
   Unix.tm_mon = 6; Unix.tm_year = 106; Unix.tm_wday = 6; Unix.tm_yday = 202;
   Unix.tm_isdst = true}
# Time.strftime "%m/%d/%y" a;;
- : string = "07/22/06"
#
```

That's it for this library. You now have a choice between two libraries that implement time commands. The second one does not have any dependencies other than the standard OCaml distribution and a working C compiler.

Logging Library

One of the first things you define in your logging library is the logging facility. This idea of a logging facility is taken from syslog, a venerable logging utility found on Unix systems. Syslog defines these levels as a way to prioritize and sort log messages. They range from debug messages, which are low-priority messages, to emerg, which is the highest level and almost certainly means that there is a major problem with your application.

A major design goal of any logging library is to enable the programmer to put calls to various logging functions into the code, but have them fire only if they are needed. This enables you to place debug statements throughout your code, but have them fire only when you are in debug mode. This kind of event filtering is very important to have settable at runtime, too, so you don't have to recompile your application to get detailed logging.

```
type facility = Debug | Info | Notice | Warn | Error | Crit | Alert | Emerg;;

val string_of_facility: facility -> string
```

You then define the module type for the LOGGER. This module has initialization and shutdown commands (init and shutdown, respectively) and has a list of tuples that describe which functions should be called for which logging facility. This module also sets a default logging level. You also then define two logging modules so that this module can be useful right away.

```
module type LOGGER =
  sig
    val outputs: (facility * (facility -> string -> unit)) list
    val default_log_level: facility
    val init: unit -> unit
    val shutdown: unit -> unit
  end


module SimpleLogger : LOGGER
module DefaultLogger : LOGGER
```

Next is the functor module for the logging actions. This functor takes a LOGGER and returns a new module. There are utility functions for all the logging facilities and functions to change the current default logging level. This ability to change the logging level is important because you might want to change the logging level in response to the current program instead of having to recompile it to change the default logging level. You then use this functor in conjunction with the preceding default LOGGERs to create two logging modules.

```
module Make :
  functor (L : LOGGER) ->
sig
  val log_level : facility ref
  val set_new_log_level : facility -> unit
  val log : facility -> string -> unit
  val debug : string -> unit
  val info : string -> unit
  val notice : string -> unit
  val warn : string -> unit
  val error : string -> unit
  val crit : string -> unit
  val alert : string -> unit
  val emerg : string -> unit
  val init : unit -> unit
  val close : unit -> unit
end
```

```
module SimpleLog :
  sig
    val log_level : facility ref
    val set_new_log_level : facility -> unit
    val log : facility -> string -> unit
    val debug : string -> unit
    val info : string -> unit
    val notice : string -> unit
    val warn : string -> unit
    val error : string -> unit
    val crit : string -> unit
    val alert : string -> unit
    val emerg : string -> unit
    val init : unit -> unit
    val close : unit -> unit
  end

module Log :
  sig
    val log_level : facility ref
    val set_new_log_level : facility -> unit
    val log : facility -> string -> unit
    val debug : string -> unit
    val info : string -> unit
    val notice : string -> unit
    val warn : string -> unit
    val error : string -> unit
    val crit : string -> unit
    val alert : string -> unit
    val emerg : string -> unit
    val init : unit -> unit
    val close : unit -> unit
  end
```

Now you move on the actual implementation code. The type definitions in this file for the code are provided, as well as a simple conversion function for facilities.

```
type facility = Debug | Info | Notice | Warn | Error | Crit | Alert | Emerg;;

let string_of_facility fac = match fac with
    Debug -> "Debug"
  | Info -> "Info"
  | Notice -> "Notice"
  | Warn -> "Warn"
  | Error -> "Error"
  | Crit -> "Crit"
  | Alert -> "Alert"
  | Emerg -> "Emerg";;
```

```
module type LOGGER =
  sig
    val outputs: (facility * (facility -> string -> unit)) list
    val default_log_level: facility
    val init: unit -> unit
    val shutdown: unit -> unit
  end
```

Next is the very simple logger. It just uses Printf for formatted output and doesn't include timestamps because formatting timestamps is somewhat difficult in OCaml. You have defined only three elements in the outputs array.

```
module SimpleLogger:LOGGER =
  struct
    let strmesg x y = let n = string_of_facility x in
                                      Printf.printf "%s %s\n" n y;;
    let strerrmesg x y = let n = string_of_facility x in
                                  Printf.eprintf "%s %s\n" n y;;
    let outputs = [
      (Error,strmesg);
      (Warn,strmesg);
      (Info,strmesg);
      (Error,strerrmesg)
    ]
    let default_log_level = Info
    let init () = ()
    let shutdown () = ()
  end;;
```

The default logger uses an external C function to do most of the actual work. You are passing a Unix.file_descr to the function, which is really just an integer that describes a Unix file handle. You are also passing a strftime format string to this function to do timestamps. The shutdown function in this module is actually important. Without that function, you could not close the open file handles you have created.

After this function is the functor, which is actually a very simple module. Most of the utility functions are just calls to the main log function with arguments provided. The only real work here is the logic that decides which of the output functions will be called. The algorithm is very simple: if the facility called is greater than or equal to the current log level and greater than or equal to the facility of the output, that function is called. So, if the current log level is Warn, and an Error message is sent, it would be sent to all four outputs in the DefaultLogger. If the current log level is Info, and a Debug message is sent, nothing would happen. This allows for a lot of granular control over log files and messages.

```
module DefaultLogger:LOGGER =
  struct
    let debug_file = Unix.openfile "debug.out" [Unix.O_CREAT;
                                                Unix.O_APPEND;
                                                Unix.O_WRONLY] 0o644
```

```
    external write_log_message: Unix.file_descr -> string -> facility -> string ➥
-> unit = "write_log_message"
    let outputs = [
      (Error,(write_log_message Unix.stderr "%m/%d/%Y %H:%M:%S %z"));
      (Warn,(write_log_message Unix.stdout "%m/%d/%Y %H:%M:%S %z"));
      (Info,(write_log_message Unix.stdout "%m/%d/%Y %H:%M:%S %z"));
      (Debug,(write_log_message debug_file "%m/%d/%Y %H:%M:%S %z"));
    ]
    let default_log_level = Info
    let init () = ()
    let shutdown () = try
      Unix.close debug_file
    with (Unix.Unix_error (Unix.EBADF,"close","")) -> ()
  end;;

module Make =
  functor (L: LOGGER) ->
struct
  let log_level = ref L.default_log_level
  let set_new_log_level fac = log_level := fac
  let log fac msg = List.iter
    (fun (m,n) -> match m with
                    q when ((fac >= m) && (fac >= !log_level)) -> n fac msg
      | _ -> ()) L.outputs
  let debug msg = log Debug msg
  let info msg = log Info msg
  let notice msg = log Notice msg
  let warn msg = log Warn msg
  let error msg = log Error msg
  let crit msg = log Crit msg
  let alert msg = log Alert msg
  let emerg msg = log Emerg msg
  let init () = L.init ()
  let close () = L.shutdown ()
end;;

module SimpleLog = Make(SimpleLogger);;
module Log = Make(DefaultLogger);;
```

To use the preceding functions, you need to have some C functions to call. Instead of defining your own enum for the levels, you are using the syslog-defined levels. The code for this is pretty straightforward. You could modify this code to be able to handle any output you wanted, and these side effects would be invisible to the OCaml code that calls it.

```c
#include <stdio.h>
#include <caml/mlvalues.h>
#include <caml/alloc.h>
#include <caml/memory.h>
#include <caml/fail.h>
#include <caml/callback.h>
#include <time.h>
#include <memory.h>
#include <syslog.h>
#include <string.h>
#include <unistd.h>
#include <errno.h>
#define TIMEBUF_LEN 40

static int facility_flag_table[] = { LOG_DEBUG, LOG_INFO, LOG_NOTICE,
                                     LOG_WARNING, LOG_ERR,LOG_CRIT,
                                     LOG_ALERT, LOG_EMERG };

void write_mesg(int fd,const char *fac,char *timefmt,char *msg)
{
  char *strfbuf = (char *)malloc(sizeof(' ')*TIMEBUF_LEN);
  time_t epoch = time(NULL);
  struct tm *tmst = localtime(&epoch);
  strftime(strfbuf,TIMEBUF_LEN,timefmt,tmst);

  if ((write(fd,strfbuf,strlen(strfbuf))) == -1) {
    perror("Failed writing to file");
    caml_failwith("Writing to file failed!");
  }

  if ((write(fd,fac,strlen(fac))) == -1) {
    perror("Failed writing to file");
    caml_failwith("Failed writing to file");
  }
  if ((write(fd,msg,strlen(msg))) == -1) {
    perror("Failed writing to file");
    caml_failwith("Failed writing to file");
  }
  if ((write(fd,"\n",1)) == -1) {
    perror("Failed writing to file");
    caml_failwith("Failed writing to file");
  }
  free(strfbuf);
}
```

```
void write_log_message(value fd,
                       value timefmt,
                       value facility,
                       value msg)
{
  CAMLparam4(fd,timefmt,facility,msg);

  int fac_flag = facility_flag_table[Int_val(facility)];
  int true_fd = Int_val(fd);
  char *tf = String_val(timefmt);
  char *mesg = String_val(msg);

  switch(fac_flag) {
  case LOG_DEBUG:
    write_mesg(true_fd," [DEBUG] ",tf,mesg);
    break;
  case LOG_INFO:
    write_mesg(true_fd," [INFO] ",tf,mesg);
    break;
  case LOG_NOTICE:
    write_mesg(true_fd," [NOTICE] ",tf,mesg);
    break;
  case LOG_WARNING:
    write_mesg(true_fd," [WARNING] ",tf,mesg);
    break;
  case LOG_ERR:
    write_mesg(true_fd," [ERROR] ",tf,mesg);
    break;
  case LOG_CRIT:
    write_mesg(true_fd," [CRIT] ",tf,mesg);
    break;
  case LOG_ALERT:
    write_mesg(true_fd," [ALERT] ",tf,mesg);
    break;
  case LOG_EMERG:
    write_mesg(true_fd," [EMERG] ",tf,mesg);
    break;
  }

  CAMLreturn0;
}
```

Make a META File for this Library

For this example, I created both a Makefile and a findlib META file. The Makefile enables you
to build the code, and findlib helps you install it. This Makefile is a gmake file, but any compliant make should work just as well. Also, note that the paths for the include and libraries might
need to be changed for your environment.

```
.PHONY: depends all clean doc

all: logging.cma logging.cmxa usage usage.opt doc
depend:
                ocamldep logging.ml{,i} > .depends
-include .depends
%.o:%.c
                gcc -fPIC -c -O3 -Wall -I/usr/lib/ocaml/3.09.1/ $<


%.cmi:%.mli
                ocamlc -c $<
%.cmo:%.ml
                ocamlc -c $<
%.cmx:%.ml
                ocamlopt -c $<
%.ml:%.idl
                camlidl -no-include $<

%_stubs.c: %.idl
                camlidl -no-include $<


logging.cma: write.o logging.cmo
                ocamlmklib -o logging write.o logging.cmo

logging.cmxa: write.o logging.cmx
                ocamlmklib -o logging write.o logging.cmx

install:
                ocamlfind install logging META logging.cmi logging.cma ➡
liblogging.a -dll dlllogging.so

uninstall:
                ocamlfind remove logging
doc:
                -mkdir -p html
                ocamldoc -html -d ./html *.ml
                ocamldoc -html -d ./html *.mli
                -mkdir -p man
                ocamldoc -man -d ./man *.ml
                ocamldoc -man -d ./man *.mli


clean:
                -rm *.cmo *.cmi *.cmx *.o *.so *.a
                -rm logging.cma logging.cmxa usage usage.opt
                -rm .depends
```

```
distclean:
                -rm *.cmo *.cmi *.cmx *.o *.so *.a
                -rm logging.cma logging.cmxa usage usage.opt
                -rm .depends
                -rm *~
                -rm -rf html
                -rm -rf man
```

You then define the META file, which in this case is pretty simple. This file enables findlib to do the stuff that findlib does and manage the dependencies and installation of the library.

```
name = "logging"
version = "1.0"
description = "logging library"
requires = "unix"
archive(byte) = "logging.cma"
archive(native) = "logging.cmxa"
```

If you then put all this together, you can build, install, and use this library simply and easily. Don't forget to make depend; your build will fail if you do.

```
liar@bebop:~/writing/OcamlBook/code/logging$ make depend
ocamldep *.ml > .depends
liar@bebop:~/writing/OcamlBook/code/logging$ make
gcc -fPIC -c -O3 -Wall -I/usr/lib/ocaml/3.09.1/ write.c
ocamlc -c logging.mli
ocamlc -c logging.ml
ocamlmklib -o logging write.o logging.cmo
ocamlopt -c logging.ml
ocamlmklib -o logging write.o logging.cmx
mkdir html
ocamldoc -html -d ./html *.ml
ocamldoc -html -d ./html *.mli
mkdir man
ocamldoc -man -d ./man *.ml
ocamldoc -man -d ./man *.mli
liar@bebop:~/writing/OcamlBook/code/logging$ sudo make install
ocamlfind install logging META logging.cmi logging.cma liblogging.a -dll dlllog
ing.so
Installed /usr/local/lib/ocaml/3.09.1/logging/liblogging.a
Installed /usr/local/lib/ocaml/3.09.1/logging/logging.cma
Installed /usr/local/lib/ocaml/3.09.1/logging/logging.cmi
Installed /usr/local/lib/ocaml/3.09.1/logging/META
Installed /usr/local/lib/ocaml/3.09.1/stublibs/dlllogging.so
Installed /usr/local/lib/ocaml/3.09.1/stublibs/dlllogging.so.owner
liar@bebop:~/writing/OcamlBook/code/logging$ ledit ocaml
        Objective Caml version 3.09.1
```

```
# #use "topfind";;
- : unit = ()
Findlib has been successfully loaded. Additional directives:
  #require "package";;        to load a package
  #list;;                     to list the available packages
  #camlp4o;;                  to load camlp4 (standard syntax)
  #camlp4r;;                  to load camlp4 (revised syntax)
  #predicates "p,q,...";;     to set these predicates
  Topfind.reset();;           to force that packages will be reloaded
  #thread;;                   to enable threads

- : unit = ()
# #require "logging";;
/usr/lib/ocaml/3.09.1/unix.cma: loaded
/usr/local/lib/ocaml/3.09.1/logging: added to search path
/usr/local/lib/ocaml/3.09.1/logging/logging.cma: loaded
# Logging.Log.error "I think it may not have worked....";;
07/24/2006 23:37:30 -0400 [ERROR] I think it may not have worked....
07/24/2006 23:37:30 -0400 [ERROR] I think it may not have worked....
07/24/2006 23:37:30 -0400 [ERROR] I think it may not have worked....
- : unit = ()
#
```

This library is simple in its output strategy and is quite fast. It provides flexible ways to route output and it also enables efficiency with regard to peppering one's code with debug statements and not calling unnecessary functions on them.

Conclusion

Interfacing OCaml code with C code is a good way to provide functionality for your OCaml programs. You can use a tool such as ILD or write your own primitives to accomplish this integration. If you write your own primitives in C, they are indistinguishable from OCaml functions (except for the keyword in their signature).

The next chapter discusses the OCaml debugger, profiler, and other programmer tools. You also learn more about findlib, which was introduced in detail in this chapter.

CHAPTER 27

■ ■ ■

Processing Binary Files

All data is not text. Binary data is used in all kinds of applications. Often, accessing binary data is faster than text data, and it is space-efficient, too. Until now we have not talked about what you need to do differently to process binary data in OCaml.

This is actually for two reasons. The first is that many programmers and programs are often concerned with text instead of binary data. Text and other human-readable formats are the easiest way to electronically communicate information to people. The second reason, and most important, is because there is no difference.

When dealing with binary files, a lot of information is presented in hexadecimal. If you are not familiar with hex, it can take awhile to get used to using a base 16 representation. Hex is base 16, which is different from normal decimal numbers that are base 10. These numbers are displayed using A–F (or a–f) for the extra numbers. For example, in decimal notation, 10 is 10. In hex, 10 is 16. But don't worry: OCaml can help you with this. You just prefix numbers with 0x, and the OCaml interpreter will understand these are hex numbers and convert them. You can even perform calculations on hex numbers.

```
# 0x10;;
- : int = 16
# 0x10 + 10;;
- : int = 26
```

Hex isn't used to confuse you. It is used because it is much easier to convert back to base 2 (like binary), which is what computers use. You don't have to be able to read hex with the same ease as decimal notation, but you should be able to recognize it, at least.

Endianness

You may be unfamiliar with the term *Endianness* when applied to computers. There are some computers and operating systems that store binary data with the most significant bits first. The Big Endian systems store information the opposite way from Little Endian systems, which store the data with the least significant bits first.

For example, if you take the hexadecimal number 0x23AF39 (which is 2338617 in decimal), a Big Endian system would store that number in three chunks: 23, AF, and 39. A Little Endian system would store that number as 39,AF,23. The result is that if you interpret the other order, you get the wrong results, which has some serious ramifications on the portability of binary data.

■**Note** The term *Endian* comes from Jonathan Swift's "Gulliver's Travels." The king felt that breaking an egg on its Big End was primitive, and made his subjects break their eggs on the Little End. Those who felt that the king was wrong rebelled, and war broke out between the Big Endians and the Little Endians.

If you are using OCaml programs only, you don't have to worry about Endianness. The OCaml libraries store binary data in a format known as Network Byte Order, which was created to address the Endian issue discussed in this section. If, however, you are reading a data format that has Endian issues, you have to deal with that yourself. This situation is often very platform-specific, so we can't even provide any code to help. We can, however, wish you luck and tell you that you should never write binary data files that are Endian-specific.

Support for Binary Files and Data

Not all operating systems distinguish between binary and nonbinary files. Microsoft Windows is one notable system that does distinguish between the two. To support this distinction, there are options to the open file commands: open_in_bin and open_out_bin, as well as the normal open_*_gen functions that accept arguments to specify a binary file.

The reason to make sure that you use the appropriate open function is that the OCaml I/O (input/output) routines automatically handle end-of-line conversions unless the file is a binary file. Besides, it is always a good idea to use the correct open function instead of relying on the fact that any one of them will work most of the time. Other than the I/O routines, the rest of the OCaml system handles binary files just as well (in fact, in the exact same manner) as nonbinary files.

First Example

On many Unix and Unix-like systems, there exists a utility called xxd, which can do hex dumps of files and reassemble hex dumps into files. This can be a very useful tool because it provides much of the functionality of an interactive hex editor without the real-time danger of using a hex editor. Following is the code, which takes a little more than 60 lines of code to implement.

If you have never seen a hex dump of a file, the following is a hex dump of the hosts file on one of my Linux machines. The first column shows the position of the next 16 bytes of the file (in hexadecimal). The next eight columns are 2-byte values (in hexadecimal) of the information. The last column is the ASCII representation of those bytes. Because this is a text file, it is shown as text. If the char value is unprintable, a "." is displayed instead.

```
0000000: 3132 372e 302e 302e 3120 6c6f 6361 6c68  127.0.0.1 localh
0000010: 6f73 7420 6265 626f 700a 3132 372e 302e  ost bebop.127.0.
0000020: 312e 3120 6265 626f 700a 0a23 2054 6865  1.1 bebop..# The
0000030: 2066 6f6c 6c6f 7769 6e67 206c 696e 6573   following lines
0000040: 2061 7265 2064 6573 6972 6162 6c65 2066   are desirable f
0000050: 6f72 2049 5076 3620 6361 7061 626c 6520  or IPv6 capable
```

```
0000060: 686f 7374 730a 3a3a 3120 6970 362d 6c6f  hosts.::1 ip6-lo
0000070: 6361 6c68 6f73 7420 6970 362d 6c6f 6f70  calhost ip6-loop
0000080: 6261 636b 0a66 6530 303a 3a30 2069 7036  back.fe00::0 ip6
0000090: 2d6c 6f63 616c 6e65 740a 6666 3030 3a3a  -localnet.ff00::
```

The Xxd module is presented as follows, and this code would be saved into a file called xxd.ml. This code implements a hex dump of any file. You can then reverse that hex dump and reconstruct the original file. The first function takes a binary data character and converts it into a printable character, if it can. A char in OCaml is not always printable. In fact, only the chars between decimal value 32 and 126 are printable (that's from the space character to the ~). You also have a function that uses Printf to provide the hex value of a given char. That value is always printable. After that, you have a function that helps this module output strings the right length. Because you are storing three columns in the buffer, this function calculates where the spaces go into the output string.

```
let make_printable i_char = match i_char with
    n when (((Char.code n) < 32) or ((Char.code n) > 126)) -> '.'
  | _ -> i_char;;

let make_hex chr = Printf.sprintf "%.2x" (Char.code chr);;

let conditional_add_st bffr ch = match bffr with
    n when ((Buffer.length bffr) = 0) -> Buffer.add_string bffr ch
  | n when ((Buffer.length bffr) = 4) -> Buffer.add_string bffr (" " ^ ch)
  | n when (((Buffer.length bffr) mod 5) = 4) -> Buffer.add_string bffr (" " ^ ch)
  | _ -> Buffer.add_string bffr ch;;
```

The next function provides a map function for strings. The String module provides only an iteration function, not a map function. The function you define applies the function argument to each character in the string. You build the result list backward, so you have to reverse it at the end.

```
let string_map str fnc =
  let rec strmap st acc =
    match st with
      "" -> List.rev acc
    | _ -> strmap (String.sub st 1 ((String.length st) - 1)) ((fnc st.[0]) :: acc)
  in
  strmap str [];;
```

The next function, output_lines, does the heavy lifting for the outputting of a binary file. This function reads in a binary file 16 bytes at a time, applies the preceding functions to that data, and outputs the three-column representation you want. There is some extra code that handles the last line in the file (when the last read is smaller than 16 bytes), too.

```
let rec output_lines fle f_buf s_buf curpos =
  let str_buf = String.create 16 in
  let res = input fle str_buf 0 16 in
  (
    if (res < 16) then
      (List.iter (conditional_add_st f_buf)
        (string_map (String.sub str_buf 0 res) make_hex);
       List.iter (Buffer.add_char s_buf)
        (string_map (String.sub str_buf 0 res ) make_printable))
    else
      (List.iter (conditional_add_st f_buf) (string_map str_buf make_hex);
       List.iter (Buffer.add_char s_buf) (string_map str_buf make_printable))
  );
  Printf.printf "%0.7x: %-40s  %s\n" curpos (Buffer.contents f_buf)
    (Buffer.contents s_buf);
  if (res < 16) then
    exit(0)
  else
    Buffer.clear f_buf;
  Buffer.clear s_buf;
  output_lines fle f_buf s_buf (curpos + res);;

let output_file fname =
  let fo = open_in_bin fname in
  let res = output_lines fo (Buffer.create 16) (Buffer.create 16) 0 in
  close_in fo;res;;
```

This library also rebuilds a file from a dump. To do this, you do the opposite of what was done before. However, you don't have to use a lot of the data in the dump file to rebuild the file. Basically, only the middle column of data (the hex data) is important to rebuild the file. Converting from the hex chars to binary data is more complicated than the reverse, but this is not something that people do very often. You have also defined a utility function to convert each line into a list of chars, which you then write to the file.

```
let rec build_char_list sb acc =
  let nval = try
    Some (Scanf.bscanf sb "%2x" (fun x -> Char.chr x))
  with End_of_file -> None
  in match nval with
      Some n -> build_char_list sb (n :: acc)
    | None -> List.rev acc;;
```

```ocaml
let rec input_lines source_chan dest_chan =
  let write_line sc dc =
    try
      let istr = String.sub (input_line sc) 9 39 in
      let buf = Buffer.create 32 in
              String.iter (fun x -> match x with
                                    ' ' -> ()
                                  | _ -> Buffer.add_char buf x) istr;
              let scanbuf = Scanf.Scanning.from_string (Buffer.contents buf) in
              let vals = build_char_list scanbuf [] in
              List.iter (fun x -> output_char dc x) vals;
              true
    with End_of_file -> false
  in
  let do_more = write_line source_chan dest_chan in
    match do_more with
                true -> input_lines source_chan dest_chan
      | false -> ();;

let input_file source_file dest_file =
  let ic = open_in_bin source_file in
  let oc = open_out_bin dest_file in
  input_lines ic oc;
  close_in ic;
  close_out oc;;
```

This code can be compiled like any other OCaml module. You can even create a command-line program using this module so the implementation of the original program is complete (this code would be saved into a file called xxd_command.ml).

```ocaml
let usage = (Printf.sprintf "%s <FILENAME>\n" Sys.argv.(0)) ^
  "\nDump or unDump an xxd style hexdump\n";;

let _ = try
  if (Array.length Sys.argv) < 2 then
    try
      while (true) do
        Xxd.output_lines stdin (Buffer.create 16) (Buffer.create 16) 0
      done
    with End_of_file -> ()
  else
    Arg.parse [
      ("-r",Arg.String (fun x -> Xxd.input_file x (x ^ ".rebuilt"))),
        "Build a Binary file from a hexdump")] (fun x -> Xxd.output_file x)
      usage
with unexpected_exn -> print_string (Printexc.to_string unexpected_exn);
  print_string ("\n" ^ usage);;
```

You can also see a warning (depending on the version of OCaml you are using) that enables you to know that your program might not return normally. This is because of the `while (true)` loop that was used. After you compile this program into an executable, you can run it; following is some sample output from this program. You can see from the md5 checksums that the rebuilt file is the same as the original.

```
liar@bebop:~/OcamlBook$ ocamlc -o xxd xxd.ml xxd_command.ml
File "xxd_command.ml", line 8, characters 1-63:
Warning X: this statement never returns.
liar@bebop:~/OcamlBook$ ./xxd `which ocamlc` > ocamlc.dump
liar@bebop:~/OcamlBook$ head ocamlc.dump
0000000: 2321 2f75 7372 2f62 696e 2f6f 6361 6d6c   #!/usr/bin/ocaml
0000010: 7275 6e0a 5400 0000 df03 0000 2900 0000   run.T.......)...
0000020: 2a00 0000 0100 0000 0000 5600 0000         *...........V...
0000030: 0e00 0000 0000 0000 4400 0000 0b00 0000   ........D.......
0000040: 4300 0000 0d00 0000 0c00 0000 3200 0000   C...........2...
0000050: 2200 0000 0b00 0000 4000 0000 0000 0000   ".......@.......
0000060: 2800 0000 0400 0000 0100 0000 2800 0000   (...........(...
0000070: 0200 0000 2900 0000 2a00 0000 0300 0000   ....)...*.......
0000080: 0300 0000 8500 0000 0000 0000 0400 0000   ................
0000090: 6300 0000 2800 0000 0400 0000 0300 0000   c...(...........
liar@bebop:~/OcamlBook$ ./xxd -r ocamlc.dump
liar@bebop:~/OcamlBook$ md5sum ocamlc.dump.rebuilt `which ocamlc`
21eabb5e3709d93c6a95410d6bb5f70d  ocamlc.dump.rebuilt
21eabb5e3709d93c6a95410d6bb5f70d  /usr/bin/ocamlc
```

Finding Matches Between Binary Files

On Unix systems, there is a command called `diff` that displays the differences between two files. This command is line-oriented and displays the differing lines. Binary files do not normally contain data that can be operated on in terms of lines. Also, `diff` works best on text, so doing a `diff` on a pair of binary files does not provide you with very good results.

What if you want to compare two binary files? You could write your own program to do that. Look at the three functions that are exposed from the module shown. The first returns the length and the start and end position of the longest matching segment between two files. The second returns all matching segments larger than `min_match` (which defaults to 2). The last function returns the number of matches of n length between the two files; for example, there were 500 matches of length 3 between the two files. These three signatures would be stored in an `.mli` file with the same name as the library. In this example, this module is called Binary_match, so the `.mli` would be `binary_match.mli`, and the rest of the code would be in `binary_match.ml`.

```
val longest_match : string -> string -> int * (int * int)
val find_matching_locations :  ?min_match:int -> ➡
string -> string -> (int * int) list
val show_distribution : string -> string -> unit
```

And the code for this follows. Note that this code opens the Unix module—this is done mostly for convenience. The first real function is a loading function that loads a file into a list of chars. It also means that you probably shouldn't use this function on very large binary files (less than 4 GB because OCaml lists have size limitations).

The second function creates a list of Boolean values of whether or not the two files match at that position. We wrote this function instead of using the `List.iter2` function because the function enables the lists to be of differing lengths. Because you only want matching segments, you don't care about the parts of the file that are longer than the other; you know they don't match.

```
open Unix;;

let load filename =
  let ic = open_in_bin filename in
  let size = (Unix.stat filename).st_size in
  let rec loader fl acc remaining = match remaining with
      0 -> List.rev acc
    | _ -> loader fl ((input_char fl) :: acc) (remaining - 1)
  in
  let res = loader ic [] size in
  close_in ic; res;;

let rec mapper ar ar' acc = match ar,ar' with
    [],_ -> acc
  | _,[] -> acc
  | h :: t,h' :: t' -> mapper t t' ((h = h') :: acc);;
```

After creating the map, you define a function that finds the beginning and the end of matches (simply segments of the list that are all true). This function creates a list of positions indicating the start and end of a given matching segment. After that, you define your filter/utility function for finding the matching segments and the longest matching segment.

```
let rec find_matches (in_match,loc) lst idx acc = match lst with
    h :: t -> if (in_match && h) then
      find_matches (in_match,loc) t (idx + 1) acc
    else
      if (h) then
              find_matches (h,idx) t (idx + 1) acc
      else if (not h && not in_match) then
              find_matches (h,idx) t (idx + 1) acc
      else
              find_matches (h,idx) t (idx + 1) ((loc,idx) :: acc)
  | [] -> if (in_match) then
      ((loc,idx) :: acc)
    else
    acc
```

```
let find_matching_locations ?(min_match=1) file1 file2 = let bl = mapper ⮞
 (load file1) (load file2) [] in
  List.filter (fun (n,m) -> (m - n) > min_match) (find_matches (false,0) bl 0 []);;


let longest_match file1 file2 =
  let bl = mapper (load file1) (load file2) [] in
    List.fold_left
      (fun (m,(n,o)) (p,q) -> if (m < (q - p)) then
                  ((q - p),(p,q))
        else
                  (m,(n,o))) (0,(0,0)) (find_matches (false,0) bl 0 []);;
```

To find the distribution of the lengths of the matching segments, you need to count the frequency of each length. First, you create a Map module (using integers). This type is hidden by the signature and is not used by the module user. After that, you build a map of match length -> count. You use a Map because you want to have the data displayed in an ordered manner (instead of unordered, as with a Hashmap). After you build the map, you print it out.

```
module IntMap = Map.Make(struct type t = int let compare = compare end);;


let show_distribution file1 file2 = let bl = mapper (load file1) (load file2) [] in
let rec disp_distribution boolist acc = match boolist with
    [] -> acc
  | (m,n) :: t -> let existing_value = try
       IntMap.find (n - m) acc
     with Not_found -> 0 in
      disp_distribution t (IntMap.add (n - m) (existing_value + 1) acc)
in
let matches = find_matches (false,0) bl 0 [] in
let distrib = disp_distribution matches IntMap.empty in
  IntMap.iter (fun x y -> Printf.printf "%d %d\n" x y) distrib;;
```

Now that you have the code, you can compile and run it. Because you have a signature file, it must be compiled first. Otherwise, the compilation of this module is straightforward. It can be imported and used (sample output is shown).

```
liar@bebop:~/OcamlBook/$ ocamlc -c binary_match.mli
liar@bebop:~/OcamlBook/$ ocamlc -c binary_match.ml
liar@bebop:~/OcamlBook/$ ledit ocaml
# #load "unix.cma";;
# #load "binary_match.cmo";;
# Binary_match.find_matching_locations "/bin/ls" "/usr/bin/who";;
- : (int * int) list =
[(22180, 22204); (22172, 22178); (22072, 22169); (22052, 22065);
 (22036, 22038); (22020, 22034); (22004, 22007); (21956, 22003);
 (21940, 21943); (21844, 21939); (21840, 21843); (21836, 21839);
 (21832, 21835); (21828, 21831); (21824, 21827); (21820, 21823);
 (21808, 21819); (21804, 21807); (21800, 21803); (21796, 21799);
```

```
(21792, 21795); (21788, 21791); (21784, 21787); (21780, 21783);
(21776, 21779); (21772, 21775); (21768, 21771); (21764, 21767);
(21760, 21763); (21756, 21759); (21752, 21755); (21748, 21751);
(21744, 21747); (21740, 21743); (21736, 21739); (21732, 21735);
(21728, 21731); (21724, 21727); (21720, 21723); (21716, 21719);
---- Lots of output CUT -----
# Binary_match.find_matching_locations ~min_match:3 "/bin/ls" "/usr/bin/who";;
- : (int * int) list =
[(22180, 22204); (22172, 22178); (22072, 22169); (22052, 22065);
 (22020, 22034); (21956, 22003); (21844, 21939); (21808, 21819);
 (21672, 21679); (21656, 21671); (21640, 21647); (21616, 21627);
 (21592, 21599); (21580, 21587); (21496, 21503); (21464, 21471);
 (21444, 21451); (21436, 21443); (21420, 21426); (21404, 21411);
 (21388, 21394); (21356, 21362); (21340, 21346); (21324, 21331);
 (21308, 21314); (21292, 21299); (21276, 21282); (21228, 21235);
 (21180, 21186); (21116, 21123); (21068, 21074); (21052, 21059);
 (21004, 21010); (20795, 20799); (19807, 19811); (14067, 14071);
 (12551, 12555); (9898, 9902); (5261, 5265); (5107, 5111); (1805, 1809);
 (1728, 1732); (1278, 1282); (467, 471); (211, 215)]
# Binary_match.longest_match "/bin/ls" "/usr/bin/who";;
- : int * (int * int) = (97, (22072, 22169))
# Binary_match.show_distribution "/bin/ls" "/usr/bin/who";;
1 415
2 208
3 236
4 12
6 10
7 14
11 2
13 1
14 1
15 1
24 1
47 1
95 1
97 1
- : unit = ()
```

The matching algorithm is pretty brute force, and there are probably improvements that could be made.

Reading Bitmaps

One of the most common places to find binary data is in image files. In this chapter, you will be operating only on bitmaps, which enjoy several features that make writing tools to read, write, and operate on them attractive. The first (and arguably the most important) is that they are a very well-documented format. The second thing about bitmaps is that they are actually very easy to manipulate, especially in their uncompressed form. The last feature that bitmaps have over many other image formats is that they are completely unencumbered by patents. Bitmaps are not the only unencumbered format, but their free status gives a trifecta when combined with the first two benefits.

Bitmaps have a 54-byte header. This header makes for some ugly OCaml code, but it is a small price to pay. Table 27-1 describes the header for Windows bitmap files. Remember: most of the numbers in these files will be in hex.

Table 27-1. *Bitmap Header Definition*

Index	Length (in bytes)	Description
0	2	"Magic" number (or "BM" for this file)
2	4	Size of the file (in bytes)
6	4	Reserved; should always be Char \000
10	4	Offset of where the image starts
14	4	Size of bitmap header (0x40 in this case; decimal 54 in hex)
18	4	Width of the image (in pixels)
22	4	Height of the image (in pixels)
26	2	Number of image planes; there is only one for BMP
28	2	Bits per pixel (24 in this case)
30	4	Compression type (0 because you are not compressing)
34	4	Size of compressed image (or a zero if not compressed)
38	4	Horizontal resolution; should be zeros
42	4	Vertical resolution; again, should be zeros
46	4	Number of colors used; should be zeros
50	4	Number of important colors; also can be zero
54	4	Color map, which is zero for all of our examples (we don't use mapped colors)

Bitmaps use a three-byte unit to define colors in units of red, green, and blue (or RGB). Pure red, for example, would be 0xFF0000. Pure green would be 0x00FF00. You can create almost any color by combining values of red, green, and blue in this manner. This also makes the colors easy to read in from a file—each pixel is three bytes. Now you define a module that operates on bitmaps (you'll save it to `bitmap.mli` and `bitmap.ml`, respectively). The signatures for the functions in this module (in the `bitmap.mli` file) are as follows.

```
val fourbitstring : int -> string
val int_of_fourbitstring : string -> int
val gen_header : int -> int -> string
val emptybmp : string -> int -> int -> unit
val custom_emptybmp : string -> int -> int -> (int -> char) -> unit
val operate_on_image :   string -> string -> string -> (int -> int -> int) -> unit
val xorimage : string -> string -> string -> unit
val landimage : string -> string -> string -> unit
```

Much of the information in the header is contained in four-byte fields. They are Little Endian fields, so you have to be aware of that when you convert the field into an integer. You perform this conversion by calculating the modulo of each location in the four-byte field. You can convert integers to four-byte strings via the fourbitstring function. You can also convert four-byte strings into integers using the int_of_fourbitstring function.

```
let fourbitstring numb =
  let lb = Buffer.create 4 in
  let rmost = numb mod 256 in
  let nextr = (numb / 256) mod 256 in
  let nextrr = (numb / (256 * 256)) mod 256 in
  let nextrrr = (numb / (256 * 256 * 256)) mod 256 in
  Buffer.add_char lb (Char.chr rmost);
  Buffer.add_char lb (Char.chr nextr);
  Buffer.add_char lb (Char.chr nextrr);
  Buffer.add_char lb(Char.chr nextrrr);
  Buffer.contents lb;;

let int_of_fourbitstring frbtst =
  (Char.code frbtst.[0]) + ((Char.code frbtst.[1]) * 256) +
  ((Char.code frbtst.[2]) * 256 * 256) + ((Char.code frbtst.[3]) ➡
  * 256 * 256 * 256);;
```

You learned about the bitmap header earlier. Following is a hand-rolled header that uses Printf to supply the important parts. This header is, quite honestly, the hardest part of dealing with bitmaps. Because each pixel is really three bytes, you see a lot of multiplication by three. After the header function, you see a function that creates an "empty" (or all white) bitmap of arbitrary size.

```
let gen_header xdim ydim = Printf.sprintf ➡
"BM%s\000\000\000\0006\000\000\000(\000 ➡
\000\000%s%s\001\000\024\000\000\000\000 ➡
\000%s\000\000\000\000\000\000\000\000\000 ➡
\000\000\000\000\000\000\000" (fourbitstring ➡
(((xdim * ydim) * 3)+54)) (fourbitstring xdim) ➡
(fourbitstring ydim) (fourbitstring ((xdim * ydim) * 3));;

let emptybmp fname xdim ydim =
  let oc = open_out_bin fname in
  let qqq = Array.init ((xdim * ydim) * 3) (fun x -> '\255') in
  output_string oc (gen_header xdim ydim);
  Array.iter (fun x -> output_char oc x) qqq;
  close_out oc;;
```

In addition to being able to generate a blank bitmap, we also present a function, emptybmp, that allows the creation of a bitmap according to a function. After that, we define a generic function, open_out_bin, that takes two bitmaps (that must be the same size) and operates on them, creating a new bitmap. This enables you to compost bitmaps or combine them in arbitrary ways.

```
let custom_emptybmp fname xdim ydim appfunc =
  let oc = open_out_bin fname in
  let qqq = Array.init ((xdim * ydim) * 3) appfunc in
  output_string oc (gen_header xdim ydim);
  Array.iter (fun x -> output_char oc x) qqq;
  close_out oc;;

let operate_on_image img_one img_two newfile oper =
  let newc = open_out_bin newfile in
  let ic = open_in_bin img_one in
  let ic' = open_in_bin img_two in
  seek_in ic 18;
  seek_in ic' 18;
  let xdim = Scanf.fscanf ic "%4s" (fun x -> int_of_fourbitstring x) in
  let ydim = Scanf.fscanf ic "%4s" (fun x -> int_of_fourbitstring x) in
  let xdim' = Scanf.fscanf ic' "%4s" (fun x -> int_of_fourbitstring x) in
  let ydim' = Scanf.fscanf ic' "%4s" (fun x -> int_of_fourbitstring x) in
  if ((xdim = xdim') & (ydim = ydim')) then
        (output_string newc (gen_header xdim ydim);
          seek_in ic 54;
          seek_in ic' 54;
          try
          while (true) do
            let c = input_char ic in
            let c' = input_char ic' in
              output_char newc (Char.chr (oper (Char.code c) (Char.code c')))
          done
          with End_of_file -> close_out newc;close_in ic;close_in ic')
    else
        raise (Invalid_argument "image files are not the same size");;

let xorimage imgone imgtwo newfile = operate_on_image imgone imgtwo newfile
( lxor );;

let landimage imgone imgtwo newfile = operate_on_image imgone imgtwo newfile
( land );;
```

This module can be compiled simply because it has no external library dependencies. Then it can be used. I have created a sample BMP file with the right dimensions (420x300 for these examples). It was saved as a file named sample.bmp for the following examples. It can be seen in Figure 27-1.

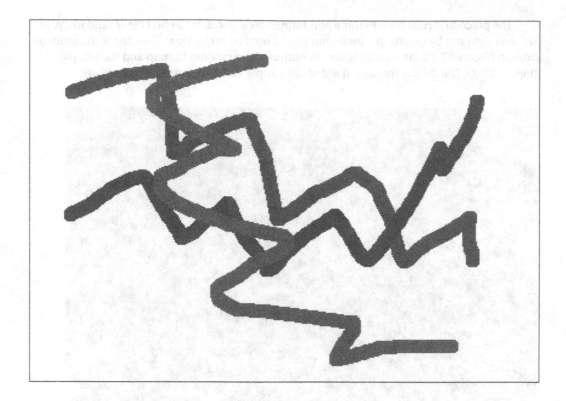

Figure 27-1. *Sample BMP File*

```
liar@bebop:~/OcamlBook/$ ocamlc -c bitmap.mli
liar@bebop:~/OcamlBook/$ ocamlc -c bitmap.ml
liar@bebop:~/OcamlBook/$ ledit ocaml
        Objective Caml version 3.09.0

# #load "bitmap.cmo";;
# Bitmap.custom_emptybmp "random.bmp" 420 300 (fun x -> Char.chr (Random.int 255));;
- : unit = ()
# Bitmap.xorimage "random.bmp" "sample.bmp" "random3.bmp";;
- : unit = ()
# Bitmap.landimage "random.bmp" "sample.bmp" "random4.bmp";;
- : unit = ()
#
```

The preceding code creates three new bitmap files. Because the first file is random, your results might not be exactly like them, but they should be pretty close. The first is the random bitmap (Figure 27-2); the second is the xor output of the random bitmap and the sample (Figure 27-3). The third is the logical and of the sample and the random (Figure 27-4).

Figure 27-2. *Random BMP*

Figure 27-3. xor *BMP*

Figure 27-4. and *BMP*

Conway's Game of Life

In 1970, a British mathematician named John Conway created the field of cellular automata when he published the first article on the subject. Conway's "game" isn't so much a game played by people as it is a mathematical experiment. The game is an example of emergent behavior because there are only four simple rules that generate an amazing amount of complexity. Conway's game is also Turing Complete, which means that (given the right initial conditions) the game is as powerful as any "real" computer. The game itself is represented (in its original version) by a matrix of cells. These cells can be either alive or dead, as determined by the cells' neighbors and the rules of the game.

This representation of cells is why Conway's game provides an excellent graphical target to shoot for. There are only four rules in the game:

- A cell will die if it has fewer than two living neighbors.

- A cell will die if it has more than three living neighbors.

- A living cell stays the same if it has two or three living neighbors.

- A dead cell with three living neighbors becomes a living cell.

You define a module type first because it will be needed for the functor later. This module includes the dimensions of the image, a function that takes the nine cell locations that are important (the current cell and all its neighbors), and returns an integer. The other two functions define what colors map to what integers (for input and output).

You then define two default modules: one is black and white, and the other is multicolor. You'll focus on the black-and-white modules first. After that, there is the signature for version of Conway's game that outputs bitmaps. This is handy because you can then save different frames of the game and use them to examine the results. There are two output functions: the first one outputs the end of the game; the other outputs a frame at different intervals (for example, in a 10,000-generation game, you could save one bitmap frame every 100 generations). The game functions take arguments of the filenames to use, the number of generations, and the percentage of the map to fill randomly for the initial conditions.

The last module is the game, except it uses the OCaml graphics module to display the results in real time. We'll talk more about this module later. The signature file should be stored in a file named life.mli.

```
module type LIFER =
  sig
    val xdim: int
    val ydim: int
    val results: int * int * int * int * int * int * int * int  -> int -> int
    val default_colormap: int -> char * char * char
    val default_mapcolor: char -> char -> char -> int
  end

module Default:LIFER

module DefaultColor:LIFER
```

```
module Game:
  functor (L:LIFER) ->
sig
  val game_of_life : string -> int -> int -> unit
  val game_of_life_from_file : string -> int -> unit
  val make_record : int -> int -> string -> int -> unit
end

module GraphicGame:
  functor (L:LIFER) ->
sig
  val init: unit -> unit
  val close: unit -> unit
  val game_of_life : int -> int -> unit
end
```

Now you get to the implementation. First, you define the black-and-white version. This module has a result function that conforms to the original Conway rules. The module type definition for the LIFER module is included so the definition is available to the code in this module.

```
module type LIFER =
  sig
    val xdim: int
    val ydim: int
    val results: int * int * int * int * int * int * int * int -> int -> int
    val default_colormap: int -> char * char * char
    val default_mapcolor: char -> char -> char -> int
  end

module Default:LIFER =
  struct
    let xdim = 100
    let ydim = 100
    let results (l,m,n,o,p,q,r,s) x =
      let res = l + m + n + o + p + q + r + s in
      match res with
          remain when (res = 2) -> x
        | live when (res = 3) -> 1
        | _ -> 0

    let default_colormap x = match x with
        0 -> ('\000','\000','\000')
      | 1 -> ('\255','\255','\255')
      | _ -> assert(false)
```

```
    let default_mapcolor x y z = match x,y,z with
        '\000','\000','\000' -> 0
      | _ -> 1
end;;
```

The next module is the colorized module. This function does not conform to the original Conway rules. The module is colorful, but almost completely chaotic. It does give a good example of how to implement your own functions, though.

```
module DefaultColor:LIFER =
  struct
    let xdim = 100
    let ydim = 100
    let results (l,m,n,o,p,q,r,s) x = match x with
        1 -> (let res = l + m + n + o + p + q + r + s in
                 match res with
                     remain when (res = 2) -> x
                   | live when (res = 3) -> 1
                   | gain when (res = 4) -> 2
                   | more when (res = 5) -> 3
                   | more' when (res = 6) -> 4
                   | more'' when (res = 7) -> 5
                   | _ -> 0)
      | 2 -> (let res = l + m + n + o + p + q + r + s in
                 match res with
                     remain when (res = 2) -> x
                   | live when (res = 3) -> 1
                   | gain when (res = 4) -> 2
                   | more when (res = 5) -> 3
                   | more' when (res = 6) -> 4
                   | more'' when (res = 7) -> 5
                   | _ -> 0)
      | 3 -> (let res = l + m + n + o + p + q + r + s in
                 match res with
                     remain when (res = 2) -> x
                   | live when (res = 3) -> 1
                   | gain when (res = 4) -> 2
                   | more when (res = 5) -> 3
                   | more' when (res = 6) -> 4
                   | more'' when (res = 7) -> 5
                   | _ -> 0)
      | 4 -> (let res = l + m + n + o + p + q + r + s in
                 match res with
                     remain when (res = 2) -> x
                   | live when (res = 3) -> 1
                   | gain when (res = 4) -> 2
```

```
                   | more when (res = 5) -> 3
                   | more' when (res = 6) -> 4
                   | more'' when (res = 7) -> 5
                   | _ -> 0)
        | 5 -> (let res = l + m + n + o + p + q + r + s in
                 match res with
                   remain when (res = 2) -> x
                   | live when (res = 3) -> 1
                   | gain when (res = 4) -> 2
                   | more when (res = 5) -> 3
                   | more' when (res = 6) -> 4
                   | more'' when (res = 7) -> 5
                   | _ -> 0)
        | _ -> (let res = l + m + n + o + p + q + r + s in
                 match res with
                   remain when (res = 2) -> x
                   | live when (res = 3) -> 1
                   | gain when (res = 4) -> 2
                   | more when (res = 5) -> 3
                   | more' when (res = 6) -> 4
                   | more'' when (res = 7) -> 5
                   | _ -> 0)

let default_colormap x = match x with
    0 -> ('\000','\000','\000')
  | 1 -> ('\255','\255','\255')
  | 2 -> ('\255','\000','\000')
  | 3 -> ('\000','\255','\000')
  | 4 -> ('\000','\000','\255')
  | 5 -> ('\200','\000','\200')
  | _ -> assert(false)

let default_mapcolor x y z = match x,y,z with
    '\000','\000','\000' -> 0
  | '\255','\255','\255' -> 1
  | '\255','\000','\000' -> 2
  | '\000','\255','\000' -> 3
  | '\000','\000','\255' -> 4
  | '\200','\000','\200' -> 5
  | _ -> 1;;
end;;
```

The next module is the functor that actually runs the game. You probably recognize some of the bitmap functions.

```
module Game =
  functor (L:LIFER) ->
struct
  let fourbitstring numb = let lb = Buffer.create 4 in
  let rmost = numb mod 256 in
  let nextr = (numb / 256) mod 256 in
  let nextrr = (numb / (256 * 256)) mod 256 in
  let nextrrr = (numb / (256 * 256 * 256)) mod 256 in
    Buffer.add_char lb (Char.chr rmost);
    Buffer.add_char lb (Char.chr nextr);
    Buffer.add_char lb (Char.chr nextrr);
    Buffer.add_char lb(Char.chr nextrrr);
    Buffer.contents lb;;

  let gen_header xdim ydim = Printf.sprintf ➥
  "BM%s\000\000\000\0006\000\000\000(\000 ➥
\000\000%s%s\001\000\024\000\000\000\000 ➥
\000%s\000\000\000\000\000\000\000\000\000 ➥
\000\000\000\000\000\000\000" (fourbitstring ➥
(((xdim * ydim) * 3)+54)) (fourbitstring xdim) ➥
(fourbitstring ydim) (fourbitstring ((xdim * ydim) * 3));;

  let int_of_fourbitstring frbtst = (Char.code frbtst.[0]) + ➥
((Char.code frbtst.[1]) * 256) + ((Char.code frbtst.[2]) * 256 * 256) + ➥
 ((Char.code frbtst.[3]) * 256 * 256 * 256);;

  let life_seeder xdim ydim percent_fill = Array.init (xdim * ydim)
    (fun x -> let nval = Random.int 100 in
       match nval with
          n when n <= (99 - percent_fill) -> 0
        | _ -> 1);;

  let safeget ar idex  = match idex with
     n when idex < 0 -> let newidex = idex + (L.xdim * L.ydim) in ar.(newidex)
   | m when idex >= (L.xdim * L.ydim) -> let newidex = idex - ➥
(L.xdim * L.ydim) in ar.(newidex)
   | _  -> ar.(idex);;
```

The previous function, when combined with the next function, runner, uses a single array to create a borderless playing area. This avoids some of the edge conditions that can occur if you simply define off-board cells as dead. The run functions work in concert with the saving functions to save bitmaps of the game board.

```
let rec runner lifemat numiter = match numiter with
    0 -> lifemat
  | _ -> let newmatrix = Array.mapi (fun x y -> let a = safeget lifemat ➥
(x - (L.xdim + 1)) in
                                let b = safeget lifemat (x - L.xdim) in
                                let c = safeget lifemat (x - (L.xdim - 1)) in
                                let d = safeget lifemat (x - 1) in
                                let f = safeget lifemat (x + 1) in
                                let g = safeget lifemat (x + (L.xdim - 1)) in
                                let h = safeget lifemat (x + L.xdim) in
                                let i = safeget lifemat (x + (L.xdim + 1)) in
                                    L.results (a,b,c,d,f,g,h,i) y) lifemat in
        runner newmatrix (numiter - 1)

let save_game xdim ydim newarr filename colormap = let oc = open_out_bin filename
in
  output_string oc (gen_header xdim ydim);
  Array.iter (fun n -> let (x,y,z) = colormap n in
                output_char oc x;
                output_char oc y;
                output_char oc z) newarr;
  close_out oc;;

let game_of_life filename iterations percent_fill =
  let initial = life_seeder L.xdim L.ydim percent_fill in
  let run = runner initial iterations in
  save_game L.xdim L.ydim run filename L.default_colormap;;
```

We also provide a function, load_game, that loads a previous game from a file. This allows you to continue running a given game from any saved bitmap.

```
let load_game filename mapcolor =
  let ic = open_in_bin filename in
  seek_in ic 18;
  let xdim = Scanf.fscanf ic "%4s" (fun x -> int_of_fourbitstring x) in
  let ydim = Scanf.fscanf ic "%4s" (fun x -> int_of_fourbitstring x) in
    seek_in ic 54;
    let newmat = Array.create (xdim * ydim) 0 in
      Array.iteri (fun x y ->
                    newmat.(x) <- Scanf.fscanf ic "%c%c%c" mapcolor)
        newmat;
      close_in ic; ((xdim,ydim),newmat)
```

```
let fcopy fn newfn = let newoc = open_out_bin newfn in
let ic = open_in_bin fn in
  try
    while (true) do
      Scanf.fscanf ic "%c" (fun x -> Printf.fprintf newoc "%c" x)
    done
  with _ -> close_in ic;close_out newoc;;
```

The previous function enabled you to copy old game files. The next function, game_of_
life_from_file, is a wrapper around the rest that enables you to actually run the game.

```
let game_of_life_from_file filename iterations =
  let ((xdim,ydim),initial) = load_game filename L.default_mapcolor in
    save_game xdim ydim (runner initial iterations) filename L.default_colormap;;

let rec save_record tng curcount se fname = if (curcount < tng) then
  (
    game_of_life_from_file fname se;
    fcopy fname ((string_of_int curcount) ^ fname);
    save_record tng (curcount + se) se fname
  )
else
  ();;

let make_record totalgames save_every filename initial_fill =
  game_of_life filename save_every initial_fill;
  fcopy filename ("0" ^ filename);
  save_record totalgames save_every save_every filename;;
end;;
```

And that's it. This module can be compiled and run directly or as a library.

```
liar@bebop:~/writing/OcamlBook/new_book$ ocamlc -c -dtypes life.mli
liar@bebop:~/writing/OcamlBook/new_book$ ocamlc -c life.ml
liar@bebop:~/writing/OcamlBook/new_book$ ledit ocaml
        Objective Caml version 3.09.1

# #load "graphics.cma";;
# #load "life.cmo";;
# module CGL = Life.Game(Life.Default);;
module CGL :
  sig
    val game_of_life : string -> int -> int -> unit
    val game_of_life_from_file : string -> int -> unit
    val make_record : int -> int -> string -> int -> unit
  end
# CGL.game_of_life "outputfile.bmp" 10 10;;
- : unit = ()
# CGL.make_record 100 10 "output-string.bmp" 10;;
- : unit = ()
#
```

This has created 11 bitmaps (only two are shown). Figure 27-5 is after 10 generations, with 10 percent of the field populated at random. Figure 27-6 generates 10 bitmaps, with 10 generations between them and the initial field having been populated at 10 percent with random units.

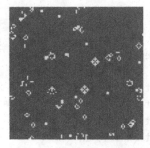

Figure 27-5. *Sample output*

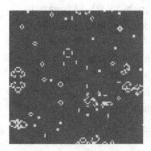

Figure 27-6. *More sample output*

Next, you define the module that enables you to run these simulations in real time. Instead of generating bitmaps, this module uses the graphics module to display the 2D graphics.

```
open Graphics;;
module GraphicGame =
  functor (L:LIFER) ->
struct

  let init () = open_graph (Printf.sprintf " %dx%d" L.xdim L.ydim)
  let close () = close_graph ()

  let life_seeder xdim ydim percent_fill = Array.init (xdim * ydim)
    (fun x -> let nval = Random.int 100 in
      match nval with
          n when n <= (99 - percent_fill) -> 0
        | _ -> 1);;
```

```
  let safeget ar idex  = match idex with
      n when idex < 0 -> let newidex = idex + (L.xdim * L.ydim) in ar.(newidex)
    | m when idex >= (L.xdim * L.ydim) -> let newidex = idex - (L.xdim * L.ydim) ➥
in ar.(newidex)
    | _  -> ar.(idex);;

  let rec runner lifemat numiter = match numiter with
      0 -> lifemat
    | _ -> let newmatrix = Array.mapi (fun x y -> let a = safeget lifemat (x - ➥
(L.xdim + 1)) in
                                    let b = safeget lifemat (x - L.xdim) in
                                    let c = safeget lifemat (x - (L.xdim - 1)) in
                                    let d = safeget lifemat (x - 1) in
                                    let f = safeget lifemat (x + 1) in
                                    let g = safeget lifemat (x + (L.xdim - 1)) in
                                    let h = safeget lifemat (x + L.xdim) in
                                    let i = safeget lifemat (x + (L.xdim + 1)) in
                                    L.results (a,b,c,d,f,g,h,i) y) lifemat in
      let newcolors = Array.map (fun cell -> let (r,g,b) = L.default_colormap ➥
cell in
                                    int_of_string (Printf.sprintf "0x%X%X%X"
                                              (int_of_char r)
                                              (int_of_char g)
                                              (int_of_char b))) newmatrix in
      let old_image = get_image 0 0 L.xdim L.ydim in
      let matr = dump_image old_image in
        Array.iteri (fun idx cell -> let xcord = idx / L.xdim in
                      let ycord = idx - (xcord * L.xdim) in
                        matr.(xcord).(ycord) <- cell) newcolors;
      draw_image (make_image matr) 0 0;
      runner newmatrix (numiter - 1);;

  let game_of_life iterations percent_fill =
    let initial = life_seeder L.xdim L.ydim percent_fill in
      ignore(runner initial iterations)

end;;
```

You can then create a new module using the graphics system and run the simulation with similar arguments.

```
# module GraGCL = Life.GraphicGame(Life.Default);;
module GraGCL :
  sig
    val init : unit -> unit
    val close : unit -> unit
    val game_of_life : int -> int -> unit
  end
```

```
# GraGCL.init ();;
- : unit = ()
# GraGCL.game_of_life 100 20;;
- : unit = ()
# GraGCL.close ();;
- : unit = ()
#
```

The graphics module is supported on most OCaml systems, but if it's not on yours you can still use the bitmap-generating module.

Graphics in OCaml

The OCaml graphics module does not work with image files. Instead, it provides a platform-independent way to display and manipulate a two-dimensional canvas. When we say "platform-independent," don't mistake it for a Java-esque platform independence. The Graphics module is linked with native graphics primitives for the operating system you are running. That also means that it's "platform-independent" to the degree that the feature has been ported to your operating system.

The Graphics module provides rudimentary interfaces for interactive input (both mouse and keyboard) and sound generation as well as 2D graphics. It also has double-buffering support as well as definitions for 2D primitives (such as squares and circles).

The Graphics module does not provide enough functionality for complex games or heavy animation. It does, however, provide a convenient way to display rudimentary graphics, such as the Game of Life. You use only a fraction of the capabilities of the module.

For a complicated graphics display, you might want to check out the SDL libraries, which have OCaml bindings. OCaml also has some well-developed OpenGL bindings, if you have need of 3D graphics.

Conclusion

This chapter covered a lot of ground. Now you should have a basic understanding of the difference between binary files and ASCII files—and how to handle both of them. You should also have a grasp of creating simple graphics files in OCaml and manipulating them.

■ ■ ■

OCaml Development Tools

Having a programming language is not the only thing you need to actually do development in that language. You also need tools that make the process of developing and debugging code easier.

Even though OCaml code is terse and often easy to understand, there are times when you might want to have more than a text editor in which to develop code.

Integrated development environments are not the only tools available when developing code. The compiler is also a tool, and the OCaml compiler has many features that can aid your development efforts. There are also profiles, debuggers, build tools, and a host of other little things that can make you a happier and (hopefully) more productive OCaml coder.

Build Tools

Unlike some languages (such as Eiffel or SML/NJ), OCaml does not have a native compilation manager. So if you want automated compilation, you have to do it yourself.

This is a mixed blessing. Although you can use whatever build tools you are comfortable with, you also have to create a build environment.

If you are familiar with Make, you can use it with OCaml code just like any other source code/compiler combination. The OCaml distribution also includes the ocamldep utility, which can create dependency information for Makefiles.

Typically, you would add lines similar to the ones that follow to your Makefile to create a depend target in the Makefile. You could then do a make dep;make all and be confident that the dependency information would be included into your Makefile. In this example, the minus sign that prepends the include makes it so that the Make will not fail if the file is not found. If you want the Make to fail if the file is not found, do not include the minus sign.

```
depend:
        ocamldep *.mli *.ml > .depend


-include .depend
```

There is also Markus Mottl's OCamlMakefile, which is basically a preconfigured Makefile with every option you can think of set up (it has been used several times in this book).

There is also limited support for the autotools package. Configure and Makefile.in macros have been written by Jean-Christophe Filliatre and can be downloaded from his web site at http://www.lri.fr/~filliatr/index.en.html.

The Great Outdoors Digital Indoors (GODI) system also has a build system built into it. You can use GODI packages to build and distribute your applications. The GODI package system is well-documented, and several examples can be found at http://www.ocaml-programming.de.

Editors and Integrated Development Environments (IDEs)

If you prefer an environment like Visual Studio, you might be disappointed by what is available for OCaml development. There is currently no Visual Studio integration for OCaml, although Microsoft Research has developed a language based on OCaml called F# that has some Visual Studio support. Most of the OCaml development utilities follow the Unix approach of many modular tools instead of a monolithic development environment. (You can find out all about F# and the work Microsoft Research is doing on this topic at http://research.microsoft.com/fsharp/fsharp.aspx).

Of the utilities discussed here, Emacs has the most complete and far-reaching support for OCaml. This is probably not surprising to anyone who uses Emacs. The Tuareg mode allows you easy access to the toplevel and provides many niceties for developing OCaml code.

There are also Emacs Lisp libraries that come in the standard OCaml distribution and provide a mode for editing OCaml code and other features. They are not automatically installed, so if you want access to them, you have to manually install them into your Emacs environment.

There is an alpha-level support for OCaml in Eclipse. The Eclipse-fp environment, which has support for both Haskel and OCaml, can be found at http://eclipsefp.sourceforge.net/.

You can also use Vim to edit OCaml code with syntax highlighting. The Vim syntax file is written and maintained by Markus Mottl at http://www.ocaml.info/vim/syntax/ocaml.vim.

Both OCamlWinPlus and the camlbrowser have editors built into them, but they are not the kind of full-featured editor that Vim or Emacs provides. They can, however, be useful editors, especially when editing code that is primarily to be used in the interactive toplevel.

Using the OCaml Profiler

The profiler cannot be used on all compiled OCaml code. Byte code that you want to profile must be compiled with the ocamlcp compiler, which takes the same arguments as the normal batch compiler. Native code can be profiled using gprof, but this requires the addition of the -p flag when compiling the code.

Any modules from which you want to get profiling information also must be compiled with the appropriate compiler and flags. The following code outlines how the profiler can be used. The code is compiled and then executed. During its execution, a data file is created that can be read by the ocamlprof utility. That utility displays the source code of the program and the number of times each program element (function, and so on) was called.

```
let _ = Random.self_init ();;

type success = Failed of (int * float) | Succeed of (int * float);;

let avg lst =
  let sum = List.fold_left (fun x y -> x +. y) 0. lst in
  sum /. (float_of_int (List.length lst));;
```

```
let rec run_until v acc = match v with
    n when v > (avg acc) -> run_until v ((Random.float 1.) :: acc)
  | n when List.length acc > 1000 -> Failed ((List.length acc),(avg acc))
  | _ -> Succeed ((List.length acc),(avg acc));;


let _ =
  let res = run_until 0.5 [0.41] in
  match res with
    Succeed (m,n) ->  Printf.printf "List of length: %d and average: %f\n" m n
  | Failed (m,n) -> Printf.printf "Failed at length: %d and average:
  %f\n" m n;;
```

The code is compiled using the ocamlcp compiler instead of the normal batch compiler.
The output of the command is also shown. The command will not always get to such a high
list length as shown; often it will find a solution with far fewer items. Note the number of times
each function is called contained within the (* and *).

```
$ ocamlcp -o prof prof.ml
$ ./prof
List of length: 278 and average: 0.500143
$ ocamlprof prof.ml
let _ = Random.self_init ();;

    type success = Failed of (int * float) | Succeed of (int * float);;

let avg lst = (* 347 *)
  let sum = List.fold_left
    (fun x y -> (* 39919 *) x +. y) 0. lst in
    sum /. (float_of_int (List.length lst));;

let rec run_until v acc = (* 340 *) match v with
    n when (* 340 *) v > (avg acc) -> (* 333 *) run_until v
                                          ((Random.float 1.) :: acc)
  | n when (* 7 *) List.length acc > 1000 ->
              (* 0 *) Failed ((List.length acc),(avg acc))
  | _ -> (* 7 *) Succeed ((List.length acc),(avg acc));;


let _ =
  let res = run_until 0.5 [0.41] in
  match res with
    Succeed (m,n) ->  (* 7 *) Printf.printf
    "List of length: %d and average: %f" m n
  | Failed (m,n) -> (* 0 *) Printf.printf
    "Failed at length: %d and average: %f" m n;;
```

One problem with the byte-code profiler is that it counts only the number of times each
function was called. It does not show the amount of time that was spent or other metrics provided by utilities such as gprof. You can use gprof on native code to get that information.

I cannot stress enough how valuable the profiler can be for a programmer. The profiler can tell you where to focus your attention when trying to optimize code. The profiler also does not make guesses or have hunches; it tells you exactly what is going on. Before you attempt to make optimizations to any code, you should always use the profiler.

Using the OCaml Debugger

At some point, if you are doing development of any kind, you will have a need for a debugger. The OCaml debugger (ocamldebug) is a byte code–only debugger for OCaml programs. You can also use gdb on native code, but it does not understand OCaml source code, so you are left interpreting stack information.

The basic use of the debugger can be very simple: start the application in the debugger by using ocamldebug *<APPNAME>* (replace *<APPNAME>* with your application name). This command puts you into the debugger shell. You can set breakpoints (using the break command) and use most normal debugger commands.

One of the interesting advantages of using the OCaml debugger is that you can navigate a program in time as well as line. You do this via the goto command, which can act as an undo for the step and next commands. You can also install and uninstall custom type printers from the debugger. This is done via the load_printer function, and these printers are used via the install_printer function. You can uninstall printers by using the uninstall_printer function.

You can view the source code of the file you are debugging by using the list command. You can list any module and lines by passing them as arguments—you can also specify a line range. If you were debugging the previous prof command and wanted to see lines 8 through 17, you could do that, too.

```
(ocd) list prof 9 17
9 let rec run_until v acc = match v with
10    n when v > (avg acc) -> run_until v ((Random.float 1.) :: acc)
11    | n when List.length acc > 1000 -> Failed ((List.length acc),(avg acc))
12    | _ -> Succeed ((List.length acc),(avg acc));;
13
14
15 let _ = let res = run_until 0.5 [0.41] in match res with
16    Succeed (m,n) ->  Printf.printf "List of length: %d and average: %f" m n
17    | Failed (m,n) -> Printf.printf "Failed at length: %d and average: %f" m n;
;
```

The debugger can also be used in Emacs. The files are included in the source distribution, but you have to install them yourself.

Shells

The utilities described here are called *shells*, mostly for lack of a better term. They are utilities that run an OCaml process and provide services such as enhanced line editing.

Most of the utilities were discussed before. Ledit, for example, is a tool that makes using the OCaml toplevel much easier. It is not the only tool that performs this function; a utility called rlwrap can be found at http://utopia.knoware.nl/~hlub/rlwrap. It is very similar to Ledit except that rlwrap uses the GNU Readline utility.

OCamlWin is a very nice shell found in the Windows distribution of OCaml. As a shell, it provides many of the features found in Ledit or rlwrap, but has the advantage of being mouse-aware. It also provides a (basic) editor for your OCaml code.

The camlbrowser is not strictly the same kind of utility as the other shells that have been discussed, but it can be a very useful tool when developing OCaml applications. On Windows, the camlbrowser requires that Tcl/Tk be installed, which you can find at http://www.tcl.tk/.

The camlbrowser enables you to browse the installed OCaml libraries and view function signatures, documentation, and other information associated with the library. It also provides a (basic) editor much like OCamlWinPlus.

OCaml Compiler

OCaml offers two compilers: ocamlc and ocamlopt. The first is the OCaml batch compiler; the second is the OCaml native compiler. *Batch* refers to the fact that many source files can be specified on the command line to be compiled. Both compilers are batch compilers. The real difference is that the ocamlc compiler produces byte-code files that require only that the OCaml runtime and the ocamlopt compiler produce native binary code. Both compilers produce executables that can be considered stand-alone.

All the arguments passed to the compiler are processed sequentially. Among other things, it means that you must specify the dependent libraries after the libraries they depend on.

If you pass a file that the compiler cannot handle or doesn't understand, it displays an error message (Don't know what to do with <FILE>) and displays the (rather long) usage message.

Basic Compiler Flags

-where: Prints the path for the standard library and then exits. This flag is useful in Makefiles and Shell scripts to find out where the standard library path is.

-o OUTPUTFILE: Sets the name of the generated executable or library.

-a: Instead of creating an executable, tells the compiler to build a library. If you use this option, build a library (.cma file) with the object files (.cmo files) given on the command line instead of linking them into an executable file. The name of the library must be set with the -o option.

-c: Compiles the file or files, but skips the linking phase. This option is used to compile modules separately and does not generate an executable or a library.

-g: Adds debugging information to the compiled files and adds the information to the file required by the OCaml debugger. It can be used with the -c and -o flags and also on objects and source files.

-impl FILENAME: Compiles the FILENAME as if it were an .ml file, even if the extension is not .ml. This is useful to match signature (.mli) files to implementation (.ml) files if the implementation file does not have the .ml extension.

-intf FILENAME: Compiles the FILENAME as if it were an .mli file, even if the extension is not .mli (similar to the -impl flag).

-pp PREPROC: Tells the compiler to preprocess the source files with the given command. It creates a transient file containing the output of the command that is deleted when compilation is finished. This command is often used with Camlp4.

-verbose: Displays all the external commands executed by the compiler.

-linkall: Forces all modules of the modules contained in libraries to be linked in. Normally, unreferenced modules are not linked in. Also causes all libraries linked to the module to have the -linkall flag set.

-I <DIR>: Adds the directory specified by <DIR> to the search path for compiled objects, interface files, and libraries (including C libraries). The current directory is searched first by default, followed by the standard library directory. If you add directories with the -I flag, they are searched after the current directory. You can also add a + to the directory name, which will be interpreted as a path relative to the standard library directory.

Type Information Compiler Flags

-i: Enables the compiler to type check the code but not produce .cmo or .cmi files. The output is in interface syntax, which means it can be used to generate .mli files from extant .ml files.

-rectypes: If you don't know what arbitrary recursive types are, you do not need this flag. If you do, you should know that you need to include this flag when defining these types.

-dtypes: Dumps detailed type information to a file that can be used by the caml-types.el file. The Emacs file (caml-types.el) can then display interactive type information while editing the associated source code. This file is called FILENAME.annot (the original source filename would have been FILENAME.ml).

-principal: Causes the compiler to make sure that all types are derived in a principal way. This flag enables you to be confident that future versions of the compiler will be able to infer the types in your program correctly. All programs that are acceptable with this flag are acceptable in the default mode. This option will probably slow down type checking of your program, although you should always run it at least once on your code. This option can be thought of as similar to the -pedantic option used by the GNU C compiler.

Flags Relating to C/Binary Code

-cc <CCNAME>: Enables you to use a different compiler for C files. The default is the compiler that was used to compile OCaml.

-cclib -lLIBNAME: Passes the -lLIBNAME option to the linker when using the -custom flag. Any number of libraries can be specified. This option is stored in the library produced and is set for users of this library unless the -noautolink option is used.

-ccopt OPTION: Passes the options to the C compiler and linker (for example, -ccopt -I/usr/include/MYSTUFF -L passes the -I and -L flags to the compiler and linker). This option is stored in the library produced and is set for users of this library unless the -noautolink option is used.

-noautolink: Tells the compiler to ignore -custom, -cclib, and -ccopt flags contained in the libraries passed to the compiler. This enables you to pass C library and option information to the compiler that is different from the ones contained within the libraries. This option is especially useful in situations in which the libraries might contain incorrect information.

-dllib -l<LIBNAME>: Informs the runtime system that it should load the dynamic library given by <LIBNAME> at startup. Dynamic libraries that are used must be named dll<LIBNAME>.dll on Windows systems or dll<LIBNAME>.so on Unix systems.

-dllpath <DIR>: Adds <DIR> to the runtime search path for shared libraries.

Runtime-Related Flags

-make-runtime: Enables you to build your own runtime, which can be used to execute byte code instead of the default.

-use-runtime RUNTIME: Tells the compiler to use the given runtime instead of the default. This flag enables you to specify a runtime that you created with the -make-runtime flag.

-custom: Tells the compiler to link the custom runtime instead of just the shared runtime. It also causes the compiled files to be larger than those using the shared runtime. However, the custom runtime enables the program to run even if the runtime is not installed. You can also use this flag if you need to link in static libraries or C object files. This custom runtime is not necessarily the one from the -make-runtime call; there is (confusingly) a runtime in the standard distribution called the custom runtime. This option is stored in the library produced and is set for users of this library unless the -noautolink option is used.

Threading-Related Flags

-thread: Compiles the program as a threaded program, which automatically adds path and library information needed to use threads.

-vmthread: Similar to the -thread flag, but uses the VM thread library.

Miscellaneous Flags

-noassert: Turns assertion checking off. It works only when compiling source files and has no effect on object files of any kind. You should carefully consider the ramifications of using this option.

-nolabels: Makes parameter order strict and ignores optional parameters. This only affects code that uses labels.

-unsafe: Turns bounds checking off on arrays and strings, so strings accessed via the x.(i) and arrays accessed via x.[i] do not check to see whether the index is valid. Programs compiled without bounds checking are slightly faster; however, if your program accesses an array or a string outside of their bounds, anything can happen. The performance benefit that it might generate is something to be carefully weighed against the chance of bad things happening.

-v: Prints the version of the compiler in long form and the location of the standard library.

-version: Similar to the -v flag, except it prints the version number in short form and does not display the standard library path.

-p (only for ocamlopt): Compiles in profiling information.

-disntr: Shows the opcodes of the OCaml byte code. This is an undocumented flag that can be useful for understanding the internals of OCaml.

-pack: Enables you to break a module into several compilation units. For example, if you have a module Top_module that contains modules One, Two, and Three, you can compile one.ml, two.ml, and three.ml separately. You can then build your main module using these three, accessing them as Top_module.One, and so on.

```
ocamlc -pack -o top_module.cmo one.cmo two.cmo three.cmo
```

-w [WARNING LIST]: Enables or disables warnings as specified in the supplied list. The supplied list is formatted by using capital letters to indicate enable and by using lower-case letters to indicate disable. The complete list of warnings can be found using ocamlc -help (it is a pretty long list). For now, we can tell you that, by default, the compiler uses -w Aelz, which translates to having all warnings enabled except fragile matchings, omitted labels, and other unused variables (suspicious unused variables are enabled by default).

-warn-error [WARNING LIST]: Turns the specified warnings into errors, which stop compilation. It takes the same arguments as the [WARNING LIST] in the previous flag.

File Extensions Used

The following list shows what files are accepted and what their output files are.

.mli: Treated as interface files. The output file for x.mli is x.cmi.

.ml: Treated as source code files. The output file for x.ml is x.cmo. If x.cmi exists, the type information in the interface is used to verify the type information in the .ml file. If an appropriate .mli file exists, but the .cmi file does not, the compiler gives an error. The compiler does not automatically resolve these issues.

.cmo: Treated as byte-code files. These files can be linked together with other .cmo files or .ml files. The output file for this file is a byte-code executable or library (.cma file).

.cma: These files are byte-code libraries. These can be made from .ml or .cmo files using the -a option to the ocamlc compiler. If a .cma file or .cmo file that is not referenced anywhere in the resulting program is passed as an argument, it is not linked in.

.c: These files are treated as C language files and are passed to the c compiler. If the -custom flag is set, the resulting object file (.o) is linked with the program.

.o: These files are assumed to be C object files (or libraries if they end in .a). When the -custom flag is set, they are linked into the program. On Microsoft Windows, they are .obj or .lib, respectively.

.so: These files are assumed to be shared libraries.

■**Caution** You should not use the `strip` command on OCaml byte-code executables or any executables produced using the `-custom` flag. It will strip important byte code and leave you with a useless file.

.`cma`: Treated as libraries of OCaml byte code. This kind of library packs a set of OCaml byte-code files. You can build libraries with the ocamlc compiler using the –a flag or with the `ocamlmklib` command. The compiler does not link in segments of the library that are not referenced in the application being built. These libraries are platform-independent, although they are compiler version–dependent.

.`cmx`: Treated as libraries of OCaml native code. They are like the byte-code libraries (.`cma`) files, except they are native code and are therefore platform-specific. These files are also compiler version–dependent.

Findlib

Findlib is a set of utilities written by Gerd Stolpmann, the creator of GODI. Findlib provides meta information that enables dependencies to be described in a useful way for module writers. It is essentially a package manager, in which the files stored have a strict directory structure and metadata repository. Findlib does not modify your OCaml installation, nor does it use any special internal OCaml functions. Findlib is not a replacement for package managers you might already use (such as RPM or DEB); instead, it deals with OCaml packages.

Findlib can be downloaded from `http://www.ocaml-programming.de/programming/ findlib.html` and installed if you have Make and a working OCaml installation.

```
$ ledit ocaml
        Objective Caml version 3.09.0

# #use "topfind";;
- : unit = ()
Findlib has been successfully loaded. Additional directives:
  #require "package";;      to load a package
  #list;;                   to list the available packages
  #camlp4o;;                to load camlp4 (standard syntax)
  #camlp4r;;                to load camlp4 (revised syntax)
  #predicates "p,q,...";;   to set these predicates
  Topfind.reset();;         to force that packages will be reloaded
  #thread;;                 to enable threads

- : unit = ()
#
```

This utility makes loading the correct files in the toplevel simple, and it can also be used to simplify interactions with the OCaml compiler. The findlib utilities include a Makefile wizard that helps you create a Makefile for your project. The command-line utility `make wizard` creates a customized Makefile for your project. You then need to supply a META file and the project code. The only problem you might encounter with the wizard is that it requires the Tk module. For more detailed information, consult the findlib documentation.

Conclusion

This chapter helped you understand which tools are available for developing OCaml tools. The OCaml documentation also includes complete documentation for all the tools shipped in the standard distribution.

The next chapter covers Camlp4, which is one of the most powerful aspects of the OCaml language. Although only a small part of the Camlp4 functions capabilities is discussed, it should be helpful if you want to use Camlp4 in your own programs.

■ ■ ■

## CHAPTER 29

Camlp4

Camlp4, which provides a very interesting and powerful way to extend and change the OCaml language, enables the easy definition of domain-specific languages (DSLs) based on OCaml. The name *Camlp4* refers to the fact that it is a preprocessor and pretty printer (four Ps) for OCaml.

As a preprocessor, you can use Camlp4 to extend the syntax of OCaml programs. This means that you can add or modify the syntax of the language.

In C, you can use the C preprocessor (cpp) to do macro expansion and to change the syntax of C. The C preprocessor is not able to make changes in the language that cannot be accomplished via macro expansion.

Camlp4 can be a very difficult application to understand, let alone use. It shares some similarities with tools such as the C preprocessor, Lisp, and scheme macros.

Revised Syntax

One important thing about programming in Camlp4: you need to use the revised syntax, which is slightly different from the traditional syntax. The differences are designed to create less ambiguity in the OCaml language. This syntax is designed to be more logical and easier to parse than the traditional syntax.

That said, the fact that the revised syntax is not frequently used makes it a source of ambiguity for people still learning the language. The fact that the revised syntax is so infrequently used is sometimes cited as a benefit. It is easier to make changes to the revised syntax without needing to take backward compatibility into consideration.

You could write all your own programs in the revised syntax, if you wanted. There is a Camlp4 preprocessor (camlp4r) that is designed to deal with revised syntax files. You can also use the revised syntax from within the toplevel.

Following are a few of the differences between the revised and traditional syntax.

```
# let m = 10 in
    match m with
        0 -> false
      | 10 -> true
      |  _ -> assert false;;
- : bool = true
# let mylist = [1;2;3;4];;
val mylist : int list = [1; 2; 3; 4]
```

```
# let mytuple = 1,2,34;;
val mytuple : int * int * int = (1, 2, 34)
```

If you now load the camlp4r library and attempt to do what you did in the revised syntax, you can see the differences.

```
# #load "camlp4r.cma";;
        Camlp4 Parsing version 3.09.1

# let m = 10 in
    match m with
  [
      0 -> False
  | 10 -> True
  |  _ -> assert False ];
- : bool = True
# let mylist = [1;2;3;4];
Toplevel input:
# let mylist = [1;2;3;4];
                    ^
Parse error: 'and' or 'in' expected (in [expr])
# value mylist = [1;2;3;4];
value mylist : list int = [1; 2; 3; 4]
# value mytuple = 1,2,3;
Toplevel input:
# value mytuple = 1,2,3;
                     ^
Parse error: ';' expected after [str_item] (in [phrase])
# value mytuple = (1,2,3);
value mytuple : (int * int * int) = (1, 2, 3)
```

You also can see that the error messages generated by the revised syntax are very different from the error messages of the traditional syntax. This is another issue to bear in mind when working in the revised syntax. Finally, values can be defined only by using the value keyword, whereas let is reserved only for expressions. This also means that functions must be defined like value f = fun [x -> x + 1], which is considerably different from the traditional syntax.

What Is Camlp4?

Camlp4 is a preprocessor that operates at the source level of OCaml code, which has some important ramifications. One of the most important is that Camlp4 can generate code that does not compile because Camlp4 rewrites the input files based on rules and actions you specify. This rewrite is done without regard to correct OCaml source code (although the way Camlp4 works makes it difficult to write Camlp4 expansions that result in unparseable OCaml code).

As a preprocessor, the action of Camlp4 comes before the compilation of a given source file. This also means that code you have that takes advantage of Camlp4 must be processed with Camlp4.

Camlp4 is also a pretty printer, but it is not a source-code beautifier. In this case, pretty printing refers to the capability to create automatic actions based on types. This functionality is not as good as using the Format module in the standard library. Creating pretty printers is one of the areas not covered in this book.

Streams and Parsers

The Camlp4 system provides streams and parsers. Streams are lazily evaluated sequences (that can be infinite) of a given type. Parsers operate on streams. The term *parser* can be confusing because there is a module named *Parsing* that has nothing to do with the stream-based parsers discussed in this chapter—those parsers are for ocamlyacc.

Understanding Streams

Streams can be created by hand using the [< >] syntax, which is the same syntax used by parsers. Streams created by hand are mostly the same as those created by the functions in the Stream module. However, you cannot use any of the functions in the Stream module on streams that are created by hand. Basically, it is almost always best to use the stream creation functions in the Stream library.

```
# #load "camlp4o.cma";;
        Camlp4 Parsing version 3.09.1
# let rec nextint n = [< 'n;nextint (n + 1) >];;
val nextint : int -> int Stream.t = <fun>
# let str = nextint 3;;
val str : int Stream.t = <abstr>
# Stream.next str;;
- : int = 3
# Stream.next str;;
- : int = 4
# Array.init;;
- : int -> (int -> 'a) -> 'a array = <fun>
# let ar = Array.init 10 (fun _ -> Stream.next str);;
val ar : int array = [|5; 6; 7; 8; 9; 10; 11; 12; 13; 14|]
# let ar = Array.init 10 (fun _ -> Stream.next str);;
val ar : int array = [|15; 16; 17; 18; 19; 20; 21; 22; 23; 24|]
```

Streams can be built from a variety of sources: functions, strings, lists, and channels. All stream builder functions return a stream that can be operated on by the functions in the Stream module. Besides the next function (which predictably returns the next token in a given stream), there are few interesting functions noted here. The next function is actually listed as a built-in parser. In this next example, an infinite stream is created. It will not be shown, but it is unwise to call Stream.iter on a stream that never ends.

```
# let stream = Stream.from (fun _ -> Some (Random.int 100));;
val stream : int Stream.t = <abstr>
# Stream.peek;;
- : 'a Stream.t -> 'a option = <fun>
# Stream.peek stream;;
- : int option = Some 0
# Stream.next;;
- : 'a Stream.t -> 'a = <fun>
# Stream.next stream;;
- : int = 0
# Stream.peek stream;;
- : int option = Some 17
# Stream.junk;;
- : 'a Stream.t -> unit = <fun>
# Stream.junk stream;;
- : unit = ()
# Stream.peek stream;;
- : int option = Some 65
# Stream.next stream;;
- : int = 65
# Stream.npeek;;
- : int -> 'a Stream.t -> 'a list = <fun>
# Stream.npeek 3 stream;;
- : int list = [57; 76; 60]
# Stream.next stream;;
- : int = 57
# Stream.junk stream;;
- : unit = ()
# Stream.next stream;;
- : int = 60
# Stream.count;;
- : 'a Stream.t -> int = <fun>
# Stream.count stream;;
- : int = 6
# Stream.empty;;
- : 'a Stream.t -> unit = <fun>
# Stream.empty stream;;
Exception: Stream.Failure.
# Stream.empty [< >];;
- : unit = ()
```

The functions in the Stream module can throw exceptions. They will throw a Failure exception if none of the stream pattern's first elements is accepted (more on that later). They might also throw an Error errorstring exception, in which more information about the nature of the error is contained within the errorstring.

Understanding Parsers

The parsers operate on the token type defined in the Genlex module. This type consists of six enumerated types describing string keywords (Kwd of_string), which are special characters such as (, string identifiers (Ident of_string) that are strings such as + or *, integers (Int of_int), floating-point numbers (Float of_float), strings (String of_string), and characters (Char of_char).

```
# let example = parser
        [< 'Genlex.Kwd "(";'Genlex.Int n;'Genlex.Kwd ")" >] -> n;;
val example : Genlex.token Stream.t -> int = <fun>
# let lex = Genlex.make_lexer ["(";")"];;
val lex : char Stream.t -> Genlex.token Stream.t = <fun>
# let stream = lex(Stream.of_string "( 10 )");;
val stream : Genlex.token Stream.t = <abstr>
# example stream;;
- : int = 10
#
```

Parsers are created by using the parser keyword and the [< >] syntax. Parsers can return any valid OCaml data type. These parsers are recursive descent parsers instead of parsers that ocamlyacc creates. You should also pay attention to the ' before each type in the parser; this syntax is required.

Example Configuration File Parser

For this example, you will design a very small DSL that describes a configuration file. This configuration file will have nestable values and be typesafe (an example file is shown here). It would be nice if we could also support comments in the file. Another feature of the configuration file is the capability to set string values from environment variables (env) and from command output (exec).

```
hi {
(** hello *)
            set bill = "100";
            set ted = env "PATH";
            set harry = 3.14159;
            set tom = exec "echo 1 + 2";
            works {
                set other = 3;
                nested {
                            set reallynest = 40;
                }
            }
}

another {

            set bill = 100.0;
}
```

You are in luck. The OCaml stream-based parser can handle all this, and the Genlex module even enables you to support comments without any real effort. The code used to generate the module that supports configuration files such as the preceding one is shown next.

The Unix and Genlex modules are opened for convenience. The lexer includes a few elements that are not normal OCaml keywords. The Genlex module implements a lexical analyzer that is roughly based on OCaml syntax and can be extended somewhat by passing it a list of string tokens. This module then can be used to create a stream of tokens, which is used by the parser.

```
open Genlex;;
open Unix;;


let lexer = make_lexer ["{";"}";"set";"=";"env";";";"exec"];;
```

Next up is the parser itself. You define the recursive-descent parser here. This code also flattens out the namespace for the nested elements. They are accessed via a dot notation, but inside strings. This is somewhat crude, but you can update the implementation to whatever way you want to handle it.

```
let rec section = parser
  [< 'Ident q;'Kwd "{"; l = getvals q []; 'Kwd "}"; >] -> l
and getvals m p = parser
  [< 'Kwd "set";'Ident s;'Kwd "="; n = get_res; 'Kwd ";";
     j = let newlist = try
                List.assoc m p
     with Not_found -> [] in
                getvals m ((m,((s,n) :: newlist)) :: (List.remove_assoc m ⮥
p)) >] -> j
  | [< 'Ident q;'Kwd "{"; l = getvals (m ^ "." ^ q) p; 'Kwd "}" >] -> l
  | [< >] -> p
and get_res = parser
  [< 'Kwd "env"; 'String n; >] ->
    (try
              String (Sys.getenv n)
     with Not_found -> String (""))
  | [< 'Kwd "exec"; 'String n; >] ->
    String (
    let strbuf = String.create 1024 in
    let ic,oc = Unix.open_process n in
    let res = input ic strbuf 0 1024 in
    let proc_status = Unix.close_process (ic,oc) in
              match proc_status with
                  Unix.WEXITED 0 -> String.sub strbuf 0 res
                | _ -> failwith "Process ended abnormally")
  | [< 'Float f; >] -> Float f
  | [< 'Int i; >] -> Int i
  | [< 'String s; >] -> String s;;
```

```
let rec get_all_sections acc str =
  let next =
    try
      Some (section str)
    with Stream.Error m ->
      print_endline "Problem reading file";print_int (Stream.count str);
      None
      | Stream.Failure -> None
  in match next with
      None -> acc
    | Some t -> get_all_sections (t :: acc) str;;
```

The previous function calls the parser function in a loop and processes all the sections in a given file. That is pretty much it for the real code. The rest of the code in this module is here to make accessing the configuration file data easier. All the real work—the parsing and lexing—has been done already.

This supporting code adds a couple of exceptions for access problems. A class that represents the information within the configuration file is also defined. The class is pretty verbose because of the use of option types in the configuration file data and because methods must not be polymorphic.

```
exception Bad_Section of string;;
exception Bad_value of string;;

class configfile cdata =
object
  val data = cdata
  method add_more cdata' = {< data = List.concat [cdata'; data] >}
  method get_sections = List.fold_left (fun y (m,n) -> m :: y) [] data
  method get_val sec va =
          let m = try
                    List.assoc sec data
                  with Not_found -> raise (Bad_Section sec)
          in
          let a = try
                    List.assoc va m
                  with Not_found -> raise (Bad_value va)
          in
             a
  method get_float_val sec va =
          let m = try
                    List.assoc sec data
          with Not_found -> raise (Bad_Section sec)
          in
          let a = try
                    List.assoc va m
                  with Not_found -> raise (Bad_value va)
```

```
              in
          match a with
              Float f -> f
            | _ -> raise (Bad_value "Requested value is not Float")
      method get_string_val sec va =
          let m = try
                    List.assoc sec data
                  with Not_found -> raise (Bad_Section sec)
          in
          let a = try
                    List.assoc va m
                  with Not_found -> raise (Bad_value va)
          in
          match a with
              String s -> s
            | _ -> raise (Bad_value "Requested value is not String")
      method get_int_val sec va =
          let m = try
                    List.assoc sec data
                  with Not_found -> raise (Bad_Section sec)
          in
          let a = try
                    List.assoc va m
                  with Not_found -> raise (Bad_value va)
          in
          match a with
           Int s -> s
        | _ -> raise (Bad_value "Requested value is not Int")
end;;

let load_file fname =
  let ic = open_in fname in
  let stream = (Stream.of_channel ic) in
  try
    let res = get_all_sections [] (lexer(stream))
    in
      close_in ic;new configfile (List.concat res)
  with (Stream.Error m) ->

    close_in ic;
    raise (Invalid_argument m);;
```

For this code to compile, you must preprocess with the camlp4o command by using the
-pp flag with the OCaml compiler. Once compiled, this module can be loaded and used just
as any other OCaml module.

```
$~/camlp4$ ocamlc -pp 'camlp4o' unix.cma config.ml
$~/camlp4$ ledit ocaml
        Objective Caml version 3.09.1

# #load "unix.cma";;
# #load "config.cmo";;
# let n = Config.load_file "testconfig";;
val n : Config.configfile = <obj>
# n#get_string_val "hi" "ted";;
- : string =
"/usr/local/sbin:/usr/local/bin:/usr/sbin:/usr/bin"
# n#get_string_val "hi" "harry";;
Exception: Config.Bad_value "Requested value is not String".
# n#get_float_val "hi" "harry";;
- : float = 3.14159
```

Domain-Specific Languages (DSLs)

DSLs have come up many times in this book because OCaml provides access to tools that make creating DSLs easy.

Until now, though, we have talked mainly about external DSLs. Camlp4 gives the programmer the opportunity to create internal DSLs, which are much more in the tradition of Lisp and scheme DSLs. Internal DSLs can also be thought of as syntax extensions of an existing language.

It is also important to remember that there is a difference between creating a DSL and a data file. The configuration file example shown previously is really a data file instead of a DSL. Although there is no widely accepted definition of what is or is not a DSL, we can talk about action versus information. The configuration file does not perform any computation (well, that's not entirely true); it simply creates a list of key/value pairs for data. However, the fact that shell scripts can be executed indicates that there might be some computation performed. This is another example of the fluidity of definitions regarding DSLs.

A good rule of thumb for DSLs is that the users of your DSL should be able to understand it very quickly. The advantage of DSLs is that they can be very expressive in their limited domain (which also affects their learning curve). By their very existence, DSLs contain and convey domain knowledge.

DSLs do have a downside, however. The biggest downside is that you must create the DSL itself. This can be a time-consuming and possibly error-prone process. It can also be difficult to control the scope of a DSL after you have created it. Feature creep can be a real problem for DSLs, and you can quickly get beyond the design limitations of a small language.

There are no real rules about when you should or should not create a DSL. It is often a good idea to create a DSL when you have a focused problem domain that can be expressed more elegantly in your DSLs than in the programming language you are using. You probably should not create a DSL when a data file is more appropriate. Basically, if you are simply specifying things, use a data file. However, if you are doing things in a narrow domain, you might want to create a DSL.

Extending OCaml

Camlp4 can also be used to extend the syntax of OCaml. Extending the OCaml syntax is not like writing a function to perform some action. Although the end result may be the same, the syntax extension operates at the source level, which enables you to do things that you cannot do via functions or any other OCaml syntax.

Consider the following code segment. Is it valid OCaml code? What does it do?

```
let t = 5;;
hey man bob is t and ted is (t * 10) so addem
```

By itself, it is not valid OCaml code. However, if you were to preprocess it through a suitable Camlp4 extension, perhaps like the one following, it would be valid OCaml code.

```
open Pcaml;;

EXTEND
  expr:
  [[
     "hey"; "man"; v = LIDENT; "is"; vi = expr;"and";
     t = LIDENT; "is"; ti = expr; "so"; "addem" -> <:expr<
       let $lid:v$ = $vi$ in let $lid:t$ = $ti$ in
                 Printf.printf "%d\n" ($lid:v$ + $lid:t$) >>
  ]];
END
```

This code would be compiled and then the compiled module would be used to transform the input file into an OCaml source file.

```
ocamlc -c -I +camlp4 -pp 'camlp4o pa_extend.cmo q_MLast.cmo pr_dump.cmo'
pa_simple.ml
```

After you have compiled the module, you can use the pr_o.cmo module to output the OCaml source code that is generated from the input file. Normally, you would use the pr_dump.cmo module if you want to actually compile this code. The difference is that using the pr_o.cmo module requires the compilation to be done twice, whereas the pr_dump.cmo module does the compilation only once.

```
~/camlp4$ camlp4o pa_extend.cmo q_MLast.cmo pr_o.cmo ./pa_simple.cmo simple.ml

let t = 5
let _ = let bob = t in let ted = t * 10 in Printf.printf "%d\n" (bob + ted)
```

The syntax extension is defined using a system of levels and quotations. In this case, the extension is done at the expr level. The quotation is the <:expr< STUFF >> where STUFF is the revised syntax OCaml code we want generated.

These quotations have several different types, although in this chapter we use only expr and str_item. These quotations correspond to the expr and str_item levels of the OCaml abstract syntax tree.

More About Quotations and Levels

This chapter glosses over some topics, especially some of the more complex aspects of quotations and levels. You can use the quotation that matches the level you are working in. For example, you cannot use an expr in a str_item because expressions are not structs (which is what str_item refers to).

A Longer Example

In this example, you create a syntax extension that has two parts. The first is a new keyword, "open_safe_in", which enables you to open a new in_channel and automatically registers a finalise handler to close the file. The second creates a new keyword ("client_socket") that takes a hostname and a port and returns a connected client socket.

These two extensions could be done using only OCaml functions. However, defining them as a syntax extension gives you flexibility because you cannot have a function in OCaml that has the same name but returns a different type. You could link two different versions of a given library to accomplish this, but by using syntax extensions you can do it while maintaining only one library. You could define two syntax extensions that output different code and then use one or the other, depending on the situation. The benefit here is that the syntax extensions would be less code to maintain.

```
open Pcaml;;

EXTEND
 expr:
  [[
     "open_safe_in"; fname = STRING ->
      <:expr<
        let newic = open_in $str:fname$ in
        let _ = Gc.finalise (fun x -> let _ = print_endline ("Closing:" $str:fname$)
                                        in
                                      close_in  x) newic
      in
       newic
      >>
  ]
  | ["client_socket"; sock_name = STRING; port = INT  ->
      <:expr< let socket = Unix.socket Unix.PF_INET Unix.SOCK_STREAM 0
      in
      let hostinfo = Unix.gethostbyname $str:sock_name$ in
      let server_address = hostinfo.Unix.h_addr_list.(0) in
      let _ =
               Unix.connect socket (Unix.ADDR_INET (server_address,$int:port$))
```

```
        in
        let (n,m,o) = Unix.select [] [socket] [] 30. in match m with
                [
                    [] -> failwith "Failed to connect!"
                    | [ h :: t ] -> h ] >>
    ]
  ];
END;;
```

Note Any number of extensions can be added to any given level.

The following source file (saved to a file called simple_example.ml) shows the input code for the syntax extension. If the syntax extension is saved to a file called open_safe.ml, the compilation steps shown after the source code would compile each file.

```
let ic = open_safe_in "/etc/hosts" in close_in ic;;
let _ = Gc.major ();;

let s = client_socket "www.apress.com" 80 in
  Unix.close s;;
```

```
$ ocamlc -c -I +camlp4 -pp 'camlp4o pa_extend.cmo q_MLast.cmo ↪
pr_dump.cmo' open_safe.ml
```

You can then use the pr_o.cmo module and generate the source code to see exactly how the source code was transformed. The generated code is well-formed, but not as simple as the input file.

```
$ camlp4o pa_extend.cmo q_MLast.cmo pr_o.cmo ./open_safe.cmo simple_example.ml
let _ =
  let ic =
    let newic = open_in "/etc/hosts" in
    let _ =
      Gc.finalise
        (fun x ->
           let _ = print_endline ("Closing:" ^ "/etc/hosts") in close_in x)
        newic
    in
    newic
  in
  print_newline (input_line ic); close_in ic

let _ = Gc.major ()
```

```
let _ =
  let s =
    let socket = Unix.socket Unix.PF_INET Unix.SOCK_STREAM 0 in
    let hostinfo = Unix.gethostbyname "www.apress.com" in
    let server_address = hostinfo.Unix.h_addr_list.(0) in
    let _ = Unix.connect socket (Unix.ADDR_INET (server_address, 80)) in
    let (n, m, o) = Unix.select [] [socket] [] 30. in
    match m with
      [] -> failwith "Failed to connect!"
    | h :: t -> h
  in
  Unix.close s
```

Complex Example

Here is a more complex example. The following code shows a syntax extension that handles
lists and optional elements. This syntax is used to describe a DSL that creates groups of
checks for files. The checks are for the MD5 sum of the file, file permissions, and the optional
parameter of the file ownership. This code is likely to work only on Unix and Unix-like systems because of the use of the stat function.

You should pay careful attention to the way lists are handled. The LIST1 keyword (which
describes a list with a minimum of one element; there is a LIST0 keyword, too) is used when
you have to work with lists. Camlp4 cannot automatically create lists, so you need to use a
function—for example, the expr_list function. Keep in mind that [   ] in the revised syntax
is also used instead of normal parentheses in some places and it does not always mean lists.
This can be very confusing for beginners (and everybody else).

You add three levels to the extension to make the parsing easier to write; it doesn't have
anything to do with the intrinsic aspects of those levels.

```
open Pcaml;;

let items = Grammar.Entry.create gram "items"
let owner = Grammar.Entry.create gram "owner"
let owner_calc = Grammar.Entry.create gram "owner_calc"

let expr_list _loc l = List.fold_right
  (fun h t -> <:expr< [ $h$ :: $t$ ] >>) l <:expr< [] >>

EXTEND

  str_item:
              [[
                "check"; s = LIDENT; "{"; l = LIST1 items SEP ";"; "}" ->
                let nlist = expr_list _loc l in
                      <:str_item< value $lid:s$ = fun () -> [ $list:nlist$ ] >>
              ]];
```

```
owner:
  [
    [ "owner"; ":"; ostr = STRING ->
              <:expr< fun x -> try
                  (Unix.getpwnam $str:ostr$).Unix.pw_uid = x
              with [ Not_found -> False ]
              >> ]];
owner_calc:
  [
    [ x = OPT owner -> (match x with
                        Some o -> o
                      | None -> <:expr< fun x -> True >> )
    ]
  ];
items:
  [[
            fname = STRING; chkstr = STRING; perm = INT;
            owner_info = owner_calc ->
              <:expr<
              try
                  let correct_owner = $owner_info$ in
                  let chk = $str:chkstr$ in
                  let cperm = $int:perm$ in
                  let ic = open_in $str:fname$ in
                  let d = Digest.channel ic (-1) in
                  let st_d = Digest.to_hex d in
                  let _ = close_in ic in
                  let statinfo = Unix.stat $str:fname$ in
                  let perm = statinfo.Unix.st_perm in
                  let mybuf = Buffer.create 20 in
                  let _ = print_string ($str:fname$ ^ ": ") in
                  let _ = if (not (chk = st_d)) then
                          Buffer.add_string mybuf "\n\tChecksum Failed!"
                        else
                          ()
                  in
                  let _ = if (perm != cperm) then
                          Buffer.add_string mybuf "\n\tPermissions Failed!"
                        else
                          ()
                  in
                   let _ = if (not (correct_owner statinfo.Unix.st_uid)) then
                          Buffer.add_string mybuf "\n\tOwner Failed!"
                        else
                          ()
```

```
                     in
                   if ((Buffer.length mybuf) = 0) then
                             print_string "OK\n"
                   else
                    let _ = try
                     match Sys.argv.(1) with [
                        "-v" -> let _ = Buffer.add_char mybuf '\n'
                                in
                                   print_string (Buffer.contents mybuf)
                      | _ -> print_string "Failed\n"]
                     with [ (Invalid_argument x) -> print_string "Failed\n" ]
                    in
                       ()
               with exn ->
                   Printf.printf "Error! %s\n" (Printexc.to_string exn) >>
      ]];
  expr:
    [[
       "run"; s = LIDENT; ";" -> <:expr< $lid:s$ () >>
     ]];
END
```

If you use the preceding syntax extension, you can write the files in the new DSL you have created. A short example follows. Using this syntax, you can define groups of files to be checked and can run those groups selectively. For the examples in this section, the following code is saved into a file named check_test_two.ml.

```
(* we automatically have comments *)
check hello {
  "/etc/hosts" "bbabbababbbabba" 0o655 owner:"josh";
  "/etc/init.d/ppp" "Iknowthiswillnotmatch" 0o657
}

check world {
  "/etc/init.d/ppp" "9745d3baaeb1165f402a202463121f81" 0o0755
}

run hello;
run world;
```

After compiling the extension, you can use that extension to expand the previous code into valid OCaml source code (as follows). This code can be compiled and run in the normal way. Note that the camlp4o command does not compile any of the code.

```
$ ocamlc +camlp4 -pp 'camlp4o pa_extend.cmo q_MLast.cmo pr_dump.cmo' -c ➥
check_test_two.ml
$ camlp4o pa_extend.cmo q_MLast.cmo pr_o.cmo ./check_two.cmo check_test_two.ml
(* we automatically have comments *)
let hello () =
  [begin try
    let correct_owner x =
      try (Unix.getpwnam "josh").Unix.pw_uid = x with
        Not_found -> false
    in
    let chk = "bbabbababbbabba" in
    let cperm = Oo655 in
    let ic = open_in "/etc/hosts" in
    let d = Digest.channel ic (-1) in
    let st_d = Digest.to_hex d in
    let _ = close_in ic in
    let statinfo = Unix.stat "/etc/hosts" in
    let perm = statinfo.Unix.st_perm in
    let mybuf = Buffer.create 20 in
    let _ = print_string ("/etc/hosts" ^ ": ") in
    let _ =
      if not (chk = st_d) then Buffer.add_string mybuf "\n\tChecksum Failed!"
    in
    let _ =
      if perm != cperm then Buffer.add_string mybuf "\n\tPermissions Failed!"
    in
    let _ =
      if not (correct_owner statinfo.Unix.st_uid) then
        Buffer.add_string mybuf "\n\tOwner Failed!"
    in
    if Buffer.length mybuf = 0 then print_string "OK\n"
    else
      let _ =
        try
          match Sys.argv.(1) with
            "-v" ->
              let _ = Buffer.add_char mybuf '\n' in
              print_string (Buffer.contents mybuf)
          | _ -> print_string "Failed\n"
        with
          Invalid_argument x -> print_string "Failed\n"
      in
      ()
  with
    exn -> Printf.printf "Error! %s\n" (Printexc.to_string exn)
  end;
```

```
    try
      let correct_owner x = true in
      let chk = "Iknowthiswillnotmatch" in
      let cperm = 0o657 in
      let ic = open_in "/etc/init.d/ppp" in
      let d = Digest.channel ic (-1) in
      let st_d = Digest.to_hex d in
      let _ = close_in ic in
      let statinfo = Unix.stat "/etc/init.d/ppp" in
      let perm = statinfo.Unix.st_perm in
      let mybuf = Buffer.create 20 in
      let _ = print_string ("/etc/init.d/ppp" ^ ": ") in
      let _ =
        if not (chk = st_d) then Buffer.add_string mybuf "\n\tChecksum Failed!"
      in
      let _ =
        if perm != cperm then Buffer.add_string mybuf "\n\tPermissions Failed!"
      in
      let _ =
        if not (correct_owner statinfo.Unix.st_uid) then
          Buffer.add_string mybuf "\n\tOwner Failed!"
      in
      if Buffer.length mybuf = 0 then print_string "OK\n"
      else
        let _ =
          try
            match Sys.argv.(1) with
              "-v" ->
                let _ = Buffer.add_char mybuf '\n' in
                print_string (Buffer.contents mybuf)
            | _ -> print_string "Failed\n"
          with
            Invalid_argument x -> print_string "Failed\n"
        in
        ()
    with
      exn -> Printf.printf "Error! %s\n" (Printexc.to_string exn)]

let world () =
  [try
    let correct_owner x = true in
    let chk = "9745d3baaeb1165f402a202463121f81" in
    let cperm = 0o0755 in
    let ic = open_in "/etc/init.d/ppp" in
    let d = Digest.channel ic (-1) in
    let st_d = Digest.to_hex d in
```

```
      let _ = close_in ic in
      let statinfo = Unix.stat "/etc/init.d/ppp" in
      let perm = statinfo.Unix.st_perm in
      let mybuf = Buffer.create 20 in
      let _ = print_string ("/etc/init.d/ppp" ^ ": ") in
      let _ =
        if not (chk = st_d) then Buffer.add_string mybuf "\n\tChecksum Failed!"
      in
      let _ =
        if perm != cperm then Buffer.add_string mybuf "\n\tPermissions Failed!"
      in
      let _ =
        if not (correct_owner statinfo.Unix.st_uid) then
          Buffer.add_string mybuf "\n\tOwner Failed!"
      in
      if Buffer.length mybuf = 0 then print_string "OK\n"
      else
        let _ =
          try
            match Sys.argv.(1) with
              "-v" ->
                let _ = Buffer.add_char mybuf '\n' in
                print_string (Buffer.contents mybuf)
            | _ -> print_string "Failed\n"
          with
            Invalid_argument x -> print_string "Failed\n"
        in
        ()
    with
      exn -> Printf.printf "Error! %s\n" (Printexc.to_string exn)]

let _ = hello ()
let _ = world ()
```

You now can compile the code, which you can do in one step. Notice that the Unix module is linked in as well. After the code is compiled, the following output is shown.

```
~/camlp4$ ocamlc -o checker -I +camlp4 -pp 'camlp4o pa_extend.cmo q_MLast.cmo ➡
pr_dump.cmo ./check_two.cmo' unix.cma check_test_two.ml
~/camlp4$ ./checker
/etc/init.d/ppp: Failed
/etc/hosts: Failed
/etc/init.d/ppp: OK
~/camlp4$ ./checker -v
```

```
/etc/init.d/ppp:
        Checksum Failed!
        Permissions Failed!
/etc/hosts:
        Checksum Failed!
        Permissions Failed!
        Owner Failed!
/etc/init.d/ppp: OK
```

Conclusion

Believe it or not, this chapter really only scratches the surface of what you can do with Camlp4. We have covered streams and parsers, and how they are used. We also have shown how to extend the OCaml syntax and create embedded DSLs in your own code.

Camlp4 is probably one of the most complicated aspects of OCaml programming. Meta programming often is. There are a few online resources that can help you understand the rest of Camlp4 (which can be found on the OCaml web site).

CHAPTER 30

■■■

Conclusion

You have now arrived at the last chapter of this book. Although this book does not cover all aspects of OCaml programming, I have tried to present information that can help you become an OCaml programmer if you are not one yet—or a better OCaml programmer if you are.

There is still much that remains for you if you choose to pursue programming in OCaml. Not only are there several (high-quality) resources online but there are also a few other books on the subject. OCaml is taught at the university level in several places, too, if you're into that sort of thing.

Although this chapter may be the end of this book, I hope that it is not the end of OCaml for you. The syntax of OCaml is simple, and the language is easy to learn. However, learning how to use it effectively is as difficult as any other language, and it might take more than this book to make you an OCaml guru.

What This Book Covered

This book covered most of the OCaml programming language and associated utilities and tools. You also saw a lot of OCaml code and created various utilities, programs, and libraries.

```ocaml
(* We learned about Ocaml Types *)
type wwl = WhatWeLearned of string;;

(* and records *)
type wwwlrecord = {from_the_simple:int;to_the_complex:string};;

type wwwlmore = From_Records | To_Basic_Types | To_Others;;

(* Hopefully, what you have learned will *)
let you_define_functions () = print_string "And use them";;
let you_curry_functions with_values = (+) with_values;;
let you_compose_functions with_other_functions = with_other_functions in
  "Your Code";;
```

```ocaml
module AndModules =
  struct
    let you_make_large_programs = `Easy_to_build
    let you_group_functionality _in _easy _units = `And_allow_easy_compilation
    let you_hide_implementation details = `In_Easy_groups;;
    let you_control_interfaces = () in "Your Code"
  end

module type CONSTRUCTS =
  sig
    val let_you_define_modules: int
    val let_you_constrain_modules: string
    val and_do_stuff: string
  end

module Functors(C:CONSTRUCTS) =
struct
  let you_can_create_functors from_modules = C.and_do_stuff
end

(* Ocaml provides robust *)
exception Handling;;

external functions_can_be_defined: unit -> unit = "in_c_code";;

class ocaml_objects =
object
  val object_oriented_programming = true
  val functional_programming = true
  val imperative_programming = true
end

let you_create = new ocaml_objects;;
```

ocamllex and ocamlyacc

This book discussed ocamllex and ocamlyacc in some detail. The lexer generator, ocamllex, is a general lexer and can handle almost any lexing task. The ocamlyacc parser, created in the spirit of Yacc and Bison, enables you to create parsers for unambiguous grammars. These tools together are a powerful compiler construction toolkit, text-processing powerhouse, and unbeatable utilities for many kinds of text processing.

Camlp4 and Stream Parsers

If ocamllex and ocamlyacc aren't the tools for you, there is also Camlp4. Not only does it provide stream parsers and utilities to create recursive descent parsers but it also actually enables you to rewrite the syntax of OCaml. This facility is more powerful than Lisp macros, typesafe, and everything that OCaml is—plus whatever you write into it.

Where to Go from Here

Now that you can see the end, where should you go from here? That largely depends on what you want to do. OCaml is under active development and is used in research and corporate groups all over the world. If OCaml is your first exposure to strong-typed languages, you might want to learn more about types and their impact on programming. Unfortunately, type theory and category theory are not very approachable without a fairly serious formal mathematics background. You can read a few books on the subject that might be useful to nonmathematicians, however.

Then there is OCaml itself. We have scratched only the surface of some powerful and complicated tools in this book. Camlp4 is one of the notable examples.

More Functional Programming

OCaml is not the only functional programming language out there. Besides the other metalanguage (ML) dialects, other languages such as Haskell and Scheme are functional programming languages with ways of handling problems differently from OCaml.

Although these other languages are not better, or worse, than OCaml, it can often be useful to view a problem from another perspective to enhance your understanding. This is especially true with very difficult problems (see the final example in this chapter for more on that).

Camlp4

Camlp4 is probably one of the most difficult parts of OCaml to understand and use. There is a small amount of online documentation about Camlp4, but questions of any depth probably need to be asked on one of the mailing lists.

Resources

There are a number of resources to help you in your future study and use of the OCaml language. Many of these resources are online, and there is a vibrant community surrounding OCaml. You can find assistance in several languages, but English and French are widely available.

Mailing Lists

Several OCaml mailing lists are hosted at a variety of locations. The place to start is probably the OCaml beginners list (Ocaml_beginners@yahoo.com, which is a Yahoo! group). Don't let the term *beginners* scare you away; remember that the community is pretty small, so all kinds of problems get addressed on this list, and the definition of a beginner question is pretty broad. The best way to describe this list is that it is geared toward people using the OCaml language.

The next list is the main OCaml list, which deals with more complicated questions, especially internal questions. People from the Institut National de Recherche en Informatique et en Automatique (INRIA) regularly contribute both questions and answers to this list. If the beginners list is for people using the language, this list is for people who understand the language. If you have a question about type inference and the ramifications of a given string-handling algorithm, this is the list for you.

The Great Outdoors Digital Indoors (GODI) mailing list is the most popular nonofficial distribution of the OCaml system. You can find the mailing list for GODI at http://www.ocaml-programming.de. This is a relatively low-frequency list, but it is the perfect place to ask questions about GODI, GODI packages, and associated stuff.

The OCaml community, which is pretty small compared with languages like Java, is generally a friendly place. This book, for example, would not have been possible if not for the community at large.

Other Resources

Several Usenet news groups exist that are loosely focused on OCaml. Comp.lang.ml and fa.caml are the two most likely to be of assistance. Comp.lang.functional is also a good place to check.

You can find several other books on the subject of OCaml. There are more on ML, although most are directed at standard ML, which is similar but not the same as OCaml. The good news is that many of the concepts covered in ML-oriented books are applicable to Ocaml.

Thank You

Before we get to the final example, I want to thank you for purchasing this book. You make it possible for publishers and authors to create books like this. I hope you have found the material practical and useful.

Final Example

I will leave you with a final example. Several years ago, I found myself interested in applying for a job for which I was grossly unqualified. Because "they can't say yes if you don't ask," I tried to find a way to apply that would (hopefully) make them overlook the fact that I wasn't really qualified.

My solution was to write my resume in Python, which I thought was a very clever solution to my problem. I didn't get the job, but I did learn a lot more about Python by performing this exercise. Since then, I always attempt to write my resume in any language that I am learning.

A resume is a good showcase for the problem. It can be thought if as an object, a data type, a collection of data types, and so on. Operating on this data and outputting text is a good approximation for many common programming tasks.

First, look at the signature of the Resume module. The first type defined is the date type, which is designed to be simpler than the Unix.tm type because the problem doesn't need resolution greater than month. Next is a compare function for the date type, which is important because dates are an ordered type. Also, a function to convert dates to strings is provided.

```
type date = { month : int; year : int; }
val compare_date : date -> date -> int
type jobtype = Contract | FullTime | Temp
```

Next comes the job_date class, which describes the duration of time at a given job. One of the main reasons why this is a class and not a module is because there will be several instances of it instead of a module, which would require a new type and functions to operate on this type. The end result would be the same, but it is easier to understand an object in this case.

```
class job_date :
  date * date ->
  object
    val end_date : date
    val start_date : date
    method duration : unit -> int
    method to_string : unit -> string
  end
```

Unlike the date class, the corporation is a data type because a corporation is really (in this code) just a data element. Unlike job_date, which has a duration that must be calculated, the corporation contains only information. After that is the accomplishment data type, which contains accomplishments (or bullet points) for the resume. After that comes job_type, which contains all the types so far.

```
type corp = { corp_name : string; corp_location : string; }
type accomplishment = { acc_level : int; acc_descr : string; }
type job = {
  dates : job_date;
  company : corp;
  title : string;
  job_type : jobtype;
  description : string;
  b_points : accomplishment list;
}
```

After the corporate stuff comes the rest. I included a type for academic degrees and publications. They are limited and can be made much more complicated. You could probably even create functions to generate bibtex entries from publications if you added more information.

```
type academic_degree = {
  ad_dates : job_date;
  degree : string;
  institution : corp;
}
type publication = { pub_date : date; pub_title : string; publisher : corp; }
```

The next two functions, is_whitespace and breakstring, would usually not be available outside the module; they are involved in line-breaking for the text output. Although there will be more on these functions later, I will say now that line-breaking is a surprisingly difficult problem. The line-break algorithm I implemented for this module is pretty crude. It works, but only because implementing Knuth's optimal line-breaking algorithm would be overkill for an example like this (and it is impossible to deal with kerning issues when using a console font).

```
val is_whitespace : char -> bool
val breakstring : ?flinepad:string -> string -> int -> string -> string
```

The OUTPUT module type is used for the resume functor. It defines the module type for the module that actually outputs the resume data. In this example, the data and the outputting of the data are totally separate. The module has only one publicly accessible function: output. This function takes all the resume data via arguments and outputs the resume in whatever form is defined by the module.

```
module type OUTPUT =
  sig
    val do_output :
      string * string * string ->
      string * string * string * int * string ->
      job list -> academic_degree list -> publication list -> int -> unit
  end
```

Now you come to the Resume module itself. This functor takes an OUTPUT module type. A module of type RESUME is where the actual data would reside. The module created by the functor would output that data.

```
module type RESUME =
  functor (O : OUTPUT) ->
    sig
      val name : string * string * string
      val address : string * string * string * int * string
      val version : float
      val license : string
      val jobs : job list
      val degrees : academic_degree list
      val publications : publication list
      val output : unit -> unit
    end
```

Now, you move on to the implementation. First, you open Scanf and define two of the main types. You also define a comparator function for the date type because it is an ordered type.

```
open Scanf;;
type jobtype = Contract | FullTime | Temp;;
type date = {month:int;year:int}

let compare_date x y = if (x.year < y.year) then
  -1
else if (x.year > y.year) then
  1
else
  if (x.month < y.month) then
    -1
```

```
    else if (x.month > y.month) then
                1
    else
                0
```

Then you define the job_date class, which simplifies handling date ranges. It also provides a convenient to_string method that we will take advantage of. The initializer prevents using dates that are mismatched (you can't have negative time).

```
class job_date(x,y) =
object(jd)
  val start_date = x
  val end_date =  y
  method duration () =  if (start_date.year < end_date.year) then
            let next_year_dist = 12 - start_date.month in
                (12 * ((end_date.year - 1) -
                  start_date.year)) + next_year_dist +
                    end_date.month
    else
end_date.month - start_date.month
  method to_string () = if ((jd#duration ()) < 12) then
              Printf.sprintf "%i/%i - %i/%i" start_date.month start_date.year
              end_date.month end_date.year
    else
              Printf.sprintf "%i - %i" start_date.year end_date.year

  initializer assert ((compare_date x y) < 1)
end
```

The next five types (corp, accomplishment, job, academic_degree, and publication) define the basic blocks of the resume, which are the same as the preceding signature.

```
type corp = { corp_name:string;corp_location:string}
type accomplishment = { acc_level:int;acc_descr:string }
type job = { dates:job_date;
                          company:corp;
                          title:string;
                          job_type:jobtype;
                          description:string;
                          b_points:accomplishment list }
type academic_degree = {ad_dates:job_date;degree:string;institution:corp}
type publication = {pub_date:date;pub_title:string;publisher:corp }

let is_whitespace c = match c with
              ' ' -> true
  | '\n' -> true
  | '\013' -> true
  | '\t' -> true
  | _ -> false;;
```

These two functions (the previous one and the one following) are the implementation of the line-breaking algorithm. It is pretty easy to describe, but the code can be a little convoluted. Basically, if the current character is whitespace, and the last character is whitespace, dump the current character. Replace all whitespace characters with spaces unless they get dumped. If the line length exceeds a given threshold, break the line at the next whitespace character. As you can see, it takes a lot of code to do that simple action.

```ocaml
let breakstring ?(flinepad="") str brk pad = let strbuf =
  Buffer.create (String.length str) in
let sb = Scanf.Scanning.from_string str in
let do_break = ref false in
Buffer.add_string strbuf flinepad;
  try
    let _ = while (true) do
              Scanf.bscanf sb "%c"
              (fun x ->
                let cnt =
                 let tmplen = Buffer.length strbuf
                in
                match tmplen with
                  0 -> 1
                | _ -> tmplen
                in
                match x with
                n when is_whitespace x && (((cnt mod brk) = 0) || ➡
do_break.contents) ->
                        Buffer.add_string strbuf ("\n" ^ pad);
                        do_break := false
              | n when is_whitespace x ->
                        let lastchar = Buffer.nth strbuf (
                          (Buffer.length strbuf) - 1
                        )
                        in
                          let should_break = (cnt mod brk) = 0 in
                        ( match should_break with
                            true -> Buffer.add_char strbuf '\n'
                          | false -> if is_whitespace lastchar then
                                        ()
                                     else
                                        Buffer.add_char strbuf ' ')
              | n when (cnt mod brk) = 0 -> (
                        if (is_whitespace n) then
                                (Buffer.add_string strbuf ("\n" ^ pad);
                          do_break := false)
                        else
                          do_break := true);
                        Buffer.add_char strbuf x
```

```
                    | _ -> (if (cnt mod brk) = 0 then
                                         do_break := true);
                              Buffer.add_char strbuf x)
            done
            in
                Buffer.contents strbuf
      with End_of_file -> Buffer.contents strbuf;;

    module type OUTPUT =
      sig
                val do_output: string * string * string ->
                   string * string * string * int * string ->
                     job list -> academic_degree list -> publication ➡
list -> int -> unit
      end


    module type RESUME = functor (O: OUTPUT) ->
    sig
      val name: string * string * string
      val address: string * string * string * int * string
      val version: float
      val license: string
      val jobs: job list
      val degrees: academic_degree list
      val publications: publication list
      val output: unit -> unit
    end
```

The TextOutput module is the implemented plain text output module, which just uses creative Printf statements to accomplish this. It is not very complicated, but thanks to all the conversions, it can be difficult to follow.

```
module TextOutput: OUTPUT = struct

    let hsep () = let str = String.create 80 in
            String.fill str 0 80 '-';
            print_endline str;;

    let string_of_name x = match x with
            (m,n,o) -> Printf.sprintf "%s %s %s" m n o

    let string_of_address x = match x with
                (m,n,o,p,e) -> Printf.sprintf "%s\n%s,%s,%i\n%s\n" m n o p e

    let rec print_corps x afl = match x with
            [] -> ()
            | h :: t -> (
                Printf.printf "\n%-18s|%-20s|%28s\n%s\n" (h.dates#to_string ())
```

```
                              h.company.corp_name h.title (breakstring
                              h.description 71 "");
                      List.iter (fun x ->  if (x.acc_level >= afl) then
                                           Printf.printf "\n%s\n" (
                                           breakstring ~flinepad:"            * "
                                           x.acc_descr 50 "            ")) h.b_points);
                  print_corps t afl


      let rec print_degrees x = match x with
              [] -> ()
            | h :: t -> Printf.printf "%s %-13s %s\n"
                        (h.ad_dates#to_string ())
                         h.degree h.institution.corp_name;
                      print_degrees t


      let rec print_pubs x = match x with
              [] -> ()
            | h :: t -> Printf.printf "%i/%i [%13s] %s\n" h.pub_date.month
                 h.pub_date.year h.pub_title h.publisher.corp_name


      let do_output nme addr jobz degz pubz acc_filter =
              Printf.printf "%s\n%s\n" (string_of_name nme) ➡
(string_of_address addr);
              hsep (); Printf.printf "Work History\n"; hsep ();
              print_corps jobz acc_filter;
              hsep (); Printf.printf "Academic History\n"; hsep ();
              print_degrees degz;
              hsep (); Printf.printf "Publications\n"; hsep ();
              print_pubs pubz
    end
```

The next module is the actual data from the resume that is encoded in the functor. Any output module could be used with this data. The following data is mostly fabricated, except the stuff about playing Nethack (which, in my opinion, is the greatest game of all time).

```
module JoshResume: RESUME =
  functor(O:OUTPUT) ->
struct
  let name = ("Joshua","B.","Smith")
  let address = ("1 O. Caml Way",
                         "Functional",
                         "CA",
                         90210,
                         "josh@apress.com")
  let version = 0.03
  let license = "GPL"
```

```
let jobs = [{dates=new job_date(
                        {month=6;year=2005},
                        {month=8;year=2005});
                    company={corp_name="Kognitive, Inc.";
                    corp_location = "Chicago, IL, USA"};
                title="Consultant";
                job_type=Contract;
                description="Worked as a project management and ➥
                business consultant for a small consulting firm in
                Chicago.";
                b_points = [
                  {acc_level=1;
                        acc_descr = "Did some cool stuff for local
                                        Fortune 5 company"};
                  {acc_level=1;
                        acc_descr = "Created training materials"}]};
                {dates=new job_date(
                {month=9;year=2000},
                {month=6;year=2005});
                 company={corp_name="Some Firm, LLC";
                            corp_location = "Chicago, IL, USA"};
                 title="Caml Wrangler";
                 job_type=FullTime;
                 description="Did all kinds of stuff, but didn't
                 worry about linebreaks.";
                 b_points = [
                 {acc_level=1;
                        acc_descr = "Introduced people to Ocaml."};
                 {acc_level=1;
                        acc_descr = "Wrote very little software,
                        and a whole lot of documentation."};
                {acc_level=1;
                        acc_descr = "Frequently got coffee
                        for people."}]};
                 {dates = new job_date(
                 {month=5;year=1998},
                 {month=5;year=2000});
                    company={corp_name="Another Big Corp.";
                            corp_location = "Chicago, IL, USA"};
                    title = "Unix Systems Administrator";
                job_type=FullTime;
                description = "Made sure the server room was
                free from dust.";
```

```
                               b_points = [
                                 {acc_level=1;
                                       acc_descr = "Used Ping a great deal."};
                                 {acc_level=1;
                                  acc_descr = "Install Nethack on SunOS 4.13
                               systems and verified they were Y2K compliant."}]}]
          let acc_filter_level = 1
          let degrees = [{ad_dates=new job_date({month=2;year=2003},
                                           {month=8;year=2005});
                             degree="MBA";
                             institution = {corp_name="Lake Forest Graduate
                                             School of Management";
                                            corp_location = "Chicago, IL, USA"
                             }};
                             {ad_dates=new job_date({month=8;year=1992},
                                                 {month=6;year=1996});
                             degree="BA (English)";
                             institution = {corp_name = "Denison University";
                                            corp_location = "Granville,
                                                             OH, USA" }}]
          let publications = [{pub_date={month=8;year=2006};
                             pub_title="Practical Ocaml";
                             publisher={corp_name = "Apress, Inc.";
                         corp_location = "Berkeley, CA, USA"}}]

        let output () = O.do_output name address jobs degrees
                  publications acc_filter_level
      end

      module MyResume = JoshResume(TextOutput)

      let _ = MyResume.output ();;
```

After this code is compiled (by using ocamlc), you can then run the resulting executable and get the text version of the resume. It is a lot of work to create a resume this way, but you should (after reading this book) be able to easily understand and modify the code in this module.

Joshua B. Smith
1 O. Caml Way
Functional,CA,90210
josh@apress.com

```
--------------------------------------------------------------------------
Work History
--------------------------------------------------------------------------


6/2005 - 8/2005   |Kognitive, Inc.     |                  Consultant
Worked as a project management and business consultant for a small consulting
firm in Chicago.

        * Did some cool stuff for local Fortune 5 company

        * Created training materials

2000 - 2005       |Some Firm, LLC      |                  Caml Wrangler
Did all kinds of stuff , but didn't worry about linebreaks.

        * Introduced people to Ocaml.

        * Wrote very little software, and a whole lot of
   documentation.

        * Frequently got coffee for people.

1998 - 2000       |Another Big Corp.  |  Unix Systems Administrator
Made sure the server room was free from dust.

        * Used Ping a great deal.

        * Install Nethack on SunOS 4.13 systems and verified
   they were Y2K compliant.
--------------------------------------------------------------------------
Academic History
--------------------------------------------------------------------------
2003 - 2005 MBA          Lake Forest Graduate School of Management
1992 - 1996 BA (English)  Denison University
--------------------------------------------------------------------------
Publications
--------------------------------------------------------------------------
10/2006 [Practical Ocaml] Apress, Inc.
```

Good luck and enjoy your future of OCaml hacking!

Index

forums.apress.com

JOIN THE APRESS FORUMS AND BE PART OF OUR COMMUNITY. You'll find discussions that cover topics of interest to IT professionals, programmers, and enthusiasts just like you. If you post a query to one of our forums, you can expect that some of the best minds in the business—especially Apress authors, who all write with *The Expert's Voice*™—will chime in to help you. Why not aim to become one of our most valuable participants (MVPs) and win cool stuff? Here's a sampling of what you'll find:

DATABASES

Data drives everything.

Share information, exchange ideas, and discuss any database programming or administration issues.

INTERNET TECHNOLOGIES AND NETWORKING

Try living without plumbing (and eventually IPv6).

Talk about networking topics including protocols, design, administration, wireless, wired, storage, backup, certifications, trends, and new technologies.

JAVA

We've come a long way from the old Oak tree.

Hang out and discuss Java in whatever flavor you choose: J2SE, J2EE, J2ME, Jakarta, and so on.

MAC OS X

All about the Zen of OS X.

OS X is both the present and the future for Mac apps. Make suggestions, offer up ideas, or boast about your new hardware.

OPEN SOURCE

Source code is good; understanding (open) source is better.

Discuss open source technologies and related topics such as PHP, MySQL, Linux, Perl, Apache, Python, and more.

PROGRAMMING/BUSINESS

Unfortunately, it is.

Talk about the Apress line of books that cover software methodology, best practices, and how programmers interact with the "suits."

WEB DEVELOPMENT/DESIGN

Ugly doesn't cut it anymore, and CGI is absurd.

Help is in sight for your site. Find design solutions for your projects and get ideas for building an interactive Web site.

SECURITY

Lots of bad guys out there—the good guys need help.

Discuss computer and network security issues here. Just don't let anyone else know the answers!

TECHNOLOGY IN ACTION

Cool things. Fun things.

It's after hours. It's time to play. Whether you're into LEGO® MINDSTORMS™ or turning an old PC into a DVR, this is where technology turns into fun.

WINDOWS

No defenestration here.

Ask questions about all aspects of Windows programming, get help on Microsoft technologies covered in Apress books, or provide feedback on any Apress Windows book.

HOW TO PARTICIPATE:

Go to the Apress Forums site at **http://forums.apress.com/**.
Click the New User link.

JOIN THE APRESS COMMUNITY

READ THE NEW AND IMPROVED ABLOG!

Offering regular posts from Apress authors, technical reviewers, editors, and employees, Ablog offers an assortment of expert advice, industry talk, insider gossip, and tips, tricks, and hacks to keep you one step ahead of the competition.

What Ablog Can Offer You:

- Tips to keep your Linux shop running smoothly

- The value of Vista—Is it worth the wait?

- Taking the leap of faith with new technologies, including Ajax and Ruby on Rails

- IPv4 v. IPv6—Is the transition right for you?

http://ablog.apress.com/

Ablog

FIND IT FAST
with the Apress *SuperIndex*™

Quickly Find Out What the Experts Know

Leading by innovation, Apress now offers you its *SuperIndex*™, a turbocharged companion to the fine index in this book. The Apress *SuperIndex*™ is a keyword and phrase-enabled search tool that lets you search through the entire Apress library. Powered by dtSearch™, it delivers results instantly.

Instead of paging through a book or a PDF, you can electronically access the topic of your choice from a vast array of Apress titles. The Apress *SuperIndex*™ is the perfect tool to find critical snippets of code or an obscure reference. The Apress *SuperIndex*™ enables all users to harness essential information and data from the best minds in technology.

No registration is required, and the Apress *SuperIndex*™ is free to use.

❶ Thorough and comprehensive searches of over 300 titles

❷ No registration required

❸ Instantaneous results

❹ A single destination to find what you need

❺ Engineered for speed and accuracy

❻ Will spare your time, application, and anxiety level

Search now: *http://superindex.apress.com*

You Need the Companion eBook

Your purchase of this book entitles you to buy the companion PDF-version eBook for only $10. Take the weightless companion with you anywhere.

We believe this Apress title will prove so indispensable that you'll want to carry it with you everywhere, which is why we are offering the companion eBook (in PDF format) for $10 to customers who purchase this book now. Convenient and fully searchable, the PDF version of any content-rich, page-heavy Apress book makes a valuable addition to your programming library. You can easily find and copy code—or perform examples by quickly toggling between instructions and the application. Even simultaneously tackling a donut, diet soda, and complex code becomes simplified with hands-free eBooks!

Once you purchase your book, getting the $10 companion eBook is simple:

❶ Visit **www.apress.com/promo/tendollars/**.

❷ Complete a basic registration form to receive a randomly generated question about this title.

❸ Answer the question correctly in 60 seconds, and you will receive a promotional code to redeem for the $10.00 eBook.

2560 Ninth Street • Suite 219 • Berkeley, CA 94710

eBookshop

THE EXPERT'S VOICE™